CW00959986

P-51B MUSTANG

JAMES WILLIAM MARSHALL AND LOWELL F. FORD

P-51B MUSTANG

NORTH AMERICAN'S BASTARD STEPCHILD THAT SAVED THE EIGHTH AIR FORCE

OSPREY PUBLISHING
Bloomsbury Publishing Plc
PO Box 883, Oxford, OX1 9PL, UK
1385 Broadway, 5th Floor, New York, NY 10018, USA
E-mail: info@ospreypublishing.com
www.ospreypublishing.com

OSPREY is a trademark of Osprey Publishing Ltd

First published in Great Britain in 2020

A catalogue record for this book is available from the British Library.

ISBN: HB 978 1 4728 3966 4;
eBook 978 1 4728 3967 1;
ePDF 978 1 4728 3964 0;
XML 978 1 4728 3965 7

20 21 22 23 24 10 9 8 7 6 5 4 3 2 1

Edited by Tony Holmes and Philip Jarrett
Map on page 317 by www.bounford.com
Charts on pages 321, 324, and 326 by www.bounford.com
Charts on pages 330 and 331 by Robert Gruenhagen
Index by Zoe Ross.
Originated by PDQ Digital Media Solutions, Bungay, UK
Printed and bound in India by Replika Press Private Ltd.

Front cover: 1Lt Lee Mendenhall of the 354th FS/355th FG slow times the Packard Merlin engine in P-51B-10 42-106950 *The Iowa Beaut*. The B-model's inboard wing leading edge extensions where smaller than those fitted to the P-51D. This aircraft was lost in action on September 11, 1944 when it was shot down by flak during a bomber escort mission to Magdeburg, in Germany. Its pilot, 1Lt Kevin G. Rafferty, was killed. (*USAF, sourced by William Marshall Collection*)
Back cover image (top) © Rolls-Royce; all other back cover images © The Boeing Company.

Authors' note: The primary sources for the plotted performance values for the P-38, P-47 and P-51 in Appendix B were from Mike Williams and Spitfireperformance.com website. The primary source for Bf 109 and Fw 190 variation data and notes in Appendix B were from Dr. Milliei Adam, PhD email exchanges December 2019 and Kurfurts.com website.

CONTENTS

ACKNOWLEDGMENTS

THE BOEING COMPANY

The authors extend our most warranted appreciation to Michael Lombardi of The Boeing Company Archives for his support in making this history possible and the effort The Boeing Company Archives expends in the preservation of North American Aviation, Inc. (NAA) historical records. Thanks to Carlton Wilkerson for assistance in securing images from The Boeing Company online ordering process.

EDITORS AND SPECIAL CONTRIBUTORS

Walter Beachell was especially helpful in sharing his finds from The National Archives, which gave much insight into the early development of the Mustang, including the first evidence of the Millikan Report, and the French order for 20 NA-73s. Grateful appreciation goes to Christopher Wamsley, who provided many images of the different Mustangs and greatly simplified selection of the photographs used in this book. The patience and knowledge contributed by Robert W. Gruenhagen during his exhaustive review, contributions to fact-checking the narrative, and the loan of his original materials for this project cannot be overstated. Bob was the primary go-to person for the authors when arcane questions needed discussion. Much appreciation must also be conveyed to Don Caldwell, who spent significant time fact-checking the sections devoted to the Luftwaffe and Germany's response to Operations *Argument* and *Pointblank* leading up to D-Day. Steve Brooking, Chris Fahey, Colin Ford, Tom Griffith, Steve Hinton, Pete Law, and John Terrell were extremely helpful during the fact-checking process before submission of the draft to Osprey. Steve Brooking and Colin Ford were key contributors for both general review and specifically Royal Air Force (RAF) developments.

THE NORTH AMERICAN AVIATION FAMILY

Most grateful thanks to Michelle Ratcliff and Gerald Vandervort, whose records-management skills preserved NAA's engineering design and communications history and allowed access to those records to support this writing. Special gratitude is due to Gerald Landry, who aided in the search for the Millikan Report by accessing long unopened files in the storage area at the Guggenheim Aeronautical Laboratory at the

California Institute of Technology (GALCIT). With Gerald's assistance, access was gained to the Mustang wind tunnel reports and other technical data used to support this writing.

Meetings, conversations and manuscripts with and by J. L. Atwood, before his passing, gave personal insight into the workings of the NAA team that was so cohesive in the contract proposal effort, development and production of the Mustang airplane and its unique cooling system. Thank you also to Rolph Schmued, who allowed access to Edgar Schmued's scrapbooks and notes on his career as Chief Designer with NAA. Ralph Ruud, Plant Production Manager, supplied information on the assembly line in meetings before his passing, and in his papers published in NAA periodicals. His description of the teamwork involved in the development of the Mustang airplane fully illustrated the close relationship of the engineering and production departments at NAA. Ed Horkey, Chief Aerodynamicist, verified with conversations before his untimely passing the wing design effort that led to the High Speed Wing and other attributes that made the Mustang a great airplane. Conversations with Irving Ashkenas, and the discovery of his thesis paper in the GALCIT search, confirmed his involvement in the Mustang cooling system design and his place in the continuous improvement process.

Joe Beerer provided an overview of the challenges faced with the cooling system design for the Mustang in a meeting at his apartment in Santa Barbara, California, before his passing. His published papers in thermodynamics point to his expertise, not only in the Mustang cooling system, but in the intercooler design for the NAA XB-28 bomber. Secretarial notes on Lee Atwood's involvement in the Mustang contract negotiations and other details of his letters were meticulously documented by his secretary, Ms. Patti Hyatt, and her daughter, Ms. Stefani Operez, and her husband, Ray, provided copies of these very explicit papers to support this work by Atwood. Access was graciously granted to the many files in their possession to ferret out any details respective to the Mustang. Other employees of NAA and Rockwell who supported this work in varying degrees were Morgan Blair, George Capp, Frank Compton, Joseph Goss, Bill Larkin, Rick Miller, and Earl Theaker, and James Hughes, who related his experiences while working in the Experimental Department under Carl Walterhoffer while the X73 was being hand-crafted in secrecy.

THE P-51 EXPERTS IN THE INTERNET COMMUNITY

Other special key contributors not associated with NAA or Boeing who need to be highlighted include key research sources and authors, from which many of the facts underlying the narrative have been drawn. They are, in alphabetical order, Dr. Millei Adam, PhD, Steve Blake, Warren Bodie, Gary Boyd, Steve Brooking, Don Caldwell, Jack Cook, Ted Damick, Francis Dean, Chris Fahey, Colin Ford, the late Roger Freeman, David Jones, Nigel Julian, David Lednicer, Paul Ludwig, John Mazula II, Tim McCann, Kent Miller, Danny Morris, Dr. Richard Muller, PhD, John Nichols, the late Merle Olmstead, Dr. Frank Olynyk, PhD, Rich Palmer, Greg Pascal, Peter Randall, Joe Shea, Jeff Stephens, the late Ray Wagner, Horst Weber, Ken Wells, and Mike Williams. All made substantial contributions in thought and time over the years, particularly during the dreary editing process and deep dives for photos and documents in development of the Appendices.

The P51SIG.com community was very helpful, and this is a great place for serious research for all things Mustang. Beginning with Craig Quattlebaum, site owner, and knowledgeable friends Christian Alamy, Jim Azleton, Robert Bourlier, Steve Brooking, Colin Ford, Mike Gleichman, Tom Griffith, Jim Harley, Jennings Heilig, Martin Kyburz, John Maybee, John Melson, David Muir, Charles Neely, Michael Scalingi, Bob Sikkel, the late Michael Vorrasi, Glen Wegman, and Matt Willis. Deep apologies to any that we missed. At the time this book was in production with Osprey, P51SIG.com was struggling with financial support issues. Hopefully the issues will be resolved, or the single most important site for exchange of "all things Mustang" will be lost to researchers in the future.

The WW2Aircraft.net forum group has many who were particularly helpful in the 15-plus years of engagement, and a number of contributors cross over to the Facebook "forum exchanges" as well. They include Damon Boehner, John Breitenbach, Rick Brown, Dan Case, Chris Cox, Michael Glenn, Steve Hogan, Dale Karger, Marcel Kirkveld, Dave Lilley, Paul McDrow, Joe Morales, Grant Newman, Tomislav Pavic, and Steve Rusling. Apologies to those who contributed to the Mustang discussions whom we have overlooked.

Key contributors on the Facebook Mustang community, some of whom also belong to P51SIG.com, include Chris Fahey, Tom Griffith, Chris Henry, John Maszula II, John Nichols, Rich Palmer, John Terrell, and Matt Willis.

Robert Bennett, Hank Bille, Jack Cook, Jeff Ethell, Walter Gresham, Billy Hovde, Chuck Lenfest, Cal Sloan, Ed McNeff, Lee Mendenhall, Fred Ramsdell, Peter Randall, Fred Robinson, Glynn Williams, and Bob Woody and were long-time major contributors to the European Theater of Operations (ETO) photos, and in particular the cover photograph of Lee Mendenhall slow-timing P-51B 42-106950 WR-P of the 354th FS/355th FG in August 1944 after an engine change. Finally, we must include the many fighter pilots who contributed to the background knowledge of the P-51B and P-51D during combat operations: Bud Anderson, Hank Bille, Don Blakeslee, Jim Brooks, Henry "Junior" Brown, Bill Cullerton, Irvin Ethell, Norman "Bud" Fortier, Gordon Graham, Walter Gresham, David "Tex" Hill, Billy Hovde, Claiborne Kinnard, Jr, Chuck Lenfest, Bill Lyons, Bert W. Marshall, Jr, Lee Mendenhall, Robin Olds, Royce "Deacon" Priest, Fred Ramsdell, Joe Shea, Johnny Sublett, Alvin White, Robert M. White, and Bill Whisner. All contributed their photo albums and scrapbooks to various projects in the past.

DEDICATION

In thinking about this, we asked the fundamental question, "To who or whom does the United States Army Air Force owe the most for the great and very important fighter aircraft necessary at the right place and time from December 1943 through D-Day, when hundreds of thousands of lives were at stake on the beaches of Normandy if confronted by an intact Luftwaffe to support the Wehrmacht, as it existed on January 1, 1944?"

The answer is neither simple nor attributable to one or several persons. Obviously, the NAA "team," and specifically the key leaders with both a vision of building a great "High Speed Pursuit" and the perseverance and talent to design and produce what became one of the best fighter aircraft of World War II, are extremely important. Equally obvious are the fighter pilots and crews and support personnel that launched the Mustang deep into Germany to fight the Luftwaffe's best aircraft and pilots.

Then there is Lt Col (then Maj) Thomas "Tommy" Hitchcock, a World War I fighter pilot, world famous polo champion scorer and possessor of very important connections to US political and military leaders. He was on "ground zero" at the time of the grand experiment to convert a quarter-horse to a lethal thoroughbred via installation of the superb Rolls-Royce engine. His perseverance and his fighter pilot background, combined with his ability to politically navigate at Cabinet level, enabled him to present the case for the Mustang in the face of what can only be described as unimaginative bureaucrats. This might have been the tipping point, at least to the extent that the Mustang was realized for the superb potential killing machine that it became in time to make a difference.

One cannot ignore the fact that the final tipping point was when the "Boss," Gen Henry "Hap" Arnold, stepped in directly to drive the continuation of the A-36 to the P-51A as the great Merlin experiment ran in parallel in California and Great Britain. But what about Maj Gen James "Jimmy" Doolittle, who recognized that, with the short window between his assumption of the command of the Eighth Air Force and the looming *Overlord* operation less than five months away, he had to do something drastic to light a fire under VIII Fighter Command and risk the fury of his bomb wing commanders by making the destruction of the Luftwaffe the number one priority. His famous directive "Destroy the Luftwaffe, in the Air and on the Ground," allowing destruction of aircraft on the ground to count the same as an aerial victory, and freeing the Eighth Air Force fighters from close bomber escort to indulge in "freewheeling hell" across the airfields of the European Continent, were huge factors.

FOREWORD

Some 55 years have passed since I started to research the history and the development of the P-51 Mustang fighter. My original interest was stimulated by six years of hands-on daily maintenance of this wonderful machine. Today, Bill Marshall and Lowell Ford have teamed up to peruse the archives and collections now available. The authors add a new perspective to interpreting and explaining the history of the P-51 in detail, incorporating new information from the Boeing and NAA archives and contacts. Now, I am proud to contribute my words to these continued efforts to complete the story.

Bill Marshall and Lowell Ford have many years of experience in the aerospace industry. Bill is an engineer, historian, and published author. Lowell Ford, a long-time researcher on the P-51, worked with NAA, Rockwell, and Boeing, and contributed as the archivist for this book. Resources for the volume were gathered from private, personal, and corporate holdings, as well as from material in descendants' possessions. Their combined efforts have resulted in the detailed recording of the events that created the P-51B Mustang, an aircraft which was produced and became available at a time of need during a period when the theories of the US Army Air Force (USAAF) planners and leaders had been proved wrong.

The theory that "the bombers will always get through" had caused the USAAF planners to create a fleet of bombers, each manned by ten men, to fly over Europe at freezing altitudes to bomb and destroy the war-making machine of the enemy. By 1943 the fighter force of the Luftwaffe had risen to the task of destroying this bomber force before it had reached its targets. The USAAF's military planners believed it was not possible to build a fighter that could travel the distance required to escort the bombers to Germany. The Mustang was available when this period was reached, and had the longest range. The first deliveries of the Mustang to the theater had been assigned to squadrons of the Ninth Air Force, whose mission was tactical air support. This mistake was corrected by reassignment of these aircraft to Eighth Air Force escort missions.

In this book, the story of the design and evolution of the Mustang is enhanced by the events in industry and in the high levels of USAAF command. These events delayed the acceptance and assignment of the fighter to the role that would establish its place in history. Marshall and Ford have compiled the history of this period with documents and correspondence which takes the story to a level of understanding and completeness that has not been presented before. The inclusion in the story of the development and use of the competing fighter aircraft available to the USAAF provides a comparison, and awards the final diploma to the Mustang as the outstanding member in its class.

Robert W. Gruenhagen
March 2019

INTRODUCTION

D-DAY – CULMINATION OF FOUR YEARS OF HARD WORK AND PREPARATION

In the opinion of most Allied senior commanders in the European Theater of Operations (ETO), including Gen Dwight Eisenhower, Supreme Allied Commander of the Supreme Headquarters Allied Expeditionary Force (SHAEF), destruction of the Luftwaffe's ability to organize and attack the invasion fleet and troops would be a critical factor in achieving success during Operation *Overlord*. Specifically, Chief of the Air Staff Air Chief Marshal Sir Charles Portal reported to the Combined Chiefs of Staff on December 3, 1943, "that *Pointblank* [the Allied bomber offensive designed to destroy German fighter strength] was a full three months behind schedule and that the success of *Pointblank* would determine the date of *Overlord*."[1]

The single most important agent of *Argument* (five days of focused tactical actions to defeat the Luftwaffe in the air and on the ground that had commenced on February 20, 1944) was the North American Aviation P-51B Mustang, which, in limited numbers compared with total fighter assets based in Britain, carried the fight beyond the German capital. Outnumbered, the aircraft engaged the Luftwaffe in deadly day-after-day combat while flying deep target escort for the Eighth Air Force.

On the eve of D-Day, June 5, 1944, across USAAF fighter bases in East Anglia, a force of thoroughbred Lockheed P-38, Republic P-47, and NAA P-51 fighters were being prepped for the invasion of France. Operation *Overlord* was scheduled to launch on time because Operation *Argument* had been a resounding success.

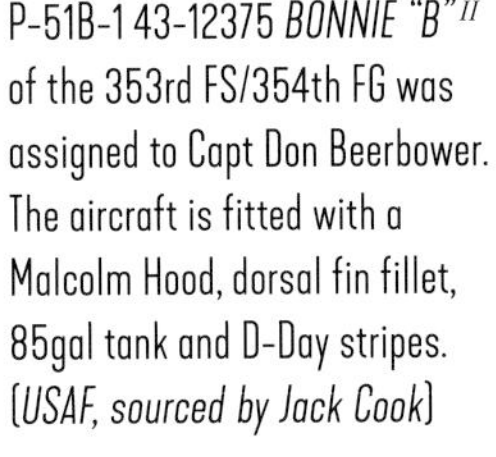

P-51B-1 43-12375 *BONNIE "B" II* of the 353rd FS/354th FG was assigned to Capt Don Beerbower. The aircraft is fitted with a Malcolm Hood, dorsal fin fillet, 85gal tank and D-Day stripes. (*USAF, sourced by Jack Cook*)

Similarly, but with a later start, the Mustangs of the Fifteenth Air Force performed deep target attacks from Italy. USAAF Spitfire fighter groups in-theater that had begun converting to Mustangs in April 1944 were able to provide bomber escorts into Rumania and southern and eastern Germany – targets beyond the range of Fifteenth Air Force P-38F/G/Hs until the improved P-38J-15 arrived in sufficient numbers from May 1944.[2]

Looking at the P-51B/C as it existed on June 5, there are several notable changes to the airframe from the lively Mustang I, on which the British Purchasing Commission (BPC) had gambled four years earlier. Most were major, some were minor, but they were all important to the air superiority narrative and the inherent ability to engage the Luftwaffe over its own capital and places "beyond."

A differentiating feature of the Merlin-powered P-51B from the earlier Allison-engined Mustang was the relocation of the carburetor intake from the top of the cowl to the "chin" behind and under the propeller. The change was necessary to accommodate the updraft carburation under the engine that was required when the Merlin was introduced. Following the lower cowl line from spinner to wing reveals a slightly deeper profile of the fuselage by three inches to accommodate the lowering of the wing. Also noticeable is the radiator/oil cooler duct intake profile, and the deeper lower aft cowl to accommodate the necessarily larger radiator for the Merlin and improve the radiator cooling Meredith Effect.

The new intake cowl design (the "Scoop") featured a "raked intake" as well as more separation of the upper intake lip from the lower wing, designed as a "gutter" to bleed low-energy boundary-layer shedding from the lower cowl from the scoop inlet. Only by this change in intake cowl, coolant radiator sizing, and location, plus changes to improve internal aerodynamic flow to the radiator rear air scoop, was the famed Meredith Effect, producing near-net thrust over cooling drag, truly achieved.[3]

Other noticeable external features include the visible high-octane filler cap just aft of the canopy left rear panel, denoting the presence of the new internal 85gal fuselage tank. This extra fuel tank gave the P-51B the longest range, compared with the P-38J and P-47D, by a significant measure. Later D-model Thunderbolt versions, post-D-Day, had improved combat radius, but the P-51B/D's range exclusively permitted target escort to central Poland and Czechoslovakia.

Also identifiable is the white "cross" notation added below the left-side data block above the leading edge of the wing for those Mustangs modified with the 85gal kits. On or about November 24, 1943, USAAF Materiel Command instructed the air depots in the US and Britain to apply a 6in. x 6in. white cross below the data block to denote center of gravity issues with a full tank. It also issued instructions to denote the modified P-51-1 and P-51B-5 as the P-51B-7, and the P-51C-1 as the P-51C-2 within the data block, but those instructions were not fully complied with.[4]

The "cross" remained for some time, into the P-51D release, but was eventually discontinued in the summer of 1944. Those earlier P-51B-1s and -5s and C-1s that left the factory without the 85gal tank were modified at air depots with a kit to rearrange the area aft of the cockpit, relocate the Identification Friend or Foe (IFF) equipment,

ABOVE This P-51B-5 of the 355th FG's 354th FS was assigned to squadron CO Lt Col Claiborne "Clay" Kinnard Jr. Note the filler cap for the 85gal tank installed behind the cockpit at the Buffalo Depot. *(USAF, sourced by William Marshall Collection)*

TOP RIGHT P-51B-5 43-6893 was assigned to 355th FG Deputy Group CO Lt Col Everett "Ev" Stewart. The white cross at the wing root denoted that the fighter was fitted with an 85gal tank. *(USAF, sourced by William Marshall Collection)*

RIGHT A P-51B-1 in the No. 5 Hangar at BAD2 Warton receives ETO mods, including the fitment of an 85gal fuselage tank. Other work carried out here included the fitting of the Malcolm Hood and external fuel tank pressurization modifications – the latter were performed on every Merlin Mustang prior to the aircraft being delivered to a frontline fighter group. BAD2 Warton was the final stop for newly arrived Mustangs. *(USAAF, sourced by BAD2.co.uk)*

add the 85gal fuselage tank, change the plumbing, and increase the oxygen supply. NAA added the white cross to its top decal/markings drawing in December 1943 for all new P-51B-10s emerging with factory-installed 85gal tanks.[5] A total of 1,200 complete kits were shipped from NAA in the fall of 1943, primarily to the Buffalo Air Depot in New York and Base Air Deport No. 2 at Warton, in Lancashire.

Beneath each wing was a pylon, which was originally introduced on the A-36 close air support version of the Mustang. The design change to accommodate it also included additional internal fuel lines to the pylon so that droppable fuel tanks could be carried for ferry purposes or for bomber escort. It was an extremely important modification, adding fuel capacity to available internal tankage.

The wing of the Mustang I was considerably strengthened in order to become the A-36 production wing, with dive brakes and bomb-carrying capability. It was further strengthened for the P-51B/C when the aileron "throw" angle was increased to improve roll rate.

Not as noticeable were five important changes from the earlier Allison Mustang. First, the aileron throw was increased from +/-10 degrees only, to adjustable rigging of +/-10, 12, and 15 degrees deflection, yielding significantly better roll performance.

355th FG P-51B-10 42-106450 *Miss Behave/Lil Lo* was flown by the CO of the 354th FS, Maj Henry Kucheman. It had a factory-installed 85gal fuselage tank and a reverse rudder boost tab. The fighter is also carrying 110gal underwing drop tanks. (*USAF, sourced by William Marshall Collection*)

The second change of note was the inclusion of the main landing gear door up-locks in the wheel well to eliminate the unwelcome main gear deployment under high-G forces during dive pull-out. The third was the addition of extra oxygen capacity to accommodate the increased endurance. The fourth feature was repositioning of the radio, battery, and IFF to accommodate the aft fuselage 85gal gasoline tank, along with internal plumbing and the five fuel tank selector switches and gages. Last, but not least, was the incorporation of a production pressurization system for both internal and external fuel tanks – the last critical enhancement that enabled the reliable use of combat tanks at ETO bomber altitudes.

Flying alongside the P-51B/Cs on D-Day were a small number of brand new P-51D-5-NA Mustangs. The aircraft had entered serial production in late January 1944, but only began to dribble out from Base Air Depot No. 2 at Warton to operational P-51-equipped fighter groups in late May. The notable key differences between the B and D were: the bubble canopy in the form of a sliding, clear, 360-degree-view Plexiglas cockpit enclosure, first tested in November 1943;[6] and the addition of one more Browning AN/M2 0.50cal heavy machine gun, with 400 more rounds of ammunition, per wing. The 50 percent increase in firepower over the P-51B/C also necessitated some structural changes to the wing leading edge (owing to a longer root chord at the centerline) to allow the wing to incorporate new main-

P-51D-5 44-13316 *"MILDRED"* (later *Nooky Booky II*) of the 62nd FS/357th FG was Capt Leonard "Kit" Carson's first D-model Mustang. He commenced operations with it shortly after D-Day. (*© IWM (FRE 3170)*)

wheel door fairings. Viewed from above, the wing now had a more pronounced "crank" from Wing Station 61 near the guns, back to the fuselage, necessitated by the need to meet the leading edge of the new root chord. Not as noticeable was the change to the leading edge angle of incidence of the wing between the nose of the root chord at the centerline to Wing Station 61.

OPPOSITE A newly-built P-51D is put through its paces by a NAA pilot prior to the fighter being delivered to the USAAF. The enlarged inboard wing leading edge extensions and new main landing gear fairing doors can be clearly seen from this angle. (*© The Boeing Company*)

ABOUT THE BOOK

The authors have had several objectives in mind when compiling this volume. The first and dominant purpose was to organize and disseminate volumes upon volumes of NAA files of correspondence, reports, project logs, and drawings to present much more detail than previous publications regarding the Mustang's development milestones.

A specific disclaimer must be noted here. Namely, while the NAA sources from The Boeing Company were used extensively, the opinions presented by the authors are not expressed or implied by The Boeing Company. Additionally, for brevity in sources citing The Boeing Company, "Boeing" will be used to reference The Boeing Company and The Boeing Company Archives.

The narrative includes the NAA team assembly; the drive to build the highest quality/best performing aircraft in each class; the innovation of production processes, new fasteners, plating processes, and simplification of airframe assembly; the risks taken to introduce and achieve major performance increases for a new low-drag/high-speed airfoil; the introduction of analytical geometry for aerodynamically superior fuselage lines development; and the transformation of the theory of Meredith jet thrust for radiator cooling systems into a practical and efficient system yielding major speed performance improvements for the Mustang.

The narrative follows the evolution, chronologically, of a peacetime USAAC between 1935 and 1942, as the leaders envisioned a separate air force with the mission to "destroy the enemy's capacity to wage war"; and the story summarizes the leadership from "Hap" Arnold and his lieutenants to transform a small peacetime component of the US Army through the explosive growth of 1938–41 as the USAAC, then the USAAF, shaped the Air Force Doctrine of Air Power by trial and error. The different roles of separate aircraft types to support components of the Air Mission evolved as the intelligence from, first, the Spanish Civil War, and then from the wider conflict in Europe, became clearer. In the authors' opinion, those actions and events greatly influenced both the NAA struggle to have a pursuit airplane accepted by the USAAC/USAAF and also the success that the Mustang achieved – particularly in the strategic bombing campaign prior to D-Day.

Various developments of the Lockheed P-38, Republic P-47, Focke-Wulf Fw 190, and Messerschmitt Bf 109 are presented in milestone format to contrast with parallel Mustang developments. They will be referred to as "Mustang Rival Notes" in the text. The actions of the Luftwaffe to respond to the Eighth Air Force as it gained strength and experience led to many innovations in fighter armament, better altitude performance, excellent early warning systems, better radar, and better command and central control. The industrial leaders of the Third Reich in the form of Erhard Milch and Albert Speer, were able to overcome Adolf Hitler's objections and ramp up day fighter production and decentralize critical industries to lessen the effect of the daylight bombing campaign.

Lastly, the narrative will also point out parallel events that were important to the struggle to bring the P-38 and P-47 into the critical long-range escort niche as the Luftwaffe reacted strongly to the Eighth Air Force. The early failure to provide USAAF heavy bombers with effective air cover created the vacuum that the P-51B managed to fill just in the nick of time.

WHY DID THE P-51B MATTER?

Without the P-51B-1-NA Mustang's introduction to combat operations in December 1943, Operation *Argument* (also known as "Big Week," which commenced on February 20, 1944) would have resulted in far higher heavy bomber losses than those suffered months earlier by the Eighth Air Force on August 17 and October 14, 1943. The mass daylight assault on Luftwaffe day fighters and aircraft industries in central and eastern Germany were beyond the escort range of P-47Ds. Apart from the major high-altitude operational issues experienced in the ETO, the presence of only two operational P-38-equipped fighter groups in England by February 20, 1944 was wholly inadequate to protect the Eighth Air Force's strikes deep into Germany. Only one more fighter group would start operations in March, and three more (one Eighth Air Force and two Ninth Air Force) by the middle of May. The comparative results of the two operational Mustang units were far greater than those of the two Lightning groups, and nearly the same as the combined nine Eighth and Ninth Air Force P-47 groups performing escort to the limit of their endurance.

ABOUT THE BOOK TITLE

The title of this narrative history, *P-51B Mustang: North American's Bastard Stepchild that Saved the Eighth Air Force*, leans to hyperbole, as the relay system of bomber escort enabled virtually all the arriving P-51B/Cs to be tasked with providing the deep target escort – where most of the defending Luftwaffe day fighters were positioned. That said, all three USAAF escort fighter types performed great service toward drastically reducing the losses of VIII Bomber Command to Luftwaffe day fighters.

Thus, the stage is set to tell the story of how the P-51B Mustang came into being at the right time. It was a difficult path requiring a combination of factors to achieve conception and delivery of the airframe at the critical moment in history, where it perhaps made saving contributions to *Overlord*. Some of the very fine Mustang books preceding this one tend to cover the internal politics of the USAAF, as well as the necessary incremental stages of NAA Mustang engineering development, with fewer details than the narrative presented in this book. This presentation may be thought of as "The Nerd's Guide to the Mustang – Step by Step," from unknown aircraft company through "blocked entry to USAAC Pursuit aircraft bidding," to "rejection by USAAF," to "USAAF decision to buy the Mustang," to "the perfect marriage between Rolls-Royce Merlin," to the "just in time arrival in the ETO during the Eighth Air Force's darkest hour."

It may be argued whether the P-51B/D Mustang was the greatest fighter of World War II, but it embodied the best combination of any US-produced fighter developed for air superiority at long range, performance at all altitudes, reliability and maintainability, ease of handling, and cost to buy and operate.

Although Gen Arnold later accepted blame for the USAAF not ordering the Mustang earlier, and thus introducing it sooner as the answer to the long-range escort problem, the authors believe that perhaps only two months' delay occurred, primarily due to production delivery issues affecting the Packard Motor Company. The unquestionable key to Mustang performance was the Merlin 60 series two-speed/two-stage supercharged engine. Packard performed outstanding work, receiving the Rolls-Royce Merlin 60 series blueprints in late 1941, making improvements to the supercharger, tooling up for the Packard Merlin 1650-3, submitting to the USAAC Materiel Command (USAAC-MC) for testing and acceptance, and delivering the first two production units to NAA by October–November 1942. That said, the next one was delivered more than 45 days after the first P-51B-1-NA airframe was completed. NAA's P-51B airframe completions far exceeded deliveries of the 1650-3 through to July 1943.

Also worth detailing are the important innovations made to the P-38 and P-47 in an effort to deliver crucial escort capability to daylight strategic bombers in the ETO and the Mediterranean Theater of Operations (MTO). Like NAA, both Lockheed and Republic were innovative and responsive to the rapidly changing future requirements of the daylight strategic bombing campaign in both the ETO and MTO, but failed to deliver the combination of extended ranges, maneuverability, and reliability required in time to be the escort fighter of choice in Europe for 1944.

The Luftwaffe was not idle in this period, not only improving its daylight interception/bomber destroyer capability, but also organizing computer-guided anti-aircraft artillery and the command and control capability to cause heavy and unacceptable losses to the Eighth Air Force in the last quarter of 1943. Some of those important milestones, as well as the development of the principal Mustang opponents, the Bf 109 and Fw 190, will also be introduced and expanded upon in this book. Those introductions, as well as the developments of the primary Luftwaffe fighters, are highlighted in "Mustang Rival Notes."

CHAPTER 1

THE CREATION OF NAA

The road of success from NAA's creation as an airframe manufacturing company on January 1, 1935, to the assembly of an exceptional design and manufacturing team, to the introduction of excellence in trainer and observation and light bomber aircraft, contrasted with its struggles to build a pursuit fighter for the USAAC.

Much happened in the years between General Motors' decision to rename the General Aviation Manufacturing Corporation (GAMC) holding corporation to North American Aviation, Incorporated in 1935 and the delivery of NAA Reports 1592 and 1593, along with three-view and side profile drawings of the P-509-1 "High Speed Pursuit (Allison)" proposal to the British Purchasing Commission (BPC) in New York City in mid-March 1940. The first chapter concludes after three weeks of intense discussion and changes between the technical staff of the BPC and the NAA's Vice President Lee Atwood and his technical staff, led by Chief of Engineering Ray Rice and supported by Chief of Preliminary Design Edgar Schmued.

President of NAA, James Howard "Dutch" Kindelberger, seen here in the 1940s, was Vice President Engineering at Douglas when he was hired by Ernest Breech in 1935. (*Photo by Hulton Archive/Getty Images*)

The end result was a Letter of Intent signed by the civil servant Sir Henry Self (responsible for arranging the purchase of American aircraft to fulfill the needs of the RAF during World War II) for the NAA X73 High Speed Pursuit on April 11, 1940.

THE FORMATION OF NORTH AMERICAN AVIATION

North American Aviation was founded in 1928 by Clement Keys, who observed that "ten per cent of aviation was in the air and 90 per cent was on the ground." Following an extended illness, Keys put NAA on the market and it was acquired by General Motors Corporation (GMC) at the urging of World War I ace Eddie Rickenbacker in 1932. There followed a session of acquisitions by GMC that added to its aviation stable.

The company formed GAMC in May 1930 to operate Fokker Aircraft Corporation. The assets of the latter were acquired in whole by NAA the following month, with Anthony Fokker continuing as Chief Engineer for GAMC. NAA then acquired a majority interest in Berliner-Joyce Aircraft. The fatalities resulting from a crash of a Fokker F-10 airliner in 1931, which killed Notre Dame coach Knute Rockne, caused Fokker transport sales to dry up. Following Fokker's resignation, the Fokker plant near Teterboro airport, New Jersey, closed and some remaining employees, including Schmued, transferred to the Berliner-Joyce plant near Baltimore, Maryland. All GAMC personnel then moved to Dundalk, about five miles from the Berliner-Joyce plant at Baltimore's Logan Airport.[1] One more reorganization occurred in 1934, when the Dundalk plant closed and the remaining employees were transferred to the Berliner-Joyce factory in Baltimore.[2]

Post-war group photograph of the Dundalk Gang at the Bald Eagles Reunion showing most of the key GAMC personnel who moved to NAA in 1935. (© *The Boeing Company*)

At about the same time, the Air Mail Act of June 1934 forced companies owning both airlines and aircraft manufacturers to divest one or the other to open competition. "Dutch" Kindelberger was hired by GMC chairman Ernest R. Breech the following month, becoming president of GAMC. In December 1934 GMC committed $125,000[3] toward the development of the General Order GA-15 three-seat single-engined monoplane to compete in a USAAC observation plane competition.

The Kindelberger-Schmued relationship began when Kindelberger encouraged Schmued to pursue design concepts for the GA-15/XO-47.[4]

On January 1, 1935, GAMC took the name of the holding company, North American Aviation.

Ernest R. Breech was a GMC Board member that took over GAMC, hired John "Dutch" Kindelberger and was chief executive officer of NAA during World War II. (© *The Boeing Company*)

THE EXECUTIVE TEAM

To set the stage for this story of the first Mustang, it must be pointed out that the aviation pioneers and future giants of the aircraft industry were not financial managers or accountants brought in to control cash. They were engineers.

The Boss

John Howard "Dutch" Kindelberger took a two-year correspondence course and qualified as a civilian inspector and draftsman for the US Army Corps of Engineers. He subsequently entered Carnegie Institute of Technology, was President of his Freshman Class, then joined the US Army in 1917 and was posted to the Engineering Corps. An afternoon watching stunt pilot Lincoln Beachy fly over the Wheeling Fair Grounds convinced Kindelberger that his future was in aviation.[5]

After transferring to the Aviation Section of the Signal Corps, Kindelberger became a pilot and duly served as an instructor on the Curtiss JN-4 Jenny biplane for the rest of the war. Following the end of hostilities, the Signal Corps dramatically scaled back its aviation section, and the ex-lieutenant went to work as a draftsman for the Glenn L. Martin Company. In 1920, company president, Glenn Martin, his factory manager Donald Douglas, Chief Engineer Lawrence Bell, and "Dutch" Kindelberger all worked under the same roof. These four went on to found and guide organizations that, 40 years later, had a combined gross value of well over a billion dollars.[6]

Donald Douglas went west to form the Davis-Douglas Aircraft Company, but "Dutch," having an option to join Douglas, remained with Martin. While there, until 1925, he became Chief Draftsman, then assistant Chief Engineer.[7] Kindelberger joined the Douglas Aircraft Company as Assistant Chief Engineer in 1925, and was promoted to Vice President–Engineering three years later. Included in his engineering projects were the Douglas Dolphin Amphibian, the introduction of cowls to reduce the drag associated with radial engines, and the DC-1, DC-2, and DC-3, which essentially cornered the air transport market for the next 25 years. During his tenure at Douglas, Kindelberger hired John Leland "Lee" Atwood in 1930.

In 1935 Kindelberger was approached by Ernie Breech to head up GAMC. He accepted the offer and, after reviewing the stable of obsolete projects in hand, set about thinning out the commercial designs and concentrating on securing government business, particularly with the USAAC.

NAA Engineering and Production Leaders

Lee Atwood's first taste of the aviation industry was with the OK Airplane Company in Oklahoma. Before joining Douglas Aircraft, Atwood received his Bachelor of Arts degree at Hardin-Simmons University, followed by a Bachelor of Science degree in engineering from the University of Texas, with primary minors in physics and mathematics to round out his Major in Structural Analysis. Following graduation, he took a job at the United States Army Air Corps Materiel Division (USAAC-MD), based at Wright Field, Ohio – his first entry into the field of aeronautics. One of the most important aspects of that job was exposure to, and adherence to, the USAAC-MD Handbook of Instructions for Aircraft Designers. That document set the conformal standards (for both the USAAC and the US Navy) by which government and civilian engineering designs were examined with respect to structural analysis, aerodynamics, performance estimates, etc. Atwood brought these disciplines to Douglas and NAA.

When Atwood left the USAAC-MD he took a senior engineering role at the Moreland Aircraft Company, with new president Fred Herman. The venture failed

RIGHT NAA Vice President James Leland "Lee" Atwood was brought in by Kindelberger from Douglas to be Chief Engineer in 1935. (© *The Boeing Company*)

FAR RIGHT Stanley Smithson also joined NAA from Douglas. He was a key Production Executive and Project Engineer who ensured NAA's manufacturing/production excellence. (© *The Boeing Company*)

soon afterwards, and when Herman moved to Douglas Aircraft as a Project Engineer, Atwood followed as Structural Engineer – both men were hired by "Dutch" Kindelberger. Atwood rose from Aircraft Structural Design Engineer to Chief – Airframe Structures during the development of the DC-1, DC-2, and DC-3.[8]

NAA also recruited Stanley "Stan" Smithson shortly thereafter. Also a talented engineer, he had a flair for designing airframes combined with a perspective of how they would be assembled. Smithson's contributions toward NAA's capability to continuously improve manufacturing processes in order to speed up the progress of airframes on the production floor, reduce labor costs, and improve quality, cannot be overstated. Having followed Atwood and Kindelberger to NAA from Douglas, Smithson was also made a Project Engineer – a role he had previously fulfilled with his former employer. He became Head of Production near the time NAA began producing the BT-9 primary trainer for the USAAC.

Ralph Ruud, who was initially employed as a toolmaker at GAMC, rose quickly through production ranks to an illustrious 40-year executive career with NAA. He was a key leader in driving labor hours down via innovative production improvements. (© *The Boeing Company*)

As a side note regarding Smithson, the future phrase "Airframe on the half shell" related to one of his innovative processes of keeping the right and left sides of the Mustang fuselage unassembled so that the shop floor technicians could easily access the inside of the fuselage prior to the two halves being brought together toward the end of the aircraft's construction. Such a method allowed several people to work together and simultaneously attach special brackets and install conduit and fuel lines and control systems in a dramatically reduced time frame compared to conventional manufacturing processes that required technicians to reach into cramped spaces to attempt the same tasks. Even so, it should be noted here that credit is owed to the people of short stature at NAA, whose size became an asset for the company, and the wartime aircraft industry as a whole.

Ralph H. Ruud joined the Berliner-Joyce Company at Dundalk as a toolmaker and structural steel fabricator. When the firm was absorbed into NAA and then transferred to Inglewood, California, Ruud moved too. His first assignment was supervisor of the Tool Design Department, which brought him constant work assignments from Kindelberger and Smithson. His talent and thoughtful innovation led to many improvements to both labor efficiency and throughput time on the assembly lines. Ruud's merit-based promotions included being named supervisor of the Tooling Department (1940), Assistant Factory Supervisor and then General Supervisor (1941), followed by Assistant Factory Manager in 1942. Finally, he became Vice President of Manufacturing for all NAA factories in 1951.

Richard "Dick" Schleicher was yet another NAA recruit from Douglas. He became Chief – Airframe Structures, reporting to Raymond Rice. (© *The Boeing Company*)

Numerous factory floor innovations were introduced by Ruud, including changing the panel drilling and countersinking tool from a heavy vertical steel jig to a horizontal tool set-up. The panels in each jig were gang drilled and countersunk via a rail-based battery of radial vertical drills along a track on both sides of the panel. In the case of fuselage side panels, they went to a station where formers and panels were installed and then moved on to an assembly line for the installation of hydraulic and fuel lines and electrical conduits as part of the "Airframe on the Half Shell" process previously mentioned. This single innovation of drilling and riveting the panels reduced labor time from 300 to 77.5 hours – a dramatic reduction in both cost and time. Notably, during

ABOVE Ed Horkey (seated, left) discusses the new P-51D canopy – seen here in wooden model form – with other NAA aero team engineers. (© *The Boeing Company*)

ABOVE CENTER Carl "Red" Hansen was Chief – Project Engineering as well as Asstistant Chief Engineer – Administration. He was the key Project Engineer for the B-25. (© *The Boeing Company*)

ABOVE RIGHT Raymond Rice, who was Chief – Structures at Douglas, reporting to Atwood. He came to NAA as Assistant Chief of Engineering in 1938. (© *The Boeing Company*)

the peak of NAA's explosive growth, Ruud pursued an engineering degree three to five nights a week for 11 years. His career culminated in 1970 when he was named Vice President of Operations for North American-Rockwell.[9]

Engineering Team

Lee Atwood led NAA engineering with a hands-on approach until he hired Raymond Rice as Assistant Chief of Engineering in 1938. Between 1935 and 1938 NAA assembled a design group headed by Atwood, Rice (Assistant Chief Engineer), Richard Schleicher (Chief Structures), Edgar Schmued (Chief Preliminary Design), Edward Horkey (head of Aerodynamics and Flight Performance), and Harold Raynor (head of Weights and Balances). Key Project Engineers Ken Bowen, Herbert Baldwin, George Gehrkens, and Carl "Red" Hansen were also recruited.

RIGHT Ed Horkey with famed Bf 109 designer Willy Messerschmitt during a post-war visit by the latter to NAA. (© *The Boeing Company*)

Rice joined Kindelberger at Dundalk and was originally Chief – Structures before a promotion that saw him reporting directly to Atwood as Assistant Chief – Engineering. Baldwin was another Douglas alumnus, holding a position of draftsman before joining NAA.[10] Rice was Assistant Chief – Engineering when Edward Horkey was employed in June 1938. When Atwood was promoted to First Vice President and his duties spanned Engineering, Operations, and, jointly with Kindelberger, Sales, Rice was promoted to Chief – Engineering in late 1939.

Dr. Clark B. Millikan, PhD and Professor of Aeronautics, California Institute of Technology, was a key consultant drawn upon by Kindelberger and the author of the report "Performance Estimate for the Idealized 1938 Pursuit." Commissioned by NAA, it was delivered on March 29, 1938 to Gen Arnold in answer to his request for information from the aviation industry on what the next generation pursuit should look like. The report detailed the desired design engineering efficiencies, including drag reduction, powerplant, and propeller technology, and outlined the care that needed to be taken during the airframe design manufacturing process to eliminate as much parasite drag from rivets, sheet metal construction, and other components of parasite and profile drag, including the critical design of a submerged cooling system. The report, and the approach suggested by Millikan, helped shape Atwood's and Schmued's concepts for the best work practices that were instituted in the preliminary design department at NAA prior to the creation of the Mustang.

Millikan was also co-chairman of the Guggenheim Aeronautical Laboratory at the GALCIT, along with Theodore von Karman, PhD. Millikan was Ed Horkey's academic advisor, and recommended him to Kindelberger for employment at NAA as an aerodynamicist. Through the reputation and leadership of Millikan and von Karman, the GALCIT became the premier wind tunnel testing facility for several years.

BELOW LEFT Paul Balfour was a lead test pilot with NAA who made many "first" flights, including those of the BT-9, BC-1, O-47, NA-40, and P-64. (© *The Boeing Company*)

BELOW CENTER Louis S. Wait, Chief Test Pilot, made the first flights for NAA in the Harvard I, BT-14, AT-6 and production NA-73. (© *The Boeing Company*)

BELOW Joe Barton was the other NAA test pilot in place for the B-25 and P-51 test programs. He was killed in a B-25 accident in 1946. (© *The Boeing Company*)

ABOVE Bob Chilton left the USAAC (with whom he had also been a test pilot) to join NAA in 1941. Seen here about to take P-51B-10-NA 42-106435 aloft on a pre-delivery check flight, Chilton was regarded by Ed Horkey as the best test pilot he ever worked with. (© *The Boeing Company*)

ABOVE RIGHT Edgar Schmued was Chief Preliminary Design Engineer at NAA and arguably the "Father of the Mustang". He also led the design teams that created the F-86 Sabre and F-100 Super Sabre. (© *The Boeing Company*)

Ed Horkey, Chief Aerodynamicist, came to NAA directly after completing his master's degree in aeronautics. While studying for his master's, he was often to be found at the GALCIT, where he was introduced to Clarence "Kelly" Johnson from Lockheed, Arthur Hammond and Arthur "Maj" Klein from Douglas, and George Schairer from Boeing. All were leading designers of the 1930s, with "Kelly" Johnson eventually becoming perhaps the greatest US airframe design engineer and program manager of them all.[11] During Horkey's studies at Cal Tech as a student of von Karman and Millikan, he was inculcated in leading-edge theories of design principles for low-drag design concepts, performance analysis, and airfoil design for desired lift and drag attributes based on lifting line and airfoil thickness distributions. Horkey had been working in the Transportation Department at NAA when he was recommended to Kindelberger by Millikan.

During Horkey's early tenure with NAA he introduced both the performance analysis methodology and the iterative complex variable transformation methodologies pioneered by Theodorsen, Kutta-Joukowski and LaPlace that he had studied under

Millikan to compute airfoil sections based on desired pressure distributions along the chord; essential to the development of the NACA/NAA 45-100 low-drag/high-speed airfoil for the P-51.[12]

The pilots and Flight Test Services were an important part of the NAA engineering set-up. Joe Barton, Louis S. Wait, and Paul Balfour worked out of the same office area as Rice's engineering team. Perhaps the best, and certainly the most important, flight-test pilot in the Mustang story was Bob Chilton. A University of Oregon graduate and then a USAAC test pilot, Chilton joined NAA following medical issues with his eardrum. According to Ed Horkey, he was the very best test pilot during his time at NAA.[13]

Schmued, often described as "The Mustang Designer," was persuaded to move from the GMC-acquired Fokker Aircraft Corporation to NAA while the latter was still in Maryland. Although he did not attain a degree, Schmued did acquire his knowledge of aeronautics, drafting, and mechanics via intensive self-study in Germany. Before World War I, he took an engineer-apprentice job at a small engine factory. During the war itself Schmued served in the Austro-Hungarian *Luftfahrtruppen* (Aviation Troop), but his role is unclear. When the conflict ended he went to work as an engineer for an auto equipment company, where he was named in five German patents by his 22nd birthday.

The economic conditions worsened to the point that in 1925 jobs in airplane companies were nearly non-existent, so Schmued followed his brothers Erwin and Erich to Sao Paulo, Brazil. After failing to raise capital for an airplane company, he joined a GMC auto agency and was sufficiently impressive as a mechanic to be hired by GMC itself. Schmued soon obtained a visa and passport from the Austrian and American consul in Brazil and traveled to Teterboro airport, where he was hired as an engineer at the Fokker Aircraft Corporation. While here, Schmued formed the company's first Preliminary Design department and contributed significantly to the YO-27 single-engined observation monoplane for the USAAC. When the USAAC accepted the YO-27, Schmued became Project Engineer, thus acquiring significant leadership and management skills of diverse engineering teams. He expanded these at General Aviation when he took over the GA-43 single-engined monoplane transport.[14]

CHAPTER 2

NAA'S STRUGGLE TO GAIN USAAC ACCEPTANCE

NAA CHRONOLOGY FOR 1935

The aggressive actions Kindelberger initiated to gamble on building to a vision were noteworthy. The network available for counsel, military contracts intelligence, and financing was GMC, which was the parent corporation of both NAA and the Allison Engine Company. Allison was extremely important to NAA, as it provided the latter with advanced knowledge in respect to new developments of the company's V-1710 engine series. NAA was also able to glean important details regarding upcoming Proposal requests from the USAAC-MD at Wright Field. The requests for Proposals after 1935 frequently included Allison as an alternative powerplant source.

On January 15, 1935, the USAAC-MD released two open Requests for Proposals (RFP). The first, Circular Proposal 35-414 for X-602, was for a two-seat, single-engined pursuit airplane with bomb-carrying capability. The second, X-603, was an

The O-47A three-seat observation aircraft, while innovative, was too slow to survive the future demands for a World War II "battlefield observation" type. (© *The Boeing Company*)

RFP for a single-seat, single-engined pursuit airplane. The RFP asked for a profile layout and performance specifications for an all-metal-covered cantilever monoplane with retractable main gear. The request was spawned by a poorly thought-out set of aviation requirements for pursuit and attack airplanes, and was retracted several months later.[1]

NAA noted the emergence of Allison's powerful V-1710, and this led to the company submitting a proposal for the two-seat, in-line-engine pursuit to the 1935 Air Corps Pursuit competition. The lure of a 1,000hp in-line engine promised potentially efficient low-drag airframes. NAA provided internal project funding to develop an NA-35 specification and design the P-198 XP to pursue the X-602 Pursuit Airplane contract.

On April 4 Chief Engineer Lee Atwood released the detail specification, and the side profile drawing for the P-198 followed on May 5, 1935. It was the first NAA design to incorporate an in-line Allison V-1710 with a single-speed/single-stage supercharger. The USAAC canceled the Proposal request before NAA submitted the design specifications, however.[2] Unknown to NAA, the company was not considered by the then Chief of Engineering, USAAC-MD Capt (later Maj Gen) Oliver P. Echols, as a likely developer of pursuit aircraft. Instead, he selected the Seversky P-35 over the Curtiss P-36 – both conventionally powered by radial engines.[3]

Shortly after issuing the pursuit RFP, the USAAC opened a new competition for a two-seat basic trainer. The revenue-earning potential associated with providing the USAAC with hundreds of trainers stimulated another $16,000 of funding from GMC to NAA.[4] On January 25, 1935, General Order NA-16 was issued, anticipating the forthcoming USAAC Circular Proposal for the same. This effort called for the design and construction of a fixed-gear, two-seat basic trainer for anticipated USAAC requirements for the next several years.

The creation of the NA-16 exemplified the hard work and sacrifice of the NAA team. Kindelberger recalled many years later that he discovered his designers and shop personnel were clocking out in accordance with "no-overtime rules" embodied in the National Recovery Administration, leaving to get beer and sandwiches, and returning to work to "have fun finishing the plane."[5]

The BT-9 contract not only funded NAA's move from Dundalk to Inglewood, it was the progenitor for the hugely successful Harvard and AT-6 advanced trainer. (© *The Boeing Company*)

The XO-47 was the first major contribution that Edgar Schmued made as Chief Preliminary Design Engineer at GAMC before the move to Inglewood. (© *The Boeing Company*)

The two-seat trainer flew for the first time in April 1935 with Paul Balfour at the controls, and it was then flown to Wright Field on April 22, 1935 to be evaluated as the BT-9 prototype. The aircraft subsequently beat the Seversky BT-8, leading to a contract for 42 BT-9s, executed on September 19, 1935. General Order NA-19 was opened to provide funding for the production version of the BT-9.[6]

Although work had begun on the GA-15 observation plane prior to the reorganization of General Aviation into NAA, the resultant XO-47 observation aircraft was not completed until June 1935. It was well received by the USAAC, the three-seat, all-metal aircraft being designed to maximize the view of the observer, who was seated below the wing between the pilot and gunner. In addition to the unique all-metal fuselage and wing, it also featured retractable main landing gear – this feature is often believed to have reflected Schmued's early design contributions to General Aviation before he became Chief – Preliminary Design three years later.

Arguably, the BT-9 contract award was the single most important "win" for NAA because it funded the move to Mines Field, later known as Los Angeles International Airport, following the lease executed by Kindelberger on September 24, 1935. It also funded the new plant construction in Inglewood, the factory and facilities being carefully planned with respect to layout and support functions, including laboratories, wind tunnel, and hangar facilities. They were started on November 1, 1935, and triggered the recruitment of NAA employees based in Baltimore who were willing to move to the Los Angeles general area. By the end of the year, 75 of the 250 workers at the Inglewood/Mines Field plant had come from Baltimore.

During 1935 two very important papers were published in Great Britain regarding the "Meredith Effect."[7] First, on August 14, 1935, F. W. Meredith reported on radiator ducts immersed in flow, exchanging heat and exiting through a converging duct to achieve thrust. The technical paper, Report and Memoranda 1683, was published by the Aeronautical Research Council and resulted from research at the Royal Aircraft Establishment (RAE), Farnborough. It would lead to a key technical innovation incorporated into the design of the P-51 Mustang several years in the future. The Meredith Effect paper discussed the theory and practical application of the ramjet effect to improve the design of piston-engine cooling systems by lowering the net drag of coolant radiators for in-line engines. A more thorough discussion is presented in Appendix A.

It is worth noting that the Meredith Effect was attempted in the first and succeeding Supermarine Spitfires from 1936 onwards, as well as in the Bf 109, although their radiators and ducting were mounted in the wings, not in the aft fuselage. There is evidence to support the notion that Lee Atwood, as Vice President – Engineering, was aware of the paper, but the concepts were not advanced until Rice, Schmued, and Horkey embodied the ducting/aft radiator design into the P-509 in December 1939, and perhaps as early as June of that same year following the cancelation of NA-53 pursuit production.

The second major paper on the Meredith Effect, Report and Memoranda 1702, "The Cowling of Cooling Systems," by R. S. Capon, was published in March 1936. The author expanded on design concepts for cooling radiators and achieving jet exhaust effect for aircraft.[8]

MUSTANG RIVAL NOTES – 1935

The first primary future adversary of the Mustang, the Bf 109, completed manufacturer's flight tests at the end of October 1935, and was then delivered to the Luftwaffe at Rechlin. The first all-metal monoplane fighter accepted by the Luftwaffe, it remained in service through to VE Day on May 8, 1945.[9] The later Bf 109G variant was the single most encountered enemy fighter engaged by the Mustang during World War II.

The Bf 109 prototype would lead to the Luftwaffe's most widely produced (almost 34,000 built between 1937 and 1945) and longest serving fighter both before and during World War II. (*Tony Holmes Collection*)

The NA-21 (XB-21) Dragon prototype was faster and carried a larger bombload than the B-17. A USAAC contract went to the rival Douglas B-18, however, due to the NA-21's high cost and the troubled performance of its turbo-supercharged engines. (© *The Boeing Company*)

NAA EARLY EXPANSION NOTES FOR JANUARY THROUGH DECEMBER 1936

Schmued's impending arrival at Inglewood from Maryland was interrupted by a fatal automobile accident on November 22, 1935 in which his wife Luisa was killed and Schmued injured. He eventually reported for work to Lee Atwood in February 1936. The previous month, construction had begun on General Order NA-21 for the XB-21 bomber to compete for USAAC Circular Proposal CP36-528.[10]

Schmued designed the power-driven nose turret for the advanced Pratt & Whitney R-2180 turbo-supercharged twin-engined bomber. Although the aircraft lost to the less novel Douglas B-18 due to cost, it also suffered many disruptions in flight testing owing to problems with the engines' turbo-superchargers.[11] During flight tests, beginning in December 1936, several issues were also encountered with the powered turrets' drive motors, and they were removed. In the following spring the XB-21 crash-landed at Wright Field. During repair under General Order NA-39, several improvements were made. The XB-21 had impressed the USAAC sufficiently enough for it to be purchased from NAA (for $555,000) so that the aircraft could be used for further evaluation as a test bed.

The reasons for mentioning the XB-21 in this narrative include, (1) lessons learned in development of high-performance twin-engined bomber aircraft led to innovative designs for NA-40 and the highly successful NA-62 (B-25), and (2) further increasing USAAC confidence in NAA competency as an aircraft designer and manufacturer by adding yet another successful design and build to the BT-9 and XO-47.

In Britain, the Spitfire prototype flew in March 1936 from Eastleigh Airport, in Hampshire.[12] It would remain in serial production beyond the end of World War II and was undoubtedly one of the two or three greatest fighters of that conflict. Indeed, it is usually the single aircraft with which the Mustang is compared as the "best fighter of World War II." Noteworthy was the airfoil selected for the Spitfire, the NACA 2200 series. NAA selected the same series for the BT-9, BC-1, and AT-6 trainers, but alternated tip airfoils until the NACA 4412 was implemented to improve stall characteristics at low speeds.[13]

ABOVE The Supermarine Spitfire – this is the first prototype, K5054 – would arguably be considered, along with the Messerschmitt Bf 109 and NAA Mustang, to be the greatest fighter aircraft of all time. (*Tony Holmes Collection*)

RIGHT The BC-1 was an armed development of the BT-9 built in response to Brig Gen Arnold's request that NAA construct a Basic Combat Trainer for the USAAC. (*© The Boeing Company*)

The first production BT-9 flew on April 15, 1936, with Balfour at the controls. A series of BT-9 variations were sold to foreign countries, and it was then further developed into a retractable-gear version, with more power and armament, as the Basic Combat BC-1 trainer.

Project NA-25, dated August 15, 1936, was initiated for the production run for the O-47A three-seat observation aircraft with an upgraded engine. The O-47A incorporated changes requested by the USAAC following trials, these being incorporated into the XO-47 while it was being repaired.

In October 1936 NAA opened Charge Number NA-26 in response to USAAC Circular Proposal CP37-220 to design and construct an airplane to fill the role of the Army Basic Combat Trainer. Brig Gen Arnold, Assistant Chief of Staff of the USAAC, directly engaged NAA in order to encourage the company to compete for the new trainer contract, based on the BT-9 results. The resulting BC-1 had a larger Pratt & Whitney R-1340 engine, retractable gear, 0.30cal machine guns, and an all-metal fuselage built in modular sub-sections for ease of manufacture and maintenance.

The addition of armament to the BC-1 not only enabled NAA to fulfill the significant USAAC requirement for an aircraft suitable for advanced fighter pilot training, but also led to a proliferation of export variants, including the Harvard I for Britain. An appreciably modified version in the form of the Commonwealth Aircraft Corporation Wirraway also saw extensive combat with the Royal Australian Air Force in the Pacific during the early stages of World War II. The NA-26 project first resulted in the prototype of the BC-1, and this was subsequently demonstrated to the Royal Canadian Air Force. After flight trials began in February 1938 the USAAC asked for modifications that resulted in the creation of the NA-36 (Harvard, then AT-6 variants) later that same year.

Aspects of this aircraft that were important to future development of the Mustang were (1) introduction into the foreign sales markets, (2) introduction to modular designs based on coordination between production and design departments at NAA, and (3) the initial orders placed by the USAAC for NA-36 resulted in the most produced basic combat trainer of World War II, providing extremely important financing for NAA from before the initial designs for the B-25 and the Mustang all the way through to the mid-1950s.

In the fall and winter of 1936 Kindelberger met and established a relationship with World War I ace Oberst Ernst Udet at the Bendix Trophy Races at Mines Field. When Kindelberger went to Europe in June 1938 at the behest of Brig Gen Arnold, Udet personally hosted him when he inspected the Heinkel, Messerschmitt, and Junkers plants, giving him a first-hand view of German manufacturing techniques. Udet mentioned to Kindelberger that assembly line techniques from the American automobile industry had been introduced into German aircraft production. At that time Udet was Director – Technical Office of the new Luftwaffe, and was instrumental in developing dive-bombing as a tactical close air support (CAS) doctrine, as well as the Junkers Ju 87 Stuka.

BELOW LEFT In addition to being in the "inner circle" of the peacetime Nazi Party, World War I ace Oberst Ernst Udet was also a very skilled pilot who competed in air races as an "ambassador" for Germany. He is shown here performing his "Scarf Trick" in a Bücker Bu 133 Jungmeister at Mines Field, Los Angeles, which hosted the 1936 Bendix Trophy Race. It was during this event that Udet met Kindelberger. (© *The Boeing Company*)

BELOW Oberst Ernst Udet was Director – Technical Office of the new Luftwaffe, and instrumental in developing dive-bombing as a tactical CAS doctrine. He was also a staunch supporter of the Junkers Ju 87 Stuka. (*Philip Jarrett Collection*)

TOP RIGHT The first Y1P-36 was modified so that is could be fitted with a Pratt & Whitney R-1830-13 radial engine. It was duly chosen for frontline service with the USAAC as the P-36A, this particular example being assigned to the 55th PS/20th PG at Barksdale Field, Louisiana, in 1940. (*Tony Holmes Collection*)

RIGHT The second Y1P-36 was modified to install the V-1710 engine/turbo-supercharger combination. It was re-designated XP-37. (*Philip Jarrett Collection*)

US President Franklin D. Roosevelt placed a two-year wait on foreign delivery of new aircraft in November, and the Allison XV-1710-7 made its first flight in the Consolidated XA-11A on December 15, 1936.

In two years NAA, under the leadership of Kindelberger and Atwood, placed two new, innovative and well-made aircraft into military service. The BT-9 became the backbone of the USAAC's pilot extension program while it prepared for massive growth over the next three years. The O-47A was the first relatively high-performing observation aircraft, combining an all-metal fuselage and monoplane wings with retractable landing gear. Although failing to enter production, the advanced XB-21 twin-engined bomber had an internal bomb load the same as that of the four-engined Boeing B-17 Flying Fortress, plus a high-altitude capability with turbo-boosted supercharged engines and powered retractable turrets to reduce drag. Thus, NAA had secured a reputation for quality and performance in the building of trainers, bombers, and observation aircraft. However, Kindelberger and Atwood also wanted an NAA type in the USAAC's pursuit stable.

Also during 1936, both the Curtiss Model 75 (fitted with an 850hp Wright XR-1820-39 Cyclone) and Seversky P-35 (fitted with a Pratt & Whitney R-1830-9

Twin Wasp) were acquired by the USAAC for testing. Three Model 75s (designated Y1P-36s) and 77 P-35s were purchased. When the USAAC reopened the pursuit competition in early April 1937, the first Y1P-36 was re-engined with the R-1830-13 to conform to new policy to standardize on the Twin Wasp engine for pursuit aircraft. It was delivered to Wright Field in March 1937, and the production P-36A, B, and C were duly developed. The second Y1P-36 was modified for the new Allison V-1710-11, with an exhaust-driven turbo-supercharger. Designated the XP-37, it joined the Y1P-36 at Wright Field seven weeks later, on April 20, 1937.[14]

As Curtiss and Seversky prepared to compete for the order for 220 pursuit aircraft, the USAAC developed specifications for two new pursuit types incorporating the turbo-supercharged Allison. The latter promised lower drag, more horsepower and better high altitude capability than the Pratt & Whitney R-1830.

NAA CHRONOLOGY FOR 1937

In January and March 1937 the USAAC-MD, via Lt Benjamin Kelsey and Capt David Schlatter in the Fighter Projects Office, issued CP37-608 for a twin-engined pursuit and CP37-609 for a single-engined pursuit. These Circular Proposals were sent to nine manufacturers, but NAA was not included. Kindelberger, discouraged because his company had been specifically precluded from receiving an invitation to bid, continued his efforts to gain recognition for NAA.

The purpose of the new requests was primarily to serve the future intercept role. In the case of CP37-608, the winner was to be the Lockheed XP-38 Lightning, and the Bell XP-39 was chosen for CP37-609. The lightweight XP-39 Airacobra, with heavy armament but low fuel fraction, was, in the words of Lt Kelsey, "The small solution." Nevertheless, the production versions of the P-38, P-39, and later Curtiss P-40 would serve as the primary wartime fighters for the United States Army Air Force (USAAF, successor to the USAAC from June 20, 1941) in the first 12 months of World War II following the Japanese attack on Pearl Harbor on December 7, 1941.

BELOW The gleaming XP-38 prototype. The sharp, strong futuristic lines of Lockheed's new fighter are evident, the aircraft being a complete departure from the standard single-engined designs of the period. The XP-38 was also large, weighing in at more than 15,000lb and boasting a wingspan of 52ft. (*Tony Holmes Collection*)

NEXT PAGES Five YP-38s are seen here lined up on the Lockheed ramp at the company's Burbank, California, facility on November 17, 1941. While the XP-38 had been hand built in response to the USAAC-MD's CP37-608 requirement for a twin-engined pursuit, the follow-on YP-38 was designed with efficient mass production firmly in mind. (*Tony Holmes Collection*)

TOP RIGHT The Bell XP-39 was chosen by the USAAC-MD as the answer to its CP37-609 requirement for a single-engined pursuit, the aircraft being equipped with the new Allison V-1710 and its General Electric turbo-supercharger. The intercooler and waste gates for the latter are clearly visible here mid-fuselage. (*Tony Holmes Collection*)

CENTER RIGHT The Curtiss XP-40 was a P-36 modification incorporating the Allison V-1710 and General Electric turbo-supercharger for improved high altitude performance. The prototype is seen here with its original mid-lower-fuselage mounted radiator. Overheating issues forced Curtiss to move the radiator and oil cooler to a position in the nose, directly below the engine. (*Tony Holmes Collection*)

BOTTOM RIGHT The modified XP-40 is seen in the NACA full scale wind tunnel at Langley Field, Virginia, on April 24, 1939. Just 48 hours after this photograph was taken the USAAC ordered 524 examples as the P-40 Warhawk. (*Tony Holmes Collection*)

The NA-44, developed from the BC-1 airframe, was designed as a two-seat light bomber with a bigger engine than its progenitor. The aircraft also featured underwing pylons for external bombs. (© *The Boeing Company*)

The Allison V-1710-C5 completed the USAAC-MD Bench Test for 150 hours of continuous operation in April, and on July 17 it ordered that one be installed in a P-36. The aircraft so modified became the XP-40. The first installation also included a turbocharger, signaling the USAAC's commitment to attaining high-altitude performance via such a system.[15] These decisions to mandate turbocharging to achieve high-altitude performance hindered Allison's development of two-speed/two-stage supercharging for several years.[16] The USAAC did not believe that two-speed/two-stage supercharging was a practical expectation. Allison was a research engineering company with little in the way of development resources available to pursue such technological improvement. Allison further compounded the challenges it faced when developing the V-1710 into a high-altitude-capable engine by failing to ask its parent company GMC for funding to help move two-speed/two-stage supercharger technology along.

Fortunately, Rolls-Royce was not deterred in its own pursuit of such technology. In March 1936 the Merlin I was on the cusp of entering frontline service with a single-stage/single-speed supercharger giving 1,050hp at 5,250ft. Rolls-Royce delivered the first production Merlin II on August 10, 1937, while the first two-speed supercharger was delivered with the Merlin X on December 5, 1938. The company's research and development continued, resulting in the first bench test for the Merlin 60 in April 1941, and the first production two-speed/two-stage Merlin 60 series entered production exactly a year later. The Packard Motor Company delivered two pre-production Merlin 1650-3s (Merlin 61s) to NAA in October–November 1942 for the XP-51B, but serial production deliveries did not begin until May 1943.

In China, the date defined as the start of continuous engaged conflict between Japan and China was July 7, 1937, at Marco Polo Bridge. On that night Japanese troops attacked nearby Wunming in China.[17]

On December 9, NA-44 Charge Number was opened to cover the building of a two-seat light bomber variant of the BC-1. It incorporated an all-metal fuselage that became NAA's standard for all future designs, plus guns and provisions for bomb racks.[18]

TOP RIGHT Built in response to the USAAC's CP38-385 Light Attack Bomber requirement, the NA-40 and Douglas Model 7B (DB-7)/A-20 did not secure orders despite both types being well received. (*© The Boeing Company*)

CENTER RIGHT Like the DB-7/A-20, the NA-40's fuselage was narrow, placing the co-pilot in tandem with the pilot. This was Lee Atwood's last design project as NAA's Chief Engineer. (*© The Boeing Company*)

BOTTOM RIGHT The Douglas Model 7B (seen here in A-20A form in 1941) was favored by the French *Armée de l'Air* over the NA-40, and it placed an order for the light bomber shortly after the prototype first flew in January 1939. (*Tony Holmes Collection*)

The USAAC released CP38-385 for the Light Attack Bomber competition. Pleased with the design of the XB-21, the USAAC encouraged NAA to compete, and the latter opened NA-40 on December 9, with Lee Atwood leading the design effort.[19] The resulting clean airframe exhibited the same efficient low-slung nacelles as the XB-21, with an improved top speed. In addition, the narrow fuselage placed the co-pilot behind the pilot, and the aircraft included NAA's first design for a tricycle landing gear. The USAAC deemed the aircraft "underpowered" when it was first flown on January 1, 1939, so the Pratt & Whitney R-1830s were replaced by Wright R-2600 A71 Cyclones. The NA-40-2's first flight in March 1939 demonstrated its excellent speed and handling characteristics. Both the Douglas Model 7B and NA-40 were deemed superior to the Stearman X-100 and Martin 167F. While neither aircraft achieved USAAC orders, the British and French were impressed and placed an order for the Douglas DB-7 Boston and Martin 167 Maryland. The French Maryland I and British Maryland II had different cockpit controls and instrument layouts.

The NA-40 design left a highly favorable impression with the USAAC-MC, which recommended improvements following extensive flight testing that resulted in the future NA-62 (B-25) design. Sadly, the NA-40 prototype was lost in a flight test crash at Wright Field on April 11, 1939.

The introduction of the BT-9 and BC-1, plus foreign sales of derivatives of these aircraft, ensured the financial health of NAA and would subsequently enable Kindelberger to gamble by rejecting the 1940 USAAC request for NAA to build P-40s under subcontract. Indeed, the company closed out 1937 with explosive growth in the export market for BT-9 and BC-1 variants based on the NA-26 design. From mid-1937 through to February 1938 NAA also built demonstrators and conveyed licensed manufacturing rights to Australia, Japan, Great Britain, and Sweden for variants of the BT-9.

NAA CHRONOLOGY FOR JANUARY THROUGH AUGUST 1938

On February 2, 1938, Allison engaged in dialogue with NAA regarding USAAC interest in the V-1710 configuration, augmented with a General Electric turbo-supercharger driven by exhaust gas and new 100-octane fuel, for the forthcoming pursuit fighter competition.[20]

Nine days later Vance "Van" Breese flew the new BC-1, and shortly thereafter preliminary design layouts and specifications were begun for export and light fighter variants of the aircraft – these would feature a larger engine and more armament.

After Kindelberger received back-channel information from Allison regarding the impending release of the USAAC-MD's Circular Proposals for single- and twin-engined pursuit aircraft, he contacted Dr. Millikan at the GALCIT. NAA requested a consulting study for an optimized "High Speed Pursuit" based on a 1,050hp in-line engine and a projected design, with best industry practices for both aerodynamics and manufacturing processes. Millikan was a key member of the National Research Council, and was being drawn upon with increasing frequency to help solve significant scientific problems out of the domain of USAAC expertise. He was also well-liked by Brig Gen Arnold.[21] Around the time of Millikan being commissioned to do his report on what the next generation pursuit should look like, Kindelberger met with a foreign visitor to the GALCIT. Prof. Dr. Ing. Georg Madelung, manager at the Deutsche Versuchsanstalt für Luftfahrt, was Willy Messerschmitt's brother-in-law, and he worked for him as an advising engineer. Although no records have been found detailing the content of their conversation, surely the topic of pursuit design was visited.

Additionally, Millikan employed as yet unpublished aircraft performance methods developed by Oswald and improved upon by W. C. Rockefeller at the GALCIT.[22] The performance analysis techniques taught by Millikan and von Karman were brought to NAA by Millikan graduate student Edward J. Horkey in June. Horkey and NAA used these analytical performance analysis techniques for the duration of World War II.

The British Air Ministry, impressed by the BC-1, ordered the Harvard I for the RAF – the aircraft delivered to the latter incorporated many customer-specific changes. This was a very important deal for NAA, and it begat numerous foreign sales. Harvard I N7033 of No. 2 Service Flying Training School, based at Brize Norton, in Oxfordshire, was photographed with its undercarriage and flaps extended during a solo student flight in 1940. (*Tony Holmes Collection*)

Millikan later published *Aerodynamics of the Airplane* in 1941.[23] In his text he presented both fundamental and advanced analytical techniques required to design an airplane. The textbook was intended for graduate engineers who had not specialized in aerodynamics, performance, and stability and control.

Millikan's analysis, leading to the report "Performance Estimate for Idealized High Speed 1938 Pursuit Airplane," began sometime in mid-March. The objective of the report was to analyze potential speed and climb performance of a single-engined, single-seat fighter built to the latest industry standards possible around a 1,150hp powerplant in 1938 with respect to finish, with flush rivets where necessary, minimum gaps between sheet metal, and an aerodynamically clean airframe design. Kindelberger sent a letter to Arnold on March 29 telling him about the study, to set comparisons with known Spitfire and Bf 109 fighter designs and to confirm that he (Kindelberger) was preparing to visit European aircraft manufacturing centers in Germany, Great Britain, and Holland soon.

On April 15, in another letter to Arnold, Kindelberger discussed Millikan's findings, which pointed to current propeller efficiencies as the greatest uncertainty in the report's projected performance findings. He concluded by mentioning that he had sent Lt Col Echols his findings, that Atwood would visit Arnold the following week, and that he (Kindelberger) would report his observations gleaned from his travels upon returning from his impending European trip of May 29, 1938.[24] Kindelberger and Gerald Brophy (of Contracts) embarked on a three-month trip to visit German, Dutch, and British aircraft companies, as well as to conclude business for the BC-1/Harvard I order.[25] Impressed by the BC-1, Britain's Air Ministry duly ordered the Harvard I, requiring several equipment changes to conform to RAF specifications.

The Millikan Report was circulated by Brig Gen Arnold to Lt Col Echols, then Chief, Engineering Section of the USAAC-MD at Wright Field. Presumably, Kindelberger was hoping that NAA would be invited to create designs for the upcoming Circular Proposals for single- and twin-engined pursuit airplanes. That said, the physical characteristics of the "Idealized High-Speed 1938 Pursuit" in the Millikan Report were

The 1938 NAA Executive team come together for a group photograph outside the company's Inglewood factory. (*© The Boeing Company*)

very similar to those contained in the forthcoming USAAC Request for Comment on Single-Engine Design 345. Dated May 4, 1938, it specifically included the Allison V-1710, an embedded radiator under the cockpit and an exhaust aft of the wing. Future design layouts by NAA Preliminary Design Chief Schmued closely matched these April/May 1938 concepts, as will be shown for the lightweight P-509 design.

Also, in May, the National Advisory Committee for Aeronautics (NACA) published Technical Report Memo 896, a translation of B. Gothert's German report "Drag of Radiator with Special Reference to Heating." Contained within the document were several design concepts for intake plenum, coolant radiator, and exit nozzle, with different drag test results for each one.

TOP The NA-50, which was intended for export sales, was the first NAA project funded explicitly for the design and construction of a pursuit aircraft. (© *The Boeing Company*)

ABOVE The fixed-undercarriage NA-64 P-2 was built for the French *Armée de l'Air* (200 examples) and *Aéronavale* (30) in 1939–40. Of these, 111 had reached France by the time it surrendered to German forces in June 1940. This example was photographed in California prior to being shipped to abroad. (© *The Boeing Company*)

In June Horkey joined NAA as aerodynamicist, sharing the same office as Schmued, Rice, and Smithson. He had come to Kindelberger highly recommended by Millikan, who had first-hand knowledge of Horkey's academic excellence at Cal Tech, as well as his extensive summer work at the GALCIT's wind tunnel.

The NA-44 light bomber flew for the first time on July 7. Many subsystems from the BC-1 were incorporated into the aircraft, plus some "new wrinkles." In addition to bomb racks, it had an all-metal fuselage, which led to the same feature for the AT-6 and all subsequent NAA aircraft.

Allison continued to be helpful in support of a potential NAA entry into the forthcoming USAAC competition for single- and twin-engined pursuits, to be released in early 1939. Beginning in July 20, 1938, it sent packages of engineering data and engine cooling requirements to NAA.[26]

The GMC board of directors authorized funding for the NA-50, the NAA's first attempt at building a fighter, in July 1938. The NA-50 General Order for an export fighter began in August 1938. Created in response to a Peruvian request, the single-seat, razorback, NA-50 featured the NA-44's all-metal construction and a Wright R-1820-G3 engine. Two years later, a follow-on contract for Siam (renamed Thailand in 1940) resulted in the NA-68.[27]

By USAAC standards, and in comparison with existing frontline fighter designs in Europe, the NA-50 was underpowered and under-gunned. Nevertheless, it was desirable to foreign governments seeking low-cost, good performance fighter aircraft in second-tier countries. Both Thailand and Peru ordered them before the USAAC intervened and requisitioned the existed completed airframes, designating them P-64s.[28]

During Kindelberger's trip to Europe, his tour of aircraft plants in Holland, Germany, and Britain convinced him that Messerschmitt's construction processes were superior in respect to simplicity, as well as capacity to rapidly produce aircraft. When he was in Britain, the question of whether NAA would be interested in a license to build Spitfires was broached. Kindelberger believed that too much redesign of subcomponents would be required to achieve the ease of manufacturing that NAA had set as standard, and therefore concluded that it would not be cost effective.

Correspondence between Kindelberger and Breech in February 1940 revealed similar concerns regarding potential production of the P-40, the former writing: "The French and British will ask us to build quite a lot of Curtiss pursuit planes and we could handle that probably without much difficulty if they would permit us to change some of the detail design to better fit our processes." [29]

Before returning home, Kindelberger and Brophy closed the Harvard I production contract with Britain, and shortly after returning to Inglewood he received news of the accidental death of Gen Oscar Westover, Chief of Staff, USAAC, in a flying accident on September 21. Maj Gen Arnold was named as his successor in a temporary capacity, but it took several weeks for President Roosevelt to finally select him on a permanent basis on October 27.[30]

NAA CHRONOLOGY FOR SEPTEMBER THROUGH DECEMBER 1938

On September 28 Louis S. Wait took the Harvard I for its maiden flight. Over the following two weeks, design data and performance estimates were also completed for Model NA-53.[31] It was to be powered by a turbo-supercharged Pratt & Whitney R-1830-S3C-G developing 1,200hp for better higher-altitude performance. The design used many of the existing BC-1 and NA-50 airframe components to achieve both faster delivery and lower cost. Adding a turbo-supercharger to the R-1830-SC3-G would have improved the performance of the NA-53 when compared with the P-36 and the P-35, modified into the AP-4, in early 1939, so NAA prepared plans to similarly modify the NA-44.

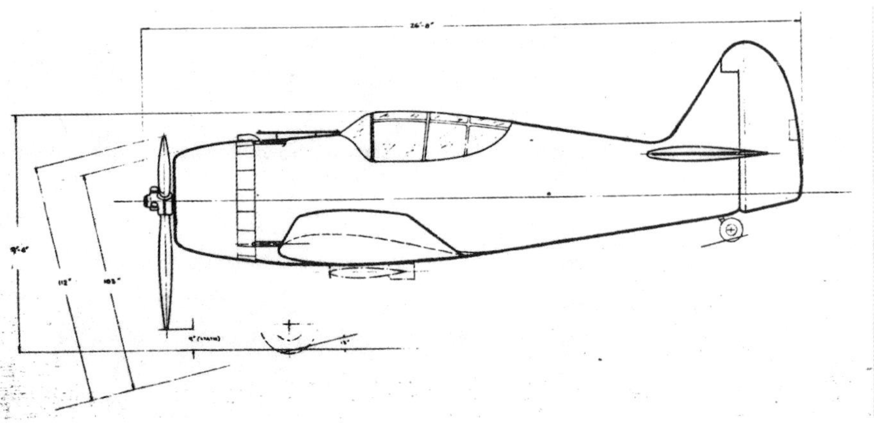

The NA-53 of 1938 was canceled in March of the following year when the USAAC mandated that an inline engine be included in the proposal. (© *The Boeing Company*)

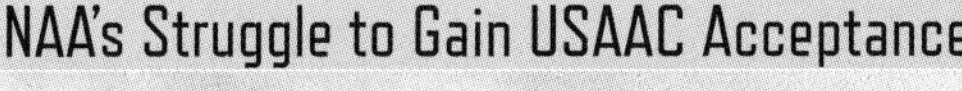

Following cooling issues with the XP-40 traced to the mid fuselage-located cooling system, the radiator and oil cooler were moved to the "chin" on all production P-40s. (*Tony Holmes Collection*)

The Seversky AP-4 was entered into the forthcoming Circular Proposal CP39-770.[32]

The Curtiss XP-40, with the Allison V-1710-19/C3 (featuring a single-speed, single-stage supercharger) installed, flew for the first time on October 14. Originally built as the tenth production P-36, it was fitted with the in-line engine under the direction of the USAAC. Two weeks later Lt Ben Kelsey flew the XP-40 from Dayton to Buffalo at an average speed of 350mph, setting a new USAAC speed record. In December the XP-40 flight tests revealed cooling issues owing to the mid-lower-fuselage-mounted radiator, and the design for the P-40 was changed to position the radiator in the nose, directly below the engine.[33]

The final addendum to the Millikan Report, with tables and graphs to illustrate high speed and climb performance with better propellers, was delivered to Echols by Kindelberger in October 1938.[34]

At the close of the year, as a result of the XB-21, BC-9, O-47, NA-50, and Harvard I deliveries, NAA had gained recognition at home and abroad as a quality and innovative airplane design and production company. It had secured an important foreign market share with both trainers and low-cost, medium-performance lightweight fighter derivatives of their trainer product line. However, NAA was still being ignored as a potential supplier of high-performance fighter aircraft at home. Combined with the urging of GMC Board member "Ernie" Breech, NAA continued to focus on fighter aviation, despite being directed by Echols to stick with the development of trainer, observation, and medium bomber airplanes.

The momentum of in-line-engined pursuit aircraft design continued into 1939 with the first flights of the turbo-supercharged, Allison V-1710-powered XP-38, XP-39 and XP-40 between October 1938 and April 1939. With this momentum came severe pressure on Allison to plan for mass production, which would require ramping up from a small design/manufacturing core to large-scale manufacturing. Furthermore, the company had to respond to almost daily Materiel Change Requests from the USAAC-MD for the V-1710. The attendant change management, liaison with both the USAAC-MD and Allison customers, and the incorporation of modifications into the production line all adversely affected the quality of the engines being built and the company's ability to meet delivery commitments.[35]

USAAC EVOLUTION SEPTEMBER THROUGH DECEMBER 1938

The fall of 1938 brought major changes to the perceived role and future direction of air power in the USA. In addition to Maj Gen Arnold's rise to chief of the USAAC, other changes in the top command structure of the US Army, combined with continuing alarming reports regarding the state of US air power in comparison with that of Germany, Great Britain, and France resulted in President Roosevelt calling a conference with the Secretaries of War, Treasury, and the US Navy (US Army Gens George Marshall, Malin Craig, and "Hap" Arnold, and the US Navy's Adm Harold Stark were also in attendance) at the White House on September 18, 1938.

During the conference, "FDR" made it clear that the meeting was to discuss aircraft production and air power in general. The goal, he stated, was "fewer alterations in production types and a speedier production line – in short, a successful mass production of combat airplanes for our friends abroad, and ourselves."[36] He set specific goals of 10,000-a-year plane production, with an objective of producing 20,000 annually. He also pointed out the need for balancing the profit of the aircraft companies with a guaranteed profit margin for making investments on a cost-plus-fixed fee basis, as well as providing government assistance in providing for new plants, tooling, and training to increase capacity.

These events, and subsequent approvals from Congress to expand military funding, placed great strains on the USAAC as it struggled to manage growth across all areas under its control. Doctrine, policy, and assignment of priorities all experienced great change over the next four years.

NAA CHRONOLOGY FOR JANUARY THROUGH DECEMBER 1939

On January 5, 1939, the BPC delivered the latest British Specification, F.18/29 Operational Requirement OR.73, to NAA.[37] Entitled "High Speed Single Seat Fighter Specification, F.18/29. Operational Requirement OR.73 for the Replacement of Spitfire and Hurricane," it presented several key requirements that served to frame NAA and Air Ministry technical discussions for what briefly became the X73 Company Sponsored Pursuit and then, later, the X73 Demonstrator. In Britain, this requirement resulted in the construction of the Martin-Baker MB 3, which would not fly until well after Mustang production was underway. Specifically, OR.73 stated:

Requirements:
To meet Operational Requirement OR.73, a high speed single-seater fighter capable of operating in any part of the world is required as a replacement for the Spitfire and Hurricane. The outstanding requirement is to obtain the greatest possible superiority in maximum speed over the contemporary bomber. There may be advantages to be obtained from a twin-engined design which would be acceptable, provided the performance was superior to that which could be obtained from a single engine aeroplane. The AUW [all-up weight] of an aircraft built to this specification is 12,000lb.

Performance:
The speed at 15,000ft must not be less than 400mph with the 37.V/12 engine and it is essential that the engine selected should be equipped with a two-speed supercharger so that speeds at altitudes below 15,000ft may be as high as possible. The normal fuel load is to be sufficient for 15 minutes of flying at maximum engine speed for take-off conditions, plus two hours at the most economical cruising air speed at 15,000ft, plus 15 minutes at 15,000ft at maximum engine speed for level flight at 15,000ft, plus 30% reserve.

Engine:
The aircraft shall be designed to accommodate a 37.V/12 engine but a Rolls-Royce RM.2SM engine is to be installed in the first instance.

Strength:
The design requirements of AP.970, any corrigenda thereto and all current ADMs applicable to TV class aeroplanes are to be satisfied at 1.1 times the AUW in the fully loaded condition at factors given in the fully loaded condition for "other than experimental aeroplanes."

Armament:
Two cannon guns in each wing set to fire along line of sight, with at least one drum of 60 rounds of ammunition per gun. Provision shall be made for the installation of a reflector gunsight and a bead sight, and a Cine Camera gun, mounted internally. Protection for the pilot against armour piercing 0.303-in. ammunition is required to cover a forward cone with an angle of 20 degrees to the thrust line of the aircraft.[38]

The French and British purchasing commissions returned in February to revisit American aircraft companies, with an eye toward augmenting their own production capacity as war in Europe loomed.[39]

March 1939 was a significant month for the USA. Most importantly, German forces crossed the Czechoslovakian border on the 15th to occupy Bohemia and Moravia after consolidating Sudetenland. Hungarian troops occupied Carpathia-

P-509-1 "High-Speed Pursuit (Allison)" proposal submitted to the BPC by NAA in mid-March 1940. (*Artwork by Jim Laurier, © Osprey Publishing*)

Sired by the Seversky AP-4J (which traced its lineage to the P-35 pursuit fighter), the Republic YP-43 featured a Pratt & Whitney R-1830-35 and a mid-fuselage mounted B-2 turbo-supercharger. This particular aircraft is a P-43A-1 originally built as part of a Lend-Lease purchase for the Republic of China Air Force but retained by the USAAC. It was powered by a 1,200hp R-1830-49 engine. (*Philip Jarrett Collection*)

Ukraine and Slovakia on the same day. This aggressive move by Germany caused major ripple effects, not only across Europe, but also in the US, as the threat of Nazi Germany was fully recognized by "FDR" and his War Department.[40]

On March 11 three Requests for Proposals were issued by the USAAC-MD. They were CP39-780, Multi-Place Pursuit, Specification C-618; CP39-775, Twin-Engine Interceptor Pursuit, Specification C-615: and CP39-770, Single-Place Pursuit Specification C-616. The Multi-Place Pursuit request was later abandoned, leaving only CP39-770 and -775. The objective of the requests was to "solicit pursuit interceptor types having substantially better performance than the P-39 and P-40 airplanes."[41] [42] Intrinsic to the new Circular Proposals was the necessary inclusion of in-line engine designs. Also, in early March, NAA canceled all work on the NA-53 project, potentially making those funds available to design work on more advanced pursuit aircraft.

CONNECTION BETWEEN THE NA-53, P-509, AND X73

It is probable that funds to start preliminary design work on the P-509 were made available near this time, as NAA realized that the NA-53 with the planned Pratt & Whitney R-1830 engine, while interesting in 1936, had no chance of outperforming the current Lockheed and Bell prototypes, much less newer proposals offered to the USAAC-MD. NA-53 was canceled in March, freeing funding for confidential design activity aimed at producing a company-sponsored pursuit. Additional funds granted by the GMC board of directors, with the approval of board member E. I. DuPont, added to the financing for the pursuit aircraft based on the conviction that NAA could design and build to Millikan's report. The company-sponsored project charges were accrued in one account going forward into April 1940.

It is probable that the new announcement by the USAAC-MD that both the single- and twin-engined pursuit proposals were permitted to be designed around in-line engines would have been sufficient stimulus for NAA to dust off the Millikan Report specifying a "1,050hp" in-line engine and think about actually designing and building one. Work probably started on P-509 on a limited project budget basis shortly after the cancelation of the NA-53.

As noted later in this chapter, the NA-53 design activity was reopened briefly on December 8, 1939, under NA-50A, probably in the hope of securing an order from the French through NAA's sales office in South America. However, the Belligerent Nations Act caused the legality of such an arrangement to come in to question. NAA duly shifted design and sales activity to an allowable fighter trainer design under shop charge SC-46, Preliminary Design P-500.

In December 1939 the SC-46/P-500 Pursuit Trainer design moved forward to address permitted foreign sales, even while the British and the USAAC-MD were prodding NAA to build P-40s under license from Curtiss. With secret design work on the Company Sponsored Pursuit progressing in the background, another "rabbit" was about to emerge from "Dutch" Kindelberger's hat – at least to the extent that NAA could present an advanced concept of a competitive fighter to the BPC.

With the determination by Kindelberger, Atwood, Rice, and Smithson that it would take approximately two years for NAA to retool in order to efficiently build the increasingly obsolete P-40, it decided to present the Company Sponsored Pursuit (the P-509) as an alternative to the Curtiss fighter. The best evidence points to the NA-73X charge number being allocated on April 24, 1940, even though work on the plane had been moving forward under Preliminary Design P-509.

Upon gaining positive interest in the P-509 design from the British, the P-500 mock-up was ordered to be hung in the rafters and the remaining project funding for SC-46 and NA-53 was moved to support the X73 prototype.[43]

As noted earlier, the last production P-35 had been modified to incorporate a turbo-supercharger system plus several other changes, leading to impressive flight tests by the USAAC of the AP-4, now designated the Seversky XP-41. On March 22, 1939, the engine caught fire in flight, forcing the pilot to bail out. With modifications,

The XB-28 was an advanced high-altitude turbo-supercharged twin-engined medium bomber. Very fast, it also featured a pressurized cabin and advanced fire control systems. The aircraft failed to secure a production contract, however, because it was incapable of carrying a B-17-size bomb load over the same range and was more expensive to build than either the B-25 or Martin B-26 Marauder medium bombers. (© *The Boeing Company*)

this same design was entered into competition for the CP39-770 when the USAAC opened up the specifications to include radial engines and other contemporary features.

The resultant AP-4J incorporated a mid-fuselage-type B-2 turbo-supercharger to augment the Pratt & Whitney R-1830-35 to achieve 1,200hp at 20,000ft. The USAAC purchased the AP-4J/XP-41 with modifications and designated it YP-43. Two YP-43s were contracted in May 1939 for delivery in 1940.[44]

In July, H. C. B. Thomas and Charles Luttman of the BPC met with NAA to discuss potential fighter designs. This was the first documented meeting between the BPC's technical representatives and the NAA engineering group.[45] As discussed later in this chapter under December events, this meeting may have been the first NAA presentation of Schmued's concepts for the "High Speed Pursuit – Allison" that he had prepared for the USAAC-MD's CP39-770, released in March.[46]

Also in July 1939, Gen George Brett, Chief, USAAC-MD, ordered increased spending devoted to a single-seat, single-engine, pursuit interceptor. An important decision by the USAAC-MD, as noted in all the 1939 Circular Proposal requests, was to request only the proposed *design* as the evaluation criteria for the winner. It no longer required an aircraft be built and tested before issuing a production quantity order for the successful design. This directive was a very important factor in the future ability of HQ-AAF Directorate, Military Requirements, and Directorate of Air-Ground Support to accelerate the deliveries of the A-36, P-51A, and P-51B from design to production.

That same month the USAAC requested bids for a new medium bomber, for which NAA submitted NA-62. The USAAC accepted the design and designated it B-25. Based on the innovative NA-40, it incorporated many modifications, including more powerful engines and a redesigned cockpit. NAA received an initial order for 184 B-25s, plus additional orders for the Harvard I and BT-14. It also entered the competition for the very advanced XB-28 research and development project.

The XB-28 combined advanced aerodynamics with a pressurized fuselage, remote-controlled gun turrets and powerful turbo-supercharged Pratt & Whitney R-2800-27 radial engines, and although the aircraft was nearly the same overall size as the B-25, it was 100mph faster. Indeed, the bomber proved to be nearly as fast as the Mustang I at 25,000ft. The contract for the first XB-28 was executed in February 1940, two months before the NA-73 Mustang. The only reason for mentioning the XB-28 here is that its first flight pre-dated the XB-29 by five months, and included all the essential innovations that characterized Boeing's Superfortress, thus demonstrating the wide range of engineering skills retained at NAA. The XB-28 was the first design released by NAA with Raymond Rice as Chief – Engineering. Despite its impressive performance, the XB-28 was a "tweener," not capable of carrying a B-17 bomb load over the same range, nor having a clear mission as a high-altitude medium bomber versus the cheaper B-25 and Martin B-26. It was, however, quite suitable for high-altitude reconnaissance work

The second YP-38 (39-690) was extensively tested in NACA's wind tunnel at Langley. Following these trials a fillet was added at the wing/fuselage joint to eliminate buffeting. (*NASA*)

The primary pursuit designs offered in the twin-engined pursuit RFPs were the Lockheed Model 322 and the Grumman XP-50. Both were powered by engines that were turbo-supercharged, but one had twin in-line Allison V-1710s and the other radial Wright R-1820s. The Model 322 duly won the CP39-775 twin-engined pursuit competition, Lockheed providing a design very similar to the YP-38 that had recently been awarded a 13-aircraft contract despite the crash of first prototype XP-38 37-457 at Mitchell Field, New York, on February 11, 1939 – the accident was caused by pilot error. The primary differences between the Model 322 and the XP-38 were the upgraded Allison V-1710-27/29 (F2) engines with new General Electric B-2 turbochargers fitted to the former. The USAAC ordered 66 Model 322s on August 10, based on Lockheed performance and delivery schedules guarantees.[47]

Exceptionally good performance by the twin-engined turbo-supercharged Grumman XP-50 was not enough to secure a contract for the manufacturer from the USAAC. Indeed, the latter wisely selected the superior YP-38. Nevertheless, the USAAC was sufficiently impressed by the XP-50 to order one for testing in November 1939 – the only Grumman aircraft ever ordered by the USAAC. (*Tony Holmes Collection*)

The Curtiss XP-46 was allegedly designed with Meredith cooling/exhaust concepts. The USAAC had very high performance expectations for the aircraft and, accordingly, placed a large order for the production version to replace the P-40. (*Tony Holmes Collection*)

The USAAC was sufficiently impressed by the competitive XP-50 to order one for testing in November 1939. Powered by twin Wright R-1820 turbo-supercharged engines, and featuring a heavy nose armament and tricycle landing gear, it proved to be the only Grumman aircraft ever ordered by the USAAC. The manufacturer claimed the fighter would attain 424mph at 25,000ft, but engine/turbo problems plagued the prototype. Indeed, it suffered severe damage when one of the engines exploded in November 1941.[48]

Following changes to the CP38-390 issued in 1938, the single-engined pursuit RFP CP39-770 was reissued to permit a wider range of top performance engine-critical altitudes, from 15,000 to 20,000ft, as well as expanding acceptable design features to allow a more conventional approach. The re-issue of CP39-770 in July 1939 was a direct action following disappointing XP-39 flight tests. It was framed around requirements for a better "single-place, single-engine, pursuit interceptor equal to any in the world." One of the conclusions arising from the Kilner–Lindbergh committee (a body created by Maj Gen Arnold in 1939 to advise him on how best to identify the key long-term requirements for the USAAC) and succeeding Emmons Board conferences was that the P-39, P-40, and the new P-46 were unsatisfactory either as interceptors or as long-range escorts.[49]

What started life as the Seversky AP-10 eventually evolved into the Republic XP-47 in 1941 following the fitment of the new turbo-supercharged Pratt & Whitney R-2800 engine. This aircraft is the XP-47B, which closely resembled the production-standard Thunderbolt that would soon follow. (*Philip Jarrett Collection*)

The USAAC had also amended CP39-770 and -775 to provide production contracts in lots of 110 to 300 aircraft. The Seversky AP-4J and AP-10, Douglas DS-312A, Bell XP-45, and Curtiss XP-46 aircraft were submitted for evaluation, and although the latter finished third behind the AP-4J and DS-312A, Gen George Brett recommended development of the XP-46 on September 1, 1939. He also assigned it top priority for testing when the aircraft arrived at Wright Field. The USAAC-MD chose the XP-46 based on Curtiss representations that it would attain "410mph at 15,000ft when fully loaded, including armor plate, armament and self-sealing tanks." The company placed great expectations on achieving significantly lower drag via an embedded radiator and duct system to achieve a "Meredith Effect."

Specifically, because of the disappointing performance of the turbo-supercharged Allison-powered XP-39, the USAAC knew it was even further behind proven European single-engined fighters already in service. Great faith was therefore placed in the new Curtiss pursuit. The XP-46 and XP-46A were exhaustively evaluated by the USAAC-MD Engineering and Flight Test pilots and engineers, as the aircraft was intended to be the primary USAAC fighter from late 1941. When it first flew, in February 1941, it was stripped, lacking armor, self-sealing tanks, or armament. Thus configured, it did nearly meet the USAAC specification for speed at 22,000ft, but when the second prototype was flown fully loaded as required in operational service, it achieved only 355mph at 12,200ft.

The USAAC also requested that Seversky design and build the AP-10 lightweight fighter with the Allison V-1710 engine. As soon as Republic became the controlling entity of Seversky, the USAAC contracted for two AP-10s, re-designated XP-47A and XP-47B. The contract was rejected by HQ-AAC in September, however.[50] Following the failure to build the Allison-powered lightweight fighter, Republic was encouraged by the USAAC-MD to take another direction, and it began preliminary designs to evaluate the installation of the new Pratt & Whitney R-2800 engine. In 1941 the revised design emerged as the XP-47B.

The reason for pointing out the collage of fighters developed by the major manufacturers for the USAAC through to the end of 1939 is that the US aircraft industry failed to produce any single-engine airframes that matched the performance of the Bf 109 or Spitfire. Nor had the USAAC (or US Navy) yet flown a radial-engined fighter to compare with the newest German entry, the Fw 190. Vought Aircraft, however, completed the XF4U-1 mock-up in February 1939 for US Navy inspection. Also unknown to the USAAC or US Navy was the presence of the Japanese Mitsubishi A6M Zero-sen fighter, first flown in April 1939. The A6M delivered startling performance against US fighters in combat in 1941–42. The Fw 190 was equally effective against all RAF fighters from September 1941, and also against USAAF fighters in 1942–43.

On September 1, 1939, Germany launched an all-out *Blitzkrieg* on Poland to start World War II in Europe.

In the fall of 1939 key aerodynamicists Irving Ashkenas and George Mellinger were hired from Cal Tech by Ed Horkey. Both were to make significant contributions to the Mustang as they gained experience.[51]

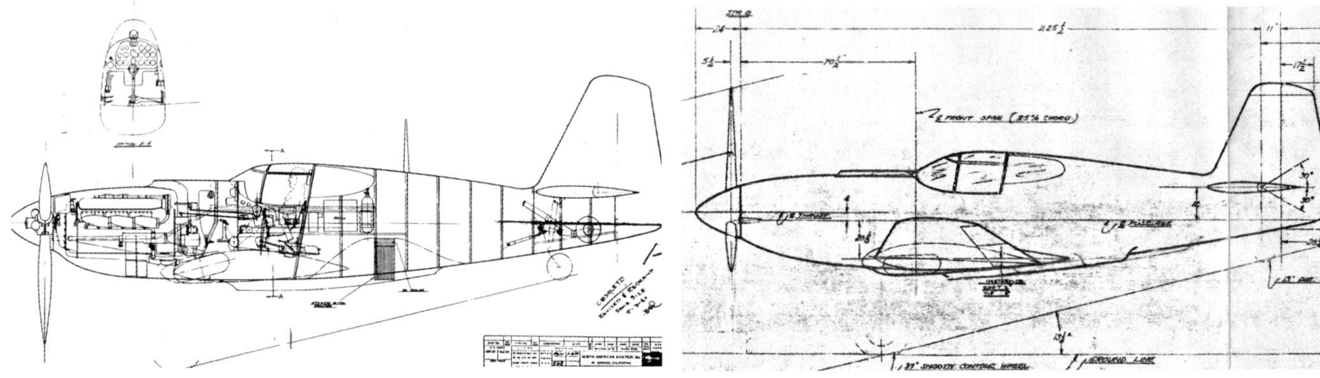

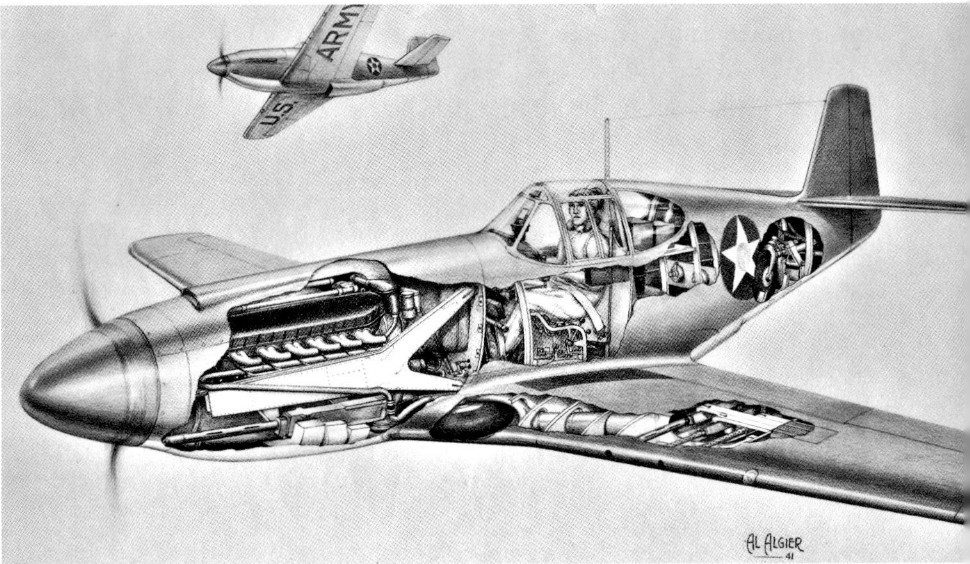

ABOVE The P-509 "High-Speed Pursuit (Allison)" shown with imbedded radiator and oil cooler – the first attempt by NAA to incorporate a Meredith Effect cooling system into an aircraft. Contrast the scoop/plenum design with that of the XP-51B. (© *The Boeing Company*)

ABOVE RIGHT The P-509 was not only shorter than the X73, it also had a smaller wingspan and different wing airfoil. In addition, the X73 front coolant scoop was positioned further aft. (© *The Boeing Company*)

RIGHT NAA artist Al Algier created this cutaway rendition of the P-509 in USAAC colors in early 1941. (© *The Boeing Company*)

In November 1939 Congress passed a version of the Neutrality Act in which the US could provide arms to Britain and France on a "cash and carry basis." The Director General of Purchases, Arthur Purvis, established the BPC US office in New York City on the 7th.[52] Now that war was a reality, the French and British (and Chinese) were anxiously seeking the newest army and navy fighters, and other arms, while trying to bypass the Neutrality Acts imposed by Congress in 1935, 1936, 1937, and 1939. During this period, a flurry of back channel diplomatic exchanges occurred between the US and British governments with the primary objective being to organize more cohesive purchasing and acquisition activities on behalf of both the French and British. Following the successful conclusion of the discussions, the highly confidential Anglo-French Purchasing Board (AFPB) was organized in New York City on November 30. Purvis was appointed Chairman and France's François Bloch-Lainé filled the role of Vice-Chairman.

The NACA began wind tunnel testing of the new NACA 45-125 high-speed/low-drag laminar-flow airfoil at this time too.

At the end of November NAA received a contract for the NA-50 export fighter and opened Charge Number NA-68.

The onset of war also accelerated changes to NAA management and design initiatives. Following Kindelberger's return from his earlier European trip in November 1938, it was clear to him that the preliminary designs embodied in the trainer-based NA-53 and lightweight P-500 pursuit concepts, as upgraded trainer airframes and underpowered export fighters, were no match for either the Bf 109 or the Hurricane and Spitfire.

Although NAA was rejected as a bidder for pursuit projects, it was invited to comment on the other designs evaluated by the USAAC Fighter Projects Department led by Lt Ben Kelsey at the USAAC-MD, Wright Field.

From mid-1939 through to December 1940, Schmued continued progress on preliminary drawings for a single-engined pursuit, with the Allison V-1710 in mind for its powerplant. According to Atwood, he and Schmued initiated sketches to embed the radiator into the fuselage aft of the cockpit in "late 1939."[53] NAA issued Charge Number SC-46 for a single-seat, lightweight Ranger-powered pursuit on December 18, 1939.[54] The drawing referenced for both the preliminary design data and associated performance estimates based on the P-500 was formally released as P-500-1. At about the same time the NA-53 was reopened as NA-50A. It is probable that Schmued was also working on the preliminary design P-509-1 High-speed Allison Pursuit between mid-December 1939 and early January 1940, as both the P-509 and P-500-6 were referenced for the Pursuit Proposal, as recounted below.[55]

Worthy of note is the single-page data sheet on page 60 extracted from Pursuit Data Analysis, circa – 1939, labeled "Pursuit Proposal."[56] The P-509 dimensional data would change over the next three months to the form submitted to the AFPB in mid-March 1940.

The P-500 was one of the alternate proposals submitted to the BPC in lieu of producing the P-40 at NAA. Although theoretically having a higher performance than the NA-50 and NA-53, it was, nevertheless, viewed by the BPC as being little more than a fast armed trainer. (© *The Boeing Company*)

PURSUIT PROPOSAL / AIRPLANE DATA SHEET			
	Specifications		**Similar to**
1.	Wing area	201sq ft	P-509 (+11sq ft)
2.	Wing loading	37.8lb/sq ft	P-509 (36.3lb/sq ft)
3.	Wing Section	2,516 Root/2,508Tip	P-500 and P-509 (High Speed Wing)
4.	Normal Gross Wt	7,600lb	P-509 (6,455lb)
5.	Vmax – Altitude	390mph at 19,000ft	P-509 (400mph at 19,000ft)
6.	Vmax – sea level	350mph	N/A
7.	Vlanding- Stalling speed, Flaps Down	84mph	N/A
8.	Vdive (applied)	595mph	N/A
9.	Vterminal	595mph	N/A
10.	Applied Positive Load Factor	Applied=8.00/Des.=12.0	N/A
11.	Applied Negative Load Factor	Applied=-4.0/Des.=6.0	N/A
12.	Applied Positive Gust Factor	Applied=5.92/Des.=8.88	N/A
13.	Applied Negative Gust Factor	Applied=-5.92/Des.=-8.88	N/A
14.	Landing Load Factor	7.0	N/A

1.) The airfoil sections above are the same as those called out on Drawing 500-6 for the Menasco-powered light weight single seat pursuit design.
2.) Other attributes favor the P-509.

USAAC CHRONOLOGY FOR JANUARY THROUGH DECEMBER 1939

By early 1939 several of the senior officers within the USAAC were beginning to recognize that single-engined interceptors such as the Spitfire and Bf 109 would soon have the performance to challenge the B-17 at altitude, and began to review future options. Both British and American observers in Spain during the Spanish Civil War reported serious doubts that bombers could prosecute long-range missions without fighter escorts.

Two years earlier, the Air Corps Tactical School (ACTS) Report "Aerial Warfare in Spain, February 1937" cited the "need for escort fighters to protect the bombers against attacking fighters."[57] Augmenting the ACTS report were further assessments from American intelligence pointing to the failings of the defensive armament carried by bombers on both sides in Spain, with the weaponry creating "no problem for the attackers" and further illustrating the need for escorted bomber formations.[58]

In March 1939 Secretary of War Henry Woodring directed the USAAC to study the entire question of air power, with definitions for the role of bombardment, pursuit, attack, observation, training, and transport to be followed by a table of organizational recommendations to support those missions, and to present its findings to the Chief of Staff.

On May 1 Maj Gen Arnold also appointed a special panel to recommend research and development priorities for USAAC research and development funding for FY 40 and beyond. Arnold asked Charles Lindbergh to join Cols Carl Spaatz, Earl Naiden, and Edwin Lyon on the Kilner–Lindbergh Board to provide extremely valuable insight on German industry, new aircraft, Luftwaffe training, and support functions. The Board, and specifically Lindbergh, produced far more information than Arnold had received from US Intelligence sources. The record-breaking aviator had just completed a nearly one-year grand tour of the European aircraft industry, secretly gathering intelligence on pursuit and bomber designs. Upon his return, Lindbergh gave Arnold a private briefing at Thayer Hotel at West Point.[59]

Ironically, despite the looming conflict in Europe and the Sino-Japanese War in China, the Board came back with an odd ranking of priorities, namely: (1) Liquid-cooled engine development, (2) Improved fire-control systems for bomber aircraft, and (3) "A fighter aircraft to rank with the best in the world."[60]

A major product of Woodring's March directive was the Army Field Manual FM 1-5 "Employment of Aviation," which was completed and released on April 15, 1940. It addressed Training; Special Purpose (non-combat aviation; Reconnaissance; Liaison – tied to Army ground units); Overseas Garrison; and GHQ Aviation (Combat). The GHQ mission focused on Combat (Striking force over long distance); Defense (close in) over most important industrial sites within the US; and Support (Logistics as well as Air–Ground (direct support) against enemy ground troops).

In November 1939 Arnold held another conference with the Air Staff. The stated purpose was to review intelligence reports from Europe regarding heavy losses of bomber-type aircraft to single-engined pursuit aircraft, and, (1) analyze European bomber/pursuit aircraft in comparison with American aircraft and methods and, (2) improve tactics and equipment for both bombers and fighters. Included in the conference were the commanding officers of GHQ, the USAAC-MD, Plans Division, and Ordnance. The group, and particularly Gen Delos Emmons, Commanding Officer, GHQ, USAAC, were instructed to solicit input from pursuit and bombardment leaders.[61]

The reason for mentioning the findings of both the Kilner–Lindbergh Board and, later, the Emmons Board is to illustrate that, independent of the technology issues associated with developing a long-range, high-altitude-capable escort, many of Arnold's direct reports remained optimistic that future belligerent powers would not be able to effectively stop the B-17 from bombing long-range targets with acceptable losses.

On December 26, however, Gen Emmons wrote a memo to Arnold, stating, "There is no question in my mind that American bombardment units could not defend themselves against American pursuit units."[62] The reported findings from all of the conferees were submitted by early January 1940. From the November 1939 conference and assembled opinions, Plans Division issued FM 1-15 "Tactical and Technology of Air Fighting" in September 1940. The two central roles for pursuit were identified as (1) "Deny the Hostile Force Freedom of the Air" and, (2) "Provide Bombardment Escort into Hostile Skies."[63] Also noted in FM 1-15 were comments that the projected

The prototype Fw 190 V1, seen here undergoing final assembly in the Focke-Wulf Bremen plant in the spring of 1939, was developed into one of the finest all-around fighters of World War II. The unusual (and unsuccessful) ducted spinner with its large circular central intake area is particularly visible. When the Fw 190A commenced operations on the Channel Front in the fall of 1941 it came as a huge shock to the RAF. (*Tony Holmes Collection*)

P-38 and P-39 were suitable for the interceptor/defense role, but the P-39, P-40, and P-46 were not deemed adequate for either interceptor or escort roles.

The conclusions drawn were that single-engined technology and current designs were inadequate to provide for both the necessary fuel fraction *and* adequate performance/maneuverability to defeat enemy single-engined fighters over the target. By inference, the second conclusion was that only twin-engined fighter aircraft might achieve the necessary escort role and air fighter attributes.[64]

Post-war, Gen Arnold wrote in his memoirs of the lessons that the USAAC failed to learn following its study of the Spanish Civil War:

> The escort of bomber formations proceeding to and from their objectives, by double or more than double their number of fighters, has been found on both sides to be a necessity, notwithstanding the ability of the bomber to shoot down fighters. Yet, we in the United States were still debating the need for fighter escort for bombers.[65]

MUSTANG RIVAL NOTES – 1939

On January 27, 1939, Lt Ben Kelsey flew the XP-38 for the first time,[66] and this was followed two weeks later by the first flight, by Paul Balfour, of the twin-engined NA-40 Attack Bomber. Also in January, the USAAC held a fighter competition to include the Curtiss XP-37, Model 75R, and XP-40, the Bell XP-39, the Seversky XP-41, and the Lockheed XP-38. In April 1940 the XP-40 was declared the winner and the manufacturer was awarded a contract for 524 P-40s.[67]

The XP-39 made its first flight on April 6, 1939.[68] In accordance with the USAAC belief in combining in-line engines with turbo-superchargers, the XP-39 was so equipped. The performance of the XP-39 was short of expected capabilities and very disappointing to the USAAC. That said, it remained as an alternative to the Mustang for tactical and reconnaissance roles through to 1943.

The USAAC was unaware of the first flight, in June 1939, of the prototype of one of World War II's finest fighters in the form of the Fw 190 V1. From July 1942 the Mustang and the Focke-Wulf would clash in deadly combat in the skies over Europe.[69]

NAA CHRONOLOGY FOR JANUARY THROUGH EARLY APRIL 1940

Between December 18, 1939 and the end of January 1940, P-500 Ranger Powered Pursuit proposal drawings released by Schmued's team included inboard profile, cowl, wings, landing gear, and three-view drawings. This package accompanied Kindelberger and Atwood to New York City to meet with the AFPB on February 1 and 2, 1940.

The British and French quickly recognized that the proposed "fighter" could not compete with Axis frontline equivalents.[70] At the end of the meeting the AFPB formally requested that NAA build P-40s instead of P-500s.

During February 1940 Schmued continued further refinement of the conceptual layouts for the P-509, earlier prepared as "High-Speed Pursuit Fighter (Allison powered)" for the CP39-770 Single Engine Pursuit. The P-509 drawing illustrated the streamlined lower inlet/radiator cowl aft of the wing to house the radiator/oil cooler and showed the lengthened exhaust fairing and exit. This is the first known example of NAA's introduction of the "Meredith Effect" ramjet exhaust cooling approach. It also used the same airfoil as the P-500, the NACA 2516-34, but with a longer fuselage and larger empennage than previous NAA proposals for fighters with less horsepower.[71]

The NAA Report "Preliminary Design Data – Single Seat Pursuit (Allison Engine) – General," completed on or about December 18, 1939, first made reference to Drawing P-509-1. The aircraft in this four-page document featured the slightly less powerful Allison V-1710-35 engine, but had no armor and no self-sealing wing fuel tanks.[72]

On February 1, 1940, Kindelberger wrote to GMC Board member Ernest Breech:

> We have studied from all the angles the idea of building a pursuit plane and it doesn't seem to pay due to the time element. It is possible that the French and British combination will ask us to build quite a few Curtiss Pursuit planes and we could handle that probably without much difficulty if they would permit us to change some of the detail design to fit better to our processes.[73]

On the 25th, the AFPB again requested that NAA build P-40s, and Lt Col Oliver Echols supported the request. NAA executives deliberated over the options of ignoring the USAAC-MD versus making one more try to convince the AFPB. (Both Schmued's taped presentation, entitled "Preliminary Design of the Mustang," at Long Beach

Auditorium on January 30, 1970, and his manuscript "Design of the P-51 Mustang," dated 1985, have been consolidated below and in future quotes of his recollections. The source reference "PM&DM" will be used from this point forward.)

From Schmued's recollections:

> One afternoon, "Dutch" Kindelberger came into my office and asked, "Ed, do we want to build P-40s here?" I replied, "Well, 'Dutch,' don't let us build an obsolete airplane, let's build a new one. We can design and build a better one." And that's exactly what he wanted to hear. So he said: "Ed, I'm going to Great Britain in about two weeks and I need an inboard profile, three-view drawing, performance estimates, weight estimate, specifications and some detail drawings on the gun installation to take along. Then I would like to sell that new airplane that you developed."
>
> He said the rules for design were simple. Make it the fastest airplane you can and build it around a man that is 5ft 10in tall and weighs 140lb. It should have two 20mm cannon in each wing and it should meet all the design requirements of the United States Air Force [Schmued meant "Army Air Corps" in 1940]. Now, with this specification, as skimpy as it was, I went to work.
>
> We looked around to find an engineer or somebody in our organization that weighed 140lb and was 5ft 10in. Right in our Engineering Department, we found a man that fitted that specification – Art Chester. He was a famous air racing pilot who joined North American because there was no speed flying with the war on. He was a well thought of man and we were happy to have him. He later became our Project Engineer on the powerplant of the P-51. That was the beginning of the P-51.[74]

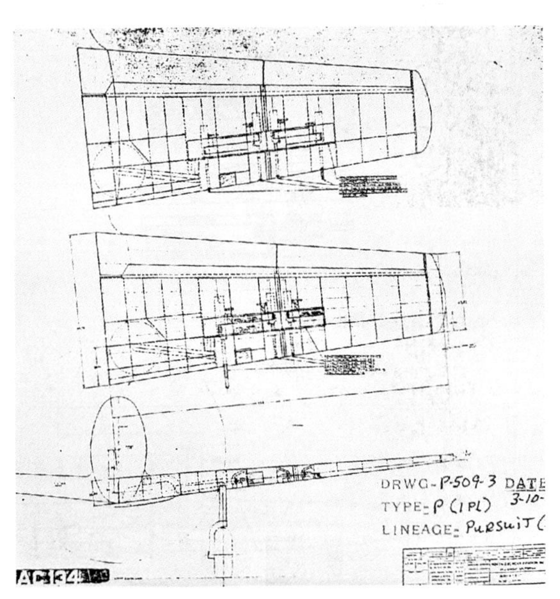

This technical drawing, dated October 3, 1940, shows the armament options for the P-509 that were presented to the BPC by Atwood. These include four 20mm Hispano II cannon, although there was no hope NAA would receive allocation of the weapon for a foreign customer from the USAAC. (© *The Boeing Company*)

Charge number NA-73X was opened for the High Speed Pursuit. Between March 6 and 11, 1940, the P-509 design data was further refined to change wing area and add self-sealing tanks and armor plating, as well as the new V-1710-39/F3R engine with increased normal horsepower and greater take-off power. All previous work on performance estimates was accordingly revised and compared against RAF Operational Requirement OR.73. The last releases of Drawing P-509-1 and P-509-3 with different armament layouts, including 20mm cannon, were completed on March 10. These two drawings reflected the pre-low-drag airfoils (NACA 2516-34) of the P-509-1 with different armament provisions.[75]

The ensuing Report No. 1592 "Preliminary Design Data, Single Place Pursuit, (Allison Engine)," dated March 11, 1940, clearly reflected dialogue with the BPC's engineering staff, as it included self-sealing tanks, armor plate, and increased power supply. American aircraft such as the P-38, P-39, and P-40 did not have those features, but the RAF deemed them essential for combat worthiness. It also had increased horsepower, achieved by adopting the newer Allison V-1710-39/F3R.[76]

Report No. 1592 reflected several important changes from the earlier preliminary design data to frame the Pursuit Fighter Specification delivered to the BPC by Kindelberger in mid-March 1939. Among the most important changes were:

1. An increase in gross weight, with "normal load" increased from 6,455lb to 6,540lb due to self-sealing fuel tanks and armor plate in accordance with known RAF requirements, as well as an increase in main-wheel tire diameters from 27in. to 30in.
2. Improved performance due to the increase in Allison V-1710-39/F3 take-off horsepower from 1,000hp to 1,200hp, 1,050hp at a military rating for 3,000rpm at 16,000ft; 950hp to 1,050hp at normal power rating, with 2,600rpm at 12,500ft. All figures based on 90-octane gasoline.
3. The wing area was changed to 180sq ft, with a 33ft span. Rate of climb and endurance decreased slightly, however, owing to higher wing loading and the slightly lower fuel capacity of self-sealing tanks.
4. A change in location of armament to include two 0.50cal AN/M2 Browning machine guns in the wing root, instead of under the cowling, but still firing through the propeller arc.
5. A specification that the airfoil would be a "NACA series airfoil developed for high speed performance," whereas the original 509-1 specified a NACA 2516-34 airfoil at the root and 2508-54R airfoil at the tip. The currently contemplated airfoil sections were NACA 23016 for the root and 23008 for the tip.
6. The incorporation of Air Ministry Specification O.R.73, as applicable to further define P-509.

NAA Report No. 1592 further identified limit and failure/destructive load limits to be +/-8G and +/-12G respectively, with negative G load limits of -4.0G and -6.0G, respectively. The applied indicial gust factor (different from high angle-of-attack (normally dive pull-out)) of sharp vertical shear loads was +/-5.92 and +/-8.88G, respectively. Each of the design criteria conformed to published USAAC standard structural design requirements for pursuit aircraft. These load factors were in accordance with the USAAC-MD at the time, but were high relative to British design standards. Several standard load factors were reduced slightly by the Schmued design team when the Lightweight XP-51F contract was initiated on January 5, 1943.

As an aside, several USAAF-MD officers attempted to derail the purchase of the A-36 in 1942 by stating that the Mustang was not designed according to the Division's Specifications for Design, which was not true. Lee Atwood, as Chief – Engineer for NAA, adhered to the very latest USAAC/USAAF specifications (and updates) for all company projects from his very first day on the job. Atwood's biography, listed in the Bibliography, details his experiences as an engineer with the USAAC-MD.

NAA Report No. 1593 "High Speed of Allison-Powered, Export Pursuit,"[77] dated one week after Report No. 1592, was a milestone in the development for the upcoming proposal to the AFPB. Prepared by the aerodynamics and thermodynamics team of Edward Horkey, Irving Ashkenas, Joe Beerer, and G. R. Mellinger, this report introduced several concepts of extreme importance to the development of the Mustang. It specifically addressed the technical innovations that were proposed for the P-509.

First, aerodynamicist Ed Horkey relied heavily on recent NACA Technical Reports of the new low-drag/high-speed airfoil wind tunnel tests at the GALCIT, which resulted in astonishing low-drag properties. Notable references included the NACA Confidential Report of August 1939, "Preliminary Investigation of Certain Laminar-Flow Airfoils for Application at High Speeds and Reynolds Numbers"; the NACA Confidential Report of January 1940, "Boundary-Layer Transition on the NACA 0012 and 23012 Airfoils in the 8-Foot High Speed Wind Tunnel"; the NACA Confidential Report of June 1939, "Preliminary Report on Laminar Flow Airfoils and New Methods Adapted for Airfoil and Boundary-Layer Investigations"; and the NACA Confidential Report of February 1940, "Wind Tunnel Tests of the NACA 45-125 Airfoil for High Speed Airplanes" Finally, several reports pertaining to exhaust gas thrust of radiator systems, including the NACA Confidential Report "Experimental Determination of Exhaust Gas Thrust" of February 1940, were cited in the NAA Report No. 1593.[78] Each of these technical papers was absorbed as Schmued's design team deliberated on the selection of the proposed airfoil selection for the wing, and the design approach to the radiator and oil cooler.

The NACA 230XX was emerging as the safe "go to" airfoil for low-drag, high-speed applications for the Fw 190, P-38, and F4U (and later the F6F and F8F as well) and was a compelling low-risk/high-performance choice. On the other hand, the potential for dramatic reductions in profile drag offered by the new NACA 45-125-type airfoil were tantalizing, but needed further validation to reduce the thickness-to-chord ratio from 20 percent thickness to a more practical 15–16 percent thickness.

Report No. 1593 carefully pointed out that the NACA and NAA were developing the algorithms to calculate an optimal "thinner" low-drag airfoil to further reduce drag compared with the "fat" NACA 45-125. The departure from an existing airfoil with valid test results demanded significant theoretical analytical exploration to select a thinner airfoil with various camber options to achieve a pressure distribution that mitigated the early onset of compressibility, yet maintained desirable lift coefficients.[79]

The team also drew heavily on both Dr. Millikan's paper in the *Journal of the Institute of Aeronautical Sciences* for September 1936 "On the Results of Aerodynamic Research and their Application to Aircraft Construction" and his aforementioned "Performance Calculations for Idealized 1938 Pursuit Airplane."[80]

The potential for additional thrust to be gained by careful selection of engine exhaust stacks and the possibility of achieving exhaust thrust from the radiator/oil cooler combination presented in the P-509 preliminary design (a large radiator submerged in the fuselage aft of the wing) were also detailed and presented in NAA Report No. 1593.[81]

The new Release of Aircraft Policy, executed on March 25, permitted the AFPB to purchase certain modern types such as the YP-38/Model 222, P-39, and P-40/XP-46, as well as other designs including the NA-73. While the AFPB acted on various selection and financial arrangements, the BPC was the primary contact for presentations, technical discussions, and contract development with NAA. It also hosted RAF and RAE technical teams at its New York City headquarters, and presented a united team to NAA for both the technical and financial arrangements. Bell Aircraft secured the first Foreign Release Agreement on April 4, convincing the AFPB that the P-39 could achieve 400mph at 15,000ft.[82] Lockheed and Republic (formerly Seversky) offered the P-38 and P-43, respectively, but Secretary of War Harry Woodring refused to allow the fitting of General Electric turbo-superchargers to the engines of either aircraft. He justified this decision by stating that they were "too secret and too scarce" for export.[83]

Thus, the stage was set when Kindelberger and Atwood made their trip to New York City to visit the BPC on around March 20. They presented the combined Nos. 1592 and 1593 Reports and P-509-1 concept as the final NAA proposal in lieu of the P-40. The British technical team, led by H. C. B. Thomas, exchanged queries and questions with NAA engineering regarding the approach to powerplant coolant and oil cooling systems. The design proposal was developed to incorporate the benefits "of negative drag/positive thrust" research offered by Meredith, Capon, and Gothert – namely to combine the lower scoop, radiator/oil cooler, exit plenum, and variable-dimension rear scoop to achieve Meredith Effect jet thrust as proposed.[84]

Other improvements in the design configuration of the new fighter were subtler but no less appealing as examples of NAA's innovative approach to design. Examples included Edgar Schmued's application of the conic projection method to develop second-degree curves for mold lines to create a structure which allowed air to flow more conformally over the surface. When the Mustang first appeared, it was obvious that the shape of the fuselage was a very clean streamlined design in which there were no bumps or bulges, or abrupt changes to the shape, with a gradual increase in cross-sectional area from the spinner to the cockpit enclosure and lower cowl for the radiator.

In most of the contemporary designs for frontline fighters the radiator was positioned under the nose and behind the propeller, which automatically obviated a "gradually increasing cross-section" immersed in the freestream and propeller vortex flows. Exceptions, in which the radiator scoop was placed behind the wing, in 1940 included the British Hurricane, the French Arsenal VG-33 and Dewoitine D.520, and the Soviet Mikoyen-Gurevich MiG-1. Their designs probably reduced drag compared with fighters that had under-nose radiators; none of the manufacturers of these aircraft claimed "net thrust" from their scoops.

As will be explained later, to achieve the promised "zero net drag" for the drag imposed by both the pressure drag of the plenum ducting and the intercooler and oil cooler radiators, significant "try and test" adjustments were made to the shape of the front scoop and its location at the bottom of the fuselage (to create the "gutter"); to intake plenum design to delay boundary-layer separation internally and move pressure stagnation regions near the radiators, to modify the radiator and heat transfer vanes; and to provide for lower turbulence aft of the radiator, with exit temperatures above 170°F. There is no evidence that "zero net drag" was ever fully achieved pre-P-51B.

The engine exhaust stacks required further investigation to achieve optimum effect (exhaust jet angle to airflow, number of exhaust stack exits, diameter of each exhaust) with minimum performance loss. The entire skin would be flush riveted with butted joints that were then puttied, accentuating the clean mold lines and reducing both friction and profile drag due to uneven surfaces. All major air leaks (flaps, ailerons, elevator, landing gear, etc.) would be sealed off to further reduce parasite drag. As noted above, successive improvements to exhaust ejectors and increased horsepower from the Allison to the Merlin significantly enhanced the exhaust thrust contribution to performance (see Appendix A for further discussion).

All this hard work eventually prevailed. The inclusion of the British theory on the potential negative drag of the cooling system (the Meredith Effect), customer relations, product reliability, and documentation (Report No. 1562 and drawings P-509-1, P-509-2, and P-509-3) regarding the new design provided the AFPB with enough confidence to elevate its support and recommend that the contract be awarded. The approval to move forward was issued by Sir Henry Self at the New York City offices of the BPC.

Based on the favorable negotiations and tentative approval by the AFPB, NAA issued Shop Order SC-1050 for construction of the mock-up of the P-509 as well as continued research into low-drag airfoil selection analytics. SC-1050 also authorized the GALCIT wind tunnel tests to study drag for different armament configurations for the P-509, and instructed the model group to complete the mock-up by April 17, 1940. NAA asked for and received confidential design data for the Allison V-1710-39/FSR engine. Ed Horkey also received the latest NACA report, No. 896, regarding the insights and opinions for consideration of including Meredith Effect radiator cooling designs.[85]

Also during the late March deliberations, Lt Col Echols repeated his request to NAA to build P-40s for the AFPB. His plan was to offload some P-40 production obligations to prepare for anticipated P-46 deliveries. Echols also planned to obtain a Foreign Release Agreement waiver to export the P-46, and use the financial arrangements to help pay Curtiss for armor and self-sealing fuel tank upgrades required by the RAF for the aircraft.

Ultimately, the introduction of the innovative P-509-1 fighter design proposal to the AFPB in March 1940 was accomplished only by the extreme perseverance of President Kindelberger and Vice President of Engineering Lee Atwood and the innovation of the outstanding NAA engineering teams. The unique design approaches to the high-speed fighter, including extraordinary drag reduction concepts and plausible radiator cooling to achieve low-drag/jet thrust, combined with the trust NAA had built up among its customers in respect to the performance and quality of the company's training aircraft, were the key factors leading to the AFPB's approval of the fighter design.

What is clear is that the approach to reduce cooling and pressure drag involved several attributes not applied by Supermarine, Hawker, and Messerschmitt in their radiator cooling designs. The refinements included first designing the intake scoop and lengthy surfaces of the forward upper and lower plenum to smooth out turbulent flow to the radiator/oil cooler face, then providing a long converging plenum aft of the radiator to a small exit rear scoop. This approach required the upper and lower plenum to extend deep into the fuselage, and the expanding of its cross-section to enclose the top and bottom of the radiator front face. Second, the design required flow speed to the radiator front face to be reduced as much as possible (with a commensurate decrease in turbulence due to boundary-layer separation) to enable the single large radiator to efficiently transfer more heat from the coolant tubes to the air passing between them. Third, the rear scoop had to be adjustable in respect to exit area so that it could be closed sufficiently enough to create pressure on the rear face of the radiator. This design enabled a pressure distribution lower than the front face, thus permitting "suction efficiency" through the radiator. Fourth, the long plenum aft of the radiator contracted ("squeezed") to enable the flow velocity of the heated air exiting from the radiator to rapidly increase to the scoop exit. This design approach provided a combination of heated and higher-velocity air through the exit scoop to create the "jet effect." Last, the rear scoop had to be designed to open and close (increase/decrease exit area) in order to also manage the temperature of the radiator coolant. The feature that was not included in the original design of the X73 was any initial attempt to create a "gutter effect" to prevent boundary-layer air from entering the front scoop.

The design of the radiator cooling system underwent many incremental improvements through to the P-51H. More discussion of coolant system design is presented in Appendix A.

Separate from the NAA effort, Curtiss had also been pursuing the sale of the XP-46 to the AFPB for manufacture in Buffalo, following the original game plan set up by the USAAC. It was also aware that the British delegation had approached NAA about building P-40s, and that NAA had proposed a Meredith Effect-based radiator design. From a Lee Atwood presentation of his recollections many years later, the events during the ten days preceding the delivery of a Letter of Intent to NAA from Sir Henry Self are noted below:[86]

> In my position as vice-president I had responsibility for contract administration, among other things, and so had occasion to go to 15 Broad Street [where the BPC had its New York City office] rather frequently to negotiate contracts, prices, spare parts, equipment, and support services. In January 1940 I told "Dutch" that I would like to try to get some kind of a fighter authorization, and that I hoped my ideas on reduced cooling drag might be a vehicle. He was generally supportive, but skeptical, as I was myself. My best hope was perhaps a contract to modify a single P-40 or possibly to build an experimental airplane.
>
> The BPC, in addition to Sir Henry, had as principal personnel Air Commodore George Baker, Col William Cave, and H. C. B. (Tommy) Thomas.

Civil servant Sir Henry Self was the leader of the BPC, and in this capacity he signed the Letter of Intent for the NA-73 High Speed Pursuit on April 11, 1940. (*Keystone Press / Alamy Stock Photo*)

> Thomas was the senior technical expert, and I used some occasions to talk to him about the cooling drag subject, making the point that my confidence in the possibilities of a major improvement was based on the Farnborough papers as well as the natural technical logic of the application.
>
> I made a point of visiting Tommy and also Bill Cave when I could, both on direct business and from Dayton and Washington, which I visited frequently. Coast-to-coast was just a long overnight trip then in DC-3s, and I could cover quite a bit of ground. I could see that my suggestion had been taken seriously after two or three visits, and I believe that Thomas established some communication with Farnborough on the subject. I used only some free-hand sketches, but Tommy was very astute and technically qualified. The questions about implementation got more concrete, but no company engineering work was started, and it seemed a long shot.
>
> I had discussed my concept with Ed Schmued, preliminary design supervisor, who, though not technically educated, had a real talent for shapes and arrangements and mechanical components, but the first work authorization, denoted NA-73, was not issued until April 1940.

Although the fact-based timeline recounting the concept of installing the radiator in the lower fuselage, then further evolutionary placement of the intake scoop protruding low and behind the wing, are fairly well known, it should be assumed that a combination of engineers at NAA and the AFPB made important contributions as the P-509 evolved into the X73, then the NA-73, and then the NA-83. Both E. C. B. Baker of the BPC and Dr. B. S. Shenstone of the RAE were consulted regarding the approach NAA was taking to these technical issues during the late March/early April 1940 discussions, and again in early 1941 when flight testing and more wind tunnel testing revealed shortfalls between theory and actual results.

In the authors' opinion, the aft placement of the radiator and cooling system design was equally in the domain of Lee Atwood (conceptual) and Edward Horkey and Edgar Schmued (practical), and was consistent with Schmued's passion for second-degree curve and area rule-based airframe design. Similarly, the refinement of the high-level detail design considerations is just as likely to have begun with the BPC/RAE technical experts, based on known issues with the Spitfire and Hurricane, and then been referred to NAA for practical designs under Schmued, Horkey, and Beerer. The key responsibility for cooling system designs lay with Horkey (aerodynamicist) and Joe Beerer (thermodynamics) in Preliminary Design. Both men worked closely to further refine and improve the cooling system through to the end of the P-51H and XP-82 designs.

Returning to the Atwood narrative:

> Finally, early in that month [April], I was invited into Sir Henry's office and was advised approximately as follows: That they had decided to accept our proposal; that I should prepare a letter contract for his signature; that it should provide for

the purchase of 320 aircraft of our design; that it provide a schedule and a not-to-exceed price per airplane; that the British-supplied equipment, including engines, would be specified; and, finally, that a definitive contract would be negotiated on the basis of this letter contract.

Burdette Wright (far left), Curtiss-Wright Aeroplane and Motor Division General Manager, negotiated the supply of P-40 and XP-46 design data to Lee Atwood so that NAA could comply with Sir Harry Self's condition for the Letter of Intent for the NA-73 contract. Wright is seen here with Maj Gen Henry "Hap" Arnold, Don R. Berlin (chief engineer of the Curtiss plant at Buffalo) and William S. Knudsen (Chairman of the National Defense Advisory Committee) on September 14, 1940. Arnold and Knudsen had come to Buffalo to inspect the Curtiss-Wright plant. *(Smithsonian National Air and Space Museum (NASM 2001-13846))*

Furthermore, he told me that since we had never produced a fighter airplane, he considered it very desirable that we have some P-40 data as a helpful guide. He specified the P-40 wind tunnel report and the flight test report. He suggested that I attempt to obtain these data. I told him I would immediately try to do so and took the night train to Buffalo, home of the Curtiss plant. Parenthetically, this was on April 10, 1940, the day Hitler seized Denmark and the Norwegian ports. I remember on that day Col Bill Cave told me that this was just one of a number of obvious moves.

In Buffalo, Burdette Wright, general manager of the Curtiss Airplane Company, was reasonable enough, considering the competitive aspects. Capt Ben Kelsey of the Air Corps is reported to have said that the Air Corps encouraged him to sell me the data. This I don't know, but it could have been the case. Later, "Dutch" Kindelberger quipped that we didn't even open the package, although I am sure that some of our technical staff did examine the reports. I gave Burdy [Burdette Wright] a marker for $56,000 for the copies and then went back to New York, and as soon as I could, presented the letter contract. After staff review, Sir Henry signed it, and I went to the LaGuardia Airport. Work Order NA-73 was issued shortly after.

Between April 4 and 7, 1940, the GALCIT completed wind tunnel testing of the different P-509 armament configuration options.[87]

The BPC technical team noted to NAA that Curtiss and the USAAC had represented that the P-46 was also designed to achieve Meredith Effect radiator cooling benefits. Verbal approval for the X73 was granted under the proviso that NAA obtain data on the XP-46 design from Curtiss that may have been beneficial to the company in the new project.

On April 10 Sir Henry Self gave verbal approval to proceed with the NA-73 prototype, with production guarantees for the aircraft based on achieving the specific schedule for delivery of both the airframe and actual performance commitments. He also specified that NAA seek and obtain technical data for the XP-46, and then instructed Atwood to draw up the agreement and present it to him for execution. On April 11, with the assistance of local GMC and NAA attorneys and staff, the agreement to purchase "400 NA-50B fighters per NAA Spec 1592 as amended" was drafted and presented the next day.[88]

The key provisions incorporated in the Purchase Agreement were (1) delivery of the first airplane by January 1, 1941, (2) delivery of 300 airplanes by September 30, 1941, and (3) conformance of aircraft delivered to Spec No. 1592 as amended by mutual consent.[89] Sir Henry Self executed the agreement on behalf of the AFPB on April 12, 1940. In addition, the French agreed to purchase 20 aircraft. Note that there was *never* a mandate to complete and fly a prototype within 120 days. As detailed above, there was the stipulation that the first airplane be delivered by January 1, 1941. Had a 120-day stipulation been agreed, NAA would have had to deliver the X73 on or about August 12, 1940. The 120-day figure stemmed from the British contract "boilerplate" term contained in all standard aircraft contracts placed by the BPC. Contract A-250 for the Mustang was an exception to the norm.

Following the signing of the agreement with the AFPB, several major events unfolded. First, as previously detailed by Atwood, he traveled to Buffalo to meet with the Curtiss-Wright Aeroplane and Motor Division General Manager, Burdette Wright, to negotiate for the XP-40, P-40, and XP-46 drag, design and flight-test report data. Atwood described the *requests* by NAA of Curtiss as follows in the first four pages of a report he submitted after meeting with Wright:[90]

> XP-40 Data – Flight test data and reports, including different layouts for cooling system designs plus issues contained therein; full-scale wind tunnel data for radiator designs and cowl designs; armament layout for wing, including wing span locations; exhaust stack design data for Allison V-1710.
> XP-46 Data – NACA full-scale wind tunnel data for a.) cooling system efficiencies for each design change; b.) drag and stability data for 400mph; c.) standard weights and balance report; d.) analysis of powerplant engine mount plus analysis of forgings vs castings; e.) high-speed analysis for cabin/ windscreen, empennage, wing and empennage fillets; f.) wing data, including planform of wing, sections, flap area, aileron area, wingtip design, and; g.) AFPB specification requests for P-46 production version.

The XP-46 was purchased by the USAAC based on performance guarantees by its manufacturer, Curtiss. Powered by the same engine as the Mustang I, the XP-46 was 30mph slower than the NAA fighter in combat weight. The USAAC placed a very high priority on the P-46, which caused the XP-51 to be virtually ignored at Wright Field until April 1942. (*USAF*)

Atwood had several discussions with Wright, based on the talking points named above, to arrive at the $56,000 payment to be made on May 13, 1940. From the files of Patti Hyatt, executive secretary to Leland J. Atwood,[91] the fifth page of the report describes how the payment was proposed by NAA/Atwood and agreed to by Burdette Wright. A summary is presented here:

The agreed upon sum of $56,000 was arrived at based on 1.) amortizing Curtiss financial costs incurred for new pursuit development of the XP-37 ($49,350), XP-40 ($39,815), XP-40 speed tests ($72,228) and pre-XP-46 ($43.789 for CP-39-13 design, model, NACA tests), for which the total was $205,182, then 2.) pro rata allocation to Curtiss and NAA based on anticipated orders for P-40 and P-46 (300 and 500 aircraft) and NA-73 (300 aircraft).
The Summary Total Cost Basis for Curtiss Development up to XP-46 = $205,182
Curtiss allocation – 500 P-40 plus 300 P-46 = 800 units
NAA New Pursuit allocation NA-73 – 300 = 300 units
Total for allocation basis (NAA payment) = 1,100 units
Curtiss Above pro-rata Ratio = 8/11 x $205,182
NAA Above pro-rata Ratio = 3/11 x $205,182 = $55,959.[92]

It is unknown whether Curtiss data which was NOT specifically related to the scoop/radiator and exit design, but requested by Atwood as above, was included in the boxes delivered to NAA in May. The shipment of data from Curtiss related to Atwood's visit with Burdette Wright was received on May 17, 1940, and it contained items and subjects from the pick list provided by Atwood. The key subject headings were Cooling and Aerodynamics, Armament, Weight and Balance, Power Plant installation, and various other documents.[93]

Both Schmued and Horkey recall that the boxes from Curtiss were delivered to Engineering, opened, and examined. Ed Horkey also recalled that Atwood asked him to review the data, including the wind tunnel test results on the XP-46 cooling system. Horkey reported to Atwood that there was nothing useful from Curtiss that could contribute to the NA-73 project, and that "He [Atwood] seemed considerably put out. I read later that he paid $50,000 for the report."[94]

Speculatively, the above data might have been useful in design trade-off discussions for the X73 with respect to the details of the empennage, wing planform, lower cowl/radiator/aft plenum, and forward mounting of the oil cooler intake/cowl located under the engine. Careful examination of the XP-46 and subsequent XP-60 reveal the major distinctions between those designs and the future final configuration of the NA-73/Mustang I.

By examination of the different designs for carburetor intake, oil cooler, short intake/exhaust plenums for radiator, empennage shape, wing planform, etc., it is obvious that there is nothing to suggest that NAA cared for, or used any, Curtiss design features. Both Horkey and Schmued have been quoted stating that NAA never used the data or designs, as its subsequent approach was far more advanced than Curtiss's in respect to the layout of the scoop, intake plenum, radiator/oil cooler, exit plenum, and exhaust gate design.

As a former aerodynamicist, I (William Marshall) would personally have been extremely interested in the actual radiator designs, the wind tunnel boundary-layer results at the radiator and separate oil cooler scoops, the flow characteristics inside the plenum forward and aft of the radiator, and the energy characteristics of the exit flow based on the P-46, as the Curtiss designs were very different from those of the X73.

The X73 is shown prior to making its first flight. Burdette Wright claimed that the X73 and NA-73/Mustang I copied Curtiss-Wright's P-40/XP-46 and XP-60 radiator cooling concepts, prompting him to ask for royalties from NAA. (*Philip Jarrett Collection*)

Ditto for the engine exhaust stacks, the wingtip and fillet designs, and wind tunnel flow and drag results for each approach. And also for casting versus forging design and manufacturing cost analysis, since the same engine was to be used in both the XP-46 and the X73. That said, as none of those features were common, we should take Horkey and Schmued at their word that the Curtiss design and test data delivered to NAA was not used in the Mustang. The inference is that only a cursory examination of the supplied data was made by NAA.

As illustrated, there was never a consideration that the final sum of $56,000 paid to Curtiss for the data acquired as a condition of Sir Henry Self's agreement for the Letter of Intent was for any purpose other than NAA (and BPC engineers) securing insight into Curtiss-Wright's stated claim to a Meredith Effect-driven cooling system and offering fair value for the research costs incurred by Curtiss when developing the XP-46. Said costs for financial discussion also included the progenitor XP-37 and XP-40 in return for the data requested. Atwood also agreed to communicate to Burdette Wright the major milestones in progress from design through to flight of the first production model (as detailed later in this chapter), as well as sharing wind tunnel results for both the cooling system and the NACA/NAA 45-100 airfoil. It is noteworthy that the post-XP-46 prototypes in the form of the Curtiss XP-60 series included both a "laminar flow" wing and an extended (but forward-mounted) cooling system.

In October 1940 the progenitor Curtiss XP-53 was ordered with the Continental XIV-1430-3 engine. It then morphed into the XP-60 prototype, which made its first flight in late 1942. The continuing XP-60 experiments included designs for the Merlin 28 and the Merlin 61 in-line engines, and then departed to incorporate the Pratt & Whitney R-2800-53 and Allison V-1710-75, fitted with both the Wright SU-504-1 and General Electric B-14 turbo-superchargers. The fundamental issues that led to cancelation of the in-line engine versions of the XP-60 were (1) too much pressure drag for the cooling system, and (2) disappointing drag numbers for the Curtiss laminar-flow wing, traced primarily to poor manufacturing control regarding the wing surface.

Burdette Wright later stated that the $56,000 payment was considered by him as a "down payment," and there is some evidence that he attempted to secure royalties for the NAA design. A flurry of letters from NAA to the AFPB, to the effect that the latter, not NAA, would be the sole source of any additional payments, were issued by GMC attorneys. A Breech letter to "Dutch" Kindelberger, dated May 13, states, in part:

> In a conversation which I had with a certain individual who had been with a Mr Smith, British purchasing agent, it was stated that they heard Mr Smith make a statement that the Curtiss people were going to insist on North American Aviation paying royalties on the pursuit ship. It is my understanding that the British Purchasing Mission had agreed to take care of any requirements of Curtiss-Wright in this respect.
>
> This note is so that you may be reminded that our contract with the British should specify that, in the event that any royalty or any other charges are to be paid to Curtiss-Wright Corporation, the British will indemnify North American Aviation.
>
> P.S. I just talked to Burla in New York and told him the above. He states that you have made an outright payment for engineering data and that the airplane is strictly a North American model and the question of further royalties should not come up.[95]

USAAC CHRONOLOGY FOR JANUARY THROUGH EARLY APRIL 1940

On January 1, 1940, Gen George Brett moved his headquarters for the USAAC-MD from Wright Field to Washington, D.C., to focus on Air Staff priorities as outlined by Maj Gen Arnold. Lt Col Oliver Echols remained at Wright Field and was promoted Chief – Materiel Division (in mid-1942 his responsibilities were expanded to include leadership of Materiel, Supply, Maintenance, Transport, and Services for the USAAF).[96]

In April Arnold received a USAAC Priorities Report from the Emmons Board that assigned development of an escort fighter with 1,500-mile range as fourth priority, behind a very-long-range heavy bomber, a twin-engined fighter interceptor, and a medium-range medium bomber. Arnold immediately moved the escort fighter priority to number one. Although many of the senior leaders of the USAAC believed that the B-17 could strike at long range without suffering unacceptable losses, the reported experiences from Arnold's key aides in Great Britain of bomber attrition in Europe due to fighters were alarming. He took to heart the December 26, 1939 memo from Gen Delos Emmons, as previously quoted in this chapter.[97] Arnold also reflected in his memoirs that although "reports of Spaatz, Kenney and others that our own tactical school theories seemed to be in accord with German tactics, most of the airplanes in Allied hands were obsolete. One thing stood out. As we had conjectured, even bombers with good armament needed fighter cover, and no fighter in the world had long enough 'legs' yet to give that cover over the distances the bombers could travel."[98]

The XP-60's radiator cooling design shared some similarities with the system installed in the XP-46. The X73's lower radiator cowl and cooling layout were entirely different, however. (*Aviation History Collection / Alamy Stock Photo*)

CHAPTER 3

BUILDING THE MUSTANG DESPITE THE USAAC-MD

NAA CHRONOLOGY FOR EARLY APRIL THROUGH MID-JUNE 1940

During the final negotiations leading to the Letter of Intent from the AFPB, Kindelberger granted Schmued an "open checkbook" to select the NA-73X prototype team from across all NAA engineering projects. In addition to the core preliminary design group, Schmued drew several key contributors from Chief Engineer Rice's organization into the NA-73X project full time, and broke up the latter into the NAA standard major airframe section groups.

The most technically challenging aspects of the NA-73X project included (1) developing the low-drag airframe envelope lofting lines – the engineering lines which actually defined the outer reference surface for the entire airframe, (2) the calculations, design, fabrication, and testing of the new wing airfoil, including leading-edge twist and planform, to ensure reduced drag while maintaining benign flight characteristics,

Group photograph of Mustang project technical leaders Louis Waite, Raymond Rice and Edgar Schmued. (© *The Boeing Company*)

and (3) designing the radiator/oil cooling system to dramatically reduce drag compared with conventional designs.

Roy Liming, Head of the Engineering Loft Mathematics group, and supervisor R. K. Weebe, both of whom were under Schmued's supervision, introduced the science of projective geometry into NAA to "control the outline or surface size, contour of the airplane – which became the foundation for utilizing the principle of projective geometry in aircraft design." Further explanation of the origin and application of projective geometry is presented in Appendix A – Aerodynamics and Performance section.

For the wing airfoil and radiator/oil cooling system design analysis, Chief Engineer Rice instructed his Technical Section, led by section chief Louis L. Waite, to place several of the team under Schmued's direction for both the wing and radiator design phases. The aerodynamics and thermodynamics department leaders (Horkey and Beerer, respectively) and structures team (led by Schleicher) began work immediately. In the aerodynamics section, Ed Horkey and his picked team planned work to incorporate the new NACA research results for the low-drag/laminar-flow airfoil into a practical high-speed/low-drag wing for the Mustang. Horkey's team worked day and night to develop the experimental wing. The methodology of conformal mapping, pioneered by advanced aerodynamicists Kutta-Joukowski Ph.D., LaPlace, and Theodorsen, is further explained in Appendix A. The conventional high-speed NACA 23016 wing was selected as the prototype wing, but work on the new low-drag wing proceeded in parallel.

The boundary conditions for airfoil selection and sizing for X73 were well articulated in Dr. Millikan's *Aerodynamic of the Airplane*. The following principles were the aerodynamicists' core objectives for design of the wing:

1. The section must have a shape suitable for enclosing the necessary structural members. In general, a thicker wing results in less weight, span and planform being equal.
2. The pitching moment coefficient (nose down) should have a value as low as practical.
3. The parasite drag coefficient should be as close to zero as possible at the flight speed for which the airplane is designed for best performance.
4. The lift coefficient should be as large as possible, but correspondingly the drag coefficient ratio to the lift coefficient should be as "flat" as possible so that profile drag will be small over a large range of lift coefficients.

Given that the NACA 23016 airfoil for the root chord and NACA 23008 for tip chord were selected as the "safe" NA-73 wing airfoil design, Horkey's team began the hard work of developing a new airfoil design to imitate the NACA low-drag attributes, while "fixing" the nominal airfoil envelope of the NACA 23xxx series. Doing so enabled the armament, landing gear, and fuel system groups to proceed with close approximation, given sections and volumes to work with.

The resultant specific airfoil dimensions were precisely modeled and handed over to Bob Davies for testing in the wind tunnel, "tweaked" as necessary, then sent in final dimensions and shape to the Engineering Lines group. Had the new low-drag/ high-speed wing disappointed, preliminary design based on the new wing would have been converted to work with the NACA 23016/23008 airfoil, being reworked and released following receipt of the new engineering lines. Schmued guaranteed that no more than "one month" would be lost as a result of the change.[1] Specific detail design changes that would have been required included rib and spar dimensional alterations (i.e., height of the rib as a function of chord location, as well as spar depths at a specific chord location). Parts and assemblies that lay within the wing envelope would have needed little change. The observable changes potentially required for the relevant wing engineering drawings were insignificant, but were huge relative to the completion of actual tooling, fixtures, jigs, and dies prepared for making those parts.

Continuing Schmued's recollections, beginning on or about March 20 to bring the narrative back to April and May 1940:

> Meanwhile, after I had prepared the drawings and reports that "Dutch" had requested, he went on his way to Great Britain, joined by Lee Atwood. When he came back, about two weeks later, we had no contract, but we started then on our mock-up of the airplane. We used everything; paper, plaster of Paris, wood, and whatever was suitable to quickly build a mock-up of the airplane. In the meantime, the British looked at our proposal carefully and concluded, that on the strength of North American's past performance of the Harvard trainer, which was delivered in large quantities to Great Britain, we would come through with a good airplane. About two to three weeks after "Dutch" Kindelberger had returned we received a contract for 400 P-51s. We made a number of changes.
>
> We had planned to use a NACA 24 Series airfoil [in his memoirs he stated NACA 24 series – which was correct for the P-509 – but Horkey and others corrected his recollection to NACA 23 series.] But we heard that NACA had developed a laminar-flow, low-drag airfoil and we decided to use it on the P-51 Mustang. This airfoil was specifically adapted to the P-51 by Ed Horkey, who was our first aerodynamicist. He and Bob Davis, head of our subsonic wind tunnel, put together a team and developed the ordinates of the laminar-flow airfoil that was used on the P-51. It was the first application of a laminar-flow airfoil in the design of an airplane. The performance of the P-51 proved that it was the best airfoil we could have used.
>
> "Dutch" Kindelberger said, "Well, suppose that wing doesn't work?" I said, "Well then, I'm going to build you a new wing in one month." Of course it was impossible; but you know it was the spirit of the time.
>
> Originally, we had planned four 20mm cannon; we then installed four 20mm cannon in the wing, and two synchronized 0.50cal guns in the engine compartment, firing through the propeller.

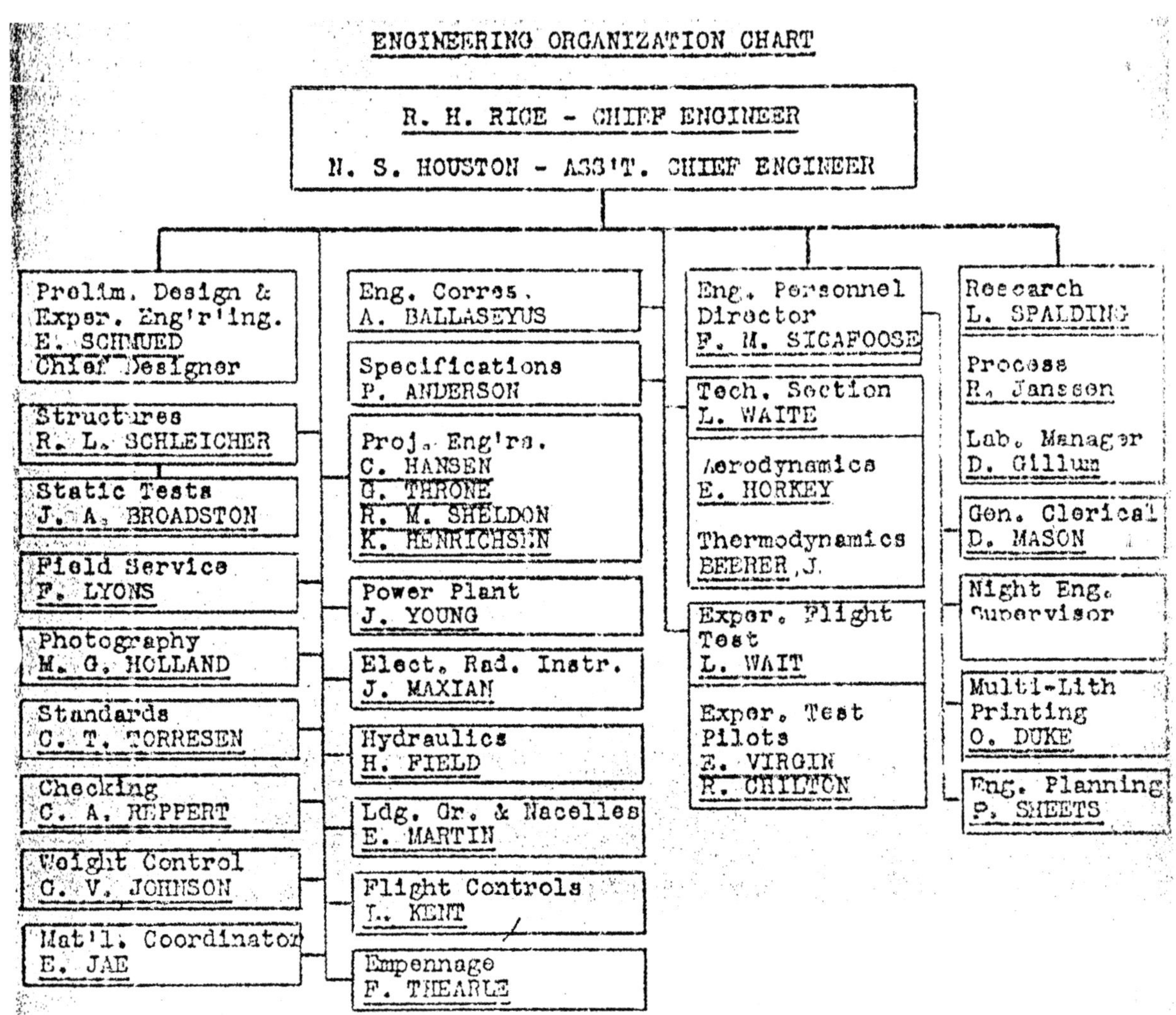

The 1941 NAA Engineering Organization Chart featured the names of most of the personnel that worked on the X73 concept in the spring of the previous year. (© *The Boeing Company*)

The NA-1620 Detail Specifications for the XP-51/NA-73 were in the process of being worked through when Kindelberger returned from New York. While in the final stages, those specifications were verbally agreed upon and Schmued was given the go-ahead by Kindelberger to pick the design team. He began detail design on the X73 on April 21.[2] The NA-1620 Detail Specification was delivered to both the USAAC and the AFPB three days later.[3]

This was the future repository for all specifications, including the final dimensions for the fuselage, wing, and empennage for X73, that would apply to future models of the Mustang through to the P-51K, with minor changes.

To continue Schmued's narrative:

> "Dutch" Kindelberger gave me free rein in selecting any engineer, irrespective if he was a project engineer or a designer. I made the best of this and picked the best people I could find. I started with eight and had about 14 or 15 two weeks after we started – and planned on growth up to 49 people, then drop down to

> 10–12. As we made this schedule, we forecast that we needed 100 days to design and build the airplane. Then, as you might say, "hell broke loose."
>
> We made a very careful time-study of this project. Each man who led a group – like wing group, fuselage group, powerplant, landing gear – was called in and made his own estimate of the time he thought he needed to get his drawings and data out to the Experimental Department.

For clarification, the X73 was "handmade" in the Experimental Department hangar. Before the completion of the flying prototype in mid-September, the project might have been released to Production Engineering on or before July 5 according to Atwood's report to Burdette Wright documented later in this chapter. Other NAA X73 project notes point to the date the Preliminary Design package was released to the Experimental Department as the start of the transition to production engineering. NAA project notes referred to the prototype funded by the NA-73 project as the "X73," and the static-test version as "XX73." Hereinafter, the X73 prototype will be differentiated from the NA-73 project charge number. Schmued's narrative continues:

> We formed an exceptional group of engineers, and there was an enthusiasm that was unequaled anywhere. We worked every day till midnight. On Sundays, we quit at 6:00 pm, so we knew we had a weekend. We scheduled completion of engineering to be completed and delivered to the Experimental Department in 100 days. It took 102 days to complete it. Unfortunately, the Allison people, who were responsible for delivering us the engine, told us that nobody ever designed an airplane in 100 days. Subsequently, we rolled the airplane out without an engine. We had no engine and the airplane was sitting on the ramp waiting for the Allison engine for another 18 days. Only prodding by our powerplant group at the Allison plant made it possible.[4]

Carl Walterhoffer was the Experimental Department supervisor who led the construction of the NA-50B/P-509 mock-up, as well as the construction of the X73. (© *The Boeing Company*)

ABOVE The mock-up for the P-509/NA-50B which was built as part of the specification discussions that led to the creation of the X73 in March-April 1940. (© *The Boeing Company*)

RIGHT This view of the NA-50B/P-509 mock-up shows the original short carburetor intake and aft radiator cooling exit. (© *The Boeing Company*)

FAR RIGHT The mock-up initially featured a curved windscreen, from which the left cockpit window was hinged. (© *The Boeing Company*)

Based on the records available to the authors, some of Schmued's recollections from his memoirs 45 years after this period were misunderstood. The design was completed in approximately 102 days, on or about August 1, when the entire package was released to the Experimental Department. According to several source references, the probable date for Schmued's authorization from Kindelberger to assemble the team was April 21. Although fabrication commenced with the early release of fuselage drawings in mid-May, the fabrication and assembly of the X73 airframe finished six weeks after completion of engineering.

After the following narrative reaches August 1, more detail from source documents will be presented to assist the reader in understanding the events and timetables between April 21 and September 9, when the completed – but engineless – X73 was rolled out of the Experimental Hangar.

The general organization of NAA Engineering, independent of the X73 project, should also be clarified. Reference has been made to several of these key contributors, most of whom were in place before the X73 project started. Many were devoted to the new B-25 and XB-28 programs before January 1940, and prior to Kindelberger tasking Schmued on April 21 to draw the best and brightest to the X73 project. The organization chart on page 80 shows the Mustang Engineering Group in July 1941, nearly a year after the Mustang I was finalized for production engineering.[5] Most of the preliminary design personnel were integrated into the Production Design team, with Schmued still tasked as lead for new designs and providing work plans for modifications and new features for proposals.

In accordance with NAA project policy, the primary groups for the X73 project mirrored the production organizations for wing, landing gear, electrical wiring, instruments, fuel systems, hydraulics, airframe, armament, radio, and powerplant. Engineering leaderships for the preliminary design groups were assigned by Schmued from Rice's overall group.

As the major effort to organize, design, and build the X73 prototype proceeded, there were many parallel activities between NAA, the USAAC, the AFPB, and RAF technical staff. First, Schmued acted swiftly to organize the work plan and engineering team assignments, discuss the manpower/task estimates with each member of his team, and deliver a schedule to Rice and Atwood before the contract negotiations were concluded. In parallel, Stan Smithson coordinated with Schmued to develop the manufacturing plan estimates for the X73. On April 17 Kindelberger cabled Ernie Breech "Mockup and Mfg. Plan complete."[6]

Although the development period for the prototype X73 airframe, from mock-up to completion, was astonishingly short, many key milestones had to be determined, debated, changed, and continued to meet Schmued's project schedule. Probably the most critical milestone was the required delivery of the V-1710-39/FSR engine from Allison. The latter was notified during the development of the final NAA Specification Report 1620 (released on April 24 for joint review by the BPC and NAA) that a V-1710-39/F3R would be required to support the scheduled installation date, approximately 120 days hence. Thus, August 20 was the engine's approximate contractual "due date." Allison responded that no new airplane had ever been built in "100 – or 120 days," so there was no reason to have it ready by then. Approximately 140 days later, on September 9, 1940, the X73 airframe was rolled out for its first photo session with only the mock-up engine installed and, so the tale goes, with its propeller tied on with a rope. The actual Allison engine (supplied by the USAAC-MD, not by Allison) was not delivered until a month later, more than 40 days after the original installation requirements passed down by NAA to Allison. The actual delivery on October 7, assisted by the USAAC-MD, was approximately 164 days after the April 21 start date. This will be discussed later.[7]

The significant airframe dimensions and attributes that changed between the P-509 of March 10, 1940 (the model described in Specifications Report 1592 dated March 11, 1940), the model described in Report 1620 dated October 1940 and then May 6, 1941, and, finally, the model A-36 defined in Report 1620 dated March 2, 1942 are shown in Table 1 on page 84. Note the changes made to aileron/tail group areas following dive tests. The most significant observable changes from the P-509 to the NA-73 were a five-foot increase to the fuselage length, as well as a three-foot increase to the wing span. The latter change resulted in an increase of 55 square feet in total wing area.

TABLE 1: Dimension Changes – Specification 1593 for P-509 through Specification 1620 for A-36						
Specification **Date**	1592 3/40	1620 4/40	1620 5/40	1620 10/40	1620 5/41	1620 3/42
Item	P-509	NA-73	NA-73	NA-83	NA-91	A-36
DIMENSIONS						
Wingspan	34ft 1in.	37ft $^{5}/_{16}$in.	37ft $^{5}/_{16}$in.	37ft $^{5}/_{16}$in.	37ft $^{5}/_{16}$in.	37ft $^{5}/_{16}$in.
Tail Span	13ft 1in.	13ft 2in.	13ft 2in.	13ft 2in.	13ft 2in.	13ft 2in.
Length	26ft 4in.	31ft 6in.	31ft 6in.	31ft 6in.	31ft 6in.	32ft $^{27}/_{8}$in.
Fuselage Width/Height	uns	35in./62in.	35in./62in.	35in./62in.	35in/62in.	35in./62in.
AREAS (sq ft)						
Wing Area	180	235.75	235.75	235.75	235.75	235.75
Aileron Area	uns	7.87	8.3	8.3	8.3	6.36
Tail Group	56.4	56.9	56.9	48.93	62.89	61.05
Horizontal Tail	uns	36.8	36.8	38.05	42.01	41.03
Vertical Tail	uns	20.22	20.22	20.88	20.88	20.02
Stabilizer	uns	10.22	10.22	10.08	25.05	27.98
Elevator	uns	16.58	16.58	17.97	16.96	13.05
Rudder	uns	10	10	10.8	10.8	10.41
Fin	uns	10.22	10.22	10.08	10.08	9.61

With the execution of the Letter of Intent, the next hurdle was the export license. Owing to the uncertainty of the new USAAC approval process for Release of Foreign Aircraft, the contract designation selected for the new plane in the Letter of Intent was NA-50B. The contract principles leading to April 11 preceded the Foreign Release Agreement execution, so the discussions were based on the NA-50 and NA-50A lineage of fighters produced for export to South America. However, those current export fighters all had radial engines and their performance was not comparable with that of the Allison-powered P-40, and thus well within the limits of the export controls in effect. A newer version of the NA-50, also having a radial engine, was being built for Siam. The latter export was eventually stopped by the USAAC and the aircraft acquired as the P-64.

When the request for export release for the NA-50B arrived at Echols' desk on or about April 20, he recognized that the engine was very different from the usual NA-50 line. Echols questioned this with his superior, Gen George Brett, at the USAAC-MD HQ in Washington, D.C., the latter responding by telegram on April 20, 1940:

> Your comments relative to the current North American situation indicate that serious complications can develop. The North American company has submitted a request for release supported by a specification for their NA-50, which appears to be similar to an airplane previously released for export to

> South America, with substantial deviations including the V-1710 engine in lieu of the 1830 and customer-furnished armament. In view of the present situation we will defer making recommendations on the release of this airplane until it can be determined if there are any features incorporated in the design that are the result of developments sponsored by the Air Corps that are secret within the meaning of the new policy.

The report titled "NAA 1620 Detail Specifications for Model XP-51/NA-73," dated April 24, reflected the USAAC demand for two production NA-73 airplanes, namely numbers 4 and 10, as per agreement between NAA and Lt Col Echols. It was in this exchange that the USAAC-MD named NAA's NA-73 the "XP-51."

This concern was soon put to rest by decisions from a higher authority, and the agreement NAA had entered into with the British proceeded.[8] Gen Brett issued clearance on the Foreign Release Agreement with respect to "forbidden technology for Export guidelines," which would be signed by the AFPB, the USAAC, and NAA two weeks later, on May 3. Considering the fact that the P-39, P-40, P-46, and Lockheed Model 222 (YP-38 without turbo-superchargers) had already been approved for export to Britain and France, and the fact that the "technology" of possessing an Allison V-1710 was the same as the proposed P-509, it seems obvious that this was the first possible attempt by Echols to hold up NAA and force the company back to building the P-40.

Additionally, the willingness of "Dutch" Kindelberger to reject the USAAC-MD's request that NAA build P-40s for the AFPB also meant that Echols' plan to assist in increasing Curtiss's capacity to build the P-46 was eliminated, thereby introducing a long-running animosity from the powerful (and future Commanding Officer of the USAAC-MD) Lt Col Oliver Echols.[9]

The period from the time NAA negotiated and executed the Foreign Release Agreement to building the X73 prototype with the AFPB on April 12, 1940, to the process of gaining acceptance by HQ-AAC for the agreement to stand, also saw the beginning of political skirmishes originated by the USAAC-MD that would continue through ultimate acceptance of the Mustang by the USAAF General Staff two years later.

In the process of bringing the proposed aircraft to fruition, basic changes were made to dimensions, weights, and systems, both for aerodynamic reasons and to meet the customer's "combat ready" requirements.

As the design team was getting organized, NAA engineer Paul Anderson drove efforts to get the NA-73 Detail Specification to conform with the AFPB directives contained in the April 11 Letter of Intent. Between April 24 and 28, questions were posed regarding armament combinations and reducing the wingspan and area (so as to reduce drag in order to achieve a higher top speed at critical altitudes), along with obvious trade-off questions when changing wing parameters.

First to be delivered was NAA Report 1620 "Detail Specification for Model XP-51 (NA-73)," which was completed on April 24. The report specified the "NACA/NAA High Speed" airfoil, but it also included the first X73-00002 three-view drawing. The latter showed the plan view and overall wing design and dimensions of the future NA-73.[10] The span, mean chord, and wing area were all the same as for the future NA-73.[11]

General Order NA-73 was opened on April 24, 1940, although detail design engineering for the airframe was started two weeks earlier. Atwood directed that the expenses associated with the business development, prototype mock-up, and engineering overheads accrued by the early X73/P-509 proposal activities, including the GALCIT wind tunnel testing under Charge Number X73, be moved to the NA-73 project account.[12] The general order from NAA to Allison was also issued, requesting delivery of one V-1710-39 engine "for delivery on or before 120 days from date of order."[13]

On April 29 Edgar Schmued and project engineer Ken Bowen hosted a design review meeting between NAA and the RAF regarding NA-1620 detail specifications. Bowen summarized the meeting in a memo to Ray Rice that included "14 points of concern," including the possible impact on the schedule for going with the P-509 wing, and performance issues due to the smaller wing.[14]

Atwood submitted to the AFPB, per request, three different armament options for the NA-73. They included 20mm cannon, as well as a mixture of 0.50cal and 0.30cal Browning machine guns. Also submitted was NA-1623, Detail Data, and NA-1623, Performance Estimates for the P-509 wing version, as requested in the meeting with the AFPB technical team on April 29.

During the final specification stage the armament package evolved again into the definitive NA-73 battery of two 0.50cal guns in the engine compartment, plus a battery of two 0.30cal and one 0.50cal in each wing. Although production of the US-manufactured AN/M2 Hispano 20mm cannon was ramping up, the US Navy and USAAC prioritized supply, and this weapon did not become available for the NAA project until late 1941.

On May 3 a general-arrangement side-profile drawing and a revised NAA X73-00002 three-view drawing showing the armament options were released from engineering.[15] The drawing package was transmitted to the AFPB's H. C. B. Thomas on the same day. Thomas and Air Vice-Marshal G. B. A. Baker approved both Specification revision 1620 and the related X73-00002 three-view drawing on the 4th. The AFPB/NAA Foreign Release Agreement for XP-51/NA-73, "estimated for 300 aircraft plus spares," was also executed that same day.[16] The French were expected to purchase 20, plus five for spares, but events in France were causing delays to approvals. It was at about this time that the dialogue regarding the NA-73 project ceased to involve the French, whose participation declined in the AFPB following the German *Blitzkrieg* on May 10, 1940.

The evolution of the NA-73 is best described as a collaboration between NAA, the RAF and the BPC, with the latter recommending improvements in view of RAF operational experience. NAA was solely responsible for the airframe, the airfoil and wing, and the powerplant installation. The team of Gp Capt Adams and H. S. Howitt of the BPC were critical in introducing specifications for self-sealing fuel tanks and cockpit instrumentation and layout, including the location of rudder pedals and control column, throttles, and gun chargers, etc.

On May 7 the "First Engineering Release of NA-73 Experimental Airplane" was issued to the Experimental Department to be fabricated in the Experimental Shop on the first floor of Building 1. From this date both the X73 prototype and the XX73 static test airframe were referred to as such, despite the project funding title for both airframes being "NA-73X." Although the time taken for X73 prototype airframe development, from mock-up to completion, was astonishingly short, many key milestones had to be reached, discussed and changed, yet still continue to meet Schmued's project schedule.

As construction of the fuselage began, a wooden mock-up of the V-1710-39 was requested from Allison to ensure the engine's proper fit in the tight space allowed for it. During the continuing development of the final NAA Specification Report 1620, Allison was once again reminded and put on notice that an engine would be required to meet the scheduled installation date of mid-August, approximately 120 days from project go-ahead. As mentioned previously, Allison responded that no new airplane had ever been built in 120 days, so there was no reason to have it ready by then. Of course, Allison was proved wrong.

To help reduce further delay in respect to engine availability, the USAAC loaned NAA a V-1710 from an order recently filled by Allison. The engine arrived at NAA on October 7 and was first run four days later. It did not meet the installation requirements originally passed down to NAA by Allison, and additional work by the Experimental Department was required to install it, as explained later in this volume.[17]

The NA-1622 Detail Specifications and revised NA-1623 Performance Analysis were submitted to Atwood on April 29. Two days later, Atwood cabled Sir Henry Self, "Proceeding with NA-73, submitting P-509-1 and -3 wings with different armament as requested." Atwood committed to "delivering all 320 NA-73s by September 30, 1941, at a fixed price of $37,590 each."[18] On May 3 the Revised X73-00002 three-view drawing per NA-1620 was completed and delivered to the AFPB. The following day, Air Vice-Marshal G. B. A. Baker, for the RAF, and H. C. B. Thomas, for the AFPB senior technical staff, approved the Foreign Release Agreement. It was then also signed by Kindelberger, the document covering the delivery of an "estimated 300 airplanes."

On May 7 Engineering Orders were released, stating, "This EO authorizes planning and all experimental department concerned to set up tickets and account Nos on X73 airplane for purposes of experimental ship." And also, "Advance release fus. Lines X73-02011 fuselage, 1 print shop." Last, and perhaps most important, was "Work can be started immediately on fuselage skin & plating jigs. Forming information is now available in loft dept. on complete fuselage lines."

Between May 11 and 13 Bowen notified Rice of changes to the NA-73 as requested by the British. Schmued wrote in a memo to Bowen, "XP-46 Aerodynamics reported. 'Doubts' accuracy of the XP-46 data." Bowen in turn sent a memo to Atwood, "13 changes for NA-73, British Commission left Wednesday for Curtiss, not impressed with their ship."

On May 13, three-view drawing X73-00002 with changes, plus detail data specifications and updated performance analysis (NA-1622 and NA-1623, respectively), were transmitted to the AFPB. Four days later, Atwood cabled

John "Dutch" Kindelberger and William Knudsen, former Chairman of the Board – GMC. The latter was appointed by President Roosevelt to manage all US military production of arms, armament and airplanes. He was the only civilian to hold the rank of lieutenant general in the USAAF. (© *The Boeing Company*)

Kindelberger, "Change requests in Pursuit Design will slow us down quite a bit but send more information Monday night."

On May 18 Atwood received the following teletype from H. C. B. Thomas regarding NA-1622/23, "TWX 05-18-40 H. C. B. Thomas to Atwood. Do not reduce the wing area on the NA-73 or reduce the strength factors because the XP-46 is being modified, reference conversation with Kindelberger and Bowen yesterday."[19] The British had correctly deduced that the smaller P-509 wing did not increase drag benefits due to reduced form drag of the smaller wingspan, or the parasite drag of reduced wing area, sufficiently to offset the higher wing loading, lower climb rate, and longer take-off and landing runs. Further, the BPC was already interested in increasing wing fuel tankage to 170gal.

This instruction from Thomas froze the X73 external design dimensions of the wing, fuselage, and empennage, and work proceeded in accordance with Specification 1620. The NA-1623 performance estimates for the "High Speed Pursuit – Export Version" continued to be updated, but were based on requested changes to the NA-1620 specification. Until the XP-51F/G/J and P-51H models appeared, there would be no further significant changes to the airplane's basic dimensions.

Rice and Johnson met with Bowen, discussing the 20 changes to Specification 1622 revised jointly by NAA and the BPC. These changes to the report due to the teletype from Thomas on the 18th resulted in it being renumbered Report 1623, effectively harmonizing all the parallel, but dissimilar, differences between P-509 and NA-73. Following the meeting to synthesize the different numbered specifications and proceed on all the changes, it was reaffirmed that the future specifications would be incorporated as changes in Specification 1620.

On May 21 the GALCIT began tests on the two alternative NAA wing designs, completing them on the 22nd (using NACA 23016 and NACA 2516 root airfoils).

Between mid-May and late June 1940, the following notable events occurred, influencing NAA, the USAAC, France, and the world in general.

On May 12 Germany invaded France. Communications with the French nearly ceased with respect to the NA-73. Also, the US Treasury Department released all Rolls-Royce Merlin drawings to the Packard Motor Company.[20]

On May 29 the NA-73 contract A-250 with the BPC was increased to 320 aircraft, plus 80 spares, to absorb the French purchase. Contract AC-15471 was executed with the USAAC for two NA-73s/XP-51s to be extracted from numbers 4 and 10 in the production ship sequence as USAAC serial numbers 41-038 and 41-039.

That same day William Knudsen, former Chairman of the Board – GMC, was appointed by President Roosevelt to manage all US military production of arms, armament, and airplanes. He was subsequently the only civilian to be a lieutenant general of the USAAF. According to Arnold, "With his arrival in Washington, the Air Corps production problems decreased as each day passed, and many of my headaches disappeared. Bill Knudsen talked our language."[21]

On or about June 26, Col J. G. Vincent, vice president of the Packard Motor Company's Aircraft Engineering Division, dedicated his efforts to developing the

OPPOSITE Evolution drawings showing progressive changes up to the production NA-73. (*Lowell Ford Collection*)

Rolls-Royce relationship, with the objective of securing an aero-engine contract for Packard. Two days earlier, Max Gilman, Packard President and general manager, and Col Vincent met with Lt Gen William Knudsen, Commissioner of Industrial Production in the Office of Production Management. Knudsen asked Packard to agree a contract with Rolls-Royce to produce 6,000 engines for the British and 3,000 for the USAAC. Following the meeting, Vincent reported that he was engaged solely in the active direction of Packard Aircraft Engineering Division. The decision was made to produce the Merlin XX.[22]

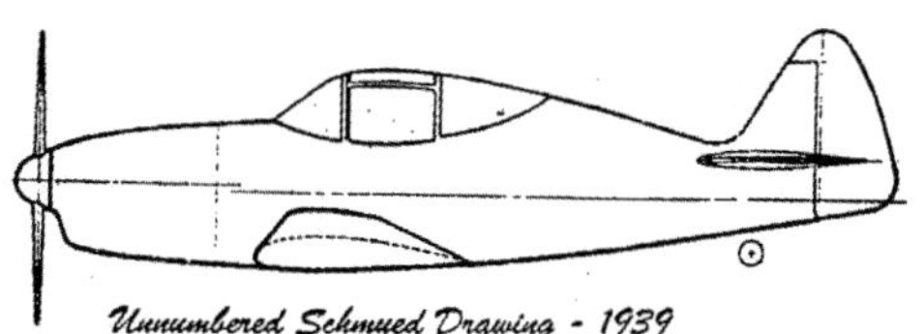

Unnumbered Schmued Drawing - 1939

On May 21 the GALCIT began tests on the two alternative NAA wing designs, completing them on the 22nd (probably using NA 23016 and NA 2516 root airfoils).

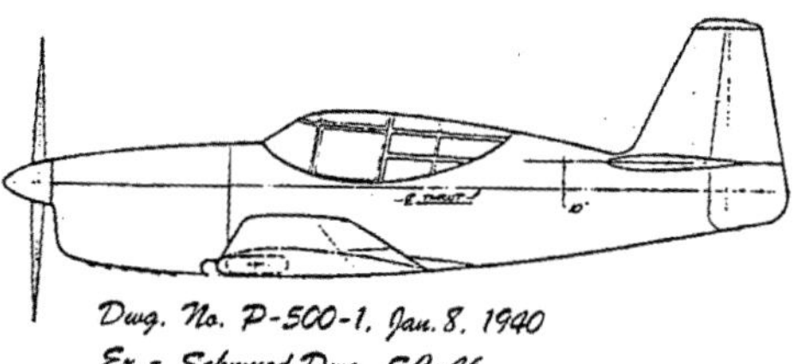

Dwg. No. P-500-1. Jan. 8. 1940
Ex - Schmued Dwg. SC-46

In mid-June Marshal Philippe Pétain surrendered to Germany, and all French contracts in the USA were subsequently absorbed by the British. Also, the US Treasury Department released all Rolls-Royce Merlin drawings to the Packard Motor Company.[23]

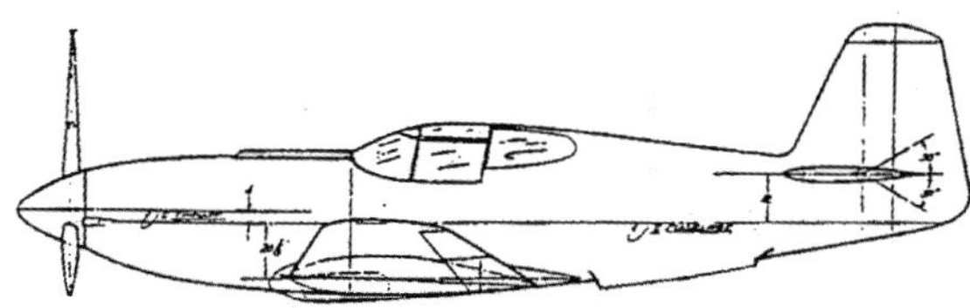

Dwg. No. P-509. Circa Feb 1940

NAA CHRONOLOGY FOR MID-JUNE THROUGH DECEMBER 1940

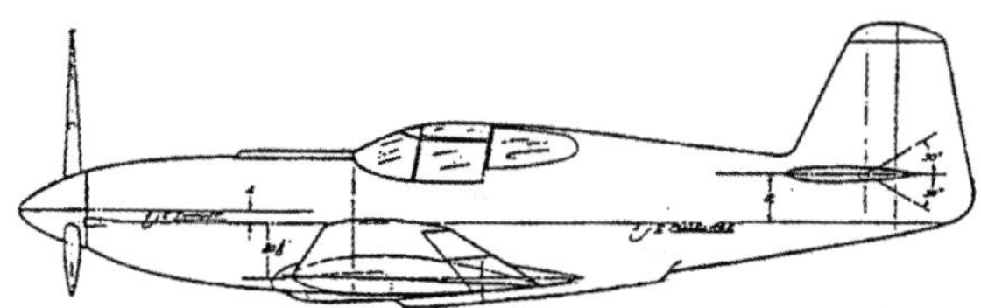

Dwg. No. P-509-1. March 10. 1940

On June 21 Rice again requested from Allison the timing for the first delivery of the engine for the X73, restating that it would be needed on August 1. Rice and Johnson met with Bowen, discussing the 20 changes to Specification 1622 revised jointly by NAA and the BPC. These changes to the report on the 18th resulted in it being renumbered Report 1623, effectively harmonizing all the parallel, but dissimilar, differences between the P-509 and NA-73.

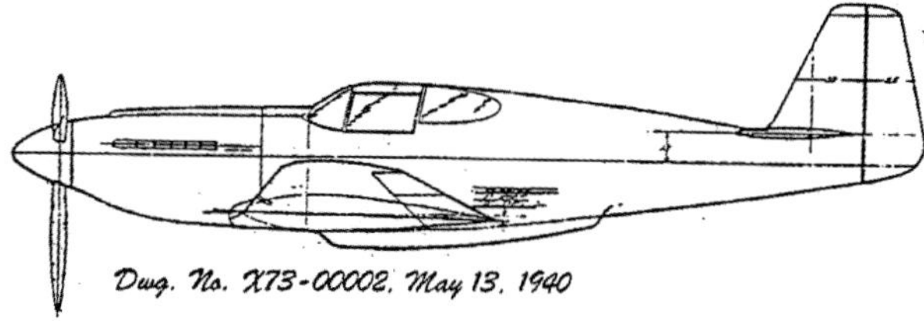

Dwg. No. X73-00002. May 13. 1940

In early July the wing/airfoil and cooling system external cowl design coordinates were released to Davies for construction of the scale model of the X73. The quarter-scale model was dispatched to the GALCIT to enable tests to begin on the new radiator/oil cooler and ducting design, as well as on the new NACA/NAA 45-100 airfoil for the wing. Between June 28 and July 26, issues were experienced regarding the recorded lift and drag coefficients of the outer

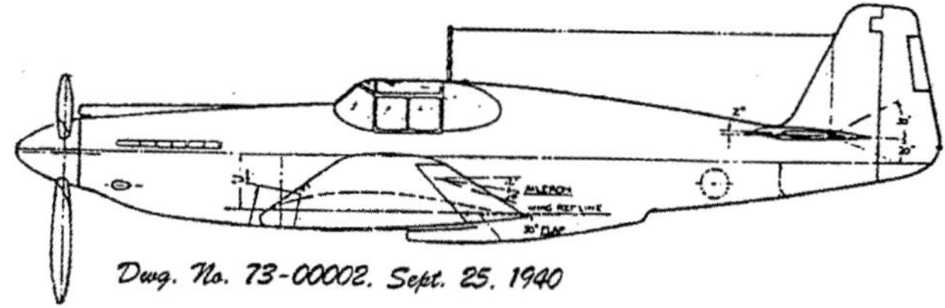

Dwg. No. 73-00002. Sept. 25. 1940

ABOVE The NA-73 Scale Model Mk 1 being evaluated in a wind tunnel With the wing airfoil remaining unchanged until the XP-51F/G/J and P-51H series, this model was used to test the dorsal fin fillet, tall fin cap, new radiator intake and exhaust scoop geometry until late 1943. (© *The Boeing Company*)

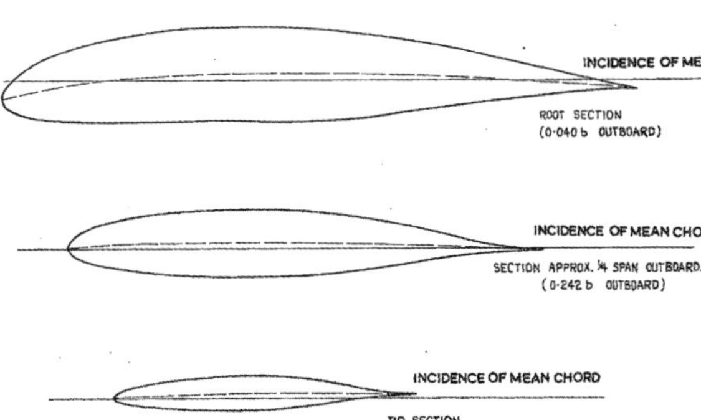

TOP RIGHT The NAA/NACA 45-100 high-speed/low-drag airfoil developed by NAA for all Mustangs from the X73 through the P-51B/C. The root chord changed length and angle of incidence from the P-51B/C to the P-51D/K out to Wing Station 61, but the overall washout to the tip chord remained approximately two degrees. (*NACA Wind Tunnel Report*)

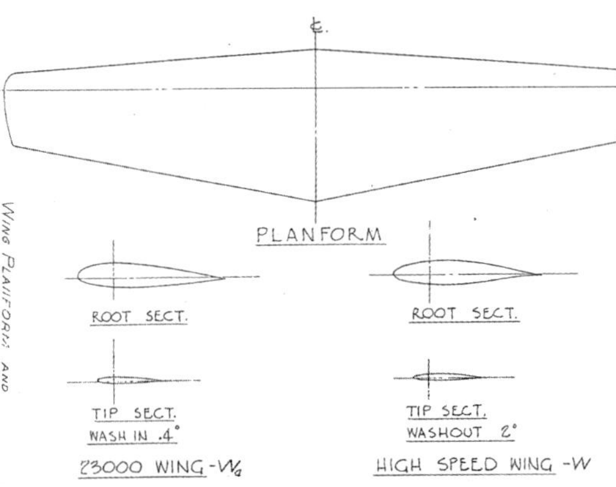

ABOVE RIGHT During the GALCIT wind tunnel testing to compare the new X73 wing using the NAA/NACA 45-100 airfoil versus the NACA 23000 series, this page served as the sketch to highlight the differences between the wings being tested. (© *The Boeing Company*)

wing, believed to be caused by interference between the GALCIT tunnel wall and wingtip. The model was moved to the larger 12ft wind tunnel at the University of Washington in Seattle. The wingtip airfoil maximum thickness position along the tip chord was changed from 37 percent to 50 percent. The wingtip design of the X73 was also changed from round to square tip. The next drag test results showed outstanding reductions compared with the wing with the NACA 23016 airfoil. The dimensions were frozen. Likewise, the drag data for the lower duct/radiator design aft of the wing was also gathered.

The disappointing results regarding less-than-expected even pressure distributions on the face of the radiator/oil cooler matrix led (correctly) to conclusions that either the inlet scoop design or the plenum controlling the airflow, or both, were inadequate to achieve the expected design goals for "Meredith Effect" drag reduction. The initial changes included adding internal vanes to provide more even flow to the radiator matrix, which improved the performance slightly. They were discontinued in 1941, however. Over the next 12 months, variations were tested to increase/decrease the areas of both the intake scoop and the aft radiator scoop, as well as adding or eliminating the internal duct flow vanes. The climb condition at high angles-of-attack to the entry scoop continued to control the changes. The cooling system improvements were incremental through to the testing of the XP-51B, when major changes were made to improve boundary-layer performance at the inlet scoop and the expansion section of the internal plenum mated to the Harrison radiator/aftercooler. More of this discussion will be presented in Appendix A.

Although the report was not completed until January 1941, Horkey released the airfoil dimensions to Roy Liming, Chief of the Engineering-Lines department, and

Project Engineer Ken Bowen in late July 1940 so that detail design using the new wing continued to proceed without delay.

On July 5, the drafting for the production NA-73 started in parallel with Schmued's continued prototype designs. In the last week of that same month the Experimental Department began assembly of the fuselage, firewall, engine mount, wing, and empennage. A wooden mock-up of the V-1710 engine was requested from Allison to ensure a proper fit.[24]

On or about August 1, the last of the design engineering drawings were released from Schmued's Preliminary Design Group to the Experimental Department after the preliminary drawings had been completed and subsequently delivered to the Experimental Shop so that fabrication and assembly work could conclude. The project engineers, assisted by approximately 100 skilled draftsmen, were tasked with converting the X73 created by Schmued's preliminary design team into NA-73 production drawings. The result was a change in final design philosophy, with careful attention to both the process and fabrication of the parts and assemblies, with mass production techniques in mind.

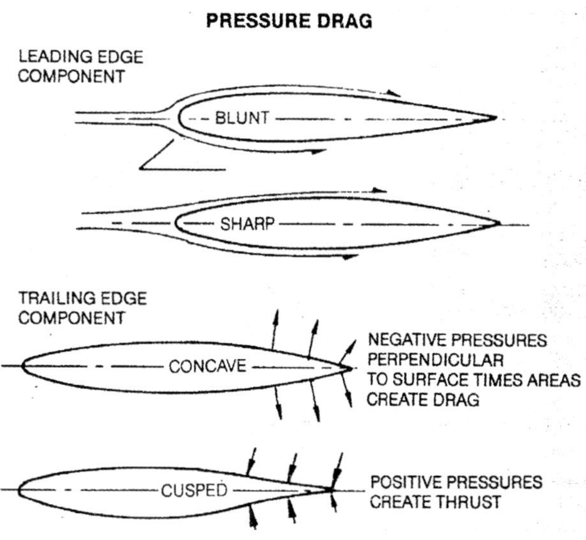

Ed Horkey's illustrated explanation for Pressure Drag comparisons between conventional (i.e. NACA 23016) and NAA low drag (NAA/NACA 45-100) airfoils, highlighting how the different shapes of leading and trailing edges contributed to drag. (*Ed Horkey Collection*)

Specific considerations for X73 designs with production in mind included features such as connection points and plugs for electrical and hydraulic lines, positioning of most normally hard to reach subsystems on the right-hand side of the fuselage for installation before the fuselage halves were joined, and developing the airframe as four separate subassemblies (powerplant/engine compartment forward of the firewall, forward fuselage section, aft fuselage section as right and left sides, and empennage with attached tail cone). In the future manufacturing process for the production Mustangs, these designs permitted easy access, allowing the subsystems to be installed rapidly with ease of quality control inspections before the aft fuselage halves were joined. Following joining of the fuselage halves, the empennage, wings, and powerplant were installed, along with "pluggable" electrical, hydraulic, and fuel lines subsystems when all major components were brought together.

Both NA-73 project engineers, Ken Bowen (then Herbert Baldwin, when Bowen was assigned to manage the Dallas plant in early 1941) and Assistant Project Engineer George Gehrkens, were placed to integrate the multiple groups, as well as to coordinate with Production Chief Stan Smithson. Bowen assigned Arthur Patch to make the new wing producible and gave John Steppe the task of translating Liming's "descriptive geometry-produced lines" of the fuselage into production drawings. They not only supervised the day-to-day design teams but worked closely with Production to ensure that best practices to fabricate, assemble, and construct the airplane were coordinated to improve ease of manufacturing.[25]

Herb Baldwin came from Douglas with Lee Atwood and headed Project Engineering management for the Mustang when his predecessor, Ken Bowen, was reassigned to manage the Dallas plant in early 1941. (*© The Boeing Company*)

RIGHT Mustang "Airframe on the half shell" production line installations of complex systems prior to closing the aft fuselage halves together greatly reduced labor hours. The latter decreased from 12,000 hours for the first Mustang Is to 2,077 for the P-51D-30-NA series in July–August 1945. (© *The Boeing Company*)

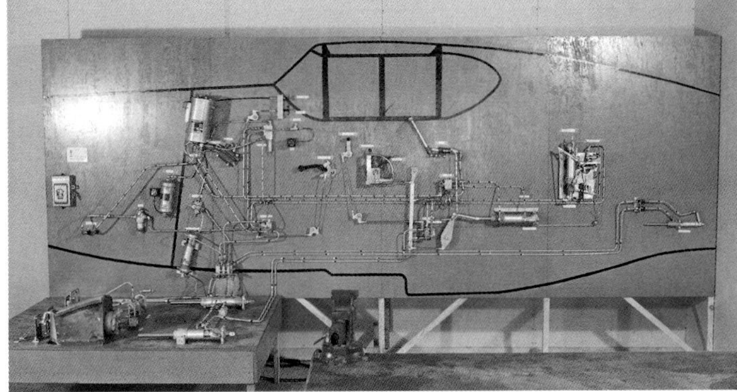

BELOW A training aid for hydraulic systems installation in the right aft fuselage sub-assembly. (© *The Boeing Company*)

Although the top NA-73 73-00009 General Airplane Assembly drawing was not retrievable for this work, the breakdown on page 198 for the future NA-106 P-51D program was very similar, and is presented to illustrate the NAA work breakdown structure.[26]

On August 9, 1940, the British requested from the Secretary of the Treasury a release of 50 Allison engines. This request was almost certainly for the NA-73, but it was turned down by Gen Arnold, who explained that his decision was based on the USAAC also waiting for engines – their absence was adversely impacting pilot/crew training needs, for P-38, P-39, and P-40 airframes were backing up at Lockheed, Bell, and Curtiss. Arnold was confronted by the demand to place the USAAC on a wartime footing, while Britain's need for the same resources was arguably far higher.[27]

The first flight of the B-25 (there was no XB-25) on August 19 heralded production of the second outstanding aircraft that NAA would contribute to the future war effort. Its success would prove to be extremely important when it came to funding the rapid increase in the number of engineering and production workers employed at the Inglewood plant. Carl "Red" Hansen was Project Engineer for the B-25. When airflow issues occurred with the straight wing, Ralph Ruud put the wings in a jig to "straighten" the outer wing section and eliminate dihedral, thereby creating the bomber's characteristic gull wing.[28]

On September 3, after a month-long negotiation, the BPC signed an agreement for the Packard Motor Company to build the Merlin XX single-stage, two-speed engine. That same month Packard received 2,000 drawings from Rolls-Royce for the Merlin XX. The company then embarked on the major task of converting most British dimensional standards to US standards, while introducing some changes to improve manufacturability and interchangeability of the engine components.

The first B-25 had a "straight wing" and displayed sub-optimal stall characteristics due to airflow issues. Ralph Ruud duly put the wings in a jig to "straighten" their outer section and eliminate the dihedral, thereby creating the bomber's characteristic gull wing. (© *The Boeing Company*)

A head-on view of the first B-25, showing its straight wing with constant dihedral, prior to Ralph Ruud "bending it". (© *The Boeing Company*)

B-25s on the vast production line at Kansas City display the gull wing for all operational versions of the Mitchell. (*© The Boeing Company*)

Throughout the relationship between Rolls-Royce and Packard there was an excellent liaison between the two companies to ensure quality and parallel interchangeability. The resultant engine was named the Packard Merlin V-1650-1 for the single-stage/two-speed supercharger versions of the Merlin XX. The V-1650-1 was the same as the latter engine except for changes to adapt to US carburetors, hydromatic propellers, propeller governors, vacuum pumps, fuel pumps, generators, and other miscellaneous US standard fittings. The BPC, Air Ministry, and USAAC negotiated a fixed percentage division for total engine production output, which was allocated to Canadian-built Avro Lancasters, Hurricanes, and de Havilland Mosquitoes, and Merlin-engined P-40F/Ls.[29]

Work on fabricating the XX73 static test article, based on the X73 design drawings, proceeded to meet static test project dates. As mentioned earlier, on September 9 the X73 airframe was rolled out with the mock-up engine installed.[30]

Pausing in the chronology of the NAA design and fabrication achievements in building the X73 prototype, it might be useful to parse what Edgar Schmued wrote about the airframe:

> It took 102 days to complete it. Unfortunately, the Allison people, who were responsible for delivering us the engine, told us that nobody ever designed an airplane in 100 days. Subsequently, we rolled the airplane out without an engine. We had no engine and the airplane was sitting on the ramp waiting for the Allison engine for another 18 days. Only prodding by our powerplant group at the Allison plant made it possible.

In the authors' opinion, this statement has led to much confusion.

To assist in the understanding of the X73 prototype and NA-73 production milestones, Atwood's telex to Burdette Wright on March 22, 1941 summarized the key achievements for both aircraft from inception:[31]

> Engineering started on experimental airplane April 21 [1940].
> First engineering release on experimental airplane May 7.
> First shop order on experimental airplane on May 29.
> First lofting on experimental airplane complete on June 3.
> Experimental airplane built from material in stock.
> Finished experimental airplane completed on September 9.
> Drafting started on production airplane July 5.
> First material ordered on production airplane June 15.
> First material received on production airplane September 1.
> First engineering release on production airplane on September 15.
> First shop order on production airplane ordered October 1 [1940].
> Revised lofting for production airplane completed February 20, 1941.
> First production airplane will have all equipment and installation complete.
> Static test completed in February 1941.
> First airplane from production will fly first week in April [1941].

From the above individual milestones telexed by Atwood to Burdette Wright, and the Schmued narratives, one can reconstruct the "102 days" stated for the start of the design of the X73 through to alleged readiness to install the Allison engine. From the telex above, beginning April 21, Atwood indicates "Engineering started." The Schmued reference to "102 days later" is approximately August 1, 1940 – a date that generally agrees with Experimental Department project logs for activities of perhaps the last 30 percent of the fabrication, assembly and installation steps to assemble the X73 airframe – not the completion date.

What is not clear from past Mustang published histories is that *only* when the prototype engineering package from Preliminary Design was suitably complete, on May 7, 1940, was there enough information to supply the Experimental Department with sufficient engineering drawings to begin construction of the prototype. In fact, the Experimental Hangar did not complete fabrication of the empennage and wings to the point that these components and the engine mounts could be installed until after August 1. That said, many tasks remained in order to complete subassembly items such as ailerons, elevators, rudder, flaps, cockpit enclosure, windscreen, cowling, guns, fuel tank, and controls, and then install hydraulics and electrical systems, landing gear, etc., before the aircraft was ready to fly. Thus, the Atwood entry "Finished experimental airplane completed on September 9" was likely closer to the milestone date of "ready to fly" had the Allison engine been delivered in mid-August as scheduled.

Perhaps a realistic marker for the release of the complete X73 by the Experimental Shop, and nearly ready for flight (apart from installation of the engine), is the notation

X73 High Speed Pursuit Prototype, Mines Field, California, November 1940. (Artwork by Jim Laurier, © Osprey Publishing)

in the Flight Department logs that work started on engine instrumentation on October 5, two days in advance of delivery of the USAAC-MD-supplied engine on October 7.[32]

For further context regarding the frustrations and delays caused by Allison, the following excerpts from correspondence and memorandums to Ernest Breech and the Board of Directors are presented below. They provide the context for Kindelberger and NAA strongly seeking "another engine solution" such as Rolls-Royce, leading to major disagreements with the GMC Board of Directors in 1941. It is also revealed in the exchanges that the USAAC seemingly expressed significant interest in the fighter to Kindelberger during the period between May 23, 1940, and May 23, 1941. The fact that the USAAC did not place orders for the P-51 raises the question "Why not?"[33]

On May 23 Kindelberger wrote to Breech, "The Army is also interested in our Pursuit and will follow it closely and expect to place large orders for it as soon as it is tested. They are also talking about our lining up to produce the new B-28 without waiting too long for experimental development on it." On July 7 Kindelberger wrote to Breech, "The Pursuit plane for the British is beginning to take shape in the experimental department and we expect to have it out in sixty days."

On September 6 Kindelberger sent the following Memorandum to all Directors:

> The Pursuit airplane is now ready to fly at any time we get an engine. The last promise for delivery here [from Allison] is September 21 so we will be fortunate to have the airplane flying by October 1. Actually, we would have been able to fly the airplane on August 20th had Allison been able to deliver the engine to our expectation. The British Air Ministry visited our plant last week and expressed their surprise and approval at the way the airplane had developed in that time. We are now under negotiation for an additional 300 of these airplanes which, with spares, will reach about fifteen million dollars without engines and propellers.

On September 25 Kindelberger wrote the following Summary of Operations for Directors:

> NA-73 – Great Britain (320 Allison single-engine pursuit) – Progress on this contract has been materially halted by failure of Allison Engineering to deliver engine required for our first airplane. Delivery is now promised for beginning of October. Engineering on this contract is approximately 15% complete, while total contract is approximately 1% complete. Delivery of first airplane is now scheduled for January 1941; however, it is hoped that this airplane will be ready for test flight considerably in advance of this date.

On November 19 Kindelberger sent the following Memorandum to Directors:

> NA-73 – Great Britain (320 Allison engine pursuit plane) – the first ship on this contract is now being test-flown. This has been made possible by the fact that the Army has loaned us the Allison engine necessary to complete the construction of this airplane for flight testing. Engineering is now 45% complete. Delivery of the first airplane is scheduled for January 1941, with an accelerated delivery thereafter, shipments being scheduled for completion on this contract by September 1941, provided engine deliveries are sufficient to keep pace with this schedule.

On January 20, 1941, Kindelberger wrote to Breech:

> We have a check on the pursuit plane for the last couple of days which indicates it will be much faster than our guarantee and there is a possibility that with future improvements it will be a real 400-mile-an-hour pursuit plane, which is something that does not exist at this moment in this country with anything like the armament and armor, etc. … The first pursuit planes will be a little late, but will be in step with the engine deliveries.

On March 11, 1941, Kindelberger wrote to Breech:

> I think it is possible that I shall go East after the opening of the Dallas plant as there is a tremendous amount of new business in the offing with the Army beyond the stuff that we already have considered. Atwood is in Dayton to conclude negotiations for 2,360 AT-6s to fill in the Dallas picture. They want even more, as well as 800 B-28 bombers, and around 1,000 pursuit planes.

On May 20, 1941, Kindelberger wrote to Breech:

> The Army and British are cutting down on the numbers of fighters all the way around. The curtailment of the fighter picture is what is throwing Bell and

> Curtiss in the four-engine field and if we finish the 700 fighter types we have on order, we will probably only get 150 for the US Army. We are still not getting Allison engines and we are not getting co-operation in any way. I find that the Army and the contractors that are working with Allison are pretty much disgusted with them. I have also found that the Allison engine in the Curtiss ships in Great Britain has not been too good. Of course, the British had the same problems with the Rolls-Royce Merlin that they are now having with the Allison, but these problems occurred a couple of years ago before the heat was on and were pretty well cleaned up by the time things began to get tough. Now they think back on the Merlin as being perfect and the Allison as being a lump of cheese.

On May 23, 1941, Kindelberger wrote to influential Australian businessman, and government advisor, W. S. Robinson:

> The Mustang fighter which we developed for the Royal Air Force is proving to be an excellent job and we are beginning to get into production. We had expected to start deliveries in January and February of this year but so far we have only been able to get three engines. The engines we received in the beginning would not work satisfactorily and we had a great deal of trouble with them. We are now about five months behind schedule but there was no use trying to get ahead of the engines. It is the sweetest airplane for production, I think, that has ever been built and we can roll them out just as fast as trainers. The performance is also excellent as we are pushing the 400-mile-per-hour mark with a 12,000-foot engine.

With its engine running, the X73 has its cockpit checked by Vance Breese prior to him taking it aloft for the first time from Mines Field on October 26, 1940. (© *The Boeing Company*)

The X73 prototype is shown in the air off the California coast during an early test flight, the aircraft featuring USAAC rudder colors expressly for this flight so that publicity photographs could be taken. (© *The Boeing Company*)

Returning to the NAA Chronology in September 1940, on the 24th of that month the BPC concluded negotiations for the second block of Mustang Is and executed contract A-1493 for 300 more Mustang Is, scheduled for final delivery in July 1942. The NA-83 as delivered included small changes to the cooling system's internal ducting geometry, increased fuel capacity to 90gal in each wing, and a strengthened wing owing to increased gross weight, plus other improvements based on the X73 and NA-73 flight tests.[34]

On September 30 NAA's Dallas plant was started, funded by the Defense Plant Corporation Act. It remained Kindelberger's and Atwood's responsibility to secure orders to be produced in Dallas when the plant neared completion. One of Schmued's key project engineers, Ken Bowen, was assigned to be Dallas plant manager and relocated to Irving, Texas, where the factory would be built.[35] George Gehrkens replaced Bowen as NA-73/P-51 production project engineer.

On October 7 a V-1710 arrived at Inglewood, loaned by the USAAC to help NAA recover from Allison's failure to deliver the engine. It came from an order recently filled by Allison, and although the engine met the installation requirements originally passed to NAA by the manufacturer, the first V-1710-39/FSR for the X73 had changes that had not been communicated to NAA. As a result, the Experimental Shop was forced to make design changes to the engine bay cowling and engine mount clearances owing to interference from electrical bundling.[36]

Ken Bowen was the X73 project engineer for preliminary design. He was later assigned as Plant Manager for NAA's Dallas factory. (© *The Boeing Company*)

Engine ground tests of the X73 with the USAAC-supplied V-1710-39/FSR installed, and with the aircraft now assigned Civil Aeronautics Authority (CAA) registration NX19998, began on October 11. Taxi tests started four days later, and the aircraft was finally declared "ready to fly" on the 26th, shortly after which Vance Breese took it aloft for the first time.

After several functional test flights between October 31 and November 13, Vance Breese concluded his contracted flights, having accumulated 3hr 20min total time. He turned over the next series of tests, including high-speed runs, to Paul Balfour for the November 20 test. Unfortunately, when Vance Breese and Schmued attempted to

ABOVE The X73 sits forlornly on its back in a plowed bean field just 150 miles west of Mines Field after it had crash-landed following fuel starvation on November 20, 1940. Test pilot Paul Balfour managed to scramble to safety via one of the canopy's side windows. (*© The Boeing Company*)

RIGHT This close up of the "propellerless" X73 reveals details of the aircraft's front radiator scoop, which then lacked both a gutter and even the simplest form of boundary-layer control. (*© The Boeing Company*)

FAR RIGHT The X73's variable-area aft radiator coolant scoop is seen in detail in this photograph of the upended prototype. (*© The Boeing Company*)

give Balfour a cockpit checkout for take-off and cruise, Balfour was uninterested, declaring that "one airplane is like another." Predictably, he erred with fuel management near the end of his speed runs. As Schmued had attempted to explain, the new selector valve required a manual switch from one tank to the other. When Balfour failed to switch to his right tank, which had nearly 32gal remaining, his engine ran dry on the left tank. After his engine stopped, Balfour made an emergency landing in a plowed field, digging in the main gear and nosing-over the X73. Balfour was uninjured, and the CAA Accident Report attributed the mishap to pilot error. Unfortunately the X73 was badly damaged.[37] After it was repaired, Vance Breese resumed testing on January 13, 1941. Fortunately, only a few issues surfaced during static testing that required significant rework for the first production Mustangs.

Between October 1940 and January 15, 1941, in a series of review meetings between the BPC and NAA regarding the X73 and NA-73, the former requested that the NA-73's wing fuel tank capacity be increased from 157gal (X73) to 170gal; that the final wing armament be fixed; and that the windshield and armor provisions be changed. US-based suppliers for RAF-mandated government-furnished equipment (GFE) such as Curtiss propellers, radio equipment, fluorescent lighting, and

Browning machine guns were secured. The final performance and gross weight specifications were also set. Except for minor changes, NA-1620 remained unchanged with respect to top speed guarantees, weight and balance, and range with both the "normal" 105gal of fuel as well as with 157gal. All agreed changes were incorporated into the 1620 Specification as revisions.

On December 1, 1940, Army Co-operation Command was activated in the RAF. There is no question that the observed effectiveness of close tactical cooperation between the Wehrmacht and the Luftwaffe was the deciding factor in its establishment. The RAF was more decisive than the USAAC in selecting fighters over slow observation types to perform tactical reconnaissance, choosing the P-40C as the first fighter type for the planned mission. Delivered as the Tomahawk I, it was deficient in armament, armor and self-sealing fuel tanks, and was eventually upgraded as the Tomahawk II. The aircraft's first deployments were primarily to North Africa's Western Desert,[38] where the experiences of the RAF's Desert Air Force contributed significantly to the USAAF's development of Tactical Air Force Doctrine.[39]

On December 9 the BPC notified NAA that the NA-73 and all succeeding models would be named Mustang.[40]

Static testing saw an incomplete airframe (designated the XX73) tested to destruction to provide accurate data on the aircraft's strength. The wings eventually failed at 105 percent of its design load, resulting in some buckling of the aft fuselage skin. This photograph was taken on January 16, 1941. (© *The Boeing Company*)

USAAC NOTES FROM MID-JUNE 1940 THROUGH DECEMBER 1940

On June 26 Col J. G. Vincent, vice president of the Packard Motor Company's Aircraft Engineering Division, dedicated his efforts to developing the Rolls-Royce relationship, with the objective of securing an aero-engine contract for Packard. Two days earlier, Max Gilman, Packard President and general manager, and Col Vincent met with Lt Gen William Knudsen, Commissioner of Industrial Production in the Office of Production Management. Knudsen asked Packard to agree a contract with Rolls-Royce to produce 6,000 engines for the British and 3,000 for the USAAC. Following the meeting, Vincent reported that he was engaged solely in the active direction of Packard Aircraft Engineering Division. The decision was made to produce the Merlin XX.[41]

On October 25 Maj Gen Arnold was made Deputy Chief of Staff for Air, in charge of all air matters. He also retained the position of Chief of the Army Air Corps. At the same time newly promoted Brig Gen Spaatz was named Chief – Plans Division. The reorganization remained confusing, as GHQ Army Air Corps was removed from Arnold's direct control and placed under the Army Chief of Staff. The separation of combat command from all the other major divisions of the USAAC would not last long. When the new reorganization defined by US Army Regulations 95-5 was issued on June 20, 1941, everything was reorganized under Arnold's leadership.[42]

SUMMARY – 1940

NAA transitioned from building radial-engined trainer derivatives for its export fighter market to the Allison-engined high-speed pursuit Mustang (from the concept embodied in the P-509 to the production NA-73) in a very short time. Also, during the period January through February, NAA fended off both the AFPB's and the USAAC-MD's desire to build P-40s in its Inglewood factory, arousing the animosity of Col Oliver Echols.

The Packard Motor Company's Aircraft Engine Division secured contracts with Rolls-Royce to build the Merlin XX engine as the Packard Merlin V-1650-1.

The USAAC experienced divisions among senior air staff regarding the vulnerability/invulnerability of the B-17 as a fast, high-altitude, bomber, leading to initial questions regarding the long-held doctrine of "the bomber will always get through."

The project cycle start date to design and construct the X73 prototype was not entirely clear, as work on the precursor, including specifications and performance estimates, proceeded apace from early 1940 and perhaps as far back as mid-1939 when the NA-53 was canceled. The halting of the latter project in March 1939 certainly ended with authorization funding remaining to be spent, and certain funds may have been diverted to further study of the Allison pursuit. If a "start date" of completion of Specification 1592 for the "High Speed Pursuit – Allison" on March 10 could be deemed "the beginning," followed by the P-509 mock-up, followed by the April 10 Letter of Intent, then completion of the airframe, minus the tardy Allison V-1710-39 engine, on September 9 may mark the "end date." That is a span of 183 days. The arrival of the V-1710 engine loaned by the USAAC on October 7, installation of the associated wiring/fuel lines and instrumentation, ground running, dispatch to Flight Test for final check out and the first flight on October 26 adds another 20 days to the project.

Newly promoted Maj Gen Henry H. "Hap" Arnold took over control of the USAAC after Maj Gen Oscar Westover perished in a flying accident at Burbank, California, on September 21, 1938. (*NARA*)

Thus, from the beginning of preliminary design (Schmued P-509) to contract, to assembly of team, to completion of engineering, to fabrication of the X73 for public roll-out, to engine and instrumentation installation, to engine tests, to taxi testing and first flight was approximately 203 days (ignoring Allison's failure to deliver a V-1710 on time). The reader may draw conclusions regarding the project timescale based on their own set of definitions. If the criteria were from "assembly of the X73 project team through to delivery of the X73 design engineering package," then the design cycle was completed in "100-plus days."

In December 1940 the first combat "customer" for the aircraft, RAF Army Co-operation Command, was established. The RAF's operational deployment of the Mustang preceded the USAAF by at least a year.

MUSTANG RIVAL NOTES – 1940

In February the fabrication of 13 YP-38s began. Between March and June 5, 1940, Lockheed received orders from the BPC for 143 Model 322s without turbo-superchargers. This was amended to an order for an additional 524 Lightning IIs with engine turbo-superchargers.[43]

In mid-June the USAAC canceled future P-43 and P-44 pursuit aircraft. Following the first flight of the Chance Vought XF4U, the USAAC-MD informed Republic that a new Pratt & Whitney R-2800-powered pursuit with a turbo-supercharger would be favorably considered. In August the USAAC specified 0.50cal armament and defensive armor, with the former quickly changing to four 0.50cals plus one 20mm Hispano II cannon.[44] On September 6 the USAAC issued a contract for a Pratt & Whitney R-2800-powered version of the XP-47, designated XP-47B – 733 production P-47Bs were ordered. Ten days later, the YP-38 was flown for the first time.

NAA CHRONOLOGY FOR JANUARY THROUGH DECEMBER 1941

January 1941 saw several milestones important to the operational Mustang. That month, evaluation of flight test observations and wind tunnel data isolated problems requiring several important changes. On the 4th the CAA reissued the Certificate of License for the X73, as the FAA Flight Department prepared for the first test on the 13th.

On January 7, R. C. Costello, Resident Technical Officer for the British Air Commission (BAC), formed in October 1940 in Washington, D.C., sent a letter requesting that NAA prepare a report on the maximum possible range of the Mustang at different speeds and maximum possible take-off gross weight, with all equipment removed save radio and navigational equipment.

The next entries, from January 7 to June 7, all relate to the extended range auxiliary tank. The narrative then resumes on January 13.

Following correspondence exchanges between the BPC and NAA, the minimum armament was fixed at two 0.50cal cowling-mounted guns, with extra fuel to be carried internally in the gun bays after ruling out lengthy design changes required for the wings, namely the lead times to design and test a bomb rack in the wings for external fuel tanks, plumbing the wings for fuel lines, and re-stressing the wings. Schmued also advanced the notion of external fuel tanks and racks when asked by the USAAC-MD to comment on the CP39-770 fighter competition. At that time, and until 1942, USAAC regulations forbade aircraft to be equipped with external tanks for combat. Horkey's estimates were summarized in a report to Rice. They specified 197.24gal of internal fuel only, and a cruising speed of 229mph at 10,000ft. It was proposed to retain the 0.50cal fuselage guns, and remove the wing armament and ammunition and replace it with a 27gal fuel cell in each of the wing bays.

On January 20 Rice wrote to R. C. Costello that NAA findings pointed to a requirement of 200 US gallons for 1,500 miles, including warm-up, take-off, and climb to 10,000ft at 75 percent rated power. The gross weight was estimated at 8,400lb, with a take-off run of 1,600ft to clear a 50ft obstacle. In parallel, quotes from the Firestone Tire and Rubber Company were requested for leak-proof fuel cells, including a 200hr test that would be carried out with 100-octane fuel. John Young of the NA-73 powerplant department issued a memo describing the fuel system as comprising two small cells for the ammunition compartment and one large one for the gun bay. Each of the three rubber tanks (for a total increase of 54gal per wing) would connect with the main tank and feed via gravity. The estimated range for the Mustang I with the auxiliary fuel cells was 1,724 miles with 220gal, for an equipment cost (to NAA) of $125.[45]

On June 7 the BAC formally requested from Rice that auxiliary tank kits be included with every Mustang I delivered. In the same correspondence it was insisted that this modification should "occasion no delay in the delivery of any of the airplanes." This last statement posed a real problem for NAA, since the results of the structural static tests of the XX73 airframe had revealed a need for several changes to strengthen the wing and fuselage to meet the tactical aircraft requirements detailed in the specification. Those changes, in concert with the post-crash analysis of the X73, had necessitated a slowdown of production to allow for essential engineering alterations and modifications of tooling and materials.

Furthermore, the Extended Range Modification was required to be provided as GFE, necessitating engineering drawings, specifications, and test results in a package for formal review. This process was not yet complete, as the fuel cells were under further development following Firestone's changes to reduce thickness of the cell walls, which resulted in an increase in capacity from 70.25gal to 76.25gal per individual wing kit. Tests showed that the cells more than exceeded requirements for leaks, contamination, and duration of contained fuel without damaging the cells.

The conversations between Costello and Rice, specifically regarding delivery issues that would arise with the requirement that the cells be included with early-production Mustangs, led to correspondence to Roy Russell of the BPC, explaining the impact on production and suggesting that the kits could be provided starting with aircraft 143 to 320, as well as following contract AC-1493 for 300 NA-83 Mustangs. Rice reiterated the 1,500-mile range guarantee, and summarized the price per kit of $245.35 per airplane. The letter was passed to the BAC, which responded by requesting that the plumbing installations necessary to accept the kits be included in the wings, and that the fuel cells be provided as separate packaged kits to be included with each airplane when crated for shipment. The economics were facilitated under "Lend-Lease."[46]

Nothing was substantiated by the authors regarding the eventual use of the three-cell auxiliary fuel tanks by the RAF. Had they entered frontline service, the Mustang I would have been the longest-range armed, single-engined fighter-reconnaissance aircraft of World War II using only internal fuel until 1943, when the 85gal fuselage tank was incorporated in the P-51B. As an illustration, a Mustang I so equipped could fly a reconnaissance sortie from London to Warsaw and back.

Continuing the narrative from January 7, flight testing with the X73 after January 13 resulted in improvements in the cockpit regarding electrical systems and control location as the change was made from USAAC standards to RAF standards (there are no recorded flights of the X73 in Chilton's logbook during this period, however). As the prototype Mustang, the X73/NA-73X was often presented in the likeness of the XP-51 and Mustang I for publicity purposes. Because it was a commercial airplane, the civil registration NX19998 was overpainted or temporarily removed and replaced by USAAC insignia or RAF camouflage, as the occasion required. In June 1941, as the first production aircraft came off the assembly line, the X73 was taken out of service and spent the remainder of the war in a corner of the Experimental Hangar. It is believed to have been scrapped post-war.

On January 14 Chilton flew AG347 (its British military serial number) with the prototype three-cell auxiliary fuel tanks installed in the gun and ammunition bay of each wing.

Four days later Rice noted in a memo to Engineering that the GALCIT tests concerning heat rejection data for the X73 cooling system pointed to the need to expand the intake scoop area to 150in., dropping the inlet air intake from the bottom surface of the wing and giving the variable aft plenum gate/exit a range of 65 to 280sq in. Britain's Air Ministry was contacted for support to assist in the redesign of the scoop.

On January 21, XX73 experienced some damage to its structural integrity at both its design ultimate angle-of-attack loading and its peak side load, which caused buckling of the spar and the airframe. The production airframe project engineers, working with structures, beefed up the longerons, the spar, and some skins to enable the changes to be incorporated into NA-73 number 11. Because of these findings, the X73 and AG345 to AG352, including USAAC 41-038 and 41-039, were deemed "disqualified" from a combat role and relegated to flight-test status.

With respect to the originally assigned NAA factory serial number sequence, USAAC 41-038 was the fourth NA-73 (73-3101) completed at Inglewood. The assigned factory serial number created confusion regarding the factory serial number identification for AG348 (the fourth in sequence of the aircraft delivered to the RAF). It is certain that AG348 was not re-designated 41-038, and that it was delivered to the RAF, and then to the Soviet Air Force in 1942. Two aircraft with the NAA factory serial numbers 73-3101 and 73-3107 were pulled for the USAAF.

The confusion was probably caused because the NAA contracts originally assigned a first block of NA-73s the factory serial numbers 73-3097 through 73-4016. However, X73 was assigned 73-3097, and the USAAF took 3101 and 3107. NAA contracts reassigned the unused 72-4767 and 4768 from NA-72 and pulled 7812 from between the NA-84 and NA-87 contract serial number assignments to complete the total of 320 NA-73 contract factory serial numbers. That said, it is still uncertain which contract factory serial numbers applied to each of the delivered RAF Mustang Is owing to the uncertainty of the production position of the new factory serial numbers pulled from other contracts.[47]

Following repair of XX73, the airframe was turned over to NAA Field Services to produce maintenance and repair instruction manuals for the Mustang.

On January 25, to explore alternatives to the Allison V-1710 for the Mustang, Atwood approved RD-1062 to study airframe and cooling system changes that

XP-51 41-038 (production aircraft No. 4), Mines Field, California, July 1941. (Artwork by Jim Laurier, © Osprey Publishing)

would arise from the installation of the Continental V-3420 engine into the NA-73 airframe. On the same date, Dr. B. S. Shenstone of the RAE arrived from Britain to consult with NAA. After reviewing flight and wind tunnel data, he suggested that the upper lip of the scoop be dropped approximately 1½in. from the bottom of the wing. At this time the new plenum design looked very much like the XB-28 aftercooler intake plenum. The results derived from the GALCIT wind tunnel testing indicated significant improvements to the radiator face pressure distribution. The new intake scoop/plenum design was sent to Production for incorporation into the NA-73 line.[48] This was the first design change to recognize the effect of boundary-layer separation in front of both the radiator and carburetor scoop.

During Dr. Shenstone's visit to NAA the wind tunnel investigations first revealed the boundary-layer interference on high-energy cooling air into the scoop. This is described as a "spilling effect" in Figures 1 and 3 on pages 22–24 of Schmued's *Design of the P-51*. The initial solution of lowering the upper lip of the scoop further away from the wing was useful in achieving significant drag reduction during the continued X73 wind tunnel tests. The next evolution of the intake scoop is illustrated photographically in this chapter. Even so, the scoop and plenum design, the radiator and oil cooler design, and the exit plenum/gate all underwent constant examination and modification through to the P-51H.[49]

On February 19 the BPC directed NAA to consider only the four-20mm configuration with belt feed in any future discussions of cannon armament, leading to the incorporation of this weaponry in the NA-91 P-51. Aircraft AG347 was the first to be given both the two-gun and four-gun installation for drag testing. After flying with these configurations in October–November 1941 it was returned to Service NA-73 condition. The data and results of the drag tests led to the installation of four 20mm cannon in NA-83 AM190 in May 1942, the aircraft serving as the prototype NA-91.[50]

ABOVE RAF Mustang I AG345 (NA-73 No. 1) with the original short carburetor scoop. It was retained by NAA to install and test RAF specific changes. (*© The Boeing Company*)

CENTER LEFT Mustang I AG345 is seen here in flight on August 19, 1941, with Bob Chilton at the controls, after the long carburetor scoop had been added. This aircraft was eventually struck off charge on December 3, 1946. (*Tony Holmes Collection*)

LEFT A close-up of the Mustang I's adjustable "alligator" front scoop and "donut" radiator/oil cooler. The scoop was adjustable so as to increase/decrease the volume of air ingested according to the engine's cooling requirements. (*© The Boeing Company*)

On February 20, the USAAC-MD released Request for Data R-40C to 13 companies for a High Speed Single-Engine Pursuit, but NAA was again excluded.[51]

Newly promoted Brig Gen Echols requested that all flight-test data for the XP-51 was to include take-off gross weight (with all installed equipment).

On February 28, based on wind tunnel results, the intake scoop design was changed to reduce the scoop area from 200sq in. to 110sq in.

Initial testing of the Hispano II 20mm cannon saw the weapons fitted in canted mountings in a mock-up wing section. This was how NAA initially intended to install them in the Mustang IA. They were later straightened out, although the design for the original canted mounts were retained for the 0.50cal weapons used by the NA-91 through NA-104 series Mustangs. (*© The Boeing Company*)

On March 1 Allison reported to NAA that the exhaust power loss was excessive, and suggested joint design and test collaboration.

On March 10 Allison Chairman O. E. Hunt wrote to Kindelberger regarding plans for a two-speed/two-stage supercharger version of the company's V-1710 engine. This had been prompted by persistent requests from the USAAC for higher performance from the V-1710, urging the manufacturer to increase supercharging capabilities to boost the engine's high-altitude capabilities. Kindelberger argued for an integral two-speed blower approach, which would minimize modification requirements of the existing Mustang airframe. Hunt responded that it would be easier (for Allison) to hang an auxiliary two-stage blower on the back of the engine, which would have created a nightmare of redesign work for NAA.

On March 11, now frustrated by the belligerence of Allison regarding a design approach that would enable a straightforward modification to allow the Mustang to take a better engine, Kindelberger fired off a request to the BPC for information on Rolls-Royce engines. This was contrary to GMC wishes, and led to serious (and continuing) discussions about keeping business within the GMC "family." Not to be deterred, Kindelberger continued to pursue the possibility of installing a Merlin XX.[52]

Testing of the repaired X73 was delayed by the installation of the new radiator intake scoop and replacement of a sick Allison V-1710-F3R. Between March 18 and 22, 1941, USAAC-MD test pilot Capt M. J. Lee flew the repaired X73 five times. He then submitted an initial and unfavorable five-line report, which included "5. unsuitable for combat."[53] Lee's negative comments initiated NAA changes to both the X73 and NA-73, including the fitting of a flat-panel windshield to eliminate distortion of the view straight ahead and changes to the elevator and aileron control systems. The X73 was grounded until the changes were completed.[54]

On March 20 test pilot Bob Chilton made his first flight at NAA, at the controls of an AT-6. Before March 16, most of his 1,170hrs of flight time as a USAAC instructor had been accumulated in Stearmans and BT-9s. He was immediately tasked to fly the B-25 and the new AT-6. His first flight in the repaired X73 was made on April 4.[55] Ed Horkey recalls that Chilton was the best and most professionally competent test pilot he ever knew. Horkey was careful to show that Chilton was so good that all of his flights were exactly to the test-flight plan in altitude and speed as demanded. In Horkey's case, the data deduced from the actual results was easily plotted with little scatter, and could be illustrated with smooth curves, whereas others with less skill had data points "all over the chart."[56]

Beginning April 12, the X73 resumed flight status.

One week later, Rolls-Royce, via US Senior Representative J. E. Ellor, sent an 18-page package of technical details for installing a Merlin XX engine, including radiator cooling and intercooler requirements relating to the P-40F and Bristol Beaufighter II (fitted with Merlin XXs) engine mount designs, etc.[57]

On April 21 Rice sent Dr. George W. Lewis at NACA test results for Allison exhaust stack designs, requesting his assistance and insight regarding why the exhaust gas thrust was lower than had been expected.

On April 23, after ten days of preparation of the aircraft in the Flight Department, Louis Wait made the first flight of the very first Mustang I (AG345) with the production flat-panel windshield. Various problems were encountered and solved between April 23 and June 30, including tailwheel shimmy; stiff control/roll rate with existing cusped ailerons; engine surge in dives, which was traced to the carburetor intake; the Prestone thermostat control; overheating, which was solved by a new scoop and radiator/oil cooler; and cockpit illumination with British fluorescent lights.

LEFT A heavily retouched early view of AG348 (which would become XP-51 41-038), with its flat windscreen and short carburetor intake. (© *The Boeing Company*)

BOTTOM LEFT Also heavily retouched, this head-on view of AG348 reveals its armament layout – two 0.30cal and one 0.50cal machines guns in each wing and two 0.50cal weapons in the lower nose. (© *The Boeing Company*)

ABOVE These comparison views from NAA documentation on the Mustang show the original X73 "round windscreen" (bottom) and improved flat windscreen (top) for the NA-73. (© *The Boeing Company*)

TOP RIGHT AG346 (only the second Mustang I completed) sits on the ramp at Mines Field before being disassembled, crated up and shipped via the Panama Canal sea route across the Atlantic to Britain. (© *The Boeing Company*)

ABOVE RIGHT Now fitted with a long carburetor intake, Mustang I AG346 – devoid of its wings – is seen in the process of being crated up for shipment by sea to Britain. (© *The Boeing Company*)

On May 20 the first flight of the USAAC's NA-73 (No. 4) Mustang 41-038 was made at Mines Field by Chilton, who flew it several more times before it was delivered to Wright Field on August 24.[58, 59] May 20 also saw Kindelberger write to Breech, "We are still not getting Allison engines or real co-operation from Allison in any way." The GMC Board was sent a summary memo stating, "grave concerns about both Allison production and service capability."[60]

Beginning on May 26, XP-51 No. 1 41-038 was deemed ready for USAAC flight testing at Mines Field after 30 Change Engineering Orders had been incorporated following initial tests in March. Capt M. J. Lee was the principal pilot for 18 flights made through to June 16. The tests in XP-51 No. 1 (and the X73) were flown to explore various configurations of different elevators to improve high-speed dive stability at one end of the flight spectrum and low-speed landing approach sensitivity at the other. Both increasing chord and changing the aerodynamic surface with a "bump" were tried, and the trials ended in July with a distinct but smaller "bump" on the top surface of the elevator. That design remained until the introduction of the metal elevator in late 1944.

The USAAC-MD requested that the XP-51 be delivered to Wright Field on or about July 12. Among other requests, it was asked that the first USAAC implementation of the automatic gun charging system be accomplished, in addition to the decision to install the modified "long" carburetor scoop at NAA rather than send it as a kit to Wright Field. The estimated completion date of August 22 at the earliest prompted the decision to send XP-51 No. 1 with the existing short carb intake. The decision to incorporate the new production carburetor scoop further delayed transport of XP-51

No. 2 to Wright Field until December, but 41-038 retained the short carb until it was modified at Wright Field in December.[61]

Rice forwarded correspondence to Atwood for inclusion of a contract addendum, and for production planning to set in motion orders to Firestone for the extended-range fuel tank kits. The contract was modified to support those orders placed on August 6, 1941.[62]

XP-51 41-038 (No. 1) as delivered to the USAAC for initial flight testing in March 1941. (*Tony Holmes Collection*)

On June 5, 1941, workers at NAA went on strike, after having voted for industrial action on May 26 and following stressful negotiations between union collective bargaining and NAA management, as well as unsuccessful pleas from national Congress of Industrial Organizations (CIO) labor union leaders. President Roosevelt and his Cabinet decided that, if the issue was not resolved immediately, the War Department would issue orders to the US Army on June 9 to seize the plant at Inglewood. During the early morning of the 9th, the commanding officer of the 15th Infantry, Lt Col Charles Branshaw, assembled 2,000 troops to await further orders. When a core of the strike leaders blocked the entrance to the plant to workers, and the Los Angeles Police Department was unsuccessful in convincing the remaining strikers to withdraw, Branshaw was ordered to seize the plant. His regiment-sized force peacefully but forcefully marched the strikers from the plant, enabling the workforce to return unmolested. The 20 union militants arrested were never tried, but were forever banned from both the plant and future union employment.[63]

After three weeks of coordinated effort by Union and NAA leadership, the situation was stabilized, with little labor–management resentment henceforth. Branshaw was able to disengage his troops and return to barracks on July 3. A formal agreement between the CIO and NAA was signed on July 18. Future concerns regarding more interference and agitation from communist influence mostly vanished when Germany invaded the USSR on June 21.

On June 30 the BPC requested 150 new Mustangs, specifying four 20mm cannon as sole armament. Defense Aid Contract DAC-140 was signed on July 7. The USAAF (which came into existence on June 20 following the reorganization of the USAAC) acquired 57 (for future delivery) on July 24 as "P-51s." One year later, on July 25, 1942, the Materiel Command (which had replaced the Materiel Division on April 1, 1942) issued the requirement to pull two aircraft from the early block of P-51s (41-37252 and 41-37421) for the NA-101 and the XP-78, later re-designated the XP-51B.[64]

On June 30 Kindelberger notified the Board that there were signature delays to the NA-83 program. This was resolved and executed as A-1483 on July 24 for 300 more Mustang Is. That same day the X73

The "bump" was one of several different designs tested for the elevator airfoil to improve stick force sensitivity in pitch following flight trials with the XP-51s. Very light control forces for pitch remained one of the few negative "handling" criticisms of the entire Mustang series until the advent of the P-51H. (*HMSO*)

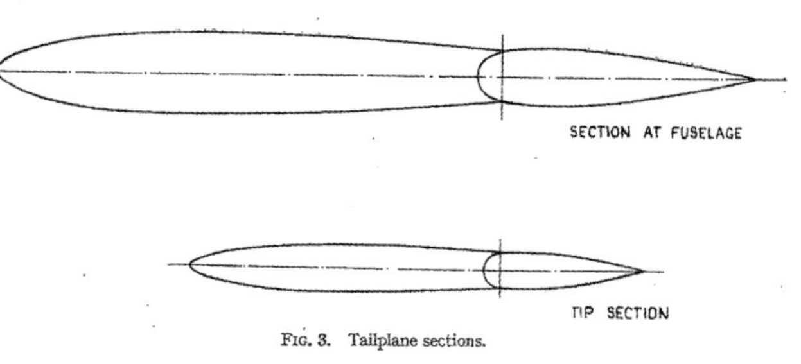

Fig. 3. Tailplane sections.

Mustang I AG346, A&AEE Boscombe Down, Wiltshire, December 1941. (*Artwork by Jim Laurier, © Osprey Publishing*)

RIGHT A page from the RAF maintenance manual for the Mustang I showing the auxiliary fuel cells installation within the ammunition and gun compartments in the left wing. (*The National Archives, ref. AIR10/2866*)

FAR RIGHT Auxiliary Fuel Cell installation schematic. As can be clearly seen in this artwork, two auxiliary tanks could be installed in the outer wing section to extend one-way flight range to 1,700-plus miles in 1941. The down side to the installation was that armament was reduced to only the two 0.50cal guns in the lower cowl. (*The National Archives, ref. AIR10/2866*)

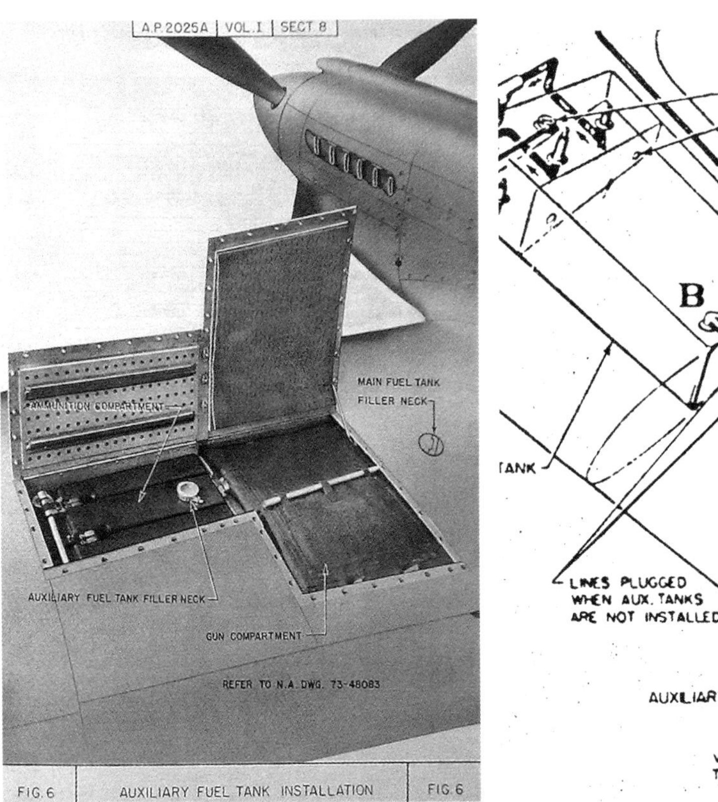

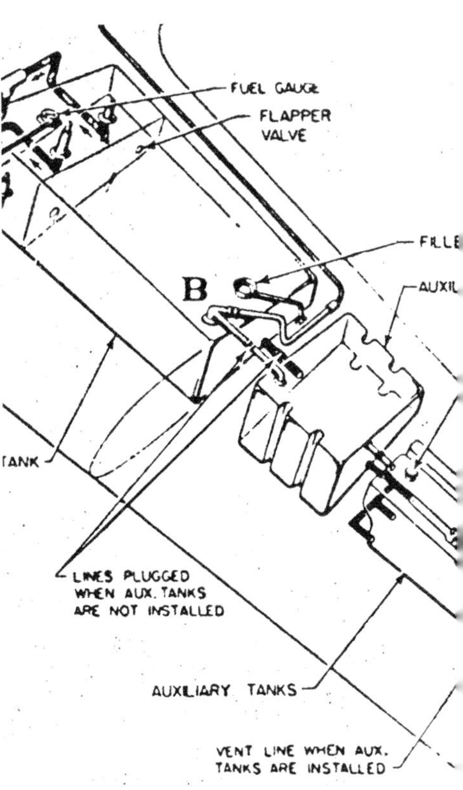

undertook its last flight, with a wake survey rake installed to record flow properties arising from the NACA/NAA low-drag/high-speed airfoil. The aircraft was then retired.

On August 1 Chilton completed the last functional tests on AG346, the second NA-73, and released it to the RAF. On the 4th, Battle of Britain ace Sqn Ldr Michael Crossley made the first "official" RAF flights of the Mustang I. Following acceptance, AG346 was crated for shipment to Britain via the Panama Canal.

The Packard Motor Company received the first drawing package for the Merlin XX/1650-1 two-speed/single-stage engine from Rolls-Royce on August 1.[65] Five days later the BPC ordered 320 long-range fuel tank kits.

XP-51 41-038 (NA-73 No. 4) was flown to Wright Field by Chilton on the 24th for delivery to the USAAC-MD.

During August, several milestones were reached. Packard completed its first Merlin V-1650-1/Merlin 28 (the same as the Merlin XX), destined for Canadian-built Lancasters and Mosquitoes. Curtiss arranged for the V-1650-1 to be delivered for its P-40F fighters, and the USAAF ordered 733 P-47B/Cs from Republic.

In September, several more events occurred that were to have a bearing on future Mustang deployments. The USAAF Army War Plans Division (AWPD) 1 mission statement simply stated "Destroy German and Italian capability to wage war."[66] The statement also set the framework for near-term global operations following the attack by Japan on December 7, 1941. The general opinion among senior staff, including Eaker and Spaatz, was that US bombers could defend themselves without escort fighters.

The NAA Dallas Plant was completed. Harold Schweder was named General Manager and Plant Manager, and Kenneth Bowen, the key NA-73 project manager, was promoted to Assistant General Manager. Bowen was credited with "design to build, ease of maintenance" concepts while working for Smithson. Gehrkens replaced Bowen as Mustang project manager.

In early October 1941 Packard delivered the first production Merlin XX/V-1650-1 – several months after the forecast dates in July. The primary issue, as relayed by Vincent, was the lack of A1 priority from the USAAC-MD, which was needed to get the necessary machine tools, raw materials and castings, fixtures, and gages. Packard began a collaborative project with Rolls-Royce engineers to assist in development of the two-speed/two-stage improvements for the Merlin 60 series. One of the first outcomes was the planetary drive, combined with aneroid-controlled altitude settings, enabling automatic supercharger impeller gear changes from low to high gear.[67]

On October 8 the USAAC-MD began flight testing XP-51 41-038 with the short carburetor scoop.[68]

Two days later, Kindelberger and Atwood, ever mindful that orders other than those from the RAF were necessary to retain the workforce trained for Mustang-related production, decided to fund preliminary design work for a new attack fighter. The authorized study to rework the NA-83 design as a low-altitude attack pursuit aircraft was to compete for funding still available for a dive-bomber-capable fast attack aircraft described in Army FM 1-15. On October 23 Structures chief Richard Schleicher informed Rice that the task of modifying the NA-83 to take the increased loadings caused by dive brakes, an external bomb/fuel load, and the increased maximum angle-of-attack loads imposed by the pull-out would require 700hrs of structural analysis to re-stress-check the new airframe. The NA-83 was already designed to a maximum gross weight in excess of 8,100lb, primarily due to increasing the main fuel tank's capacity from 170 to 180gal.[69]

TOP Mustang I AG346 was assembled by No. 1 Aircraft Assembly Unit at Speke after being shipped across the Atlantic in October 1941. It was then flown south to the A&AEE at Boscombe Down to begin Service Trials. (*Philip Jarrett Collection*)

ABOVE AG585 is reassembled in Hangar 3 at Speke by personnel from No. 1 Aircraft Assembly Unit. Note that the aircraft lacks cowl gun fairings, denoting that it was a mid-block NA-73 Mustang I. (*Philip Jarrett Collection*)

On October 15, 1941, the USAAC-MD authorized Lockheed to proceed with a design for an internal pressure pump to pressurize the external ferry tank attached to the wing racks for high-altitude transit capability.[70]

The first Mustang I shipped to Britain, AG346, arrived at Liverpool on October 24. After transport by road to Speke, it was uncrated and assembled by No. 1 Aircraft Assembly Unit and then flown to the Aeroplane and Armament Experimental Establishment (A&AEE) at Boscombe Down, Wiltshire, to begin Service Trials.[71] Of the next six Mustangs that arrived, three more (AG351, AG357, and AG359) were sent to the Air Fighting Development Unit (AFDU), and three went to the A&AEE for the accelerated testing required to evaluate the new American fighter. During December, more Mustangs were allocated both to Operational Training Units (OTUs), beginning with No. 41 OTU, and Army Co-operation Command squadrons, including Nos. 4, 26, and 241. In January 1942, No. 26 Sqn became the first operational Army Co-operation Command unit equipped with the Mustang I.[72]

On November 19 Allison informed NAA about its new "high-altitude" engine, with an auxiliary second-stage supercharger attached to the V-1710 basic design. Kindelberger requested a design study to determine the changes required to the NA-73/83 airframe to accommodate the new engine. Rice responded on December 4 that only the two-speed F11 or single-speed F3R were suitable for installation in the NA-73/83 without major design changes to the wing and fuselage to accommodate the altered center of gravity, whereas the new "high-altitude" engine (with a proposed two-speed/two-stage supercharger) required that the wing be moved 20in forward of the firewall, and that its area be increased. Rice also expressed pessimism that any current contract delivery dates could be met with such changes.[73]

From the delivery of XP-51 41-038 to Wright Field on August 24 until December 23, approximately 20 test flights were made. This Mustang's flight testing was limited by bad weather. A report was issued near the end of December 1941, and it included several constructive comments. These included noting the improved view with the flat windscreen; issues with engine surges during high-speed dives (already known to NAA); binding of the canopy top and side, creating difficulty in opening during flight; a tendency for the right gear fairing to try to open during flight; issues with right gear full extension at temperatures below freezing; and binding/scarring of the main right gear door oleo strut and an adjacent wing rib. A possible cause of the last-named problem was an extraordinarily bad landing by Capt Lee on November 26, which damaged the right main gear and destroyed the tailwheel and lower rudder surface. The airframe was inspected by NAA Structures and deemed safe, and flight tests resumed on November 30.

During early December, issues with correct gage correlation to actual fuel in the left wing reserve fuel tank were noted. Aside from the foregoing, Maj Ralph P. Swofford at Wright Field remarked that all pilots who flew the Mustang were favorably impressed with its performance and handling characteristics.[74]

On December 16 the second XP-51, 41-039, was delivered to Wright Field, where it remained untouched until April 1942, as other pursuit models were scheduled for flight testing first. However, a request to evaluate pneumatic gun chargers by both the USAAF and the US Navy in October made XP-51 41-038 a logical choice to be sent first to Langley Field, Virginia, and then to Eglin Field, Florida, for testing.[75] It was duly dispatched on December 29.

LEFT XP-51 41-039 (No. 2) looked virtually identical to 41-038, bar a slightly different anti-glare panel ahead of the cockpit. It is seen here fitted with a long carburettor scoop at NACA Langley during flight trials in March 1942. (*NASA*)

BELOW XP-51 41-039 eventually donned standard USAAF Olive Drab over Gray camouflage while at NACA Langley, as well as the "dotless" national insignia introduced from May 1942. During flight trials in March 1942 new aileron recommendations were passed to NAA following extensive testing. The aircraft has a "wake rake" airflow measuring test rig attached to the trailing edge of its left wing. (*NASA*)

USAAC/USAAF NOTES FROM JUNE THROUGH DECEMBER 1941

On June 20, 1941 the United States Army Air Corps became the United States Army Air Forces. An important letter written on that date from Assistant Secretary of War Robert Lovett to Maj Gen Arnold accompanied the announcement, stating, "Not enough attention paid to Army Co-operation and ground attack airplanes for support of Army units," and citing "effectiveness of light attack aircraft and dive-bombers for the Luftwaffe."[76]

This period of transition from USAAC to USAAF is extremely important in the story of the Mustang's US service. For the first time, a major organization in the form of the Air War Plans Division reported to the Chief, Air Forces (Arnold), and it was not a component of the primary War Department Plans Division. Prior to June 20, Lt Gen Emmons retained control of the GHQ/Combat Command as Commanding General, Air Forces Combat Command, and Maj Gen Arnold, as Chief, Air Forces, retained everything else. On June 21 the USAAC command structure was changed. Essentially Lt Gen Emmons retained leadership of the former GHQ/Combat Command, but now had two reporting lines – one to the Army Chief of Staff and another, less defined, reporting to the Chief, Air Forces, Maj Gen Arnold, who was also CO of "everything else." Contributing to the awkwardness was the fact that Emmons still outranked Arnold.

Maj Gen Brett was named Chief of the Air Corps, reporting to Arnold and being co-equal in the chain of command to Arnold as Lt Gen Emmons. Brett's organization was basically in charge of everything in the USA in respect to all procurement, materiel, transportation, maintenance, training, and supply functions for the new "Air Force." Materiel Division continued as a major entity in the newly arranged scheme, and Brig Gen Echols remained as its commanding officer, with continued oversight of engineering, procurement, flight testing, production and services.

During this period, there was much debate about suitable military aircraft types (including light-attack bombers and fighters) for the observation, reconnaissance, and ground attack roles in support of, and subordinate to, Army ground units, versus slow civilian-type aircraft for courier service and artillery spotting. Emmons, as Chief, General Headquarters and Combat Command, directed Arnold (his boss) as Chief, Army Air Forces, to (1) develop doctrines, tactics, and techniques for direct support of ground units; (2) prepare recommendations for the development of aircraft and equipment essential to Close Air Support (CAS); and (3) create an Army Close Air Support Staff Section in Air Force Combat Command and the numbered Air Forces in such a way that not only would the role of CAS and Observer units be further clarified, but they would also have a larger voice in Plans Division. Following a further reorganization in March 1942, Col David Schlatter became the first Director, Air Support Directorate, Office of Director, Military Requirements, HQ-AAF.[77]

Brig Gen Muir S. Fairchild was promoted to Assistant Chief of Staff, Plans Division, on August 5. Regarded as one of the brightest staff officers, he was highly influential in developing the USAAC Doctrine for Pursuit Aviation while Director,

Tactics and Strategy (T&S), from 1939 through June 1940. As Director T&S, his enumerated priorities for air power were to destroy hostile air forces, naval forces, ground forces, and the national industrial structure. This became the central theme for AWPD-1, completed on September 1. Fairchild was also the key contributor to USAAC FM-1-15 "Tactics and Techniques of Air Fighting," in which the mission was defined as "Destroy the Hostile Air Force's freedom of the Air."[78]

Gen Muir S. Fairchild became Director, Military Requirements, on March 1, 1942. (*USAF*)

Fairchild became Director, Military Requirements, on March 1, 1942, and his direct influence on wresting the Mustang from obscurity cannot be overstated.

Arnold was promoted again on October 20, to the Board of Chiefs of Staff as Deputy Chief of Staff, Army Air Force.[79]

On October 27 Lt Gen Emmons, Commanding General of USAAF GHQ, issued a directive which resulted in the separation of the mission and aircraft for Army Aviation for Observation into three separate types – light commercial-type aircraft to serve as couriers and battlefield observation, light twin-engined attack bombers, and fast pursuit types. The latter two evolved into having both attack and reconnaissance capability in the enemy's rear echelons. The fighters required for this mission needed to be the fastest available, and preferably faster than any fielded by the enemy. They also had to be able to carry cameras for reconnaissance.[80]

In late November/early December, pilots from the 79th Pursuit Squadron (PS)/20th Pursuit Group (PG) of the 4th Interceptor Command borrowed a P-51 to compare against the P-38D, P-40E and Vultee P-66.[81] Col Ira Eaker had been Commanding Officer (CO) of the 20th PG, based at Hamilton Field, California, until November 1941.[82] Conclusions may be drawn that Eaker, as the recent former CO of the 20th PG, became aware of the preparation of the subsequent comparison report following the flight trials and read it before the document was forwarded to Gen Ord Ryan, CO of 4th Interceptor Command. Furthermore, the authors conclude that the report caused Eaker to visit NAA to evaluate the P-51 for himself.

On December 7, 1941, the Imperial Japanese Naval Air Force executed a surprise attack on USAAF and US Navy installations, destroying most of the ships of the line at Pearl Harbor and aircraft scattered across Oahu, Hawaii. Fortunately, the Pacific Fleet's three carriers were not in harbor, and the US Navy's submarine facilities also escaped significant damaged, but apart from that, US naval and air power in the Pacific were effectively neutralized.

On December 8 Gen Arnold was named to the Joint Chiefs as Chief of Staff, Army Air Force, despite bitter resistance from the US Navy. The latter's long-cherished concept of restricting the USAAF to battlefield support and limiting its range to 100 miles offshore was over.[83]

On December 14 Col Ira Eaker flew from Hamilton Field to visit the NAA plant at Inglewood, where he flew the XP-51, expressing great admiration for its handling qualities and speed. He called Arnold and recommended that he visit NAA and inspect the P-51 personally.[84]

During the next several months Arnold's advisors from within the new USAAF Combat Command urged consideration of a fighter-type ground-attack aircraft complementary to the already approved Douglas A-20 Havoc light-attack bomber, to be armed with cannon, machine guns, and small bombs for use against enemy ground forces. The Operations Division of the Office of the Chief of the Army Air Corps called for the development of a "single-engine fighter *capable of defending itself*," in contrast to the Douglas A-24 Banshee, Curtiss A-25 Shrike, and the new Brewster XA-32 then under development.[85]

SUMMARY – 1941

Having reached the end of 1941, it is useful to summarize several important milestones and observations.

First, the rapid development of the X73, including the static-test XX73, enabled very short cycles between actual prototype evaluation in flight and wind tunnel testing. The issues that surfaced included the need to beef up the spar, longerons, and selected skin panels to achieve USAAC/USAAF Design Standards, necessary for future acceptance. It is noteworthy that NAA was not constrained earlier by the USAAC-MD looking over its shoulder to demand changes, as the Mustang was not "an Army design."

Second, the critical design feature that distinguished the Mustang from its contemporaries, most specifically the P-38, P-39, and P-40/XP-46, was the low-drag/

BELOW RIGHT The heavily armed Brewster XA-32 was canceled in favor of the A-36/P-51A. Overweight and underpowered, only two examples were built. The XA-32 was yet another failed aircraft fighter program initiated from Maj Gen Echols' Materiel Division at Wright Field in the early 1940s. (*USAF*)

BOTTOM The Douglas A-24 Banshee was the USAAF version of the US Navy's highly effective SBD Dauntless. It was deemed to be too slow for the demanding air-ground support role. (*Tony Holmes Collection*)

BOTTOM RIGHT The Curtiss A-25 Shrike was the USAAF version of the SB2C Helldiver, which was used to deadly effect by the US Navy in the Pacific War. It too was deemed to be too slow for the air-ground support role. This particular example, with WASP Helen A. Snapp at the controls, was employed as a target tug from Camp Stewart, Georgia, in 1944. (*USAF*)

high-speed wing derived from the NACA 45-100 laminar-flow airfoil research. Bell would design the P-63 wing around a NACA 66 series airfoil, and both Republic and Lockheed conducted low-drag wing research in 1943. The P-63 came closest to approaching the Mustang in respect to minimum total drag coefficient, but Republic, Lockheed, and Curtiss (XP-60 with a low-drag wing) did not appreciably reduce the parasite drag of their experimental wing designs from the production wings. Only the thin Spitfire wing, with its 20 percent less thickness-to-chord (T/C) ratio and elliptical planform, approached the Mustang wing with respect to profile drag.

Third, the descriptive/conical section methodology applied by Schmued and Roy Liming to the design of the Mustang fuselage resulted in an excellent reduction in the airframe pressure drag contribution from the chin radiators and protuberances for the gun and ammunition fairings.

Fourth, extreme care was devoted to designing fairings over retracted landing gear, the seals for flaps and ailerons, the processes applied to the fitting of butt joints and flush rivets, and to surface preparation to remove waves and ripples from the sheet metal construction of the wing.

Last, but not least, was the successful application of the Meredith exhaust gas theory to reduce cooling drag. Careful design of the intake scoop, expanding plenum designs to smooth intake flow and reduce velocity/pressure to the front face of the radiator, the insertion of a large combined oil cooler/radiator protruding deeply into the fuselage to provide efficient cooling with low-speed air, and the provision of an aft plenum long enough to provide a contracting "venturi effect" for the hot exhaust air from the aft face of the radiators to the rear scoop aft of the radiator were important contributions.

As will be explained in more detail in Appendix A – Technical Section, the coolant system variable-area scoop for the X73 through the Mustang I/IA and the P-51 changed to the new fixed intake scoop geometry for the A-36 and P-51A. The most radical changes imposed arose from the introduction of the P-51B, which brought much larger radiator demands for both the engine coolant and carburetor fuel-air charge aftercooling when passed through the two-stage/two-speed superchargers, as well as a relocation of the oil cooler.

The evidence that NAA used nothing of importance from the data acquired from Burdette Wright is exemplified by the failure to implement a low-drag wing solution to any production Curtiss airframe. Only the experimental P-40Q prototype, with a low-drag wing, was delivered 24 months after the Wright/Atwood transaction of April 1940. Furthermore, the P-40Q's radiator designs were not similar, or equal in drag reduction, to those installed in the Mustang.

The radiator cooling and engine "surge" issues experienced in the X73 flight tests were confirmed in the GALCIT wind tunnel. With the assistance of Dr. Shenstone, who arrived to consult with NAA in early 1941, the Horkey-led aerodynamics team, working with the thermodynamics team led by Joe Beerer, developed successful modifications to improve the intake scoops of the upper carburetor intake and the lower radiator duct.[86] Moving the carburetor scoops forward to near the propeller nose cone plane solved the surge issues experienced in dives.

Maj Gen Oliver P. Echols, who led the USAAC/USAAF's Materiel Division/Command for much of World War II, was a thorn in NAA's side for a number of years as the company tried to secure domestic orders for the P-51. (*USAF*)

Despite the acclaim of RAF pilots following flight tests of the Mustang, the USAAC-MD leaders at Wright Field in 1941 were curiously disinterested. On this last point, conclusions could be drawn that their boss, Maj Gen Echols, harbored animosity regarding the Mustang I, either because he was angry that NAA had rejected his request to build P-40s, or because he considered the Mustang a "British" design and was determined to prioritize and promote the American-built designs at Wright Field – or both. His future actions during March and April 1942 (explained further in the 1942 narrative) demonstrated his resistance to the decisions of the office of Chief of Staff down through Chiefs of Plans Division, Military Requirements Division, and Chief, Close Air Support, to select the A-36 for production. Those actions provide logical proof that his interest was not perfectly aligned to selecting the best available aircraft to support future combat operations.

Ultimately, impromptu flight testing of XP-51s 41-038 and 41-039 commenced in mid-1941, both with the 79th PS and at Wright Field, while Capt Ben Kelsey and his subordinates also flew the XP-51 in comparative trials against the P-40E/F from mid-December. Kelsey issued favorable report "Performance Report on North American Fighter," dated January 2, 1942, which was submitted to Col K. B. Wolfe, Chief, Production Engineering Section, Wright Field. Although Kelsey noted the tendency of the main gear doors to open, and experienced an "unpleasant shudder in dives," he concluded that the XP-51 was faster at all altitudes through 16,000ft and also in a dive. The conclusion was that "the Mustang is able to engage or break off combat at will due to its higher speed."[87] Following the test at Wright Field, 41-039 was dispatched to Eglin Field for various 20mm cannon firing and feed chute/ammunition storage tests.

MUSTANG RIVAL NOTES – 1941

On May 4 the first XP-47B was delivered simultaneously with the first production P-47B. The first flight of the XP-47B occurred two days later.[88]

On September 1 the Fw 190A-1 went operational with *Jagdgeschwader* (JG) 26 on airfields in France and Belgium. It was a shock to the RAF, the German fighter quickly attaining air superiority over the Channel and occupied coastal regions. One month later the Fw 190A-2 appeared, with the MG 151/20E 20mm cannon replacing MG 17 7.92mm machine guns in the wing roots.[89]

Lockheed's P-38E suffered structural failure during dive tests on November 4.[90] The testing and modification activities to mitigate the compressibility effects of high-speed dives finally achieved a partial solution with the introduction of dive flap kits for the P-38J in late 1943.[91]

On November 17 Generaloberst Ernst Udet, Director General of Equipment for the Luftwaffe, committed suicide. He was replaced by Generalfeldmarshall Erhard Milch, who worked tirelessly to prioritize fighter production and Air Defense capabilities.[92]

LEFT An early Fw 190A, probably an A-2 of II./JG 26, is worked on at a French or Belgian airfield. JG 26 was the first Luftwaffe fighter wing to operate the Focke-Wulf fighter, introducing the A-1 into combat on the Channel Front in September 1941. (*Tony Holmes Collection*)

BELOW LEFT A drop tank-equipped Lockheed F-5A of the 90th Photographic Reconnaissance Wing at San Severo airfield in Italy in early 1944. The windows for the aircraft's oblique and vertical cameras are clearly visible in the nose. The 90th operated both F-4 and F-5 variants of the Lightning on long-range reconnaissance missions during this period. (*USAF*)

BELOW Generalfeldmarschall Erhard Milch replaced Generaloberst Ernst Udet as Director General of Equipment for the Luftwaffe following the latter's suicide on November 17, 1941. (*Tony Holmes Collection*)

On December 21 the first P-47B was completed, but its acceptance was delayed, pending required changes.[93]

NAA CHRONOLOGY FOR JANUARY THROUGH APRIL 1942

On January 5, 1942, the first test of Mustang I AG347 equipped with extended-range wing fuel kits was undertaken by Chilton.[94] Henceforth, as per specification and contract in June, the "plumbing" would be packed in the gun bays, with six fuel cells included in the shipping crate for each Mustang destined for Britain.

On January 28 NAA completed Report NA-1778-A "Design Data Ground Attack Airplane." The aircraft detailed in this document was based on the NA-73, modified with Vultee-supplied A-31 dive brakes and 20mm armament from the

NA-91 design. It was to be powered by the low-altitude, singe-speed, single-stage Allison V-1710-87 engine, with a war emergency power of 1,500hp at 5,400ft. It also had racks both for bombs and external ferry or combat fuel tanks. The alternative engine was the V-1710-F11, which was proposed to power the A-36 to 406mph at 18,000ft, but it was discarded in favor of the more powerful low-altitude engine.

The BPC and RAF informed NAA of intentions to modify a Mustang I by fitting the wing-mounted 40mm "S" cannon.

Included in armament studies for the "Ground Attack Airplane" were drawings D-169, dated December 30, 1941, Ground Attack – with two 20mm cannon and two 500lb bombs; D-17? (rest illegible), dated January 5, 1942, Fighter with two 20mm cannon and two 0.50cal machine guns; and D-172, dated January 20, 1942, Ground Attack with two 20mm cannon and two drop tanks or two 500lb bombs.

Over the next year, the following additional studies were undertaken and illustrated in drawings: D-32000, dated March 3, 1942, Ground Attack with two 37mm cannon; D-30002, dated November 28, 1942, Fighter with six 0.50cal machine guns; D-32008, dated November 28, 1942, fighter with four 20mm cannon; D-32009, dated November 28, 1942, Ground Attack with four 37mm cannon; and, finally, D-72004, dated November 28, 1942, Ground Attack with two 37mm cannon, two 20mm cannon and six 0.50cal machine guns. The studies focused on the Hispano 20mm and Colt 37mm cannon with belt feed systems in lieu of magazine feed.

On February 3 Kindelberger wrote to Echols at the USAAC-MD, reporting that Mustang production orders would be complete in August 1942. If production was not extended, the P-51 tooling would then be stored, and manufacturing capacity would be diverted to the B-25.[95]

At NAA, some general awareness of major positive activities at USAAF Headquarters were seeping into Inglewood, but, in parallel, the company, still stinging from Allison's general poor delivery and liaison performance, began to expend research funds on alternative powerplants. Preliminary engineering and profile drawing D-111 was prepared by Schmued for the Continental V-3420 "X"

Mustang I AM106/G (the "G" suffix denoting that the aircraft was to be attended by a guard at all times when on the ground) fitted with experimental 40mm "S" cannon. (*The National Archives, ref. AIR18/732*)

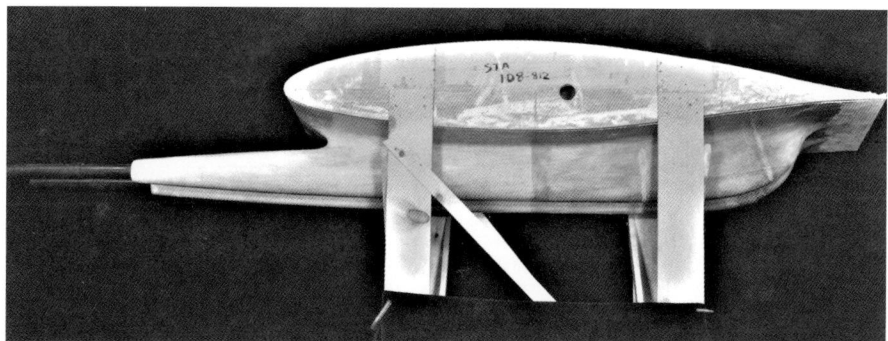

LEFT AND BELOW This experimental underwing pod housing two 37mm cannon was developed for contemplated fitment to the A-36 Apache. (© *The Boeing Company*)

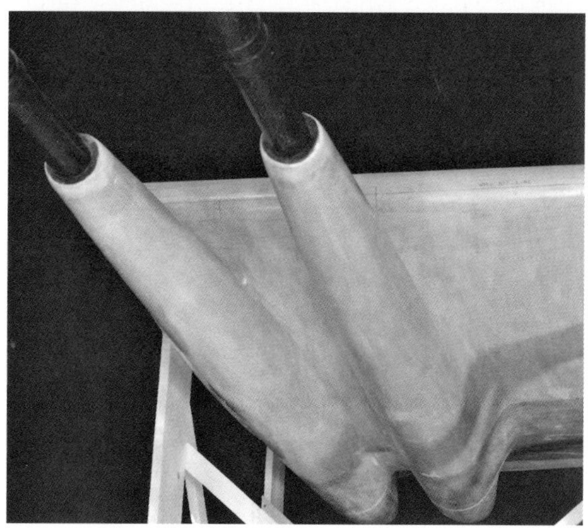

engine. Rice's engineering team began an analysis of the increased intercooler requirements and airframe changes needed to account for the extreme forward center of gravity.[96]

On February 13 NA-83 AL958 made its first test flight test, with Chilton at the controls.[97] Ten days later Rice wrote a memo to Atwood: "Cooling requirements for Continental engine require far larger radiator/intercooler, significant redesign of the airframe, and unsuitable for incorporation into the Mustang."[98]

On the 26th Atwood wrote to Allison Chairman, O. K. Hunt, to seek prioritization of the two-speed/single-stage supercharger over Allison's proposed two-speed/two-stage supercharged V-1710-45. The reason, probably not disclosed by Atwood, was that the extra length embodied in the auxiliary second-stage supercharger could not be housed in the NA-73 airframe without moving the wing further forward to accommodate the extra nose length from the firewall to the propeller.[99]

Two days later Packard received design drawings for the new Rolls-Royce Series 60 Merlin two-speed/two-stage supercharger, which it designated the Packard Merlin V-1650-3. Packard introduced the Wright supercharger drive quill to improve the design.[100] In the authors' opinion, the February 28, 1942 date for preparation by Packard to produce the Merlin 61/Packard Merlin V-1650-3 truly marks the first stage in the "birth" of the P-51B.

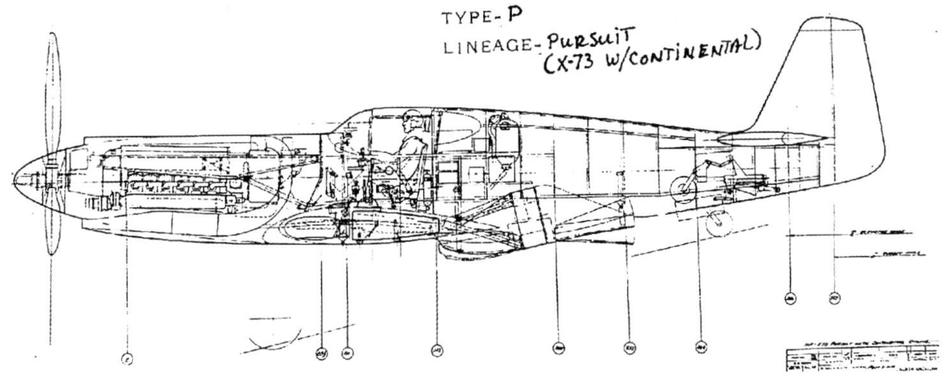

This side profile schematic view is of an NA-73 with a Continental V-3420 "X" engine installed to perform center of gravity and cooling analysis. (© *The Boeing Company*)

Britain's Air Ministry would later urge NAA to send airframes to England to allow Mustangs to be built on "home soil." The elapsed time for the British to build a Mustang assembly factory was prohibitive. Only the parallel supply of the Packard V-1650-3, installed at NAA, could ever accelerate the delivery of the P-51B/C in time to save the Eighth Air Force's daylight heavy bombing campaign in the ETO.

Following the armament/gun charging tests at Eglin Field, the USAAF dispatched the XP-51 from there to NACA Langley Field on March 1. The XP-51 commenced dive and aileron testing here eight days later.[101]

With the completion of the installation of sophisticated instrumentation to record acceleration, pressure distributions, and airspeed, USAAF and NACA pilots started a 39-flight program. The XP-51 tests were particularly focused on the high-speed/low-drag airfoil, being evaluated on an actual airframe for the first time. Over the next six months the combined test programs measured a full range of data for drag, dive, acceleration, transonic shock wave formation, buffeting, and Mach limits in dives. The XP-51's handling characteristics, stall behavior, and roll performance were also recorded. For final flights, a new series of tests was conducted to experiment

This unidentified, cannon-armed, Mustang (possibly the XP-51) was evaluated at NACA Langley in 1942. (*NASA*)

ABOVE LEFT The development of the NA-97 A-36 saw the first significant change made to the design of the front scoop, which became non-adjustable. (© *The Boeing Company*)

ABOVE NA-97 A-36 aft radiator cooling scoop, seen here in the open position. (© *The Boeing Company*)

with several different aileron airfoil shapes, as well as increasing the deflection range from +/-10 degrees all the way to +17.5/-16.5 (down) degrees left aileron, and +16.5 (up)/-17.5 degrees for right aileron. NACA also installed a flexible seal from the nose of the aileron to the aft spar to provide a seal balance for the aileron.[102]

Although the NACA Report derived from these flights was completed later, on June 20, the communication between NACA and NAA on the tests and resulting recommendations led Rice to send an earlier memo to Brig Gen Charles E. Branshaw at Materiel Command, citing major roll performance increases of 40–50 percent accomplished by increasing up and down aileron movement to +/-15 degrees. He further noted that tests with beveled ailerons plus an internal seal balance were commencing in July, but production insertion was only possible in the Merlin Mustang.[103] This NACA report with documented data resulted in design changes introduced into NA-102 P-51B-1-NA. The prototype changes were installed on the A-36 test machine AM118 and first tested by Chilton on July 15.[104]

On March 20 Ray Rice sent R. C. Costello a report summarizing the primary differences between the NA-73 and the NA-83. The principal ones were (1) addition of flame dampening exhausts, (2) redesigned windshield assembly, (3) changing from the Air Research radiator to a Harrison-designed radiator, (4) changing the forward coolant scoop fairing air scoop – not interchangeable with the NA-73, (5) addition of the N-1 gun camera to replace the W-7B, (6) redesigned hydraulic and fuel lines, and, (7) elimination of the wing-mounted floodlights.[105]

With contract AC-27396 for 500 A-36 dive-bombers issued on April 16, 1942, the NA-97 charge number was opened for project accounting. As production engineering began to transform the NA-83 airframe, Vultee was contacted for permission to use the A-31 dive brake design. Work quickly began in the Experimental Department on NA-83 AM118, which was to serve as the test bed for the A-36. Schleicher's group had the primary task of strengthening the wings to absorb the forces associated with high-speed dives and pull-outs, and to take the additional weight and drag of 500 to 1000lb bombs and external combat fuel tanks.

TOP This photograph shows the A-36's dive brakes deployed. NAA contacted Vultee for permission to use the A-31's dive brake design in its ground attack aircraft. (© *The Boeing Company*)

TOP RIGHT Top view of the dive brake control mechanism. (© *The Boeing Company*)

ABOVE Top view of the retracted dive brake, with the inspection and maintenance panels in the closed position. (© *The Boeing Company*)

The basic changes made to the NA-83 Mustang I to create the A-36 were as follows: the wing was strengthened to take the recoil of two Hispano cannon, and to accommodate dive brakes, 1,000lb bombs/or 75gal combat fuel tanks (it could carry more weight than a 75gal load of fuel, and did so later with the same strength factors in the P-51B); plumbing for the two external tanks was added; the Allison V-1710-39/F3R engine was replaced by the 1,500hp V-1710-87 low-altitude engine; and the "alligator jaw" adjustable lower radiator intake scoop, featured on NA-73/-83 and -91, was replaced by a fixed scoop.

The wing design changes included installation of the bomb rack/sway brace, incorporation of the dive brakes and controls, the slight relocation of ammunition storage and feed, and the fitting of mounts for either two 0.50cal machine guns or two 20mm Hispano cannon in each wing. The canted gun mounts were necessary to accommodate the cannon and belted 125 rounds for each gun. The main spar redesign was also to accommodate the longer Hispano cannon, per NA-91 P-51, as well as the repositioned landing lights.

The estimates for internal plumbing requirements to feed fuel from ferry tanks attached to wing pylons were essentially complete. The preliminary design for the long-range (external) ferry tank had been initiated in response to a Request for

LEFT Front view of the left underwing dive brake in the extended position and a 1,000lb AN-M44 general purpose bomb attached to the adjacent pylon. (*© The Boeing Company*)

BELOW The sole A-36 delivered to the RAF for evaluation purposes is seen here armed with two 500lb (possibly US-built AN-M43) general purpose bombs. Lacking fuselage codes, this aircraft (given the serial EW998) was assigned to the A&AEE following its delivery in March 1943. The RAF deemed dive-bombing to not be essential when it came to undertaking its tactical mission. (*Philip Jarrett Collection*)

Comments issued by the USAAC-MD in 1939, and was completed during the discussions for the long-range tank kits.[106]

The first test flight of NA-83 Mustang I AM118 with dive brakes installed, on April 30, 1942, demonstrated the advanced stage of design and fabrication that had already been reached before the contract was issued (it was not actually signed until August 21).[107] Over the next several months, as A-36 production design and assembly progressed, the necessary interim changes were made on AM118. They comprised: the addition of bomb/fuel tank racks; plumbing from the racks to a new four-place fuel tank selector switch in the cockpit; changes to the wing armament bay to accommodate either four 20mm cannon or four 0.50cal guns, including the angled gun mounts to accommodate belt-fed 20mm ammunition (the genesis of the canted gun mounts for the A-36, P-51A, and P-51B/C); and a change in inlet scoop geometry from the "alligator jaws variable opening inlet" to a fixed inlet.

To better understand the transition from the USAAF-MD's total indifference to Kindelberger's plea in his letter of February 3 ("Need orders, running out of production for the Mustang"), to a contract for 500 A-36s two months later, one needs to understand the political struggles within the USAAF high command, as narrated below. From January through to mid-April, the contest between the USAAF-MD's resistance to the Mustang and the demand for the aircraft from both Military Requirements and Air-Ground Support Directorates resulted in major breakthroughs for the fortunes of the future long-range escort fighter.

HQ-AAF NOTES FROM JANUARY THROUGH APRIL 1942

On, or about, January 1, 1942, Wright Field Experimental Engineering was asked to estimate possible improvements that might result from replacing the XP-51's Allison V-1710-39 with an Allison V-1710-61 (with an 8.8:1 blower ratio). Several speed runs in XP-51 41-039 were made to validate the critical altitudes and top speed averages with gun ports taped and in normal combat configuration. The analysis pointed to, (1) an improvement in the critical altitude from 13,000ft to 16,300ft, and (2) an increase of top speed from 370mph to 383mph in combat configuration, compared with the V-1710-39. The report was submitted on January 12 by Chief, Aircraft Laboratory to Chief, Experimental Engineering Section, Wright Field.

On January 6 the Eighth Air Force was constituted and organized under the command of Brig Gen Carl Spaatz in Savannah, Georgia.

In early January, following the conclusion of an impromptu comparison of the XP-51 and the P-38D, P-40E, and P-66 in late November and December 1941, the fighter pilots of the 79th PS/20th PG prepared a report which was forwarded to Gen Ord Ryan. In summary, the report was highly complementary of the Mustang. On January 8 Gen Ryan, CO of 4th Interceptor Command, attached the report to a letter addressed to "Chief, Air Corps," namely Gen "Hap" Arnold. In part, Ryan stated:

Attached hereto is a confidential report of the North American Mustang Fighter as compared with Army Air Force P-38D, P-40 and P-66 Pursuit Airplanes. While not complete, it is believed that this comparative report should be of extreme interest to your headquarters in view of the fact that the figures shown are actual performance in the air under identical conditions.

While it is appreciated that procurement plans for aircraft for the United States Army Air Force cannot be predicted upon reports of this nature, the undersigned considers that comparative data of this type should be given serious consideration in taking over Lend-Lease equipment scheduled for other nations.

Wm. Ord Ryan
Brigadier General USA, Command.[108]

Ryan's letter to Arnold was sent approximately three weeks after Col Ira Eaker flew the Mustang during a visit to NAA, on his way to HQ-AAF for his VIII Bomber Command assignment. He stated, "I thought that the Mustang was the best fighter that I had flown. It was somewhat underpowered, but I knew it was possible to correct that with bigger engines coming along." He later mentioned his impression of the Mustang when he arrived at HQ-AAF to meet with Spaatz (who duly notified Eaker that he was to be made CO of VIII Bomber Command).[109]

Approximately two weeks after receipt of this letter from Gen Ryan, Arnold and Spaatz visited NAA in January 1941 and came away with the impression that "the Air Force should have P-51s."[110] It is highly probable, but speculative, that Kindelberger and Atwood briefed Arnold and Spaatz that, (1) the Mustang orders were scheduled for completion in July–August, and (2) that NAA had a Mustang attack fighter version for low-altitude CAS/dive-bombing in design to compete for FY43 dive-bomber funding. It is not known whether Arnold disclosed that the Directive, Close Air Support, was pleading for just such an aircraft to replace the slow A-25 and A-31, as well as the XA-32, which was then still under development.

Several important events transpired within HQ-AAF between February 4 and March 25 to advance development of the Mustang. First, a review of the new USAAF organization might be helpful. The Office Materiel, Maintenance and Distribution (MM&D) Command was still extremely important, but no longer in "autonomous control" of aircraft program selection. While the Air Transport Division, Maintenance and Services organizations (to coordinate maintenance and modification centers and depots), Resources Division (to allocate priorities), and Materiel Division (similar duties at Wright Field, but forced to include additional test facilities for tactical trials), remained under Maj Gen Oliver Echols, other commands under the Chief, Air Staff, were exercising strong direction on aircraft type procurements.

The new (and separate Command) Office for Operations, Commitments and Requirements (OC&R) was formed to better align mission and aircraft selections, and then assign priorities for distribution of such aircraft to the different commands in the field. The Military Requirements Division in the Office of OC&R assumed the task of assessing aircraft programs for suitability to complement the missions stated in the Office of Plans. The latter was more focused (and separated from control by the Office of Army Plans), being devoted to the USAAF mission for strategic, tactical, and logistics roles.

On February 4, Col K. B. Wolfe, Assistant Chief, USAAF-MD, Production Engineering, at Wright Field sent a memo to HQ-AAF, MM&D, with copies to the Assistant Chief of Air Staff for Plans and Military Requirements, recommending: (1) cancelation of the Vultee A-35 Vengeance dive-bomber, and (2) seeking a "low altitude, dive bomber-capable, attack fighter to meet Directive – Close Air Support requirements."[111]

On February 18 authorization was issued for the creation of Modification Centers and separate reporting of HQ-AAF Director of Military Requirements from Materiel Division.[112]

Two days later, Arnold held a Fighter Conference with the Air Staff to discuss priorities for delivery of a long-range escort fighter to accompany heavy bombardment aircraft to their assigned targets. The Air Staff continued to offer development of a twin-engined fighter as the best solution, with possible "bomber convoy escort to be investigated." Increasing the internal fuel capacity of fighters, and development of pressurized, high-altitude-capable, external combat tanks emerged as the highest priorities. On February 24, Lt Col Benjamin W. Chidlaw, Assistant Chief, Air Staff, requested regular status reports from Materiel Division on combat fuel tank development.[113] One week later, on March 2, Arnold issued a Technical Instruction to Materiel Division, Wright Field, "Increase Range of Pursuit, Dive Bombers, Light Bombardment Aircraft."[114]

On February 26 President Roosevelt had elevated Arnold to Commanding General, Army Air Forces, ranking him equal to Commanding General of the US Army, and Army Commanding General of Services. Also at the end of February, three key staff at HQ-AAF Plans Division collaborated to advance the A-36. They were Col Howard A. Craig, Assistant Chief of Staff, and Director, Air War Plans Division, HQ-AAF (who, when reporting to Spaatz in the summer of 1941, led the AWPD-1 to completion and approval by Secretary of War Henry Stinson on September 11, 1941); Brig Gen Muir S. Fairchild, Assistant Chief of Staff and Director of Military Requirements HQ-AAF (prominent USAAC/USAAF planner for strategic doctrine during development of AWPD-1); and Col David M. Schlatter, Director Air-Ground Support, Office of Director, Military Requirements HQ-AAF.

Although these key officers within the Air War Plans Division, reporting to Maj Gen Carl Spaatz, Chief, Air Staff HQ-AAF, subscribed to the critical role of long-range strategic bombardment in destroying the enemy's capacity to wage war, they were vocal and persuasive regarding the need for very fast fighter and attack bombers to perform the roles of both CAS and, equipped with cameras, tactical reconnaissance.[115] In mid-February Brig Gen Fairchild, with Craig's approval, proposed the Mustang as the USAAF battlefield fighter for CAS.[116] On or about this time, the USAAF was reorganized to better align to the various missions and services defined. Specifically, Military Requirements was moved from Plans, as a separate division within OC&R.

On or about February 26, Craig issued a priority production request to Maj Gen Echols, now Commanding Officer, USAAF-MD, for "500 A-36 airplanes."

Col Patrick W. Timberlake, Chief, Production Engineering Section, Materiel Division, objected to the order (presumably with Echols' blessing), citing a serious lack of Allison engines and the adverse impact on B-25 production capacity at NAA Inglewood if the P-51 was continued. Timberlake appealed to Craig to stop the order for new Mustangs, based on the production impact that the USAAF-MD could not factually support.[117] After an exchange of memos and telexes between the USAAF-MD, Air War Plans, and Military Requirements, several actions are noteworthy.

First, Timberlake capitulated on March 22, agreeing that the Mustang could continue at NAA Inglewood at the conclusion of the British commitments.[118] Furthermore, on April 7, Col Thomas J. Hanley, Assistant Chief, Air Staff for Materiel, HQ-AAF, advised Maj Gen Millard Harmon, Chief, Air Staff, HQ-AAF, that the "only possible source for 1942 procurement funding was a ground attack version for the P-51," and further recommended that Echols be directed to issue a conversion project to modify the P-51 to a dive-bomber type "with a view to augmenting dive-bomber production in 1942." Following approval by Harmon, Hanley forwarded that memo to Echols.

It might be useful to pause the narrative here to note that in April 1942 Materiel Division was elevated to Materiel Command, and Maj Gen Echols moved his headquarters from Washington, D.C. back to Wright Field. With so many different departments and important sections (engineering, procurement, test, production, etc.), the authors will refer to each separate organization dealing with NAA as "Materiel Command" for the rest of the narrative. The reader may look to referenced sources for specific organizations noted in important correspondence.

On April 19 Fairchild formally requested of Materiel Command that 500 A-36s be procured in advance of the P-51 being tested in dive-bomber configuration. Fairchild further elaborated that "those not equipped with dive brakes can be used as fighters, fighter-bombers, [and in] observation and operational training units."[119] Finally, Materiel Command issued CTI-538 for 500 Mustangs to be modified as dive-bombers.[120]

Paul Ludwig, author of *P-51 Mustang – Development of the Long-Range Escort Fighter*, very well encapsulates the exchange of "opposing views" between the two offices of HQ-AAF Plans and HQ-AAF OC&R/Military Requirements, on one side, and Materiel Command at Wright Field on the other. He remarks that the attitude of the latter, and its leadership at Wright Field, to the Mustang is puzzling. Indeed, they seemed to go out of their way to resist acquisition of the aircraft for the USAAF, and then when forced to purchase the Mustang, limited orders to just the A-36, despite a flood of accolades and excitement from Eglin Field, OTU testing in Britain, and the Rolls-Royce experiment with the future Merlin-engined Mustang X.[121]

In parallel with the political in-fighting within the USAAF regarding the future of the aircraft, the Mustang I was soon to form the centerpiece of the grand experiment initiated by Rolls-Royce to install the Merlin 60 series engine in the airframe.

CHAPTER 4

THE BIRTH OF THE MERLIN MUSTANG

This chapter is complicated, as the parallel tracks of NAA, Rolls-Royce/RAF, USAAF senior command and bureaucracy, the beginning of Eighth Air Force operations, and the Luftwaffe's reaction are all important to the P-51B story. The narrative continues as a chronology, detailing important activities and events, but this chapter, and the subsequent ones, have been separated into more subchapters, to enable the reader to understand each important aspect. The summary at the end of each year is intended to pull the important threads together.

A pilot in World War I and a famous interwar polo player, Lt Col Tommy Hitchcock may have been the single most important figure in selling the Merlin Mustang to the USAAF leadership in 1942. (*Tony Holmes Collection*)

MERLIN MUSTANG GENESIS IN BRITAIN – ROLLS-ROYCE FROM MAY THROUGH JULY 1942

The following condensed version of the Rolls-Royce/British-driven Merlin Mustang project was taken in part from the David Birch rendition in *Rolls-Royce and the Mustang*, volume nine, in the Rolls-Royce Heritage Trust Historical Series of publications (1987). This is recommended reading for the history of the marriage of the Rolls-Royce Merlin 60 Series engines with the NA-73 and NA-83 Mustang I airframes. In the authors' opinion, this volume is the most complete and accurate presentation concerning both the facts and key individuals in the story of the Merlin Mustang.

On April 30, 1942, senior Rolls-Royce test pilot Ronnie Harker was urged to fly the Mustang I by Wg Cdr Ian Campbell-Orde, Commanding Officer of the AFDU at Duxford, in Cambridgeshire. Among other responsibilities, Harker flew aircraft powered by Rolls-Royce's competitors, so the invitation was accepted. He was intrigued by reports coming from other RAF units and pilots familiar with the Allison-powered Mustang, which were basically very positive apart from the lack of power from the V-1710 above 15,000ft. The virtues of the Mustang seemed limited only by the lack of high-altitude power to augment the impressive design attributes above 15,000ft. The following day, Harker's report of his experiences and opinion of the Mustang was dispatched to the senior officers at Rolls-Royce. Harker closed his memorandum with the comment, "The point which strikes me is that with a powerful and good engine like the Merlin 61, its performance should be outstanding as it is approximately 35mph faster than the Spitfire V with roughly the same power."[1] Between the receipt of Harker's memo by the Rolls-Royce management on May 1, and May 29, when AG518 was flown directly to the company's aerodrome at Hucknall, in Nottinghamshire, from Speke, several key decisions were made by Rolls-Royce and the RAF.

First, re-engining the Spitfire VC with the new Merlin LXI (later redesignated the Merlin 61) had resulted in a major increase (44mph) in the fighter's top speed over the standard VC with the Merlin XX. This encouraged both Ray Dorey, Manager of the Installation and Flight Test Establishment at Hucknall, and Ernst Hives, General Manager of the Rolls-Royce Engine Division, to move forward. Hives engaged with senior Air Ministry officials, beginning with Sir Wilfrid Freeman, Vice Chief of the Air Staff (VCAS), and the Assistant Chief of Air Staff (ACAS, possibly Air Vice-Marshal R. S. Sorley, ACAS Technical Requirements) for a meeting on May 14. They discussed the intention of Rolls-Royce to install a Merlin 61 or 65 into the American Mustang. The Air Ministry officials expressed grave concerns that the potential reduction in supply of the Merlin 61 would slow the introduction of the Spitfire IX to operational units.

Next, on May 19, Willoughby "Bill" Lappin, Personal Assistant to Hives, sent Dorey flight-test data on the Mustang I, the test data on the pre-converted Spitfire VC and the data on the Spitfire VC with the Merlin 61, to demonstrate the great promise for high-altitude speed and climb performance of the modified Mustang I with the Merlin 61. To assist in the evaluation of the "as is" performance baseline, the request was sent to Speke to arrange for a new Mustang I to be delivered to Hucknall.[2]

Based on events that occurred in parallel to Dorey receiving the comparative data, namely the discussions between Arnold, Air Marshal Sholto Douglas, Ambassador John G. Winant, and Lt Col Tommy Hitchcock in London to brief Arnold on the Rolls-Royce project, and the subsequent flurry of activity between HQ-AAF and NAA, it is intuitive that these comparisons were also passed to NAA's technical representative in Britain, Philip Legarra (based at Hucknall), and thence on to NAA.

On June 3 the Controller for Research and Development at the Ministry of Aircraft Production approved the project, subject to stress analysis showing that the modification could be achieved safely. Lappin requested that a set of performance estimates be prepared for comparison between the unmodified Mustang and the converted one with the Merlin 61, and a set of performance comparisons between a Mustang with the Merlin XX compared with the Merlin 61 installation. In his letter of June 3 to Dorey, Lappin also mentioned that both John G. Winant, the American Ambassador in London, and Gp Capt C. B. Wincott, British Air Ministry, Washington, D.C., had been appraised. He further noted that Winant "has given certain instructions to the Air Corps." Lappin also wrote to Hives on the same day to elaborate that Ambassador Winant had cabled instructions to Arnold to "install a Packard Merlin in the machine" immediately and give "Priority 1" to the factory.[3]

NAA's senior technical representative in Britain was Phillip Legarra, and he played a key role in liaising between Rolls-Royce, NAA and the USAAF during P-51B development and ongoing issue resolution in the ETO. (*Tony Holmes Collection*)

On June 8 Hucknall's performance engineer, Witold Challier, completed the analytical work Rolls-Royce had contracted to compare actual data for the Mustang I with projected data for the Mustang "X" with the Merlin XX and Merlin 61. On the 11th the reports were forwarded to VCAS Sir Wilfrid Freeman by Lappin, with explanations. It is probable that the performance comparisons convinced Hives to commit Rolls-Royce to converting three Mustangs at Hucknall, which he confirmed in his letter to Freeman on the 16th.[4]

On June 9 the Hucknall drawing office devoted the next week to assessing the changes required to install the Merlin 61. Four days later the drawing office released design engineering for the new hybrid Mustang, later to be named Mustang 10 or Mustang X. Fabrication of the cowling, engine mounts, the engine aftercooling system, etc., began shortly thereafter.[5] One very distinct difference between the Rolls-Royce design team's approach to the installation of the Merlin and that of NAA was the placement of the intercooler radiator under the engine, in the same space as the carburetor intake. The NAA design combined the intercooler (required for two-stage/two-speed compression of the fuel-air charge) with the engine radiator into the same radiator frame (square), whereas the Rolls-Royce team left the "donut' combination of engine radiator surrounding the oil cooler matrix, similar to the existing Mustang I (round) design. The result was a mandatory "P-40-type" lower cowl, adding drag to the hybrid compared to the XP-51B.

On June 11 Lappin wrote to VCAS Sir Wilfrid Freeman and enclosed the Challier report, which summarized the very positive results predicted for the increase in high-altitude performance for the Mustang/Merlin 61 combination.[6]

On page 14 of his book, Birch correctly surmises from the exchange of those letters that great interest had been generated in the US and steps to move forward at NAA and HQ-AAF were already in process. What remained to be done was energetic redirection for production and tooling and engine priorities from the HQ-AAF to Materiel Command to enable NAA prioritization, which had previously been withheld from Mustang production.

MERLIN MUSTANG GENESIS IN THE US – NAA/USAAF FROM MAY THROUGH JULY 1942

During May 1942, in parallel with ongoing activities at Hucknall, several important events occurred.

On the 2nd the first Mustang I combat sorties commenced with Army Co-operation Command's No. 26 Sqn.[7]

The AFDU concluded initial testing and issued a report on May 5. The combat-experienced RAF pilots of the unit were impressed with the (NA-73) Mustang as "an excellent medium altitude fighter … the best American fighter that has so far reached this country." They found it pleasant to fly, stable in all planes, easy to fly on instruments and comparing extremely well with the Spitfire, but better for low flying and for night flying. It was faster than the Spitfire VB at all heights up to 25,000ft. At 15,000ft, the rated altitude for the Allison V-1710, it was about 35mph faster than the Spitfire, and at 5,000ft about 30mph faster. The rate of climb was poor compared with that of the Spitfire, but the Mustang could dive very fast, its acceleration being particularly good. The primary criticisms concerned the pilot's view – the frames of the cockpit hood hindered the view considerably, and the sighting view (over the nose) was poor, worse than in the Spitfire. However, the internal rear-view mirror was "the best that this unit has seen."

The AFDU regarded the Mustang as well armed with a good ammunition capacity. Recent experience in the Battle of Britain attached great importance to the time taken for a quick rearm (about 11min), and for gun harmonization (30min). However, testing at AFDU identified problems with the front gun mountings in the NA-73; an issue that would also be reported later with the 20mm cannon fitted to the Mustang IA.[8]

It is probable that between May 5 and May 15 informal discussions began between Materiel Command and NAA regarding (1) intent to acquire the Mustang IA as a replacement for the P-39 in the tactical reconnaissance role, and (2) estimates to install a Merlin engine of unspecified type into a Mustang airframe. This time frame for discussions followed Legarra's awareness that Rolls-Royce was very interested in the project, and NAA's (Kindelberger/Atwood) awareness of the political changes in attitude from the USAAF regarding the value of the Mustang from both Military Requirements and Directorate of Air-Ground Support. Unmentioned was Kindelberger's obvious delight that an "escape hatch" from Allison-engined Mustangs was now a distinct probability.

In mid to late May events moved very fast when the USAAF raced to acquire the Mustang IA as both an attack and a reconnaissance fighter, and to secure priority for the very first Packard Merlin 1650-3 engines for test purposes. In internal correspondence between Atwood and Rice concerning the terms for the Merlin Mustang, it was concluded that the project would proceed far faster if NAA specified the XP-78 as a "modification" rather than a new design burdened by Materiel Command's specification cycle.[9] Accordingly, agreement was reached to specify that P-51-NA airframes 41-37352 and 41-37421 be set aside for the Merlin Mustang conversions.

Between May 14 and May 20 Arnold had several high-level meetings with Prime Minister Winston Churchill and senior Air Ministry leaders to discuss future US redistribution of agreed British Lend-Lease allocation to ensure that American crews in Britain were flying US-built aircraft. During the same meetings he and Chief of the Air Staff Air Chief Marshal Sir Charles Portal agreed that Eighth Air Force Bomber and Fighter Commands would fly US aircraft and operate under USAAF control. Arnold also met with Ambassador Winant, Lt Col Tommy Hitchcock, and Air Marshal Sholto Douglas to be briefed on the new project to pair the Rolls-Royce Merlin 61 with the Mustang I airframe. Arnold later remarked that they "didn't seem to know much about the details," but it is believed (authors' opinion) that he made the decision to order Materiel Command to deliver the Packard Merlin 1650-3 to NAA.[10]

On May 15 Col John Sessums, Fighter Projects Officer, Materiel Command, called Lee Atwood to inform him that the first two production Packard Merlin 1650-3s would be delivered to NAA following bench tests at Wright Field. In the discussion, Sessums indicated that work was proceeding to enter into a contract for NAA to build a Mustang with the new engines.[11]

On or about May 20 the USAAF decided to acquire 57 NA-91s of the 150 scheduled for delivery as Mustang IAs for the RAF. The Mustang IAs so retained were designated P-51-NAs by the USAAF. This action followed the decision that Air-Ground Command should select fast fighter aircraft for both attack and reconnaissance roles. Another decision soon followed, namely to install a vertical and oblique camera in the new P-51s and re-designate them F-6As. The eighth production P-51, 41-37327, was modified in the Experimental Department to take the K-24 camera. It was duly designated P-51-1-NA and first flown by Chilton on August 24, 1942.

On or about May 31 NAA increased design work on the Merlin modification to the P-51. It is not clear from the project notes whether the decision was based on earlier correspondence from Philip Legarra, or as part of the ongoing NAA research and development projects to find alternatives to Allison's single-stage engines. Work in parallel to date included earlier studies for the Continental engine, and the current study of the Allison V-1710-45 with an auxiliary second-stage supercharger, as well as the Griffon engine.[12]

The major design issues facing NAA engineering included a complete redesign of the coolant system to accommodate the much higher demands placed on both engine cooling and the very hot fuel-air charge from the high pressures created by the two-speed/two-stage supercharger. Additional important design changes included those introduced following the placement of the intake duct to the carburetor beneath the engine for the Merlin updraft design, ultimately resulting in the lowering of the wing to accommodate the new lower cowl and carburetor intake. There were also additional structural requirements to meet new loads imposed by the increased aileron throws, the vortex from the four-bladed propeller on the empennage, and the extra weight associated with the new Merlin 61/Packard 1650-3 engine and Hamilton Standard propeller. Based on the 1941 design studies to install the Continental engine, with far higher cooling and aftercooling requirements than the Allison V-1710, the design team had already decided to relocate the oil cooler from the radiator matrix to a more forward position with separate ducting.

OTHER IMPORTANT DESIGN CONSIDERATIONS FOR THE MERLIN MUSTANG

The Merlin 61 was more than 350lb heavier than the Allison V-1710-39, so both the engine mounts and surrounding structure needed beefing up. This further affected weight limits and ultimate allowable loads owing to the increased gross weight.

The addition of the cuffed, four-bladed Hamilton Standard propeller not only added more weight, increasing gross weight and requiring 61lb of aft ballast, but also increased the strength of the propeller vortex. Immediate requirements included some resizing of the fuselage primary longerons to accommodate the greater torque of the larger propeller/engine combination, as well as planning to move the wing lower and slightly forward for the P-51B. Future wind tunnel data pointed to several negative results due to the changes, including more profile/pressure drag of the fuselage, wing, empennage, lower cowl, carburetor intake, and cockpit enclosure immersed in the flow, increased uploads and sideloads on the empennage, and increased yaw inputs required to trim for increase/decrease of the throttle setting. The latter two structural issues caused multiple failures of the empennage in the P-51B, resulting in several design changes discussed more fully in the 1944 narrative.

Following test results and recommendations at NACA-Langley regarding aileron modifications to improve roll rate, NAA modified the existing aileron surface by incorporating a leading-edge balance strip to the forward "nose" of the aileron. This and other modifications tested by Chilton on AM118 resulted in a design change from earlier Mustang models in the form of an increased aileron throw angle rigging setting, from +/-10 degrees to +/-10, 12, and 15 degrees. The P-51B wing also had to be beefed up to take the greater loads imposed by the new increases in aileron travel.

The Packard Merlin 1650-3 had 18 changes that were not interchangeable with the Merlin 61, including a centrifugal separator to prevent oil from foaming – a feature that did not work entirely to expectations when the P-51B-1-NA went operational in the ETO.

On June 1 the BAC formally requested that, when practicable, NAA should install Malcolm Hoods on all

The aileron specifications for the NA-73 through the NA-99, showing maximum throw angles of +/-10 degrees. (© *The Boeing Company*)

NA-8419 RESTRICTED SURFACE CONTROLS

SURFACE CONTROLS

GENERAL DATA

	DEGREES	INCHES
Aileron travel (up and down)	10, 12 or 15	2¼, 2⅝, 3⅜
Rudder travel (right and left)	30	13
Elevator travel–up	30	8¾
–down	20	5¾
Trim tab travel		
Aileron (up and down)	10	¾
Rudder (right and left)	10	15/16
Elevator–up	10	¾
–down	25	1⅞
Travel tolerances (all surfaces)	½	⅛
Cables–aileron, rudder, and elevator		5/32 dia.
All trim tabs		1/16 dia.
Cable tensions (21°C-70°F)		
Ailerons		70 lbs.
Rudder		60 lbs.
Elevator		70 lbs.
All trim tabs		20 lbs.
Tolerance (all cables)		±5 lbs.

RIGGING SURFACE CONTROLS

(See figures 20 through 25.)

GENERAL RIGGING NOTES

1. Establish the exact neutral position of the controls to simplify entire rigging procedure.
2. Initial tension of cables should always be approximately 25 pounds above specified value in order to overcome stretch and seating of cables in pulleys.

RESTRICTED 29

Mustangs destined for the RAF. The BAC followed this request with details, including images, on July 2.[13] NAA analyzed the requirements and the design, and decided that the Malcolm Hood was an interim solution to the various options already being discussed, namely a sliding canopy similar to that of the Mitsubishi A6M or a bubble/teardrop canopy of clear Plexiglas. In either case the modifications discussed required redesign of the rear upper fuselage deck to permit the necessary aft travel of the canopy. The first conceptual "Packard Merlin" profiles for both a wind tunnel model and sliding-canopy version of the aircraft were begun in June and completed in July and September, respectively.

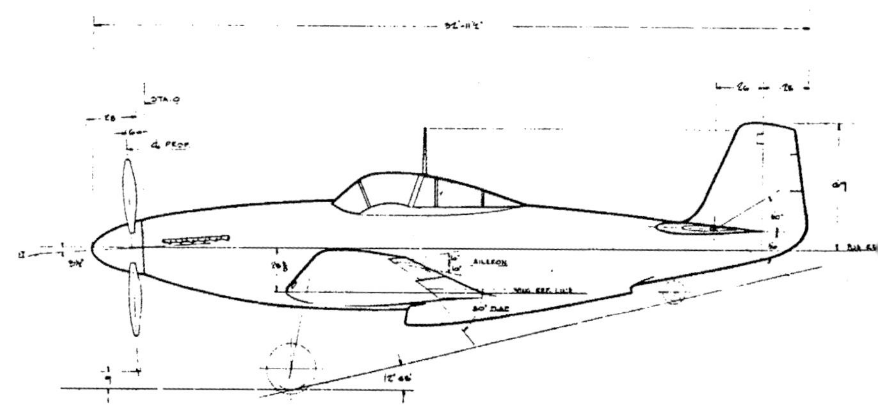

Drawing D-12011 of the "Merlin Mustang", circa September 2, 1942, was created to further explore the sliding hood concept for the re-engined fighter. NAA had various sliding hood layouts on the drawing board when the British requested Malcolm Hood installation prior to delivery of the Mustang IA. The aircraft in the drawing displays the conceptual sliding canopy, similar to the Mitsubishi A6M in configuration, with excellent visibility to the rear. This canopy design evolved into the all-clear single unit first installed on P-51B-1 43-12102 and P-51D 42-106539 – both designed, installed and tested in November 1943. (© *The Boeing Company*)

On June 5 the Directorate of Air-Ground Support further clarified the selection of 57 of the 150 Mustang IAs. The Directorate decided that the USAAF would secure the first 20 produced. From the remaining RAF Mustang IA allocation, 35 more were plucked for assignment to Training Command and two were acquired to be assigned to the construction of the NA-101 XP-78. The first 20, completed in July, were redirected and modified as F-6A reconnaissance versions. One was sent to the Air Proving Ground at Eglin Field for performance trials. The block of P-51-NAs that were modified to carry only the oblique camera – the vertical camera installation being deemed unsatisfactory – were designated P-51-2-NAs at the Memphis Depot. A few were retained by Training Command for instructional purposes. The fact that one aircraft was sent to Eglin, rather than Wright Field, was the first major action to wrest control of performance testing from Wright Field. Virtually all the combat commands had registered extreme displeasure regarding the response and delays when working with Wright Field. The last 35 Mustang IAs of the 57 acquired by the USAAF were assigned to Training Command for crew training in preparation for A-36 deliveries.[14]

On June 8 a transcribed telephone call was made between Gen Kevin B. Wolfe, Chief, Production Division, Aircraft Materiel Center, HQ-AAF, and Col Benjamin W. Chidlaw, Assistant Chief of Staff, Experimental Engineering Branch, Engineering Section, at Air Materiel Command, HQ-AAF (collectively Materiel Command internal memos). They discussed the options for installing a Merlin XX (Packard 1650-1) in the Mustang to get near-term superior performance in the Allison airframe due to existing Packard Merlin 1650-1 production, versus the much better performance expected to arise from the Merlin 61 (Packard 1650-3). Both agreed that NAA was likely to insist on the Packard 1650-3. Also discussed was "General Arnold's insistence that Mustang production continue beyond the 500 A-36s."[15]

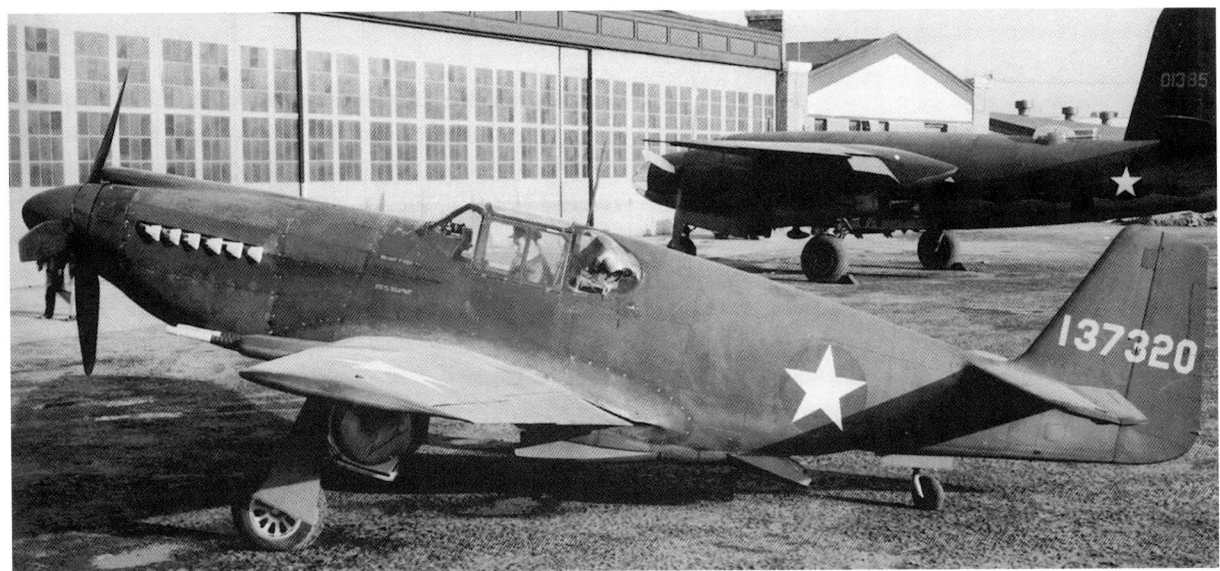

ABOVE P-51-NA No. 1 41-37420 featured the first production fitment of the US-licensed Hispano II 20mm cannon. All versions equipped with K-24 oblique cameras (as seen here behind the cockpit) were designated F-6As. (*© The Boeing Company*)

RIGHT The barrels and springs for the Hispano II 20mm cannon installed in the P-51-NA and Mustang IA were exposed to the elements. The US-built cannon were replaced with British-manufactured Hispano IIs after the Mustang IAs arrived in England. (*© The Boeing Company*)

FAR RIGHT The Hispano II 20mm cannon had a different ammunition feed and tray layout to the earlier weapon of the same caliber trialed by NAA for the Mustang IA. The RAF also strengthened the 20mm mounts for the IA, as well as those for the 0.50cal Brownings fitted in both the Mustang I and II. (*© The Boeing Company*)

On June 10 the first P-51-NA, 41-37327, was delivered to USAAF-Palm Springs by Chilton.[16]

The USAAF acquisition of 57 P-51s from the RAF order for 150 Mustang IAs (NA-91) on or about May 20, and the June 8 Wolfe/Chidlaw transcribed telephone conference referencing Arnold's decision to proceed with the Mustang, as described later, point to a positive outcome of the Arnold London meetings in May. Speculatively, high-level communications regarding the Mustang/Merlin 61 were initiated in early May between Rolls-Royce's US-based senior technical representative J. E. Ellor and NAA, based on the initial contacts established a year earlier for data on the Merlin 28/1650-1.

MERLIN 61 INSTALLATION CHALLENGES

In parallel with the start of the NA-101 XP-78 project, commencing approximately on May 31/June 1 a flurry of exchanges and actions between HQ-AAF, Wright Field, and NAA took place that influenced Merlin Mustang development.

On June 12 Materiel Command authorized NAA to engage in the development of a Mustang with the Packard Merlin 1650-3, and asked NAA to produce a Merlin Mustang specification.

The reference in the transcribed conversation to Arnold's insistence that the Mustang production continue beyond "500 A-36s" seems to indicate that Materiel Command knew that further resistance was futile. It also suggests that, while Arnold described his meeting in London with Sholto, Ambassador Winant, and Lt Col Tommy Hitchcock regarding the Hucknall project as "not very informative," he understood that a high-performance, high-altitude engine installed in an excellent fighter airframe had potential. Not only did NAA's Mustang and A-36 have the support of the USAAF Air-Ground Support Directorate leadership, it also had the backing of Arnold.

On the 15th Rice sent a memo to Brig Gen Charles E. Branshaw at Materiel Command citing a major improvement in roll performance due to the 50 percent increase in aileron movement, plus the internal seal balance being tested, but introduction of these features would begin only in the XP-78. The design accepted for the latter was one with a leading-edge balancing strip internal to the wing structure and an external seal strip from the aft wing upper and lower section housing the aileron, as well as an increased "throw" angle for the ailerons. Rice also noted that some strengthening of the wing to take the increased aerodynamic loads might not be introduced in the prototypes.[17]

Following conclusion of the flight tests, the beveled trailing edge for the ailerons on the XP-51 remained the same, as there was no reason to modify the test aircraft.

On June 23 NA-99/AC-30479 was executed for 1,200 P-51A Mustangs, subject to the provision that, with advanced notice, the P-51A contract could be converted to the future NA-104 P-51B for the balance of the order. The general differences between the P-51A and the A-36 were few, namely: replacement of the V-1710-87 low-altitude engine by the V-1710-81 for much better performance between 12,000 and 15,000ft;

ABOVE LEFT The shell ejection chutes for the production Hispano II 20mm cannon installation in the P-51-NA and Mustang IA are clearly visible in this underwing view. (© *The Boeing Company*)

ABOVE In this close-up photograph of P-51-NA No. 141-37420 both its front scoop and aft exit gate are open. Note also the K-24 camera installation behind the cockpit. (© *The Boeing Company*)

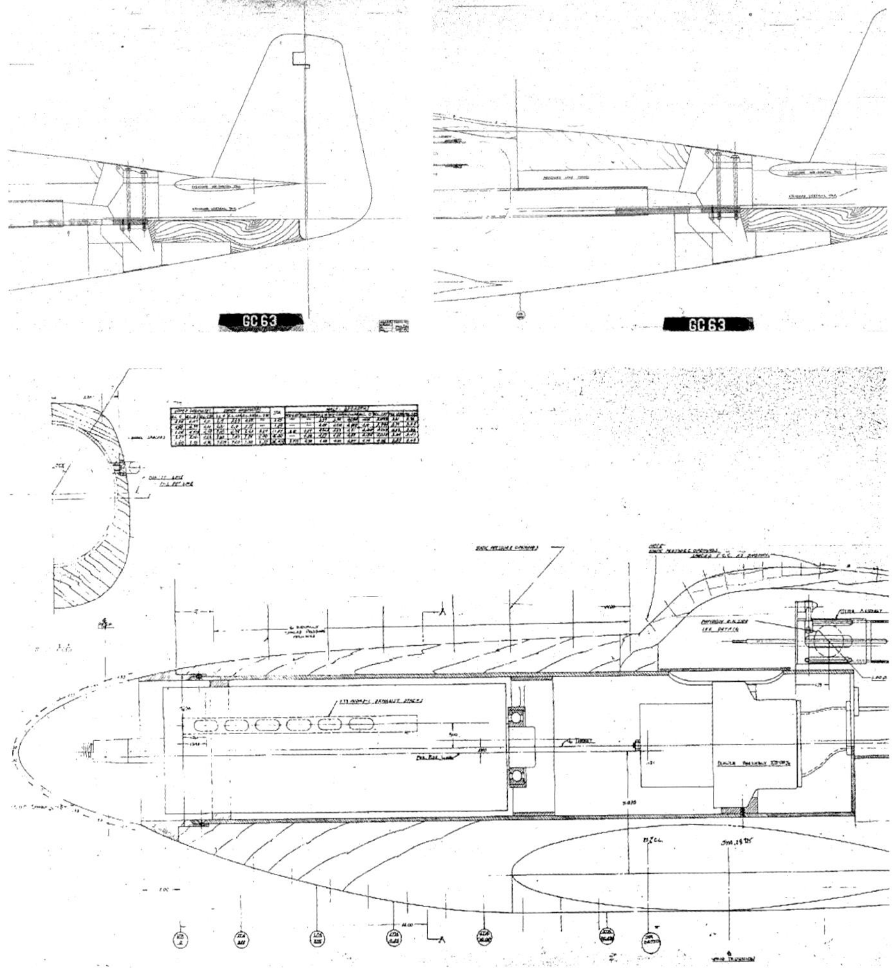

RIGHT The right side of wind tunnel model design drawing X73-01123 (Packard Pursuit/Merlin-powered Mustang), showing the modified upper rear fuselage and empennage. The model created from these drawings exhibited the lines that led to the first conceptual sliding canopy version of the Mustang, which ultimately led to the P-51D. Work was by then well underway on the XP-78 airframe, so the sliding canopy modification was deemed too extensive to incorporate into the project and still meet the proposed flight date. (© *The Boeing Company*)

TOP RIGHT The middle section of the X73-01123 wind tunnel model design drawing, showing more of the cut-down rear fuselage. (© *The Boeing Company*)

RIGHT At this early stage of the Packard Pursuit (Merlin-powered Mustang) development, the model being drawn up for wind tunnel testing had yet to incorporate definitive carburetor and radiator intake schemes. (© *The Boeing Company*)

removal of the cowl-mounted guns; removing the dive brakes and controls; re-organizing the ammunition feed bays for the two 0.50cal guns in each wing; retaining the structural modifications applied to the A-36 wing for bomb/combat tank loads, but modifying the leading edge outboard of the guns to relocate the landing lights; relocating the pitot tube; and introducing a new radiator to accommodate the increased power and cooling requirements of the replacement Allison V-1710-81 engine with water injection. Author Robert Gruenhagen notes that, for the first time, NAA was able to proceed with existing plans for production tooling and processes, dramatically improving factory throughput rates.[18]

On July 7 the NAA wind tunnel model drawing X73-01123 "Packard Pursuit" was released for construction. The first redesign for a "greenhouse" sliding canopy and lowered rear deck were immediately noticeable.

On July 9 Col William Ball, Director of Intelligence Services, wrote a letter to "J. H. Kindelberger, President, North American Aviation, Inc." Its subject was "Information Regarding the North American Mustang Fighter," and it contained elements of RAF Report No. 48,117. A summary of the letter is presented here.

The information contained in Report No. 48,117 is as follows:

> The Mustang is considered an excellent low and medium altitude fighter, being faster than a Spitfire 5B at all altitudes up to 25,000ft. The rate of climb is inferior. At 5,000ft the Mustang is 40mph faster than the Spitfire, at 15,000ft, 35mph faster, and at 25,000ft, 1 or 2 mph faster. The Merlin engine in the Spitfire 5B delivers 950hp at 25,000ft and the Allison engine delivers only 660hp at that same altitude. The Spitfire thereby draws 290 more hp to get slightly less speed. The conclusion is inescapable that the drag of the Mustang is considerably less than that of the Spitfire. This is in spite of the fact that the Mustang weight of 8,000 pounds is considerably more than the 6,475 pounds of the Spitfire. Though the poor climb of the Mustang is a disadvantage, it is more than made up for in greater speed and dive ability. It is recommended that the Mustang be speedily equipped with the Merlin 61 engine now being used in the Spitfire IX. It is estimated by Rolls-Royce people that the Mustang equipped with the 61 engine will have a top speed of 440mph and a speed curve of somewhat more than 20mph faster than the Spitfire IX.
>
> For the Commanding General of the Army Air Forces
> William Ball
> Colonel, GSC
> Director of Intelligence Services[19]

On July 10 a Letter Agreement between Materiel Command and NAA called for two P-51s, from NA-91 commitment numbers 41-37352 and 41-37421, to be modified to accept the Packard Merlin 1650-3 as the XP-78. The formal contract AC-32073, NA-101, was executed on July 25.[20] NAA and the USAAF agreed that the provisions for design autonomy of NAA engineering would follow the contractual language contained in the earlier NAA/BPC agreements attached to DA-140 for NA-91. Both Rice and Atwood expressed concerns that the USAAF would interfere "with suggestions" during the compressed schedule, and were determined to manage the NA-101 project in accordance with proven NAA project management methodology.[21]

On July 30 NAA Preliminary Design released Profile Drawing D-12001 to analyze potential design changes required to install the future Allison V-1710-45 two-speed/auxiliary second-stage supercharged engine. The issue of extending the airframe more than a foot to install the engine, combined with the change to the resulting forward center of gravity (CG), required moving the wing forward too much to be considered practical.

The design activity that led to Profile Drawing D-12001 was allegedly stimulated by a directive issued by the GMC Board to consider the new Allison engine in lieu of the Merlin 61. No citation is provided, as the order to examine the feasibility was alleged to have come via a telephone call. While this version of events is not specifically sourced, the authors believe the explanation is plausible. In addition to the design issues, NAA management had to also consider that the "new" untried Allison engine was not forecast to be ready for production in mid-1943. Given Allison's dismal track record of delivery, one might surmise that no concentrated effort to "make it work" was in the minds of the NAA team.

NAA FLIGHT TEST CHRONOLOGY FOR MAY 29 THROUGH JULY 31

On May 29 Louis Wait flew NA-91 P-51-NA 41-37320 for the first time. On the same date Chilton commenced bomb-dropping trials with AM118, and on the 30th he performed the first dive-bomb test with dive brakes extended.

On June 8, 20mm cannon firing tests using NA-83 AM190 started in an effort to improve both the fairings and the belt feed chutes for the NA-91 P-51. Reports from the British Air Ministry indicated that Martin-Baker had made important changes to the 20mm cannon recoil buffers, fairings, and belt feed chutes.[22]

On June 18 AM118 was flown with instrumentation to measure the existing aileron configuration in order to prepare for flight tests of the new aileron controls, seal, and shape.

Beginning on June 27, several tests were flown in AL958 to test new inlet scoop geometry for pressure distribution in front of the radiator and oil cooler of the new A-36 coolant system. After these tests the adjustable "alligator" scoop was discarded for the A-36 and all subsequent Mustang models.

Between July 4 and 31, AM118, serving as the test aircraft for A-36 modifications, was used for dive-bombing trials and the first 75gal combat tank drop tests. Several changes were made to the sway braces. The same aircraft was tested on July 25 following the first changes to the aileron/control. Several roll-rate tests in the modified AM118 confirmed the proof of concept for the new design.[23]

In the hoped-for objective of chronicling all important moving parts, both in the US and Britain, we have separated the timeline narrative from August through

P-51-NA/Mustang IA FD449 was photographed shortly after it had entered RAF service in 1943. (*Philip Jarrett Collection*)

December 1942 into two parts. The first segment, "NAA/AAF, Hucknall/RAF from August through December 1942," tracks the HQ-AAF and Wright Field actions to introduce existing basic Allison Mustangs into the USAAF inventory that were visible to NAA, and further developments in Britain as the project at Hucknall and Inglewood proceeded apace. The first segment also explains the HQ-AAF role in accelerating Materiel Command's actions to procure the Merlin Mustang (and some continued Wright Field foot dragging due more to imbedded bureaucracy than resistance). The second segment, "Eighth Air Force/Luftwaffe from June through December 1942," expands on the start of ETO operations for the Eighth Air Force, and the resulting response by the Luftwaffe, in 1942. The narrative will also follow this format for 1943 and 1944.

NAA/AAF, HUCKNALL/RAF FROM AUGUST THROUGH DECEMBER 1942

On August 1 S. B. Gates, Technical Office, BAC, noted in a letter to Rice the "desirability of improving rate of roll at low speed by increasing aileron travel, combined change from concave cross-section of aileron to attain 45-degree bank at 400mph in 1 sec."[24] Unbeknownst to the British, Rice was in receipt of the early results of Langley Field's XP-51 roll tests. Modifications to the ailerons, with recommendations forwarded in June, had already brought changes to the aileron throw angles and the addition of a seal balance, and experiments with cusped and wedged cross-sections were to begin on AM118 in July.

In August and September NAA made steady improvements to the Allison Mustang to introduce critically important features for the future long-range P-51B. As NAA solved conversion issues arising from the Merlin installation, Rolls-Royce continued its successful Mustang "X" project.

The fact that the American-built Mustang was already in RAF combat service in the ETO before any of the USAAF's advanced fighters, combined with the proposed British-based Rolls-Royce Merlin/Mustang hybrid, introduced many unforeseen political movements to help sway Gen Arnold ultimately to ignore the "not invented here" voices in his own staff.

On August 3 Kindelberger requested "supplementary production line funding" from the Chief, Materiel Command, at Wright Field to accelerate delivery of the Merlin Mustang. In the same correspondence, Kindelberger noted that it was agreeable to NAA to ship engineless Merlin

BELOW Preliminary design layout for a Mustang with an Allison V-1710-45 installed. Such a powerplant would have required a major re-design in order to house its auxiliary second-stage supercharger. This project to analyze the new Allison engine was initiated upon a request from GMC as a last-ditch attempt to find an "Allison Solution". (© *The Boeing Company*)

BOTTOM The preliminary design layout D-12007 prepared to explore the Rolls-Royce Griffon series engine in lieu of the Merlin 60 series. As with the projected installation of the Allison V-1710-45, it too would have required extensive redesign and disruption of production of the Mustang to incorporate the larger engine. (© *The Boeing Company*)

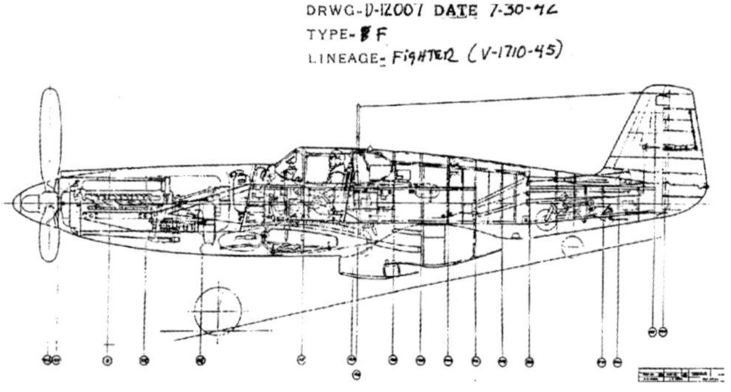

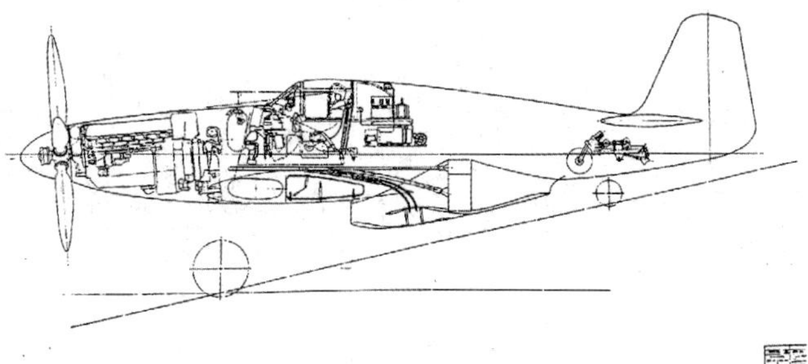

Mustangs to Britain so that the RAF could install Merlin engines should priorities for Packard Merlin 1650-3s not be made available.[25] This letter to Materiel Command almost certainly caused Echols to travel to Britain shortly afterwards with technical staff, to visit Hucknall and personally evaluate not just the production Merlin 60 series engine, but also to hear from RAF senior leaders at first-hand about their perspectives on the "project," and gage the seriousness of Air Ministry plans to produce Merlin Mustangs in Britain.[26]

On August 7 Dr. Edward P. Warner arrived at Hucknall, accompanied by Lt Col Tommy Hitchcock. Whether Warner was commissioned by Materiel Command or HQ-AAF is unclear, but his reputation as a pre-eminent aerodynamicist at Massachusetts Institute of Technology (MIT) points to a desire to review first-hand the activities required, and data, for converting the Spitfire VC into the Spitfire IX with the Merlin 61, as well as the Merlin Mustang project.[27] His report to Materiel Command upon return to the US supported the Rolls-Royce analysis.

NAA Profile Drawing D-12007, showing the Griffon engine installation in the NA-73, was released on August 8.[28] The design study concluded that too many changes would be required to install the Griffon, and these findings were passed on to the USAAF and Rolls-Royce.

That same day NAA recommended to the RAF that an immersed fuel pump in the main wing fuel cells versus "pressurization" from an engine-driven vacuum pump was an acceptable approach.[29] NAA continued to explore main fuel cell pressurization via bleed air from an engine-mounted instrument vacuum pump.

After Kindelberger sent his August 3 letter, requesting funding to set up a separate line for the P-51B and securing of the highest priorities to direct the Packard Merlin 1650-3 to the P-51B (and outlining the alternative to ship finished fuselages to Britain to have the Merlin 60 series installed), several actions by HQ-AAF and the USAAF-MC "behind the scenes" at Wright Field were very important to the Mustang story.

On August 2, by order of Brig Gen Gordon Saville, Chief, Air Defense Directorate, P-51s 41-37323, -37324, and -37325 were dispatched to the Air Forces Proving Ground at Eglin Field to undergo Tactical Trials. The testing began on August 7 and finished on November 1. These tactical trials for the Mustangs were perhaps the first example of the removal of certain test and evaluation tasks from Materiel Command at Wright Field.[30]

The following are important excerpts from the report produced after the Tactical Trials had ended:

> 3. CONCLUSIONS:
>
> It is concluded that:
>
> a. The subject aircraft is the best low altitude American fighter aircraft yet developed and should be used as the criterion for comparison of subsequent types.
>
> b. If possible, the power loadings of this fighter aircraft should be materially reduced, without increasing the wing loading.

c. To reduce the power loadings of the aircraft, both excess weight in the structure and accessories not vital to operational use should be eliminated, and engine performance increased.

d. Pilots become completely at home in this aircraft immediately after the first take-off due to the remarkable sensitivity of control, simplicity of cockpit, and excellent flying characteristics.

e. The rate of roll is not as rapid as is desired for combat operations.

6. DISCUSSION:

a. Performance. For speed, rate of climb, range and gas consumption tables, see Enclosure No. 2.

b. Maneuverability. The subject aircraft was flown in "mock" combat against the P-38F, P-39D, P-40F, P-47B, and the Mitsubishi "00" [A6M2 Zero-sen] type of aircraft.

c. The following results were obtained:

The subject aircraft was found to be superior in speed of the Mitsubishi "00," P-39D, P-40F at all altitudes, and to the P-47B and P-38F up to 15,000ft.

The subject aircraft was found to be superior in rate of climb to the P-39D, P-40F, and the P-47B up to 15,000ft.

The turning characteristics of the subject aircraft are substantially the same as the P-40F and the P-39D (and better than P-38F and P-47B). None of these appears to have any definite superior turning characteristics.

The acceleration in dives and the maximum permissible diving speed of the subject aircraft is superior to all types tested.

In close "dogfighting" the subject aircraft has the very decided advantage of being able to engage or break off combat at will. However, if neither airplane attempts to leave the combat, the P-40F is considered to have a slight advantage.

Compare the Eglin Field test pilot's comments with the comments of Wright Field test pilot Capt M. J. Lee in his March 1941 report of the XP-51 No. 1. If you read Lee's report literally, nobody of sound mind would have ever considered purchasing the P-51 for the USAAF. Was Lee's report influenced by Echols? First, the actual performance of the XP-51 was slightly superior to that of the P-51-NA for the following reasons: (1) the XP-51 had the same Allison V-1710-39 F3R engine but was 300lb lighter than the P-51-NA; (2) the speed reduction due to the drag of the 20mm cannon and fairings of the P-51-NA resulted in loss of top speed of approximately 6–8mph compared to the XP-51 configuration. So, was the Wright Field test report from Capt Lee a candid and objective evaluation of the Mustang/Mustang I?

Next, consider that the P-51-NA in these tests was (1) faster, climbed better, and also turned equally with the P-40F with a Packard Merlin 1650-1 engine, despite the drag of the 20mm cannon; (2) was faster, climbed better, and turned with the P-39D, which was lighter and had lower wing loading than the P-51-NA but had the same

The P-51-NA had been quickly adapted for the role of tactical reconnaissance, NAA modifying the airframe at the Inglewood plant so that a camera could be installed – the resulting aircraft was designated the P-51-1-NA. While not all P-51-NAs were modified for reconnaissance, subsequent aircraft with the camera installation were Depot-modified and classified as P-51-2-NAs. P-51-NA/F-6A 41-37327 was the first Mustang to boast a K-24 oblique camera installation, and it was test flown by Bob Chilton in August 1942. (© *The Boeing Company*)

Allison V-1710 single-speed/single-stage engine; (3) was faster in both horizontal flight and in a dive, turned better, and accelerated faster than the P-38F with two Allison turbo-supercharged V-1710-49/-53 F5 engines with ten percent more horsepower (each) than the Allison V-1710-39 at full-throttle height; and (4) was faster, accelerated faster, dived faster, turned better, and climbed faster than the P-47B from sea level to 15,000ft.

At approximately 15,000ft the turbo-supercharged engines for both the P-38F and P-47B continued to deliver sustained horsepower through 25,000ft (P-38F and P-47B). Additionally, the P-47B had the same engine as the P-47C and P-47D through to the D-10 (without water injection), but was 600lb lighter than the P-47C/D.[31]

Lastly, consider that, while NAA was solving the desired improvement of low-speed roll rate expressed by the RAF, the P-51 was already comparable with the P-47, which was very good indeed. Six months later NAA introduced the new ailerons on the P-51B-1-NA production line. NAA greatly improved the power loading and rate of climb with the introduction of the Packard Merlin 1650-3. The resultant rate of climb for the P-51B was superior to that of the P-38 series until Lockheed solved the aftercooler issues in 1944 and, even then, continued to be superior above mid-altitudes through 35,000ft.[32]

On August 14 Gen F. O. Carroll, Chief Experimental Engineering, Materiel Command, Wright Field, ordered the Technical Executive to "Proceed full speed on the installation of the Merlin 61 in two P-51 airplanes."[33]

During the rest of August, beginning on the 18th, Chilton flew AM118 with the four-blade Hamilton Standard propeller destined for the P-51B.[34]

On August 21 and 23 the requested modifications to install a K-24 camera on both vertical and oblique mounts in P-51-NA 41-37327 were completed, then test-flown by Chilton. The aircraft was re-designated P-51-1-NA.[35] All subsequent modifications were performed at depots, then most were shipped to the 68th Tactical Observation Group as P-51-2-NAs.[36] The designs arising for the cockpit-mounted oblique camera were used in the F-6A, F-6B, and F-6C reconnaissance Mustangs.

On August 22 Gen K. B. Wolfe, Chief, Production Division, wrote to Maj Gen Echols, Chief of Staff, Materiel Command, suggesting that NAA be awarded a contract for 400 P-51Bs, and that the P-51B Mustang be put in the Priority Preference Group 1. In addition to Materiel Command leadership, Echols was also a member of the extremely important Aircraft Directorate Board headed by Charles Wilson. This board considered and approved all Priority allocations for materiel, components, engines, and tooling for all US aircraft. Moving the Merlin Mustang at NAA to

Priority 1 not only expedited delivery of all the Packard Merlin 1650-3 and -7 production engines to NAA, but was also critical in securing expedited machine tools, subcontractor access, and raw material supply via Resources Division to support the program. Additionally, this action essentially blocked any hope Curtiss had of extending the life of the P-40 with a better engine. Although not important to this story, the assignment of Priority 1 to NAA, including the Packard Merlin 1650-3 and -7, also effectively killed any consideration for a Lockheed P-38K conversion from Allison to Merlin in 1944.

On August 26 Kindelberger sent a letter, hand-delivered by NAA's Alex Burton, to Cols Chidlaw and James Phillips, Materiel Command. Phillips in turn sent Chidlaw a memo stating "the first flight of XP-78 should be October 1st if Packard meets commitment to deliver two engines on September 1st. The second ship should follow 2–3 weeks later." Enclosed in the letters to Materiel Command were the preliminary performance estimates for the XP-78. All estimates were based on the Packard Merlin 1650-3 duplicating the performance of the Merlin 61.[37] Excerpts as follows:

> For GW = 8,350lb, 105 gallons fuel, 2x20mm cannon with 125 rounds per gun, no armor plate, or radio:
> Top speed: at SL = 340mph; @16,500ft = 420mph; at 28,000ft = 445mph
> Rate of Climb: at SL =3,460fpm; at 13,000ft = 3,520fpm; at 25,000ft = 2,400fpm
> Service Ceiling = 42,000ft
> Based on Packard Bench Horsepower Ratings (no Ram); 1,375hp at SL; 1,520hp at 13,000ft; 1,300hp at 24,000ft

The ram-air intake to the carburetor added approximately 4,100ft to the critical altitude of the Packard Merlin 1650-3. Subsequently, performance calculations for top speed and climb were based on the increase to critical altitudes for both low and high blower. In the example of estimated performance noted above, the top speed for high blower would have been attained at 28,100ft with 1,300hp at 61inHg and 3,000rpm.

The first Packard Merlin 1650-3 failed bench tests at 12in. of boost (54inHg) due to piston failure. Additionally, the carburetor was deemed inadequate to achieve design performance horsepower for the referenced manifold pressures. On or about August 26 Packard delivered a new 1650-3 to Wright Field to replace those that had failed earlier bench tests. The new engine had strengthened connecting rods and a larger carburetor to improve performance and reliability for manifold pressures greater than 12lb.[38]

Also on the 26th, preliminary results from a report entitled "Tactical Employment of Mustang P-51" were released by Air Forces Proving Ground Command at Eglin Field. In its summary it was stated, "The subject aircraft is the best low altitude American fighter aircraft yet developed and should be used as the criterion for comparison of subsequent types. The P-51 Mustang is the best fighter tested by this Command to date."[39]

Mustang I AM118, A&AEE Boscombe Down, Wiltshire, 1943.
(Artwork by Jim Laurier, © Osprey Publishing)

Again, on the 26th, Materiel Command ordered 400 Merlin-powered Mustangs as AC-33923. NAA opened charge number NA-102 for the P-51B-1-NA on the same day but, as with NA-101, significant work (such as on the wing) had already begun to transform much of the XP-78 into a production design.

On the 27th Col Chidlaw sent a letter to Brig Gen A. J. Lyons, Commanding General Eighth Air Force Air Technical Services, regarding the status of the XP-78 (XP-51B), Packard 1650-3, stating "reject Griffon as too difficult to install. Performance estimates already greater than for any AAF fighter at low and high altitude."[40] The following day Col Phillips, in a communication to Col Chidlaw, noted that NAA was "going with 1650-3, only requires small movement of wing forward and down," and "this will be a pretty good airplane if the aerodynamics aren't ruined."[41]

The 28th also saw "Bill" Lappin write a letter to Lt Col Tommy Hitchcock to summarize a visit to Hucknall and the Experimental Department by Maj Gen Echols and his entourage. In the letter he also expressed some disappointment that NAA had not installed a Packard Merlin 28 engine.[42]

On August 31 Maj Gen Fairchild directed Maj Gen Echols, "The Merlin should be introduced into P-51 production as early as that airplane engine combination is determined practical."[43]

As the critical actions by HQ-AAF and Materiel Command unfolded in August, more events important to secure the P-51B's development continued in parallel.

On September 2 the first NAA sliding-hood concept for the Merlin Mustang was shown in Drawing D-12011. The canopy design was very similar in concept to that of the A6M Zero-sen. The windscreen and aft section were fixed and the middle canopy traveled to the rear. Earlier in July the Packard pursuit wind tunnel model (Packard Pursuit Drawing X73-01123) suggested the same canopy/rear deck profile. The aft fuselage configuration was already in line with the impending P-51D to be established in February–April 1943.

On September 1 Legarra transmitted the requested NAA estimates to the British Air Ministry for estimates for plant space, tooling, labor, and materials for Britain to undertake licensed production of the Merlin Mustang, based on NAA sending airframe subassemblies to Britain. The estimated elapsed time to produce the first hybrid was deemed far too great to be practical.[44]

On September 2 the first test of the balanced, sealed aileron was undertaken on AM118 by Chilton, who noted dramatic improvements in both high- and low-speed roll rates compared with the Mustang I. Twelve days later the XP-78 was re-designated XP-51B. Then, on September 17, Chilton flew A-36A-1-NA No. 1 (43-83663) for the first time.

On September 22 Grover Loening, consultant to the War Production Board, toured US and British bases and then wrote a lengthy letter to the board's Harold Talbot, Director, Aircraft Production. In summary, he devoted much of his letter to a severe critique of the Wright Field leadership, particularly the project manager leadership (Kelsey P-38/Price P-39) because (in his opinion) they had become so wrapped up in their own projects that they were blind to other equal or better airplanes. Using the Mustang as an example of the latter, and the reference that the British considered the NAA aircraft to be the best American fighter, he (Loening) continued to elaborate on the perceived issue as viewed by senior RAF leaders.

Loening told Talbot that feedback from Air Chief Marshal Sir Wilfrid Freeman, in confidence, pointed to the Wright Field group as seriously critical of the Mustang because it was not a Materiel Command developed airplane. He further pointed out that Wright Field had flown its two Mustangs only "a couple of times" in two years. He also related that other aircraft leaving testing and delivered into the ETO from Wright Field were not only late with respect to delivery projections, but were beset by "bugs and deficiencies" that delayed their introduction into combat. This last point was extremely relevant to ongoing

An Allison V-1710 installed in a RAF Mustang I in June 1942. The identity of this aircraft cannot be positively confirmed, as both AG518 and AM121 were used by Rolls-Royce on preliminary engine performance investigation flights prior to the fitting of a Merlin 65 to a Mustang I airframe. Note the sealing of the gun ports immediately beneath the engine. (© *Rolls-Royce*)

Mustang X AL975-G, Hucknall, Nottinghamshire, October 1942.
(Artwork by Jim Laurier, © Osprey Publishing)

problems requiring Depot support in each combat theater, not only to identify the issues and provide temporary solutions, but also to communicate them back to Wright Field. The Wright Field Materiel Center was responsible for packaging the so-identified problems for distribution to the airframe manufacturing design groups, and then prodding each one to commit to insertion in production "as soon as practicable."

Among several recommendations, Loening suggested that full flight test programs be removed from Wright Field to another organization charged with testing, identifying, and resolving issues as fast as possible. Eglin Field Air Forces Proving Ground was delegated the responsibility for all tactical testing considerations.[45] In post-war years the Flight Test Center moved from Wright Field to Edwards AFB, California, with Eglin AFB remaining the Air Proving Ground for the USAF.

On October 1 the XP-51B airframe was complete and awaiting its Packard Merlin 1650-3 to enable fitment of the fuel supply system, engine controls, and instrumentation when the engine was delivered.[46]

On October 8 Lt Col Tommy Hitchcock reported on the advanced qualities of the Merlin Mustang, the resistance from Wright Field Materiel Command (HQ and Wright Field), and the British desire to locally produce the Merlin 61 version.[47]

One week earlier, the XP-51B airframe was complete, awaiting its Packard Merlin 1650-3 engine to enable fitment of the fuel supply system, engine controls, and instrumentation when the engine was delivered.[48]

On the 8th NA-103 contract AC-33940 was executed for 350 P-51C Mustangs to be built at the Dallas plant. Coordination between the Inglewood and Dallas production teams was initiated to communicate engineering and production information between the two plants to expedite the acquisition of tooling and the training of supervisors, and to duplicate all assets needed to produce the same basic airframes 1,200 miles apart.[49] The Dallas plant manager, Ken Bowen, as former Mustang Project Engineer, was uniquely qualified to assess the full slate of requirements to start production as soon as possible. The original contract was for 350 P-51Cs, but

950 more were subsequently added to NA-103 when order NA-107 P-51D-1 was canceled in fall 1943. Later, NA-111 became the contract vehicle for the last 400 P-51C-10-NTs and the 2,500 P-51Ds and K-NTs through the P-51D-20-NT series.

On October 10 Lt Col Tommy Hitchcock wrote a lengthy memo to Assistant Ambassador John Stettinius, in which he summarized: (1) the history of the NAA Mustang as a unique joint British/NAA project independent of Materiel Command; (2) the virtues of the airframe's performance with respect to comparisons with the Spitfire V and Fw 190 fighters; and (3) the very high level of support from Ambassador Winant and Assistant Secretary of War Robert A. Lovett, as well as very senior Air Ministry and RAF leaders to prioritize the development of the Merlin Mustang. He went on to recount the extreme level of indifference from the American side, pointing to the possibility of a "not invented here" syndrome, particularly with respect to no visible champion at HQ-AAF or Materiel Command.[50]

To put the timing of this letter into context, the Eighth Air Force had not yet lost the three P-38 fighter groups assigned to it as long-range escort, and had no real perceived reason to pressure HQ-AAF for "replacement" aircraft.

On October 13 the first Mustang X, AL975-G (the "G" suffix denoting that the aircraft was to be attended by a guard at all times when on the ground), was flown at

ANGLE OF PILOTS SIGHT LINE.
FUEL COOLER AND INTERCOOLER RAD.
'CONSUS' ENGINE MOUNTING
CARBURETTOR AIR INTAKE
POSITION OF INTERCOOLER RADIATOR AIR EXIT LOUVRES.
PRELIM. INSTALLATION OF MERLIN 61. IN N. A. 'MUSTANG.'

BELOW LEFT This drawing from 1942 illustrates how the Merlin 61 was to have originally been installed in the Mustang I. It shows the bifurcating of the airflow into the intercooler/fuel cooler radiator and the carburetor air intake. The Consus (Convergent Suspension) engine mounting is also clearly shown. (© *Rolls-Royce*)

BOTTOM LEFT Mustang X AL975-G flew for the first time on October 13, 1942 from Hucknall, with Rolls-Royce Chief Test Pilot Capt R. T. Shepherd at the controls. The aircraft had a Merlin 65 installed. (© *Rolls-Royce*)

BELOW Having had its engine panels removed, AL975-G reveals its Rolls-Royce Merlin 65 powerplant and Consus engine mounting. Unlike the NAA installation for the XP-78/XP-51B, Rolls-Royce installed the intercooler under the engine, retaining the "donut" coolant radiator and oil cooler intact within the fuselage. (*Philip Jarrett Collection*)

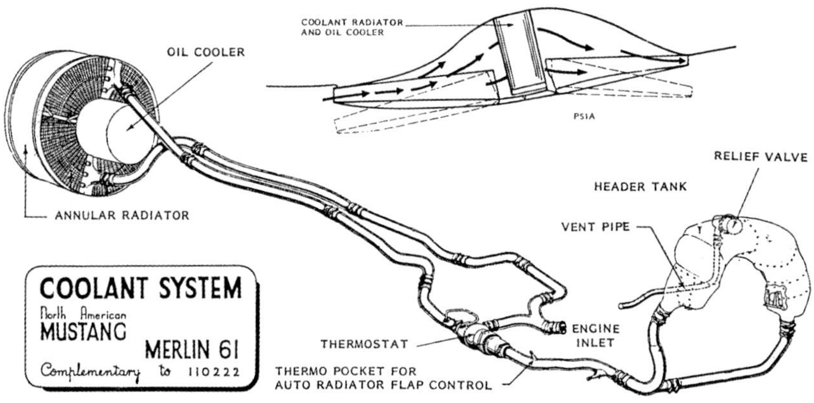

ABOVE The left side of the Merlin 65 installed in AL975-G. (© *Rolls-Royce*)

TOP RIGHT Five Mustang Is were converted into Merlin-powered Mk Xs, with this particular aircraft, AM208, being the second airframe to receive the Rolls-Royce engine. During this period and into the fall of 1943, there were serious discussions between Rolls-Royce, the British Air Ministry and NAA as they evaluated the feasibility of shipping Mustang I sub-assemblies to Britain to mate with the Merlin engine. (*Philip Jarrett Collection*)

ABOVE RIGHT This original scheme drawing details aspects of the Mustang X's cooling system. The aircraft retained the original pipework as fitted by North American, but with the addition of a radiator and oil cooler manufactured in Britain by Morris Radiators. Like the original American-made unit, the British radiator was of the curved fin and tube (secondary surface) type. It was also identical in size, although the American radiator employed a honeycomb construction. The British radiator effectively coped with a 33 percent increase in heat dissipation, although wind tunnel tests showed that a rectangular shaped matrice of the same area would perform even better. (© *Rolls-Royce*)

Hucknall by Rolls-Royce Chief Test Pilot Capt R. T. Shepherd. The engine installed was the Merlin 65. The first series of tests were prevented from extending above 18,000ft in MS supercharger stage only because the new steel tank with immersed pump to supply pressurized fuel for full operation of FS gear had not yet been installed. For the next several flights the reduction gear ratio of 0.477:1 and the 10ft 9in. propeller were changed in various combinations to a 0.42:1 reduction and an 11ft 4in. propeller, and some cowling configuration changes were made to improve streamlining around the forward-mounted intercooler radiator (to assist reducing the fuel charge mixture temperatures). Additionally, because overheating was encountered in several tests, the exit area range for the aft main radiator duct was changed, from 1.8sq ft to 0.70sq ft in closed position, and from 2.7sq ft to 1.2sq ft in the open position.

Continued modifications to the cowling shape, increasing the size of both the radiator and intercooler matrix, and experimenting with the Spitfire propeller, considerably narrowed the actual flight test results to the predicted performance. One of the more disturbing observations made was the tendency of the main gear wheel fairings to open in dives as yaw forces increased. The problem was temporarily solved at Hucknall by adjusting the cover locking mechanisms. After a series of climb-rate tests were flown in AL975-G, a main bearing failure caused future flights to be moved to A&AEE Boscombe Down, where AM208 was based.[51]

A second lingering problem was encountered during flight tests of both AL975-G and AM208, namely exacerbation of directional instability (yaw) as the throttle was applied or retarded. The root cause was believed to be the introduction of the four-bladed propeller, with higher activity factor through the blades, which required rudder inputs and constant changes in trim due to those effects. Both Rolls-Royce and NAA were consulted on solutions, leading to the installation of fin modifications for testing in February 1943.

The lingering problem of accidental opening of the main gear fairings was traced to two causes. The first was a failure of the fairing latches under high aerodynamic loads. When these failures occurred, the primary effect was an immediate change to yaw and rudder force to maintain direction. When a roll and change in direction occurred, structural failures included losing a wing. The second issue was occasional failure of the main gear uplock under high-G loads (either turning maneuver or dive pull-out) which permitted the main gear and wheel to crash the fairing door open and drop into extremely high freestream velocity. The subsequent instantaneous drag forces also caused wing failures, and were found to be the root cause of several fatal crashes of the P-51B before the "gear uplock" designs were improved at NAA and produced as kits for both the P-51B/C and early P-51D-5s in late spring 1944.

The first Packard Merlin 1650-3 was delivered to NAA on the 18th, but it failed two days later during ground tests of the installation in XP-51B 41-37352. Following successful changes to improve both reliability and power, the 1650-3 would be the standard engine supplied with all P-51B-1s and B-5-NAs as well as the P-51C-1-NT.

The standard Packard Merlin for all Inglewood Mustang deliveries, beginning with P-51B-10-NA 42-106739 and P-51C-1-NT 42-103329 in February 1944, was the 1650-7 (equivalent to the Merlin 65), with some modifications to the Merlin 65 series. The blower ratios for the 1650-7, which favored horsepower at take-off and through the middle altitudes, were greater than for the 1650-3, but provided less power above the full-throttle height of 21,400ft. Some of the thinking that prevailed was that most air fighting in the ETO was at bomber altitudes and below 24,000ft. Note that while the top speed of the P-51B with the 1650-3 at 29,000ft (full-throttle height) was faster than that of the P-51D with the 1650-7 at 24,000ft, this was not because of the drag difference between the two types (the parasite drag for both types was essentially the same total value, with small differences in separate components). It was because of the combination of different air densities at the compared full-throttle heights. These data will be further discussed in Appendix A.

Meanwhile, with the news of the Merlin Mustang successes at Hucknall, and the encouraging reports of progress from NAA, it became clear that a large potential order book for Allison-engined Mustangs was in jeopardy. This stimulated a series of investigations into Allison by GMC Board member and Vice President E. I. DuPont. Beginning on October 20, a series of high-level meetings were held between GMC Board members and the Allison executives to determine why the company's future status as the sole engine supplier for the Mustang was grim. The exchange was focused on "why Allison didn't recognize the importance of developing the two-stage supercharger."

The stated explanations from Allison's Jack C. Brown and O. E. Hunt included: (1) as a small development company Allison did not have (nor did GMC offer) research and development funding to build the engineering staff to conduct development; (2) the USAAC/USAAF was not interested in parallel development as it believed that high-altitude performance with auxiliary turbos was satisfactory, and; (3) the influx of changes to the V-1710 from its primary customer, USAAC/USAAF Materiel Command, were too much to control, both for quality and for Service demands.[52]

Between October 20 and October 30 Chilton accelerated testing of the A-36 (in 41-83663) to analyze performance for the new Allison V-1710-87F21R engine. Completed tests included speed runs, rate of climb, and endurance cruise settings.

On October 27 Col D. M. Schlatter, Chief, Air-Ground Support Directorate, issued a request for comment, titled "Fighter Aircraft for Observation," to the various combat command leaders. This Routing and Record Sheet for Comments led Brig Gen Gordon Saville, Chief, Air Defense Directorate, to order that all P-51 production allocations be to Reconnaissance and CAS units. The issuance of fighter aircraft types and quantity was in the Air Directorate Command purview at this time, although this would change in the fall of 1943 when Gen Arnold intervened to redirect both P-38 and P-51B units to the ETO.[53]

On October 30 NAA Senior Mustang Representative Philip Legarra wrote a summary report to Kindelberger, Atwood, Rice, Schmued, et al. regarding the excellent results achieved at Hucknall, including test results with varying supercharger impeller gear ratios and different propeller types.

Between November 1 and 23 more functional testing was accomplished for the new pitot tube/airspeed calibration, dive-brake testing with full bomb loads, and wing de-icing for the A-36 just as the XP-51B was being readied for its first flight.[54]

On November 5, Allison General Manager E. C. Newill appealed to Brig Gen Charles E. Branshaw, Chief, Materiel Command, for orders for the new Allison two-speed/two-stage V-1710 scheduled for production in the second quarter of 1944. Newill stated that the Allison manufacturing plan and investment for additional capacity in 1940 was now projected at 50 percent utilization for mid-1943 and beyond. He cited concerns that the last P-39Q was scheduled to roll off the Bell line with only potential orders for the P-63 on the horizon to accept the new V-1710s. The P-38K was considered a potential prospect, as well as the P-40Q, but both types were forecast deep into 1944 as potential users of the new Allison engine. In late 1942 a meeting of NAA and Materiel Command resulted in the former's agreement to put the new engine in the XP-51J.[55]

On November 6 Gen Arnold reported to President Roosevelt that 2,200 Mustangs had been ordered.[56]

On November 23 NAA Report 5567 "Weight Comparison of Spitfire IX to P-51B" was completed, leading Schmued to schedule a trip to Britain in February to meet with Supermarine and Hawker to better understand British design standards. In summary, the weight difference between the two fighters at take-off gross weight with equal fuel (100gal Spitfire, 105gal P-51B) was 1,405lb. The basic airframe differences that led to the Mustang being heavier were in the wing, fuselage, empennage, and landing gear due to several USAAF design practices, namely: (1) USAAF/NAA designed to an 8G limit load (i.e., "bend"), 12G ultimate (i.e., "break"), whereas the British standard was 7.3G limit and 11G ultimate loads for high angle-of-attack (i.e., dive pull-out and hard-banking instantaneous turn); (2) the British designed to 1G for lateral loading, whereas USAAF/NAA designed to 3G lateral (a significant difference for empennage and engine mount design weights); and (3) the British load factor for landing gear was 4.5G for landing and ground loop, whereas the US standard was 7G.[57]

Much confusion arises when reading Schmued's narrative of his London trip in February through March 1943 to personally evaluate British design standards, as well as the new RM14.SM (Merlin 100) engine.[58] Schmued's recollection was that the weight report was compiled *after* he returned, but the published NA-5567, signed by Schmued, Rice, and Schleicher, was dated three months earlier, on November 23, 1942. He also stated that Arnold called Kindelberger after receiving a copy of the Comparison Report.

However, the NA-105/AC-37857 contract for three XP-51Fs was executed on January 2, 1943, only five weeks after Weight Comparison Report NA-5567 was released.[59] In the authors' opinion, the performance and contract discussions arising from Arnold's call to Kindelberger regarding the XP-51F occurred in late December 1942.

On November 29 Brig Gen Gordon Saville expressed his written opinion in Fighter Conference 11/28-11/29 that he had "serious doubts that a [single-engine] fighter could have enough sealing gas to go to deep targets and fight."[60]

After the Flight Test Department had conducted ground tests of the second Packard 1650-3, the XP-51B was deemed ready to fly. On November 30 Chilton flew it for 15 minutes before returning with a smoking engine.

It was obvious at the beginning of the radiator/aftercooler design phase that the new radiator needed to be designed to accommodate major increases in heat transfer requirements, including a fuel-air charge aftercooler, but changes in coolant properties required to work well in the new Merlin radiator matrix were not anticipated. Following test flights that had to be aborted due to overheating, significant fouling of the radiator cooling tubes due to electrolytic reactions between the glycol coolant and the dissimilar metals in the Merlin cooling system were discovered. Flight tests of the XP-51B were suspended briefly after December 31 in order to solve the problem and test the Keg Liner solution on the bench.

Schmued consulted with the Bureau of Standards after early flight tests were halted due to overheating. The recommended solution was "Take your radiator and slosh in some Keg Liner [a lacquer used in beer cans to isolate the metal from the beer]. We used this method, sloshing the radiator with Keg Liner, and never had any more cooling trouble."[61] Additional issues associated with insufficient cooling pointed to poor airflow impinging on the upper side of the radiator matrix due to flow separation along the upper duct plenum, as well as an increase in turbulent flows behind the oil cooler (which was relocated from the center of the earlier engine coolant radiator to a position on the lower duct plenum). Work was initiated to rearrange the orientation of the Harrison radiator so that, proceeding forward, the aftercooler core now resided vertically on the right side, occupying approximately 25 percent of the radiator volume.

Furthermore, the changes to the aileron began to stack up. From December they were to be incorporated into the first production P-51B-1-NA, followed by insertion into both the P-51B-5 and C-1 (and subsequent models). A summary of the evolution includes:

All ailerons were sealed from the beginning through to the end of the Mustang series, but the early ailerons through P-51A were sealed with a "cusped" airfoil section (as described in the NACA Roll Testing), had a leading edge with weights for static balance, had only two attachment hinges for the wing mounting, and only a single aileron throw setting of +/-10 degrees. All Mustangs from Mustang I, Mustang IA/P-51, A-36, P-51A were rigged for only +/-10 degrees.

The P-51B-1-NA had a steel diaphragm in place of the leading-edge weighted strip, but retained the same two hinge/wing attachments. The new features were illustrated as dash number revisions to the original 73-16001 Aileron Assembly, the changes being sufficient enough to require the new design drawing reference 104-16001. The space required in the wing rear spar "well" created a need for structural stiffening of the wing skin, which resulted in two "fences," two on top and one on the underside. The biggest difference between the P-51B and earlier Mustangs was the increase in adjustable throw angles of +/-10, 12, and 15 degrees. The recommended factory settings were +/-12 degrees, but these could be modified in the field via coordination between pilot, crew chiefs, and technical services.

The P-51B-5 and C-1 introduced several changes that were not interchangeable with the B-1. The first was to provide three attachment points per aileron, which stiffened the aileron span-wise to provide a more effective aerodynamic surface. The steel diaphragm on the left aileron was later replaced by Technical Order, as it influenced the magnetic compass. A non-magnetic item of equal weight was used. These changes remained intact through all Inglewood production series from P-51B-5 through P-51D, and the same for Dallas series P-51C/D/Ks.[62] In the early Mustang IIIs (P-51B-1s) delivered to the RAF, their magnetic compasses were affected by the steel diaphragm, so they were "parked" until a suitable locally sourced replacement was installed.[63] When Maj Gen Spaatz requested all P-51Bs/Mustang IIIs from the RAF in December 1943, these aircraft were released to the Ninth Air Force.

Anecdotally, Robert Gruenhagen reports that Bob Hoover flew his demonstration P-51D with +/-10 degrees aileron rigging, and the authors are aware of several instances of +/-15 degrees aileron throw. That said, the NAA recommendation was to rig the P-51B/D at +/-12 degrees. When the P-51H was introduced, the ailerons were larger than those of all previous Mustangs and achieved the same roll rate with +/-10 degrees as the P-51B/D at +/-12 degrees throw.[64]

Continued flight tests during December included the first A-36 dive test with 1,000lb bombs and dive brakes extended for different dive angles up to 70 degrees. Additional evaluation included radiator scoop pressure testing, as well as evaluating performance variation between the current Curtiss Electric 10ft 6in. no-cuff propeller and the new Hamilton Standard 11ft 2in. cuffed Hydromatic propeller. The latter, while heavier, proved to be more efficient in converting horsepower into blade thrust, and became standard for the P-51B/C models. As noted earlier, however, the four-bladed propeller installations on AL975-G introduced yaw instabilities when the throttle was advanced or retarded.[65 66 67]

On December 15 a fatal A-36 accident occurred at the Eglin Field bombing and gunnery range. A witness described the aircraft in a vertical dive "past the target" with dive brakes extended and two 1,000lb bombs "trying to get back on target to the point of being near inverted." It was then observed to roll as if to perform a "reverse Immelmann," followed by a violent over-control as the pilot tried to recover from the dive, whereupon the wing separated. The airframe and wing crashed in the same area. Following this accident to 43-83666, both Materiel Command and NAA investigated the crash scene and found that the separation occurred at wing station 75, the root cause being a combination of the rolling moment with dive brakes extended at near-terminal speeds, plus the acceleration loads on the wings carrying unreleased 1,000lb bombs. After a detailed review of the structural analysis and wind tunnel data, NAA issued placard instructions in April 1944 limiting level flight speeds with extended dive brakes to 275mph at sea level and maximum bomb load to 550lb for each bomb rack.

EIGHTH AIR FORCE/LUFTWAFFE FROM JUNE THROUGH DECEMBER 1942

The 56th Fighter Group (FG) headquarters moved from New York earlier in the year to Bridgeport Municipal Airport, where the unit became the first fighter group to receive new P-47Bs in June 1942. The 56th was then essentially ordered to "debug" them.[68]

Anticipating the massive logistics required to support the Eighth Air Force, VIII Air Force Service Command established ETO headquarters in Britain, then set about organizing Depot and Service units to support VIII Bomber and Fighter Commands.

All 171 P-47Bs built by Republic (between May and September 1942) were deemed "unsuitable for combat operations" and duly assigned to train such units as the 56th FG while awaiting delivery of the improved P-47C-1-RE. (*USAF, sourced by William Marshall Collection*)

Depots had been established at Burtonwood, near Liverpool, early in the war to take shipments arriving in the port city from the US and undertake the necessary modifications to meet RAF specifications. In mid-August 1942 Langford Lodge Air Depot, near Belfast in Northern Ireland, was established, staffed primarily by Lockheed with 2,600 US civilians, including engineering personnel. Their work concerned special modifications and experimental engineering. Construction for the Warton Air Depot had begun earlier in the year. VIII Air Force Service Command reorganized shortly thereafter, first designating major centers as Base Air Depot Areas, then simply Base Depots. Burtonwood, Warton, and Langford Lodge became BAD1, BAD2, and BAD3, respectively.

The mission was then further organized, with BAD1 specializing in the B-17, P-38, and P-47 and, initially, the P-51B-1. BAD2 focused on the B-24 and the P-51B-5 and subsequent Mustangs. Radial engines were repaired at BAD1, and in-line engines at BAD2. BAD3 originally specialized in manufacturer kit modifications and propeller maintenance, but its activities gradually dwindled as Burtonwood and Warton streamlined their production capabilities in late 1943 and it was reduced to research engineering by the summer of 1944. The number one priority for BAD1 and BAD2 was to modify as required all inbound replacement aircraft for delivery to operational combat units. The Ninth Air Force was a separate entity, and is further discussed later in this chapter.[69]

Between June 8 and 15 the assignment and deployments of the P-38-equipped 1st FG to Goxhill and the P-39-equipped 31st FG to Atcham was completed. Shortly thereafter, the 31st converted to Spitfire Vs. The Eighth Air Force HQ was officially activated with the arrival of Maj Gen Spaatz, soon to be Commander, AAF-ETO.[70]

The Eighth Air Force began combat operations on July 4, shortly after which its HQ moved to Bushy Park to be close to RAF Fighter Command for improved planning and coordination. Ten days later the 31st FG flew the first VIII Fighter Command combat sorties in support of the impending Dieppe raid.

Between July 26 and 31 several notable Luftwaffe data points for the future struggles over Germany include the total day fighter strength on all fronts as 1,246 single-engined and twin-engined day fighters. The total day fighter strength in the west, facing Britain, was 442 single-engined and twin-engined fighters, of which 333 were operational with JGs 1, 2, and 26.[71]

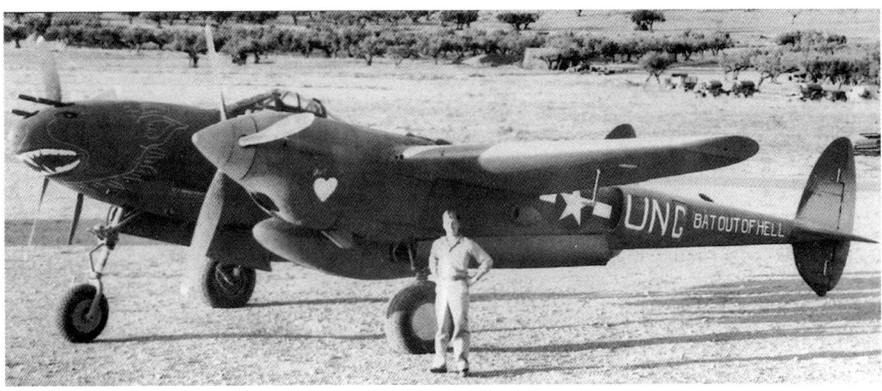

The P-38F had production ferry tank/bomb carrying capability, as well as Fowler flaps to improve maneuverability. This particular aircraft, 41-7498, was assigned to the 94th FS/1st FG at Monserrato, on Sardinia, in 1943-44. (*Tony Holmes Collection*)

On August 14 an VIII Fighter Command 1st FG P-38F claimed the first victory credit for the Lightning in the ETO. That same day Gen Arnold, over Eaker's objections, made the hard decision that the Eighth Air Force was to transfer five of its fighter groups, plus two bomb groups, to Operation *Torch* for the campaign in North Africa.[72] The immediate consequence was that the Eighth Air Force had to give up its three long-range P-38 fighter groups (1st, 14th, and 82nd FGs), as well as transfer all experienced P-38 pilots and the remaining Lightnings from the 78th FG. When the groups officially departed in November only the 4th FG remained operational in Britain, equipped with very-short-range Spitfires.

On August 17 VIII Bomber Command attacked Rouen and Sotterville in France to begin heavy bomber operations from Britain. Between the 17th and 19th the following "firsts" were recorded: the 14th FG arrived at Atcham (soon to depart for Africa); the first US-operated and flown fighter (a 31st FG Spitfire V) based in Britain destroyed a Luftwaffe fighter on the 18th; and the Royal Canadian Air Force's No. 414 Sqn recorded a Mustang I victory over an Fw 190 during the Dieppe operation on the 19th (regarding the last, author Steve Brooking has evidence of an earlier Mustang victory from a returning PoW, post-VE Day).[73]

August 19 also saw JG 1 engage VIII Bomber Command for the first time, the German pilots subsequently reporting "concerns."[74]

On August 28 AWPD/1 was revised to AWPD/2 so as to focus strategic attacks on Germany's submarine and aircraft manufacturing bases.[75] AWPD/2 was the controlling document guiding Eighth Air Force objectives for the upcoming Casablanca Conference, resulting in an agreed Combined Bomber Offensive to be conducted by the RAF and USAAF.

On September 5 the 31st FG flew its first escort mission for Douglas A-20 Havoc medium bombers attacking Le Havre. The following day the Eighth Air Force lost its first two B-17s to JGs 2 and 26 during the Méaulte attack. Conversely, B-17 gunners claimed their first Luftwaffe fighter destroyed.[76] On September 16, 11 Mustang Is of the RAF's No. 268 Sqn conducted the first long-range fighter escort operation for nine Bostons of No. 88 Sqn, RAF, undertaking a low-level bombing raid of Den Helder, in the Netherlands. This was the first time the RAF had used the Mustang in the long-range bomber escort role.[77] The RAF Eagle Squadrons (Nos. 71, 121, and 133) were absorbed into the 4th FG during September and activated in VIII Fighter Command at month-end. The group continued to operate under RAF control (as did the Spitfire-equipped 31st and 52nd FGs) until October 2.[78] [79]

On September 26, flying the new Spitfire IX, the 4th FG suffered its biggest combined loss of the war. The 336th Fighter Squadron (FS), on an escort mission, dropped below thick cloud cover near Brest. Almost immediately the squadron encountered heavy flak and an attack by two Fw 190s. The ensuing losses included seven to flak, three to crash landings due to lack of fuel, and one to an Fw 190, for a claim of one Fw 190 destroyed by Capt M. E. Jackson.[80]

On September 28 Flt Lt Janusz Lewkowicz of Mustang I-equipped No. 309 Sqn, RAF, made a solo strafing attack on various German targets at Stavanger, in Norway.

Major Egon Mayer, as *Kommodore* of JG 2, developed the deadly head-on attack from slightly higher than the 12 o'clock position on B-17s and B-24s in November 1942. He is seen here standing atop the right wing of a B-17F that he forced down amidst a field of wheat in France in the summer of 1943. It was Mayer who convinced Generalmajor Adolf Galland that a frontal pass against a B-17 offered the best chance of bringing it down, the latter duly modifying the tactic to recommend that altitude be maintained so as to eliminate the time it would take to perform a split-S and climb to allow a second attack to be made. (*EN Archive*)

He took off from Dalcross, in Scotland, and returned to land at Dunino, also in Scotland.

On October 2 the 82nd FG was officially based at Eglington, and the 1st and 4th FGs flew their first escort mission under Eighth Air Force control.[81]

The mission to Lille on October 9 suffered 4-2-46 (hereinafter shorthand for Missing in Action, Written-Off/Class E, and Damaged) of the 108 B-17s dispatched. The Eighth Air Force, after the attrition of the Lille mission, was unable to mount another 100-bomber attack until April 1943, or have P-47C-equipped fighter groups operationally ready to conduct escort missions until late April/early May 1943. A further consequence of the Lille losses was that VIII Bomber Command, due to a lack of adequate fighter escorts for missions even to northern France and Holland, was very limited in terms of its target selection for six months.[82]

Nevertheless, in his October 15 letter to Spaatz, Eaker expressed confidence that "a large force of American bombers can operate anywhere in Germany without fighter escort."[83]

On October 21, during a mission to the Dortmund-Ems Canal, in western Germany, and other objectives in Holland by aircraft from No. 268 Sqn, the Mustang I became the first single-engined fighter based in Britain to penetrate the German border. The mission was conducted by four aircraft led by Wg Cdr A. F. Anderson, with Flt Lt B. P. W. Clapin, Plt Off O. R. Chapman, and Flg Off W. T. Hawkins RNZAF flying the remaining three aircraft. This mission caused some consternation to the Luftwaffe High Command, as the presence of single-engined RAF fighters operating from Britain over Germany meant that a new level of threat had to be considered.[84]

On October 31 the 1st and 14th FGs were officially withdrawn from ETO operations for Operation *Torch* and reassigned to the Twelfth Air Force.

On November 20 Hauptmann Egon Mayer led the first "head-on" attack by JG 2, against the 1st Bomb Wing (BW), to exploit the weak forward defensive fire of the B-17E/F.[85] The tactic became known as the "Company Front" attack and was deadly, but great skill was required to assemble the attacking aircraft far enough in front of the oncoming B-17s and still retain their cohesiveness as an attacking force at closing speeds in excess of 500mph.

On November 29 the P-38F-equipped 78th FG was assigned to VIII Fighter Command at Goxhill. Unfortunately, *Torch* immediately claimed all of the group's P-38s and many of the pilots. The remaining personnel in the 78th were informed of the impending equipment change to the P-47C-2/5-RE.

On December 6, for the attack on Lille, Col Curtis LeMay's 305th Bomb Group (BG) flew his conceptual "Stagger Formation" in which the group's B-17s were arranged to achieve two primary purposes. The first was to "uncover" as many lanes of fire as possible to defend against German fighters while reducing the danger of hitting other B-17s in the formation. The second was to do so while maintaining a smaller and more compact footprint, as seen from above, with which to concentrate bombs on the target.[86] [87]

On the 12th the 44th BG went operational for the first attack by B-24s in the ETO. The 2nd BW was designated for command of the B-24 bomb groups as they arrived in the ETO. During the next several weeks the 44th was placed in formation at the same high altitudes as the B-17s, but there were found to be significant differences in performance between the two types. The B-24s were faster and had a longer range with a greater bomb load, but engines and pilots were straining to maintain formation at 25,000ft. They were typically tasked in trail as the "low box" because of the dissimilar operational characteristics.

General der Jagdflieger Generalmajor Adolf Galland was both an exceptional fighter pilot (he was credited with 104 aerial victories) and a skilled leader – he led the German fighter force from November 1941 through to January 1945. (*Robert Forsyth Collection*)

On or about December 20 *General der Jagdflieger* Generalmajor Adolf Galland published a set of tactical regulations prescribing the methods of attack on American heavy bombers. Briefly, they outlined the following: (1) concentrated attacks were preferred, both to dilute the bombers' defensive fire and to concentrate the firepower on the bombers; and (2) the fighters should fly parallel with the bomber stream until about three miles ahead, then turn and in at least Schwarm (flight) strength, attack head-on. They were to aim at the bombers' cockpits, open fire at 900m, and pass above after ceasing fire. Rear attacks were essentially to be the same, in Schwarm strength, at high speed, and pass above the bomber.

Galland emphasized that the key tactic was for the fighters to remain in formation above the bombers, in order to re-group and attack without delay. Far too many Luftwaffe pilots performed a split-S after closing with the bomber, and had to regain altitude to rejoin the fight. Over the next several weeks the fighter commanders modified the frontal assault to begin at a slightly higher altitude than the bombers, in order to concentrate fire similar to a strafing attack, in which the entire bomber vitals were exposed to a small deflection shot from above. Hence the phrase "attacks came from 12 o'clock high" became part of the Eighth Air Force lexicon during debriefings.[88]

RAF IMPROVEMENTS OF THE MUSTANG I/IA FROM LATE 1942 THROUGH 1943[89]

Cameras

Even as the very first Mustang Is were reaching Britain in early 1942, the Chief of the General Staff of the British Army was politely reminding the Senior Air Staff Officer of HQ Army Co-operation Command of the RAF that, given the impending re-equipment of Army Co-operation Command squadrons with Mustangs, these aircraft had to be fitted with cameras. Indeed, the stated requirement for said Mustangs involved in the fighter reconnaissance role stipulated that they had to be equipped with both oblique and vertical cameras in order to meet the photographic requirements of the British Army. In response, Army Co-operation Command informed the Chief of the General Staff that in keeping with the current policy regarding photography, aircraft of Army Co-operation Command squadrons should be fitted with cameras capable of taking both oblique and vertical photography. The capabilities of the current Army Co-operation Command Tomahawk and Lysander aircraft were outlined, and it was confirmed in writing on February 11, 1942 that: "Mustang aircraft are not equipped at present with cameras at all. There will be no difficulty in fitting them with oblique cameras, but it is not certain whether the vertical camera will be a practical proposition. Experiments are now being conducted on this latter point."

The discussion between Army Co-operation Command and the Chief of the General Staff continued on this matter and was escalated to within the higher levels of the Air Ministry, Ministry of Aircraft Production, and War Office. Urgent communications were made with NAA regarding the possibility of fitting a vertical camera in the Mustang, and the company's response was that "the proposed modification was considered to be impracticable." This was based on several issues, including available space in the rear fuselage, structural considerations, and center of gravity issues.

From this response the discussion escalated further, with the Chief of the General Staff and War Office launching an ambit claim to form special Army Co-operation Command squadrons to be directly under the control of the British Army. These were to be equipped with a suitable aircraft type or types that could house both vertical and oblique photography to meet the imagery requirements of the British Army. The RAF and Air Ministry subsequently proposed, as an interim measure, that work to provide the Mustang with an oblique photography capability would be a high priority. It also suggested that each Army Co-operation Command squadron would be equipped with two or three Tomahawk aircraft fitted for vertical photography until such time as another suitable solution for the Mustang could be identified. Priority in allocation of such Tomahawks would be given to units notionally directly allocated to each of the British Army Regional Commands for the Home Forces in Britain. This directive calmed the British Army's demands for a short while.

By July 1942 the question of cameras being fitted to Mustangs was still not resolved. Several installations for taking oblique photographs had been designed and trial flights were well underway. Key to these trials was the quality and usability of the photographs obtained with the oblique camera, the ease of use of the camera by the pilot, and how well the camera could be maintained and supported within the aircraft. The question of the vertical camera installation was more troublesome, with elements within the Ministry of Aircraft Production – which was having enough trouble getting all the Mustang Is being delivered Britain assembled and modified to the level the RAF required for the aircraft to be declared operational – proverbially "dragging their feet" with investigations into providing the Mustang with a vertical camera installation.

As a result, the groups within Army Co-operation Command that operated Mustangs (down to wing and squadron level) took on the challenge of how this capability might be realized in a functional and safe way.

The oblique camera installations that were originally proposed utilized the space in the fuselage immediately behind the cockpit, with the camera installation facing out to the port side, slightly downwards and to the rear. As such, this camera installation did not produce the true 90-degree oblique photographs which the British Army considered necessary for several of its requirements, particularly those related to plotting for artillery fire control and direction. Nevertheless, Army Co-operation Command persisted with the proposed installation, rather than pursuing a more complex oblique camera installation within the body of the rear fuselage, just above the exit air plenum surface aft of the radiator. This would have required significant structural work on both sides of the fuselage and greatly complicated and delayed the entry of the Mustang into service. This was notwithstanding continued negative responses from NAA regarding the proposal on several grounds.

Army Co-operation Command, therefore, pursued the refinement of the oblique camera installation in the space immediately behind the cockpit where the rear Plexiglas window cut-out was located. Early variants included complex sheet metal "cones" and panels to house and protect the lens of the installed camera and to impart a degree of rigidity to the lens – particularly when longer focal length lenses were fitted to the camera. However, these more rigid and complex installations tended not to be as successful as simpler variants, and they made it more difficult to maintain and adjust the camera and lens when installed.

As a result, the basic design that was arrived at was one of the camera being mounted on a sheet metal shelf placed on sliding rails in the area behind the cockpit that normally housed radio equipment, with the latter being relocated further down in the area behind the cockpit. The end of the lens protruded out marginally through a cut-out in the rear Plexiglas window. Quick release latches were fitted to the Plexiglas rear quarter windows behind the cockpit to allow them to be easily removed for access to the camera installation for maintenance and adjustment purposes. Through a process of further testing, adjustment of the angles of the camera and lens assembly and early operational use, the results obtained from the oblique camera installation were found to be of sufficient quality to meet the British Army's demands.

A groundcrewman prepares to mount a fully loaded F.24 camera in the oblique installation behind the cockpit of a Mustang I. (© *IWM (H 28781)*)

Standardization of the oblique camera installation then took place, with a design for the camera "shelf" mount, sliding rails upon which the shelf would be mounted, intervalometer, power and control wiring loom, and other ancillaries being established and put out for contract for manufacture and installation. Over time, as a result of operational experience, further refinements to this design would be made, all aimed at making the installation more effective and efficient. One example of this is the addition of thin sheet metal "doubler"

Mustang I AG633 of No. 2 Sqn has an early F.24 camera oblique installation behind the cockpit. This equipment was critically important for fulfilling low-level reconnaissance missions generated by Army Co-operation Command. (*USAF, sourced by Jeff Ethell Collection*)

strengthening plates around the cut-out in the rear quarter window to assist in preventing flexing and cracking of the Plexiglas.

Given the wartime demands on materials and specialist manufacturers, along with associated competing priorities of the different armed services and commands, the rate of production of the approved oblique camera installation was slower than Army Co-operation Command had expected. Despite attempts to speed up the process of manufacture and modification, competing priorities remained an issue to the end of 1943. Added to that were issues in the supply of the required F.24 reconnaissance cameras and associated lenses and camera control equipment, again competing with demands by other armed services and commands. As a result, only a quarter of Army Co-operation Command's Mustangs had been modified to carry an oblique camera by the beginning of 1943, with more than half having been modified by the middle of 1943 and the remainder by the end of that year.

The matter of aiming the camera lens at the target area on the ground was overcome by the simple expedient of painting two – normally yellow – sighting marks on the trailing edge of the aircraft's wing. If the ground target was visible just behind the wing and between the sighting marks, then it was within the area of view of the camera lens and a photo or photos could be taken. It became a part of the pre-flight check of the aircraft before a photographic sortie for the pilot to kneel at the wing trailing edge, look up at the installed oblique camera and visually check that the angle of alignment of the lens was correctly set.

It was also found that a near-vertical photograph could be taken using the oblique camera installation by placing the aircraft in a tight banking turn over the target area so that the side with the camera was literally pointing straight down at the target area, getting an "overhead" view.

Mustang IA FD449, Central Photographic Establishment, RAF Benson, Oxfordshire, 1943. (*Artwork by Jim Laurier, © Osprey Publishing*)

Depending on the tasking given to the Army Co-operation Command Mustang I, despite having been modified to use an oblique reconnaissance camera, it did not always carry this equipment. For example, if the mission assigned to the aircraft did not involve the requirement for photography, such as a "Rhubarb" to shoot up targets of opportunity in occupied Europe, or an "Arty/R" providing direction to artillery bombardment of identified targets, then a camera would not normally be fitted.

With the introduction of the Mustang IA into RAF service in mid-1943, the camera installation developed for the Mustang I was directly transferable and compatible to the new sub-type.

By the time of D-Day on June 6, 1944, much progress had been made in the overall oblique camera installation fitted to the Mustang I/IA aircraft of the RAF. A great deal of standardization had been arrived at, and the oblique camera modification was a basic requirement for a Mustang destined for the tactical reconnaissance role to be declared operational. It was the job of the Central Photographic Establishment at RAF Benson to ensure consistency and support of photographic equipment, encompassing cameras, lenses, camera mounts, camera control units, film and lens filters, wiring looms, and other essential ancillary items. Nominated as the coordinating and controlling body for this type of equipment, and managing modifications to aircraft for photographic and tactical reconnaissance purposes, the Central Photographic Establishment performed modifications and installations, or arranged the contracting out of such works to suitably qualified organizations.

Continuing the focus on the oblique camera installations, by mid-1943 it had become apparent to the RAF tactical reconnaissance squadrons that having such a camera pointing out of the port side of the aircraft only was limiting the way in which they had to plan and conduct their photographic sorties. An investigation was duly conducted into what would be required to make the oblique mounting more flexible, allowing the camera to point out to either the port or starboard side. With a few modifications to the existing mounting, a solution was arrived at and adopted.

The next phase in the oblique camera installation was to install two F.24 reconnaissance cameras fitted with shorter focal length lenses "back to back" to allow a single aircraft to take photographs from either side as required. An investigation into such a fitment was conducted, and it was found that with some compromises on the positioning of the cameras (they had to be slightly offset from each other), a dual camera installation was indeed possible. A limited number of aircraft were modified accordingly with this installation from just before D-Day onwards.

The vertical camera installation in the RAF's Mustang I aircraft remained something of a point of contention with the British Army and a "holy grail" for the technical and engineering staff of the Army Co-operation Command squadrons operating the aircraft. In the first half of 1943, with growing knowledge of the Mustang I and confidence in the solutions to issues that had been "home grown" by the Army Co-operation Command squadrons, work commenced in earnest at unit level on developing a vertical camera fitment for the aircraft. One such installation was developed that could take the full range of lenses usable with the F.24 reconnaissance camera, up to and including 14in. lenses to allow the obtaining of clear and usable reconnaissance photographs at heights of 8,000 to 10,000ft above ground level. Other installations were developed and evaluated, all with varying degrees of success.

In March 1943, a vertical camera installation developed by the Engineering Officer of No. 268 Sqn was put through a series of trials. The results of the evaluation, along with the associated technical and design documentation for the installation, was forwarded to HQ Army Co-operation Command for consideration and approval. A decision was quick in coming, with the installation being cleared in early April 1943 and directions being given for priority of manufacture for the required modification kits and for a number of aircraft – up to six within each squadron operating the Mustang I – to be modified accordingly either by Army Co-operation Command technical/engineering resources or a suitable contractor. The ultimate intention was to have all Army Co-operation Command Mustangs modified to carry the vertical camera installation, although this appears to have never been achieved. Enough Mustangs were modified, however, to provide the numbers required to meet the needs of squadrons tasked with undertaking vertical photography.

Once such a camera was installed, aiming for a vertical photo run was a bit more difficult than when using an oblique camera. Usually, the run was accomplished by placing the aircraft overhead a clearly visible ground location or landmark on the approach to the target, then flying a known set heading toward the target area from that position. If possible, the pilot would pick a point or landmark on the horizon or off to one side of the target area as a point of reference. Just prior to commencing the photo run, the pilot would quickly dip one wing to ensure the aircraft was on the correct heading, or to adjust if required, and then complete the photographic pass over the target.

As the Mustang IA entered service in mid-1943, the standard vertical camera installation for the Mustang I was directly transferable and compatible with the new sub-type. The aim was for each squadron operating the Mustang IA to have a percentage of its aircraft (somewhere in the range of one-third to one-half of the operational strength of the unit) modified with the vertical camera installation.

In the months prior to D-Day, most Mustang IAs had been modified to accept the "reversible" oblique camera installation allowing the camera to point out to either port or starboard. A smaller number of aircraft had also been modified to have the vertical camera installation as well. Most, if not all the Mustang IAs modified for the vertical camera installation also had the arrangement whereby they could carry the "back to back" oblique camera installation. A camera switch panel in the cockpit allowed the pilot to select which camera positions would take photographs – port and/or starboard and/or vertical in combination or individually.

By the time the Mustang II entered service with the RAF just before D-Day, the accepted camera installation was for aircraft to carry an oblique camera based on the Mustang IA fitment, allowing cameras facing to either side or the dual cameras, plus the vertical camera installation.

In the latter half of 1944, a limited number of Mustang IIs were further modified with the addition of "back to back" oblique installations for F.24 cameras in the lower rear fuselage down near the rear edge of the wing root above the radiator outlet – a similar location was used on the USAAF's F-6 aircraft. This produced a five-camera "rig," where the cameras could be set up to provide a 180-degree horizon to horizon coverage during a low-level reconnaissance run. This was principally employed when obtaining coverage of "linear" targets such as the immediate front line, major roads, canals, and rivers. This specific camera "rig" was used to secure coverage of both banks of the Rhine and other major rivers where "forced crossings" were planned. This entailed the aircraft flying at just above ground level along specific sections of the river, obtaining coverage of both banks and the river itself. Photographs from these sorties were used to plan the river assaults, and they allowed engineers to estimate the scalability of the river banks on both sides when it came to getting troops and amphibious vehicles into and out of the water.

One peculiarity of the Mustang II with the oblique camera mount arose as a result of the fitting of the Malcolm Hood to most of the aircraft in RAF service. Problems occurred if the length of the camera lens required for a specific sortie was a longer one that protruded beyond the cut-out in the Plexiglas quarter window behind the cockpit. The Malcolm Hood could only slide over the Plexiglas quarter windows if there were no obstructions extending out of the latter. If a protruding camera lens was in the way, the hood could not be opened or closed. As a result, when a long camera lens was required, the pilot would enter the cockpit and be strapped in ready for flight. The Malcolm Hood would then be closed, after which the Photographic Section would install the camera and associated lens and fit the Plexiglas quarter panels. The pilot would then fly the sortie with the Malcolm Hood fully closed throughout. On landing after the sortie, the pilot could not open the Malcolm Hood and exit the cockpit until the Photographic Section had removed the camera and lens.

Mustang IA AM190, A&AEE Boscombe Down, Wiltshire, 1943.
(Artwork by Jim Laurier, © Osprey Publishing)

Armament[90]

As the first of the Mustang Is were being received by RAF squadrons in mid 1942, the A&AEE at Boscombe Down was tabling its results following gunnery trials with the aircraft's armament. Trials had been conducted using early Mustang Is AG351 and AG359. Flights with the former were conducted from December 1941 through to late January 1942, with AG359 flown from February 1942 through to May 1942. The trials tested the armament as supplied by NAA and included as a part of the purchase package. The weaponry consisted of two nose-mounted 0.50cal Browning machine guns synchronized to fire through the propeller and four wing-mounted 0.30cal Brownings and two 0.50cal Brownings firing outside the propeller arc.

NA-83 AM190 was the Mustang I used as the prototype for the installation of Hispano II 20mm cannon as subsequently seen in the P-51-NA and Mustang IA. AM190 later served with No. 239 Sqn until it failed to return from an armed reconnaissance mission to Ypres, in Belgium, on July 22, 1943. *(Andrew Thomas Collection)*

The tests, which included all aspects of the aircraft armament, examined gun mounts, feed mechanisms, expended case and link arrangements, gunsights, armament servicing, and nose gun synchronizing gear. Conducted in a program of

ground firing and air firing tests, the trials revealed several issues with the armament and resulted in a long list of suggested modifications to make the weaponry fitted to the Mustang I more suitable for RAF operational use. The tests also prompted the creation of a list of recommendations in terms of maintenance and support of the installed armament, as well as changes to the aiming reticule glass fitted to the supplied gunsight.

Among the key issues revealed by the testing were inadequacies in the strength of the wing gun mounts, where, in one instance during a sustained burst during ground firing trials, a wing-mounted 0.50cal Browning broke free from its mount and caused damage to the wing. As a result, changes in the wing mounts and locking mechanisms to retain the armament in the wings were devised and recommended for implementation.

Another area of concern was faulty empty case and link ejection chutes. As supplied by NAA, these were largely of rubber construction, with some sheet metal brackets and retainers. During firing trials these caused stoppages due to ejected cases or links damaging chutes, which flexed during firing, or ejected cases becoming lodged in the chutes, blocking the empty case and link ejection paths. Additionally, the chutes deteriorated quickly due to the oil used in servicing the armament and the propellant residue chemically degrading the rubber. The effects of heat and cold fluctuations also took their toll on the chutes. The A&AEE designed and tested new empty case and link ejection chutes of a slightly different design – taking account of potential "choke points" in the chutes – made from thin sheet metal. Further testing revealed a significantly lower rate of stoppages as a result of empty case and link ejection using the A&AEE-designed chutes, and after some final refinement of the design these were recommended as a required modification for all RAF Mustang Is.

In all, more than 20 modifications were proposed, with information fed back to NAA's representatives in Britain for passing on to company HQ for their consideration for incorporation into later production batches of the aircraft.

The RAF also encountered initial problems with the gun synchronizing gear for the nose-mounted 0.50cal Brownings in the Mustang I. However, these issues were solved by improving the robustness of the electrical wiring and preventing ingress of moisture into the firing circuits, combined with a defined regime for the regular inspection and maintenance of the mechanical components of the gun synchronizer gear.

A key point to note here is that the RAF also retained the "as supplied" 0.30cal Brownings that used the standard US 0.30cal 30-06 round. This was both a different design round and machine gun compared to the standard RAF 0.303in. round chambered in the RAF version of the Browning machine gun. The RAF considered that the effort required to make the change from the US-supplied 0.30cal guns to the British-built 0.303in. weapons was not justifiable, as it would not only entail replacement of the guns, but also associated ancillary items such as ammunition feeds and empty case and link ejection chutes to take account of the differences in ammunition.

Following delivery of the Mustang IA, the testing and evaluation process for the sub-type was the same as has been applied to the Mustang I in that examples were sent to the A&AEE for armament trials of its four 20mm Hispano cannon. Initial tests had been conducted at NAA in November–December 1942 with Mustang IA prototype AM190, which was fitted with what was considered by the RAF to be a prototypical armament installation for the sub-type, but differing in a number of detailed ways from the finalized armament installation in the full production aircraft. As supplied for testing, AM190 was fitted with US-manufactured AN/M2 20mm cannon built by Oldsmobile and based on a Hispano design and specifications that had been modified to suit US manufacturing processes and design tolerances.

The trials with AM190 took the form of a series of ground and air firing tests. These revealed areas of weakness in the armament installation, including both the mounts in the wings and the empty case and link ejection chutes. The weakness of the armament installation revealed itself in flexing when the weapons were fired, allowing the cannon to move around to the point where they broke retaining brackets on the mounts and feeds. Other problems manifested themselves with lightly struck caps, varying lengths of recoil, irregularity in the firing rates, and eventually stoppages through cases jamming in ammunition feeds, breeches, or at the point of ejection of the empty case to the ejection chute.

Similar to the issues with the empty case and link ejection chutes encountered on the Mustang I, the A&AEE identified that the empty case and link ejection chutes for the 20mm cannon installation were understrength, subject to flexing and movement, and contained "choke points" where ejected cases could jam or even rebound within the chutes. The A&AEE designed new chutes using thin sheet metal, which, during subsequent tests, proved significantly more reliable than the NAA-designed items.

The A&AEE also found that the armament installation in AM190 was unsatisfactory in many aspects, but primarily that the mounting was of faulty design to the point where, under operational use, it would fail. This not only had a negative impact on the reliability of the armament, it could also cause structural damage to be inflicted on the wing.

A further trial was conducted using production aircraft FD446 during the period December 1942 to February 1943. Testing conducted by the A&AEE was similar to that undertaken with AM190, and it was soon suspended due to the front mounting tubes on all four wing-mounted cannon failing during testing. Following the issues with the US-manufactured 20mm cannon, the weapons were replaced by British-built Hispano Mk II 20mm weapons and associated feed mechanisms. The Hispano gun was a known, reliable cannon already in widespread use with the RAF, and its employment removed one set of variables that could have had a negative impact on subsequent trials during certain parts of the test program.

After modifications had been made to the armament installation, including significant "beefing up" of the cannon mounts, with a particular focus on the front mounting tubes, further testing was conducted. In conjunction with this testing, modified ammunition feeds and empty case and link ejection chute arrangements were also trialed. To add even further variety to the trials, a pair of US-manufactured AN/M2 20mm cannon was installed in one wing and British-manufactured Hispano Mk II 20mm cannon in the other.

These trials showed greater reliability, with the new mounts being able to support sustained firing without any problem. From these trials a set of recommended modifications were put forward to be implemented in all operational RAF Mustang IA aircraft. It was recommended that the US-manufactured cannon not be installed in the Mustang IA, and that they be replaced by the more reliable, and more widely supported in RAF service, Hispano Mk II 20mm cannon. One external visual clue to this change in armament and mount was the lack of external recoil springs forward of the wing cannon fairings on Mustang IAs fitted with the revised mounts and Hispano Mk II 20mm cannon.

More armament trials, using FD446, were conducted in April 1943 utilizing the Hispano Mk II 20mm cannon in all positions and all the recommended modifications from the earlier tests, in conjunction with further refined wing mounting tubes. Attention was also paid to the reliability of the US-manufactured ammunition feeds, which were closely watched for any signs of early wear on key components. These tests proved the reliability to the required operational level of the British-built Hispano Mk II 20mm cannon, the new mounts, and US-manufactured ammunition feeds. These trials also included a program of testing under all aspects of aircraft operation, including combat maneuvers and extremes of heat and cold from sustained firing and operation at altitude.

A further series of tests were conducted in late May to mid-June 1943 utilizing FD438, which trialed all available types of British-manufactured 20mm cannon ammunition for use with the installed armament incorporating all the recommended A&AEE modifications in what would represent the "operational" modification status for RAF Mustang IAs. These tests were highly successful, with no stoppages due to cannon or feed problems being recorded in an extensive firing program, and only two stoppages in total being experienced – one through electrical firing circuit failure and the other caused by a projectile/ammunition failure. During service with the RAF, the Hispano Mk II 20mm cannon used by the Mustang IA was eventually replaced by the Hispano Mk V, which was an improved sub-variant of the type.

Early operational use of the Mustang IA still provided a few issues with the 20mm cannon armament, but significantly less than anticipated with the incorporation of the A&AEE modifications. One area of concern was the US-manufactured 20mm cannon ammunition that was being used as initial supply with the Mustang IA. Examination of the ammunition revealed a number of problems, including poorly seated primer cups, poorly seated rounds in cases, bulged or swollen cases, and a high percentage of primer cup failures, even when subjected to a heavy firing pin strike. As a result, it was recommended that all US-manufactured ammunition be subject to a process of examination and physical measuring before employment. Ultimately, the RAF decided to only use British-manufactured ammunition to ensure minimal issues for operational units.

As a result, the US-manufactured AN/M2 20mm cannon and associated ammunition were passed onto the RAF Regiment, which fitted them into ground mounts for anti-aircraft use. This meant that any jams or issues could be hand-cleared by the battery gunners – something that could not be done in an aircraft installation.[91]

SUMMARY – 1942

During the significant political in-fighting between HQ-AAF and Materiel Command, the very fine NA-73 and NA-83 Mustang Is were recognized by the grass-roots USAAF and NACA test pilot community as the best "US Fighter nobody knew about from sea level to 20,000ft."

NAA became so disenchanted with its sister GMC company Allison that it first complained to the GMC Board, then quietly looked for better options, finally reaching out to Rolls-Royce in mid-1941 to discover that the new Packard Merlin 28 was a very strong contender with relatively minimal conversion issues. The Board rejected NAA's initiative, but the company continued to explore other engine possibilities in 1942, culminating in the Merlin 61 for the XP-78.

The "inner sanctum" of HQ-AAF recognized that the USAAF was still subordinate to the US Army. The major question of the role for Army Observation and Air-Ground Support, particularly in the context of Wehrmacht and Luftwaffe success on the battlefield, led the Air War Plans leaders to seek solutions that the USAAF-MC was not very well focused on.

The USAAF's aircraft procurement system and processes had already consumed FY 42 development funding for fighters in a series of abortive Pursuit Circular Proposals that left potential funding for the Mustang narrowly pigeon-holed, but NAA was aware of the funding issues. Speculatively, the company was probably also aware of the War Plans Doctrine development for Air-Ground Support, and took the gamble to invest in an attack pursuit in late 1941. The research and development specification created by NAA modified the existing high-performance low- to medium-altitude NA-73/83 fighter so that it was able to carry bombs or external fuel tanks interchangeably, and to have heavy firepower for CAS missions. The proposed design for the aircraft, known as the A-36 from April 1942, began in November 1941.

For whatever reason, not only Arnold, but Spaatz and Eaker took serious interest in the Mustang, even though it was "not an 'American' design." They all recognized its high-altitude performance limitations but, equally, they all appreciated the superior aerodynamics and performance attributes of the Allison Mustang. Unquestionably, Arnold played a role in the background after his return from London meetings with senior RAF leaders and Churchill, as well as Ambassador Winant and Lt Col Hitchcock, to nudge the Mustang along into the USAAF inventory in May.

The possibility of an existing fighter with great potential for the long-sought single-engined escort that was believed "impossible – technically" by most USAAF planners now seemed an intriguing question rather than another dead end. As 1942 drew to a close, the successful and highly acclaimed test results for both the Rolls-Royce converted Mustangs and the NAA XP-51B yielded great hopes for the aircraft's future role in the USAAF just as trouble brewed on the horizon for the well-articulated, and believed, mantra "The Bomber Will Always Get Through." That said, it would take seven more months before a substantial push by both the Eighth Air Force and HQ-AAF saw the P-51B deployed into the ETO ahead of all other theaters.

The convergence of the Rolls-Royce partnership with the Packard Motor Company, resulting in a successful conversion of the Merlin XX as the Packard Merlin 1650-1, established Packard as a reliable supplier and design partner. The introduction of the Merlin 60 series two-stage/two-speed supercharged engine in 1941 was transformational for achieving high-altitude engine performance without the turbo-supercharger auxiliary required for low-altitude engines. The active design conversion of the Merlin 61 to the Packard 1650-3 came at the precise time that the RAF discovered the major increase in performance of the converted Spitfire IX over the Spitfire VB, giving it an edge over the excellent Fw 190. The happy circumstance of Rolls-Royce's primary test pilot flying the Mustang I at the very time the Merlin 61/65 engines were entering production, and his very positive impression of the sleek but underpowered NAA fighter, could not have happened at any earlier time to accelerate the development of the Merlin Mustang.

The Eighth Air Force's initial operations in the ETO were all relatively short-range missions designed to build processes and leadership within VIII Bomber Command. The HQ-AAF dealt Eaker a severe blow when all existing P-38-equipped fighter groups were reassigned to Operation *Torch* in North Africa. Only the Spitfire-equipped 4th FG and pilots and ground staff of the 78th FG remained in VIII Fighter Command by the end of 1942. Even with the arrival of the 56th FG in early 1943, and its subsequent re-equipping with the P-47C (a type also issued to the 78th FG), the Eighth Air Force was left with only the short-range Spitfire for escort missions until April 1943.

In the fall of 1942 VIII Bomber Command struggled to initiate US-trained, but poorly prepared, B-17 crews into the ETO combat operations processes necessary to shape the Eighth Air Force into an effective weapon of war. Following initial raids, it soon became apparent that the bombing results were largely abysmal. This was traced to three factors, namely: (1) poor navigation to the target, (2) poor recognition of target features required to select and control the Aiming Point during the bomb run, and (3) poor formations/evasive action taken by the pilot during the bomb run to avoid anti-aircraft fire.

Col LeMay proposed and implemented changes, including parceling out target "sectors" and then packaging reconnaissance photos and navigation data into Sector folders to enable a core of navigators and bombardiers to become very familiar with the targets. He then tasked several navigator and bombardiers in each squadron to become experts on that specific target Sector. When a mission was selected to one of those targets, a crew with target familiarity based on intense prior study (instead of a

Albert Speer, Minister for War Production, masterfully distributed German industry to survive increasingly crippling attacks by USAAF and RAF heavy bombers. He is seen here in 1944 with Generalfeldmarschall Erhard Milch, whom Speer worked closely with to coordinate the dispersal and prioritization of Luftwaffe aircraft production. (*Tony Holmes Collection*)

cursory introduction of the target to all bombardiers at the briefing on the morning of the mission) would lead the operation. The crews were also ordered to fly a precise, "straight and level" bomb run to enable optimal target bomb drop data to be fed to the Norden bombsight. Shortly afterwards, a request was sent to Boeing through Eighth Air Force Air Technical Services for the creation of automatic flight equipment (AFE) to slave the B-17 to the bombsight controlled by the bombardier during the bomb run.[92]

When the AFE was installed, the pilot could not easily remove its autopilot function from the bombardier's control. During this period, the frontal attack was also identified as a prime cause of bomber losses. Along with the requirement for AFE, a mechanical gun turret was requested for more frontal defensive firepower, with a production capability to mirror the rumored YB-40 (Douglas-modified B-17) convoy escort due in several months.

Once introduced, these changes worked immediately, with the 305th BG becoming the lead group in the Eighth Air Force in terms of bombing results. It took several months to inculcate other bomb groups into the methods used by the 305th and develop what became known as lead crews, but by May 1943 all of the units in VIII Bomber Command had started to employ the lead crew concept, including newly arrived groups.

The Luftwaffe's reactions to the introduction of the Eighth Air Force into combat operations were mixed. Combat fighter leaders such as Mayer and Galland realized the B-17s and B-24s had formidable defensive firepower and were difficult to bring down. Aircraft industry leaders like Generalfeldmarschall Erhard Milch, the Luftwaffe Chief of Armaments, were alarmed, and began to seek a greater mix in fighter production for the future defense of the Reich. The industrial leader Albert Speer, Minister for War Production, recognized the potential threat that the Eighth Air Force posed to German industry. When ordered by Göring in 1941, and then Hitler in 1942, to increase fighter production, Milch began consolidation of the aircraft industry into large complexes to simplify construction by achieving economies of scale. This did indeed increase aircraft production through improved efficiency, but conversely made the closely grouped aircraft and engine assembly plants more vulnerable to successful large-scale attacks from the air. Speer, with the greater authority and focus on the entire industrial base, realized that industries such as those producing ball bearings and hydrocarbon were equally threatened.[93]

MUSTANG RIVAL NOTES – 1942

On January 15, 1942 the USAAF ordered 1,050 P-47Ds from Evansville and 354 P-47Gs from Curtiss-Buffalo.[94] These actions pointed to a further decline of the Curtiss Aeroplane Company as a prime contractor, and indicated the very high priority that the USAAF-MD placed on both the P-47 and P-38.

At that moment the US was at war, and the primary USAAF aircraft development plans were for bombardment aircraft tasked with "daylight strategic bombing of industrial assets to destroy the enemy's capability to wage war." The allocations of modern aircraft to the other attack support functions of the USAAF were being slowly grown for attack and medium bombers. The purchase of the A-36 was important to NAA, and it was very useful when deployed to North Africa and India, but production was not continued, demonstrating that the fast attack fighter was preferred by the Air-Ground Support division. Parallel developments under Materiel Command of twin-engined escort fighters were failing.

Additionally, the demands of the British, Soviets, and Chinese were more than industry could support, as it still had to satisfy the growth demands for both USAAF and US Navy aviation set forth by President Roosevelt. Equally noteworthy is the fact that the only two USAAF fighters in serial production with demonstrable performance above 20,000ft were turbo-supercharged – the P-38D/E and the P-47B. Only the Lightning possessed the attributes of external wing racks for ferry fuel tanks and a fuel supply system to enable fuel tanks to extend range to any significant degree. Fortunately for the Mustang story, the range of the Mustang I and P-51/A-36 with internal fuel only was superior to that of the P-38.

In late February the pressurized Bf 109G-1, equipped with GM-1 boost for better high-altitude performance, began reaching Luftwaffe reconnaissance and fighter units. Kits for underwing gondolas with a single 20mm cannon for each wing were provided for the fighter units.[95]

On March 1 Lockheed delivered the first P-38F, and that month the company concluded testing of external racks, pylons, and internal plumbing for 165gal and 310gal ferry tanks on a P-38E at Burbank, then released the kits for installation on all E-model Lightnings in the field. The modifications were incorporated in the P-38F, along with combat maneuverability settings for the Fowler flaps. The first P-38F-15 was delivered later, with external wing racks and maneuver flaps fitted during production.[96] The USAAF also accepted the first P-47B from production on March 1, the aircraft having fabric elevator and rudder coverings that would prove problematic during dive tests.[97]

On March 28 Gen Bennett Myers, Chief, Fighter Procurement, Materiel Division, proposed that the P-38E be modified to carry 175gal tanks, and that the P-47 carry two 100gal and one 410gal external tanks to increase ferry range to 3,000 miles.[98] It is important to note that although the P-38E/F could already carry two 310gal ferry tanks when this request was made by Myers, the P-47D-15, delivered to the Eighth Air Force in January 1944, was the first production version of the Thunderbolt capable of having wing pylons and plumbing from external fuel tanks to the engine installed. The Myers directive was the first official release of sanctions that generally prohibited USAAF aircraft from carrying

Reichsmarschall Hermann Göring, Supreme Commander of the Luftwaffe, is briefed by Generaloberst Hans Jeschonnek, Luftwaffe Chief of the General Staff. The latter committed suicide on August 18, 1943 following a violent haranguing from Hitler in the aftermath of RAF Bomber Command's devastating attack on Peenemünde. *(Donald Caldwell Collection)*

ABOVE The Bf 109G-1 was the first example of the Messerschmitt fighter to be fitted with a GM-1 Nitrous Oxide system to improve high-altitude performance, as well as externally mounted MG 151 20mm cannon in pods for increased effectiveness against USAAF heavy bombers. This particular G-1/R2 from II./JG 1 is fitted with tubes (for 152kg WGr. 21cm mortar shells) rather than underwing cannon, however. (*Tony Holmes Collection*)

ABOVE RIGHT Flying an Fw 190A-4 devoid of unit markings, the pilot looks up at the photographer while flying over farmland in 1943. The A-4 was a formidable foe to the Eighth Air Force thanks to its very heavy firepower and maneuverability. (*Tony Holmes Collection*)

external fuel tanks. It did not grant the authority to provide them for combat operations, but did initiate design requests from Materiel Division to provide leak-proof combat tanks.

Milch, who had replaced Udet, submitted a plan for concentrations of industrial networks to produce aircraft types. After much political maneuvering between Göring and Hitler, the latter finally approved the plan in July 1943, leading to much higher production efficiencies.[99] When first apprised of the plan, Generaloberst Hans Jeschonnek, Luftwaffe Chief of the General Staff, remarked to Milch, "I would not know what to do with more than 360 fighters per month."[100]

On May 30 the operational debut of the P-47B was deferred to permit the retrofitting of metal elevator kits.[101]

On May 31 the Bf 109G-2 was introduced to Luftwaffe fighter units. It was an unpressurized G-1 that began to replace the Fw 190A-4 for high-altitude interception.[102]

P-47B 41-5938 was modified with a proprietary manufacturer's low-drag/laminar-flow wing, being completed after wing modifications as a P-47B without a reinforced empennage in July 1942. Early tests revealed no advantage over the standard S-3 airfoil.[103] It crashed while being tested near Langley Field on October 11, 1943.

On July 31 the Fw 190A-4 was introduced to operational units.[104]

On September 30 the Bf 109G-4 with the R3 300-liter external centerline fuel tank modification began replacing the Fw 190A-4 for high-altitude actions.[105] By this date the two *Jagdgeschwaderen* on the Kanalfront, JGs 2 and 26, were largely equipped with the Fw 190A-3/4.

During September and early October, the first production P-47C-1-REs were accepted by the USAAF. The C-1 was the first Thunderbolt modified to accept the 8in. fuselage extension to incorporate the Quick Engine Change feature. Shortly afterwards, a bob weight was added to the elevator control system. In mid-September the first P-47C-2-REs were also delivered, these aircraft having the first provision for attachment of a centerline 200gal ferry tank. They duly became the first of the P-47 series to be sent to the ETO. The XP-47F, a P-47B incorporating a modified S-3 airfoil with laminar-flow characteristics, was completed in August and sent to

The centerline fuel tank modification improved the interception range and endurance of both the Bf 109G and the Fw 190A. "White 17", seen here, is a Bf 109G-6 of 9./JG 26 flown from Lille-Nord in early 1944 by 19-victory ace Hauptmann Hans-Georg Dippel. (*EN Archive*)

Wright Field on September 17. The first P-47D-1 was test-flown at Evansville two days later, and three C-1s were flown to Eglin Field for joint Tactical Suitability Trials with the P-51, P-38F, P-39D, P-40F, and A6M Zero-sen. The C-1, C-5, and future production D-1s left the factory without the bulged keel and B-7 shackles for bombs and fuel tanks.[106]

On December 27 nitrous oxide (GM-1) was introduced to boost the power of the DB 605 engine for the Bf 109G-4.[107] Two days later the Bf 109G-6 with MW-50 methanol-water injection also became available. Two 13mm MG 131 guns replaced the MG 17s, giving the new Bf 109 a three-cannon capability.[108] Compared with the bomber-destroying firepower of the Fw 190, the fighter was still regarded as deficient in its ability to shoot down the B-17. Soon afterwards, the Bf 109G-6/R6, with 20mm gondola kits for the wings, was introduced to increase the firepower to three 20mm cannon plus two 13mm cannon.

On December 31 deliveries of Fw 190A-5s began, peaking in April 1943.[109]

At the end of 1942 the Luftwaffe's day fighter operational strength aligned to protect occupied airspace across the Channel comprised JGs 2 and 26 in *Luftflotte* 3, plus JG 1 in *Luftwaffen-Befehlshaber Mitte* (*LwBfhMitte*), for a total of 442 single-engined fighters (333 operational). Most were Fw 190A-3/4s, plus two *Staffeln* of Bf 109G-1s.[110]

Increasing pressure to range more firepower against tight Eighth Air Force B-17 and B-24 formations caused the introduction of heavier weaponry for Bf 109s and Fw 190s. A large number of Bf 109G-6s were fitted with underwing MG 151 20mm cannon in pods, including this example from 5./JG 2. It was lost in action on October 20, 1943. (*Tony Holmes Collection*)

CHAPTER 5

THE LONG-HOPED-FOR SINGLE-ENGINED ESCORT FIGHTER

CHRONOLOGY FOR NAA/HQ-AAF AND HUCKNALL FROM JANUARY THROUGH JULY 1943

The testing of XP-51B No. 1 restarted after the changes to the orientation of the Harrison radiator and the introduction of the Keg Liner to protect the inner cooling tubes from chemical reactions. The first of the tests, between January 8 and 14, revealed that temperature issues had been eliminated, but a new phenomenon that Chilton labeled "rumble" emerged in high-speed dives. Experiments had been carried out at NAA to vary the scoop inlet and exit areas in line with information from the British tests at Hucknall and Boscombe Down on the Mustang X configurations. However, the differences in location of the aftercooler radiator beneath the Mustang X engine, in contrast to NAA's continued housing of the radiator, intercooler, and oil cooler in the same location under the wing, reduced the value of those information exchanges.

This front view of P-51A 43-6007 shows the experimental radiator intake scoop geometry for the NA-99. This same design, without the conformal radius in the upper intake scoop, was further modified and incorporated into the XP-51B prior to the Ames wind tunnel testing. (© *The Boeing Company*)

The new Harrison radiator was originally installed on its side to fit better into the original space permitted by the P-51-NA airframe before the wing was lowered for the production P-51B. Prior the first flight of XP-51B No. 1, multiple changes had also been made to the inlet scoop geometry, including lowering the upper lip to create a slightly larger gutter than that in the P-51A's scoop geometry – a modification credited by Horkey to Irving Ashkenas. Additionally, the A-36/P-51A's scoop upper lip, conformal to the lower surface of the wing and including provision for the wing attachment bolt fairing, had been changed to a shallow "V." Significant tests were made with the quarter-scale model in the NAA wind tunnel, including pressure and flow measurements. No vibration or excessive noise had been discovered until the radiator was reoriented to place the aftercooler matrix on top and the engine coolant radiator below the aftercooler below it to conserve space.

Chilton flew this modified XP-51B 41-37352 from January 9 to 14, following detailed flight plans to explore coolant temperatures and internal duct/plenum pressures for climb in both low and high blower. In the interest of understanding differences in behavior between the Packard Merlin 1650-3 and the 1650-1

RIGHT Front view of Harrison radiator with aftercooler on left side facing aft. (© *Rolls-Royce*)

FAR RIGHT Bottom of the cowling looking up towards the oil cooler and its bypass duct. (© *The Boeing Company, sourced by Robert Gruenhagen Collection*)

BELOW AND BELOW RIGHT The Harrison radiator included both the engine coolant and aftercooling matrix to accommodate the significantly increased cooling requirements of the Packard Merlin 1650-3 engine. The first installation had the aftercooler (smaller-diameter hose) occupying the top portion of the engine cooling radiator. Shown is a view looking aft for the production installation. (© *The Boeing Company, sourced by Robert Gruenhagen Collection*)

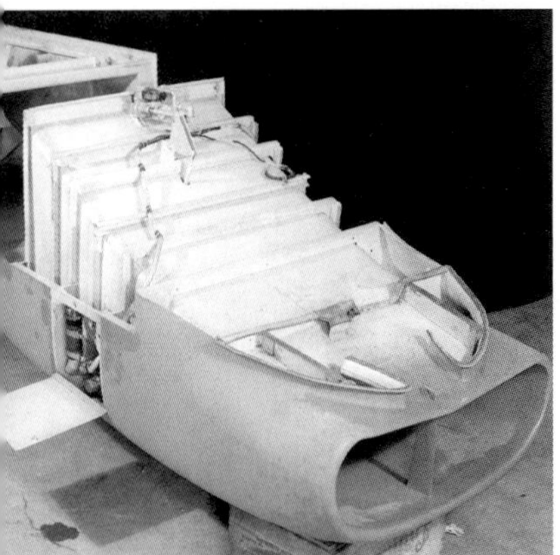

TOP LEFT The lower intake scoop underwent several changes before and during the tests at the Ames wind tunnel. Here is the XP-51B No. 2 with the original intake showing the "vertical" side view of the radiator scoop common to all previous Mustang types. This XP-51B had its 20mm cannon removed prior to making the road trip to the Ames wind tunnel to solve the duct "rumble effect" that plagued early Merlin Mustangs. (*© The Boeing Company*)

FAR LEFT The XP-51B was initially fitted with a modified P-51A/A-36 front radiator scoop. Changed from a radius center section to a "shallow V", it included a vertical splitter to improve boundary-layer control. Also visible are the structural ribs to reinforce the intake plenum to the radiator against failure at a flow rate of up to 800ft per second. (*Tony Holmes Collection*)

LEFT The original duct/plenum design to reduce flow velocity and bring even pressure distribution to the Harrison radiator was sub optimal. In fact, the intake flow still experienced a boundary-layer separation along the top surface, causing an uneven pressure distribution at the top of the radiator matrix. (*© The Boeing Company*)

single-speed/two-speed engine, Chilton also flew the 1650-1 powered P-40F on the 29th. The coolant heating issues for the aftercooler and radiator were solved, but suspicions regarding the "rumble" led to speculation that the forceful and episodic noises emanating from the radiator location might be due to boundary-layer separation of the inflow from the lower surface of the front cowl and wing into the intake plenum. The inflow plenum – top and bottom – was redesigned and improved to reduce boundary-layer separation, but was never entirely satisfactory in wartime Mustangs.

On February 1 the P-51A was ready to fly, but two extra days were spent fully testing instrumentation so as to ensure the best possible collection of flight test data. The P-51A-1-NA No. 1 43-6003 was flown for the first time on the 3rd.

On February 2 Lappin was notified from Hucknall that the fourth Mustang X conversion, AL963, had been modified with a dorsal fin fillet and was awaiting first flight at Duxford. In the same letter to Lappin, Legarra was referenced as noting that NAA also had a rudder trim installation prepared to reduce over-controlling the rudder. The modification was later known as Reverse Rudder Boost, and both modifications were introduced in the spring of 1944.[1] On the same day (2nd) a meeting was held at Hucknall to discuss recent experiences regarding directional instabilities and the main landing gear doors opening in dive tests.

NEXT PAGES Completed P-51A-1-NA 43-6007 (No. 5) emerged from the Inglewood plant near the end of February 1943 – barely a week before completion of the first production NA-102 P-51B-1-NA. P-51A-1-NA 43-6003 No. 1 had commenced flight testing on February 2, 1943. For the next two months A-36s, P-51As and P-51Bs were on the production line simultaneously at Inglewood. (*© The Boeing Company*)

831
835
822
36007

5

Mustang X AL963, Duxford, Cambridgeshire, March 1943.
(Artwork by Jim Laurier, © Osprey Publishing)

TOP RIGHT AL963 was the fourth Mustang X conversion, and the first to feature a dorsal fin fillet to improve new yaw instability experienced following replacement of the Allison engine's three-blade propeller with the Merlin's four-blade unit. After significant testing, the NAA-designed dorsal fin fillet would emerge from engineering in late March 1944. *(© Rolls-Royce)*

RIGHT Mustang X AL963 subsequently had the dorsal fin fillet removed and its fin/rudder enlarged by increasing the chord. During the flight trials that ensued it was found that the greater-chord fin was better for reducing yaw oscillation effects. However, it adversely diminished roll rates, so the dorsal fin fillet was the preferred solution. *(© The Boeing Company)*

The fitment of a dorsal fin fillet to increase effective fin area and modifying the fin by increasing its chord, which also increased effective fin/rudder area, were tried. When tested on AL963, the dorsal fin fillet proved the better solution. The greater-chord fin was better for diminishing yaw oscillation effects, but adversely affected roll rates. Despite early discovery of the trim issues due to adverse yaw tendencies, and the partial solution of adding the dorsal fin fillet, NAA did not finally develop and produce such kits for the P-51B/C and D until April 1944. Both the dorsal fin fillet and reverse rudder boost tab kits were released in April 1944 for the P-51B/Cs and P-51D-5-NAs that had already left the factories. The dorsal fin fillet was introduced on production Mustangs in July 1944, both for the P-51C-10-NT (No. 1 of NA-111 block) and P-51D-5-NA (No. 650 of N-109 block).

Included in the deliberations during the early February NAA/Rolls-Royce meeting was a commitment from the engine manufacturer to supply the "USAAF with 100,000 of the RC5/2 spark plugs," with the expectation that the British plugs would serve through 18lb (67in.) of boost. American suppliers would pick up the balance required in future.[2]

On February 10 NAA's Head of Engineering Loft Mathematics, Roy Liming, released the "Master Dimensions Book, P-51D." This document, and the associated Master Lines, established the configuration of the fuselages of the P-51B and P-51D and the six-gun P-51D wing. Although the actual P-51D Master Lines with bubble canopy were not finalized until April 2, much work had been accomplished on the "Enclosure – Sliding, Bubble" canopy in January 1943.[3]

While performing dive tests on February 14, Chilton encountered a second instance of loud noise/"rumble" in the radiator/intercooler duct below the cockpit. Other test pilots who flew the XP-51B reported the same phenomenon to Horkey, who continued to receive the information with some skepticism.

On February 15 Maj Gen Barney Giles, Chief, Air Staff, and Col William E. Kepner (future CO of VIII Fighter Command) directed that teams at NAA, Lockheed, and Republic study solutions to create added fuel capacity for both the wings and fuselage of the P-38, P-47, and P-51.

On February 20 the Merlin 61 sent by Rolls-Royce to Wright Field for bench tests was transported to NAA so that the company could consider differences in installation between the 1650-3 and the Merlin 61 for all Mustang airframes that were contemplated for final assembly in Britain, should the manufacturing arrangements be deemed feasible.

On February 24 two related actions were initiated to drive the development of external combat tanks pressurized for high altitude. First, Gen Chidlaw, Assistant Chief, Air Staff, Materiel Division, queried the Materiel Center regarding the status of the self-sealing combat tanks. Second, he requested that provision for external leak-proof combat tanks be a design requirement for current fighters.[4] Combined, these directives from HQ-AAF and the Materiel Command reversed pre-World War II USAAC restrictions prohibiting the attachment of external fuel tanks to combat aircraft. Across the Atlantic only short-range Spitfires were providing fighter cover for bombers as far as mid-France, at which point they had to break off their escort prematurely due to a lack of fuel. The longer-range P-47C-2 would not be operational for

XP-51B 41-37421 had its outer wing sections removed so as to allow it to fit into the Ames wind tunnel during NAA's investigation into the Merlin Mustang's duct rumble. Note the original intake scoop used by the XP-51B. (© *The Boeing Company*)

ABOVE XP-51B 41-37352 (the first US-based Mustang to fly powered by a Merlin) with 20mm cannon and the new production B-model intake scoop, featuring an angled radiator scoop entry and increased gutter. It was photographed at Mines Field just prior to being delivered to Air Training Command. (© *The Boeing Company*)

RIGHT Side profile of XP-51B 41-37421 after its return to Mines Field from the Ames wind tunnel, the aircraft having had its outer wing section returned and 20mm cannon re-installed. The angled intake scoop entry and increased gutter can also be clearly seen. (© *The Boeing Company*)

another two months. The situations in the China/Burma/India (CBI) and South West Pacific theaters were equally dire, given the extremely long ranges required to escort bombers in the war against Japan.

The highlights at NAA for the remainder of February through early March included the round-the-clock efforts of Ed Horkey and Irving Ashkenas to understand and solve the "rumble" and loud "banging/vibration" noises emanating from below the cockpit when Chilton put the XP-51B through high-speed runs and dive tests. From late February into early March, changes derived from the wind tunnel tests were applied, with no appreciable benefits. As late as March 2, reports to Hucknall and the USAAF revealed progress but no final solution.[5]

Chilton flew XP-51B No 2 41-37421 on March 9 and 11. After the latter test flight NAA dismantled the aircraft and shipped it without the propeller to NACA's Moffet Field full-scale Ames wind tunnel. The Mustang was accompanied by Horkey and Ashkenas, as well as Julius Villepegue from Schmued's design team, plus two very skilled sheet-metal craftsmen, with the intention of making, installing, and testing changes on site at Ames. During the first series of NACA-Ames wind tunnel tests of the actual XP-51B airframe, Horkey, who was in the cockpit as an observer, experienced first-hand the loud noises during the high-speed runs. He said they were "scaring the hell out of him." The root cause determined by NACA was "the resonant vibration of the coolant radiator at high speed, evidently caused by pulsation of the flow through the duct."[6]

Simply stated, the issue was further traced to the effect of boundary-layer separation beginning under the lower cowl and extending further under the wing around the upper scoop. It was then further exacerbated by extreme turbulence in the plenum.

During the initial investigations Horkey and Ashkenas directed changes to the scoop geometry. They modified the lower inlet duct geometry to the oil cooler and the oil cooler exit scoop to improve bypass air below the oil cooler. These improvements were achieved by dividing the intake plenum by extending the upper oil cooler plenum surface all the way to the front scoop. The first attempt at lowering the upper scoop lip further from the wing to create a boundary-layer bypass gutter between the wing and scoop further improved the situation, but did not completely solve the problem. Additionally, changes to increase and decrease the area of the radiator rear scoop were tried. Several configuration changes solved the "rumble/vibration" phenomenon, but resulted either in too much drag or too little cooling efficiencies in

BELOW LEFT A NAA factory worker prepares to install a P-51B/D oil cooler into a partially assembled scoop housing. (© *The Boeing Company*)

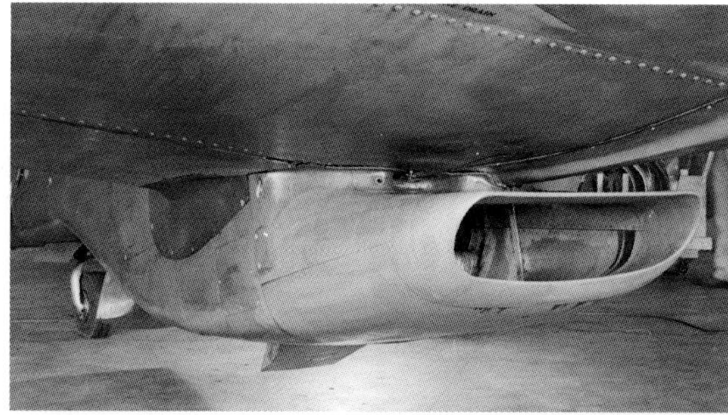

BELOW Close-up of the NA-102 P-51B-1-NA production front scoop. Note that all flow vanes save the vertical reinforcement strut have been removed. (© *The Boeing Company*)

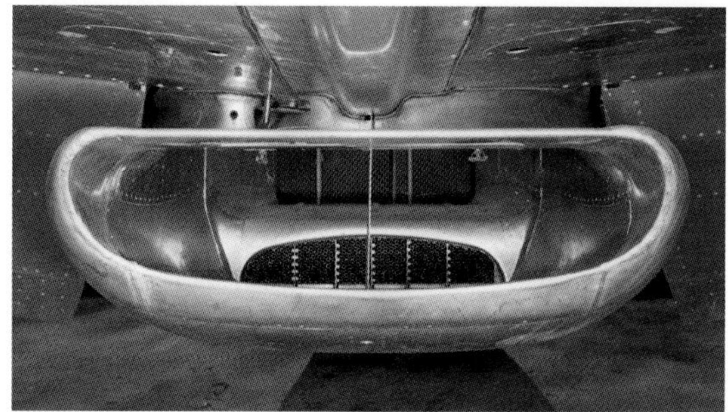

BOTTOM Front-on view of the production P-51B/C/D/K front scoop, showing the upper oil cooler face in the foreground and radiator face in the background. (© *The Boeing Company*)

climb configuration. Refer to the NACA summary tables showing changes and tabulating results in Appendix A, Section IV.

By that time most of the XP-51B flight-test program, apart from resolving the scoop/radiator-duct noise issue, had been completed. The most distinctive feature of the NACA geometrics presented in the wind tunnel scoop illustrations was the elimination of a divided plenum forward of the oil cooler, as shown in the frontal view of the production P-51B-1-NA. Although the first P-51B-1-NA was completed (awaiting its engine) with a "square/V-silhouette" intake scoop similar to that fitted to the P-51A, it was retrofitted with the final design version in May, ready to begin flight tests.

On March 22 the USAAF Dive Bomber Evaluation Board issued a final report of the "Proceedings of a Board of Officers for the Purpose of Evaluating Current Dive Bombers Now in Production." The Board had convened earlier at Wright Field to evaluate the A-24, A-25, and A-35 for suitability for the current USAAF air-support doctrine in active theaters. Materiel Command currently supported production continuation for all three, as well as issuing a large production order for the A-35. In summary, the Board's findings were as follows:

> Para. 3. The Board Finds as Follows:
>
> a. Considering the suitability of the three types (A-24, A-25 and A-35) in regard of flying characteristics, maintenance, and high speed, the types are listed in the following order of worth:
>
> (1.) A-25
>
> (2.) A-35
>
> (3.) A-24
>
> b. Suitability for active theaters:
>
> (1) The three types are not tactically suitable in an active theater. They are extremely vulnerable to hostile fighter action and need close fighter support at all times.
>
> (2) The high speed at low altitude is not sufficient to evade hostile fighters or limit the number of attacks by hostile fighters.
>
> (3) The accuracy of these types at the target will not be equal to that of the fighter-bomber type (A-36, P-51, P-39). Also, the fighter-bomber can better protect itself against hostile fighter action.
>
> (4) The low-altitude bomber types (A-26, A-20) are more accurate than the dive-bomber types against most targets.
>
> Para. 4. The Board Recommends:
>
> a. That the Commanding General, Army Air Forces, direct the Commanding General, Materiel Command, to cease procurement of dive-bomber types (A-24, A-25 and A-35) as soon as practicable.
>
> b. That all manufacturing facilities released be made available for increased production of light bombers (A-26, A-20) and fighter-bomber types (A-36, P-51, P-39).

P-51B-1-NA 43-12093 with production radiator intake scoop, Mines Field, California, May 1943. (*Artwork by Jim Laurier, © Osprey Publishing*)

The first P-51B-1-NA (43-12093) emerged from the Inglewood production line before XP-51B 41-37421 went to Ames. It is seen here in early April with the original XP-51B scoop, which was replaced before the aircraft was first taken aloft by Chilton on May 5, 1943. (© *The Boeing Company*)

c. That fighter-bomber types (A-36, P-51, P-39) be the types of aircraft used by dive-bomber groups contemplated in the present programs.

In the authors' opinion, this action by a Board constituted to critically examine Materiel Command procurement of unsuitable combat types was a major blow to Maj Gen Oliver P. Echols' prestige. Materiel Command's selection of the three attack types dismissed by the Board exemplified the disconnect between the former's view of mission requirements and those posed by both the Military Requirements and Plans Divisions. HQ-AAF was acutely aware of the successes demonstrated by the RAF's Desert Air Force against the Afrika Korps in North Africa. Second-line fighter aircraft such as the Tomahawk/Kittyhawk and Hurricane, modified with armament and bombing capability for the CAS role, were significant factors in the defeat of Rommel before American forces were engaged in-theater. Echols' continued advocacy

P-51B-1-NA 43-12093 is seen on the ramp at Mines Field in the summer of 1943, the aircraft having been fitted with a Curtiss Electric 10ft 6in no-cuff three-bladed propeller from a P-51A. Parked alongside it is brand new Mustang III FX863 painted in RAF Dark Earth and Dark Green camouflage. It also wears a mix of USAAF and RAF insignia. FX863 was one of the first Mustang IIIs shipped to the RAF for trials. 43-12093 served as a primary test vehicle for NAA. (© *The Boeing Company*)

of the poorly conceived General Motors XP-75 (too cumbersome and slow, and with notoriously dangerous flying characteristics) as a long-range escort fighter was perhaps the last straw that finally destroyed his prospects of a future leadership role in the post-war USAAF/USAF.

On March 31 the first production P-51B-1-NA airframe, 43-12093, was completed before any changes to the radiator inlet scoop arising from the wind tunnel experiments were finalized. It awaited delivery of a new 1650-3 engine for its first flight. Packard already had issues with meeting initial delivery schedules to NAA, largely compounded by the bench-test iterations at Wright Field in mid-to-late 1942. These problems were exacerbated on March 26 when 2,000 Packard employees staged a walk-out strike, followed by the entire plant on June 3. The strike ended five days later, but materially impacted 1650-3 production.

On or about March 31, flight-testing duties to evaluate fighter performance, maneuverability, and handling characteristics were assigned to Eglin Field. The most important fact about the separation of "can it fly?" and "what can it do?" was that Wright Field was not accelerating examination of the aircraft sent there, to evaluate

XP-51B 41-37352, Mines Field, California, May 1943.
(*Artwork by Jim Laurier, © Osprey Publishing*)

NAA experimented with a hidden (from side view) carburetor in the lower engine bay cowl midway back to the scoop in XP-51B 41-37421 prior to the aircraft going to Ames for wind tunnel testing. The flush lower cowl design was resurrected for the XP-51J in 1943, with the carburetor ducting originating internally above the radiator. (*© The Boeing Company*)

issues and recommend solutions quickly. Consequently, many problems affecting flight operations and the maintenance of "production" fighters were not discovered until the aircraft reached the combat theaters. Such issues were particularly noticeable with P-47C/Ds and P-38H/Js from mid-to-late 1943. To a degree this was also true for the P-51B-1s arriving in the ETO, as major unexpected operational issues surfaced upon the initiation of combat operations in December.

In April, after shop modifications based on feedback from Horkey and Ashkenas from tests of XP-51B No. 2 at Ames, final changes were made to the scoop inlet geometry that were then tested by Chilton on XP-51B No. 1 on April 8–10. The "rumble" issue was resolved.

Design NA-109 for the P-51D-5-NA was executed on April 13, 1943. The resulting aircraft was virtually identical to the P-51D and P-51D-1, save that many of the parts and subassemblies were NA-106 and new NA-109 designs, with fewer residual NA-102 and NA-104 parts. NA-109 was a natural point at which to introduce many improvements to the NA-102/104. Design NA-111 for the last block of 400 P-51C-10-NTs and the 600 P-51D-5-NTs was executed the next day.

A front view of the experimental mid-cowl carburetor intake. (© *The Boeing Company*)

The Australian contract for 100 P-51D kits plus one complete P-51D-5-NA was executed on April 23 and was followed on May 5 by the NA-111 extension for the P-51K-NT series with the Aeroproducts propeller.[7]

Between May 5 and 7, tests on the improved radiator/aftercooler efficiency and eliminated duct rumble noise were completed for P-51Bs Nos. 1 and 2. The issues with the intercooler (placed at the top third of the Harrison radiator) were not only traced to the early upper plenum shape, but also to the cooling vanes. The changes made to the cooling vanes, somewhat aligned with Hucknall experiences, resulted in satisfactory cooling for both high speeds with the rear scoop closed and taxi/high-power climb conditions with the rear scoop wide open. Various changes would be made over the next year to temperature sensing for scoop control and automatic/manual shutter controls aimed at keeping coolant temperature at 230°F. Some corrosion and quality control issues would also arise with the radiator/intercooler during early combat operations in December. Experiments with the carburetor intake continued on 41-37421, moving it back to a position ahead of the wing under the Merlin 1650-3 carburetor and flush with the cowl.

XP-51B 41-37421 subsequently had the four 20mm cannon reinstalled to match the configuration in 41-37352, and both were delivered to the USAAF on May 12, 1943. 41-37352 was sent to Eglin Field and then to Wright Field for testing, and it remained at the latter location until June 1944, when it was assigned to the 340th AAF Base Unit (AAFBU), Combat Crew Training School, at Bartow, then Hillsborough Field, both in Florida. The aircraft was surveyed on July 28, 1944. 41-37421 was assigned to Eglin Field, returned to NAA for modifications and flight tests, and was then sent to Wright Field in August 1943. In June 1944 it was assigned to the 2000th AAFBU, Air Training Command, where the fighter remained until mid-September 1945. After serving for two months at the 3502nd AAFBU (Technical School, Air Training Command) in Chanute Field, Illinois, it was surveyed on August 2, 1946.[8]

During the latter part of May 1943, Chilton had also undertaken many flights in the P-40L/N, P-39Q, P-38G/H (on the 20th), P-47D, and F6F-3 at Eglin Field until May 24. The purpose of the familiarization and mock combat with Eglin test pilots was to provide handling and performance comparisons to pass on to Rice and Schmued. Chilton later observed that the only fighter with as good, or better, handling characteristics as the XP-51B was the F6F-3.[9]

Materiel Command had already compounded the near-term Packard Merlin 1650-3 delivery problems by approving Air Services Command requests for a block of spare parts for the 1650-1 engine (required for the P-40F and L). Materiel Command then further exacerbated 1650-3 production by adding 3,000 more Merlin 1650-1 engines and spares for FY44. While these short-term issues were serious, the incremental demand for the 1650-3, and soon the 1650-7, to supply just the existing production schedules imposed by NA-102, -104, -106, -107, and -109 was far greater than Packard could meet, while also trying to keep pace with British commitments.

Because the upgrade of priority allocations to NAA and Packard had not yet been approved, the shortage of Merlin 1650-3 deliveries owing to the shift in production priority to spare parts for the 1650-1 cost an immediate 100 Packard Merlin 1650-3 engines destined for the P-51B, beginning in March. The delivery date for the 100th aircraft was pushed forward nearly 60 days into June. The order was rescinded only after Col John Sessums sent a letter to Echols, reminding him that the shift in priorities to the 1650-1, as authorized, would cost "1,200" engines for the P-51B.[10]

According to an Echols letter to Arnold on June 17, the ultimate effect of the Packard strike on the production of Merlin 1650-3s was estimated at 600,000 hours lost, and a loss of 240 two-speed/single-stage (1650-1) and 100 two-speed/two-stage (1650-3) engines scheduled for delivery that month.[11]

Many "what if" scenarios have been posed to accelerate the introduction of the P-51B-1-NA into combat operations. The lack of Merlin 1650-3 Priority Allocation and the Packard strike were the most important factors delaying the introduction of the Merlin Mustang into combat operations from as early as September 1943 to the beginning of October 1943. In other words, for the reasons posed, the Mustang was not available to mitigate the disastrous losses incurred during the October 14, 1943 Schweinfurt raid. Further consequences were the delayed formation of the Mustang-equipped 363rd and 357th FGs from mid-December to mid-February, and the delay in equipping the 4th, 352nd, and 355th FGs with Mustangs before "Big Week."

Design NA-107 was executed for the P-51E manufacturing plan at Dallas. This aircraft was the same as the P-51D-NA scheduled for Inglewood, but it was designated P-51D-1-NT. Many changes to the schedule and configuration of the "P-51D" led to consolidation of NA-107 funding and its reallocation to NA-103 and NA-104 and, possibly, NA-110 for the Australia contract. NA-107 was canceled in the fall of 1943 after all original funding moves were approved by the USAAF.[12]

On June 18 Australia issued Provisional Specification No. 4/43 (DTS 382/43) for the P-51E-1-NT, North American Model NA-107. The specification was evolved from the six-gun/birdcage P-51D but was modified to specify one 20mm cannon and one 0.50cal gun as wing armament, then changed again to agree to the NA-109 specification.[13]

On July 22 the first P-51B-1-NA, 43-12103, was ready for K-24 camera installation at the Modification Center as the first F-6C.[14]

On July 28 Army Chief of Staff Gen George Marshall approved FM 100 20.[15] This Field Manual, driven by Brig Gen Laurence Kuter, Assistant Chief/Air Staff Plans, crystallized the core mission for fighter aviation in advance of the planning for Operation *Overlord*, and set the timetable for Operation *Argument* seven months in advance of "Big Week." Kuter's perspectives were certainly shaped in part by his recent assignments as both Advisor to the Commanding General of VIII Bomber

OPPOSITE TOP This NAA Radio Equipment Installation technical drawing clearly shows that the NA-106 P-51D-NA was initially conceived with the six-gun wing and existing heavily framed P-51B cockpit. (© *The Boeing Company*)

Command in the fall of 1942, and his role as American Commander, Northwest Tactical Air Force, Tunisia. The key message from the manual read as follows:

> **Doctrine of employment** – air superiority is the requirement for the success of any major land operation. Air forces may be properly and profitably employed against enemy sea power, land power, and air power, however, land forces operating without air superiority must take such extensive security measures against hostile air attack that their mobility and ability to defeat the enemy land forces are greatly reduced. Therefore, air forces must be employed primarily against the enemy's air forces until air superiority is obtained. In this way only can destructive and demoralizing air attacks against land forces be minimized and the inherent mobility of modern land and air forces be exploited to the fullest.
>
> **Basic tasks** – The combat operations in which air force units are engaged are directed toward the accomplishment of the following basic tasks:
>
> Destroy hostile air forces. This will be accomplished by attacks against aircraft in the air and on the ground and against those enemy installations that he requires for the application of air power.
>
> Deny the establishment and destroy existing hostile bases from which an enemy can conduct operations on land, sea, or in the air.

Later in the January 1944 ETO narrative the reader will be able to reference FM 100 20 as the original source of Maj Gen Doolittle's famous order to VIII Fighter Command, "Seek the Luftwaffe and destroy them in the air and on the ground."

P-51B PRODUCTION START AND P-51D/E GENESIS

During February and early March significant engineering activity pushed the future P-51D series forward. First, on February 27, the actual contract for the P-51D was executed as NA-106 AC-30479. Shortly afterwards, it was announced that the same Mustang to be built in Dallas was to be the NA-107 P-51E. As noted earlier, beginning in August 1942, significant engineering work was performed both in preliminary design and the Engineering Lines groups to develop a sliding canopy in lieu of the Malcolm Hood.

OPPOSITE BOTTOM One week after the above Radio Equipment Installation drawing was completed, this Armament Installation drawing was created in July 1943 showing the bubble canopy cockpit enclosure. The Bubble Canopy Installation drawings had also been released to the Experimental Shop and construction commenced on P-51D-NA 42-106539. (© *The Boeing Company*)

The original configuration proposed and accepted was for both the P-51D and P-51E to have the same P-51B fuselage with a birdcage canopy, to make wing changes as the B/C by lowering the wing three inches, but incorporating six 0.50cal guns and increasing the leading-edge extension to accommodate redesigned main gear door improvements as specified in the "Master Dimensions Book, P-51D," dated February 10. Introducing the bubble canopy into production was deemed too far in the future for inclusion in the first block of P-51Ds. The initial plan was to insert this configuration into the NA-104 P-51B-5-NA series at aircraft 43-6713 (No. 401),

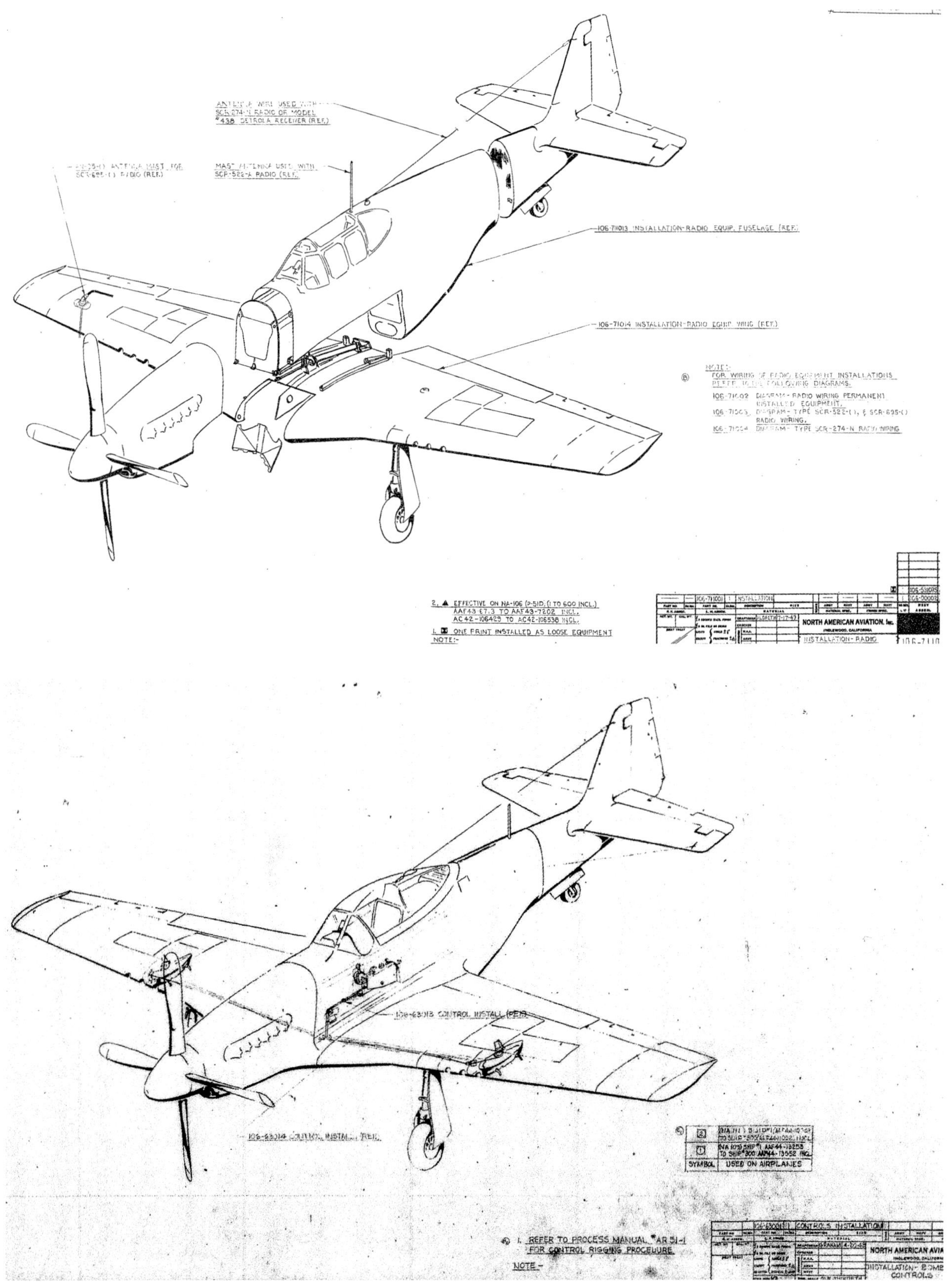

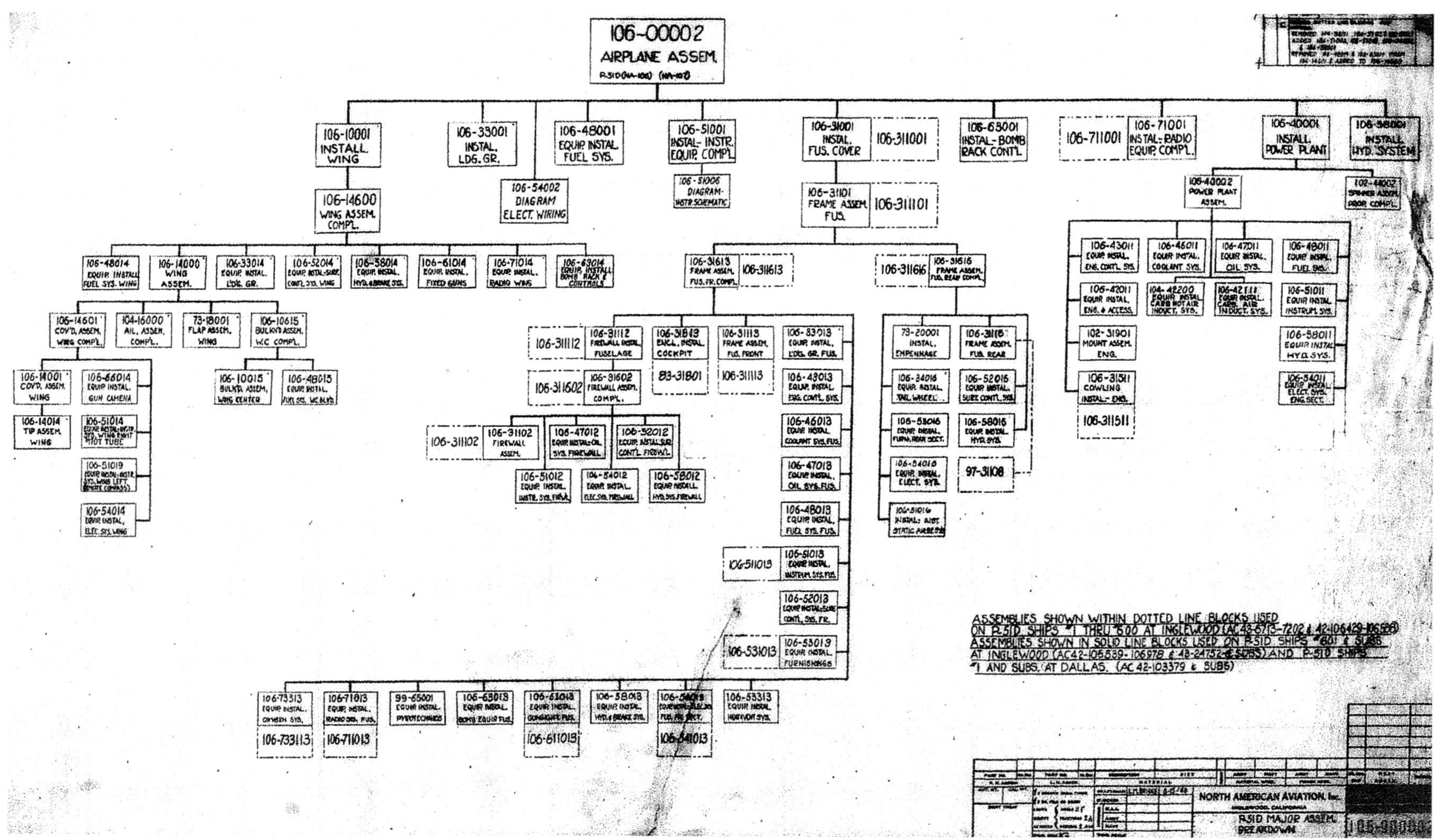
106-00002
AIRPLANE ASSEM.
106-10001 INSTALL. WING
106-33001 INSTAL. LDG. GR.
106-48001 EQUIP. INSTAL. FUEL SYS.
106-54002 DIAGRAM ELECT. WIRING
106-51001 INSTAL.- INSTR. EQUIP. COMPL.
106-51006 DIAGRAM- INSTR. SCHEMATIC
106-31001 INSTAL. FUS. COVER
106-311001
106-68001 INSTAL.- BOMB RACK CONT'L.
106-711001
106-71001 INSTAL.- RADIO EQUIP. COMPL.
106-40001 INSTALL. POWER PLANT
106-58001 INSTALL. HYD. SYSTEM
106-14600 WING ASSEM. COMPL.
106-31101 FRAME ASSEM. FUS.
106-311101
106-40002 POWER PLANT ASSEM.
102-44002 SPINNER ASSEM. PROP. COMPL.
106-48014 EQUIP. INSTALL FUEL SYS. WING
106-14000 WING ASSEM.
106-33014 EQUIP. INSTAL. LDG. GR.
106-52014
106-58014 EQUIP. INSTAL. HYD. & BRAKE SYS.
106-61014 EQUIP. INSTAL. FIXED GUNS
106-71014 EQUIP. INSTAL. RADIO WING
106-68014 EQUIP. INSTALL BOMB RACK & CONTROLS
106-14601 COV'D. ASSEM. WING COMPL.
104-16000 AIL. ASSEM. COMPL.
73-18001 FLAP ASSEM. WING
106-10615 BULKHD ASSEM. W.C. COMPL.
106-14001 COV'D. ASSEM. WING
106-14014 TIP ASSEM. WING
106-66014 EQUIP INSTAL. GUN CAMERA
106-51014
106-51019
106-54014 EQUIP INSTAL. ELEC. SYS. WING
106-10015 BULKHD. ASSEM. WING CENTER
106-48015
106-31613 FRAME ASSEM. FUS. FR. COMPL.
106-311613
106-311616
106-31616 FRAME ASSEM. FUS. REAR COMPL.
106-311112
106-31112 FIREWALL INSTAL. FUSELAGE
106-31813 ENCL. INSTAL. COCKPIT
83-31801
106-31113 FRAME ASSEM. FUS. FRONT
106-311113
106-311602
106-31602 FIREWALL ASSEM. COMPL.
106-311102
106-31102 FIREWALL ASSEM.
106-47012
106-52012
106-51012
104-54012
106-58012
106-83013 EQUIP. INSTAL. LDG. GR. FUS.
106-43013 EQUIP. INSTAL. ENG. CONT'L. SYS.
106-46013 EQUIP. INSTAL. COOLANT SYS. FUS.
106-47013 EQUIP. INSTAL. OIL SYS. FUS.
106-48013 EQUIP. INSTAL. FUEL SYS. FUS.
106-511013
106-51013 EQUIP. INSTAL. INSTRUM. SYS. FUS.
106-52013
106-531013
106-53013 EQUIP. INSTAL. FURNISHINGS
106-73313 EQUIP. INSTAL. OXYGEN SYS.
106-733113
106-71013 EQUIP. INSTAL. RADIO SYS. FUS.
106-711013
99-65001 EQUIP. INSTAL. PYROTECHNICS
106-63013
106-61013
106-611013
106-58013 EQUIP. INSTAL. HYD. & BRAKE SYS.
106-54013
106-541013
106-55313 EQUIP. INSTAL. HEAT/VENT. SYS.
73-20001 INSTAL. EMPENNAGE
106-31116 FRAME ASSEM. FUS. REAR
106-34016 EQUIP. INSTAL. TAIL WHEEL
106-52016
106-53016
106-58016 EQUIP. INSTAL. HYD. SYS.
106-54016 EQUIP. INSTAL. ELECT. SYS.
97-31108
106-51016
106-43011 EQUIP. INSTAL. ENG. CONT'L. SYS.
106-46011 EQUIP. INSTAL. COOLANT SYS.
106-47011 EQUIP. INSTAL. OIL SYS.
106-48011 EQUIP. INSTAL. FUEL SYS.
106-42011 EQUIP. INSTAL. ENG. & ACCESS.
104-42200
106-42111
106-51011 EQUIP. INSTAL. INSTRUM. SYS.
102-31901 MOUNT ASSEM. ENG.
106-58011 EQUIP. INSTAL. HYD. SYS.
106-31511 COWLING INSTAL.- ENG.
106-311511
106-54011 EQUIP. INSTAL. ELECT. SYS. ENG. SECT.
ASSEMBLIES SHOWN WITHIN DOTTED LINE BLOCKS USED ON P-51D SHIPS #1 THRU 500 AT INGLEWOOD (AC43-6713-7202 & 42-106429-106538)
ASSEMBLIES SHOWN IN SOLID LINE BLOCKS USED ON P-51D SHIPS #501 & SUBS AT INGLEWOOD (AC42-106539-106978 & 43-24752-& SUBS) AND P-51D SHIPS #1 AND SUBS. AT DALLAS. (AC 42-103379 & SUBS)
NORTH AMERICAN AVIATION, Inc.
P-51D MAJOR ASSEM. BREAKDOWN

and build the rest as NA-106 P-51Ds with the new wing. The Dallas P-51E, with the same configuration, was to start at 42-103379 (No. 351 of the old NA-103 contract).

The NAA drawing 106-90002 "P-51D Major Assembly" drawing, dated March 15, 1943, showed P-51D (NA-106) and P-51E (NA-107) in the 106-00002 "Airplane Assembly (NA-106) (NA-107)" Title Block, with all the necessary Work Breakdown "design tree" assemblies displayed in logical blocks below (i.e., wing, forward fuselage, aft fuselage, empennage, instruments, armament, and powerplant).

The 106-00002 Airplane Assembly drawing serves both as an excellent example of the NAA major assembly breakdown design tree for the NA-106 P-51D (and originally the NA-107 P-51E) and as an illustration of the changes from March 1943, when the "P-51D Major Assembly" drawing was released, to the August 1943 time frame when the final engineering drawings were released. The NA-109 P-51D production design incorporated most of the NA-106 project designs. It also illustrates the changes that were made to the basic NA-104 (P-51B-5-NA) major assembly groups, first to include the six-gun wing while initially retaining the aft fuselage/cockpit enclosure, and then to incorporate the major changes to the aft fuselage and cockpit enclosure associated with the P-51D's bubble canopy.

Those "shadow" assemblies presented in dotted lines represent the original NA-104 fuselage/cockpit enclosure/firewall that were changed and sent to the Experimental Department, as the concept of the original P-51D six-gun wing/birdcage canopy evolved into the six-gun wing/bubble canopy configuration embodied in the P-51D and D-1 being built there. Sometime in July, references to both the NA-107 and P-51E were removed as the funding for NA-106 was reduced to two P-51Ds, and funding from NA-106 and NA-107 was redistributed to NA-103 and NA-104.

On or about March 22, 1943, the title "P-51D and P-51E" was removed from the 106-9000002 Title Block and replaced by P-51D. The next associated change was to commence building P-51Ds with the bubble canopy after a 600-ship P-51B-5 and early P-51B-10 run, then redefine the P-51D to begin at aircraft 42-106539 at Inglewood and 42-103379 at Dallas.

The last contract and design changes were (1) to limit the NA-106 to two airframes, and (2) to fabricate the NA-106 P-51D and D-1 with two existing NA-102 fuselage 102-31116 "Frame Assembly, Fuselage Rear" spares, modified to the new 106-31116 Frame Assembly design, replace the older wing with the new wing, and remove the rear deck to install the "Sliding Enclosure" (bubble canopy) modification. The second airframe's designation remained P-51D-1, but both would be fabricated in the Experimental Hangar at Inglewood. The best guess regarding the fate of NA-107 is that the funding was rearranged to allocate contract dollars for the 600 P-51B-5/10s under NA-104, plus 398 P-51B-15-NAs, and contract dollars for the balance of 1,000 more P-51C-5/10-NTs in NA-103.

Beginning on March 9, Materiel Command approved the first purchase order for Materiel Change Request C-258 to the NA-102 P-51B-1-NA Specification.[16] MCR C-258-1 provided the authority to start on the "Cockpit Enclosure – Sliding (P-51D) Bubble Canopy" for the NA-106 P-51D-NA airframe. The next day, drawing

OPPOSITE The NA-106 "P-51D Major Assembly" drawing 106-00002 shows the transition from the P-51B fuselage to the P-51D and D-1, with replaced assemblies in the dotted line blocks. The original date for this top assembly drawing was March 15, 1943, which was a relatively short interval from the wind tunnel studies of the sliding enclosure for the Packard Pursuit referenced earlier in this book. (© *The Boeing Company*)

The first Mustang complete with the new bubble canopy from project MCR-258 was P-51B-1-NA 43-12102, shown here at Inglewood just prior to making its maiden flight on November 6, 1943. (© *The Boeing Company*)

106-00001, "Three-View General Arrangement," was released, dated March 10, 1943. It showed both the bubble canopy and the increased aileron throw of +/-10, 12, and 15 degrees, which were also included for all P-51B/C Series Mustangs.

Project Change Order C-258, dated March 16, stated "Covers design of a sliding enclosure to replace the hinged canopy. As the enclosure will consist entirely of an external canopy fairing, this change includes reduction in height and re-fairing of the fuselage from the cockpit aft."

On April 8, in the C-258 project logs, it was noted that the engineering for Cockpit Enclosure-Sliding (P-51D) was complete, and further noted that the design was being studied for fabrication requirements on the 15th. Following completion of shop drawings, the P-51D mock-up was started on May 19, 1943.

The first mention in the project logs for P-51B-1-NA modification was on June 19, as C-258-2 "Rework P-51B-1-NA ship No. 10 (43-12102), Installation of Sliding Enclosure. Rework ship in Dept. 9." Similarly, the entry for C-258-3 was "Rework a NA-102 Fuselage for NA-106 Static Test. Fuselage delivered on July 17."

The C-258 log comments on June 19 were more extensive regarding the tasks required to complete the installation of the cockpit enclosure, namely:

> A new enclosure being developed to provide rear vision for the pilot. This involves a complete change in structure above the upper longeron from the firewall aft to the empennage fillet, with a new windshield and a one-piece Plexiglas canopy with a travel of about 22in. This necessitates removal of the radio shelf and rearrangement of the radio equipment and some changes to the electrical system, and relocation of propeller anti-icing tank.

On July 5 the C-258 entry stated "Cockpit Enclosure – Sliding (P-51D). Rel. Sched. Rev. to work required on ships Nos. 1–600 for old type enclosure for Inglewood Drawing Release P-51D, Nos. 1-600 original type enclosures." Two weeks later, C-258-2 notes "Re-work of P-51B-1-NA ship No. 10 in process Dept. 9," and for C-258-3, "Rework NA-102 Fuselage for NA-106 Static test. Fuselage delivered to Dept. 9 on July 19."[17]

Both C-258-1 (P-51D) and C-258-3 (P-51D-1) were extracted from NA-102 spares assemblies for the complete base fuselage, coupled with NA-106 six-gun P-51D wings fabricated in Advanced Production (also as "separate" assemblies), and assigned aircraft serial numbers 42-106539 and 42-106540 from the future P-51B-10-NA series. Speculation that the P-51D 42-106539 airframe could be "pulled" from the P-51B-10-NA production line for the bubble canopy modification in the Experimental Hangar is just not plausible. The first P-51B-10 (43-7113, No. 1 of Block One) was not even completed until December, and the next one in sequence, 43-7114 No. 2, was not delivered until late that same month. Work on P-51D No. 1 42-106539 had begun in the Experimental Hangar (Hangar 9) six months earlier, in May, and it was delivered to the flight test department on October 25, 1943.

P-51B-10-NA 42-106538 (No. 110 of P-51B Block Two), immediately preceding the serial number to P-51D 42-106539, was delivered on February 7, 1944. As noted later in this chapter in discussions of Experimental Hangar project notes, both fuselages for the two P-51D modifications were NA-102 fuselage assemblies, not from NA-104 production.

The C-258 project logs in the Experimental Hangar revealed approximate timing for the decision not to insert the bubble canopy modification into the existing P-51B/C production lines – primarily owing to the delivery slowdown this would cause from P-51B-5-NA No. 400 (43-6713, projected No. 1 for NA-106 P-51D). Further project log entries will be covered in the section on July to December.

Also in July, overtime was authorized for NAA Engineering and Production to expedite the design releases for both the NA-106 and the new internal fuselage tank modifications for the NA-102 and NA-104.

EVENTS LEADING TO THE P-51B 85GAL FUSELAGE TANK – JUNE THROUGH JULY 1943

Although the Mustang I auxiliary ammunition/gun-bay fuel tank kit of 1941 significantly extended the aircraft's range, it was not a practical solution to the long-range escort requirements for the P-51B. When the USAAF, in the person of Maj Gen Barney Giles, Chief of Air Staff, pushed Lockheed, Republic, and NAA to add significantly more internal fuel to the P-38, P-47, and P-51, NAA was prepared, and immediately discarded any wing locations for extra internal fuel as impractical. The long-range task force led by Chidlaw from February 1943 received a huge push from

Gen Arnold four months later when, on June 19, the latter delivered the right message to the right man. He wrote to Maj Gen Giles, saying, in part:

> This brings to mind very clearly the absolute necessity for building a fighter airplane that can go in and out with the bombers. Moreover, this fighter has to go into Germany. Perhaps we can modify some existing type to do the job. The P-38 has been doing a fine job from North Africa in escorting our B-17s 400 hundred miles or so. Whether this airplane can furnish the same escort against the GAF [German Air Force] on the Western Front is debatable.
>
> Our fighter people in the UK claim they can't stay with the bombers because they are too slow [in cruise mode] and because they [the fighter escort] must have top speed by the time they hit the bombers. The P-38 is not notable for great acceleration, so perhaps it too will not be able to meet the FW's and 109's [sic]. About six months remains before deep penetrations of Germany begin. Within this next six months, you have got to get a fighter that can protect our bombers. Whether you use an existing type or have to start from scratch is your problem. Get to work on this right way because in January, '44, I want a fighter escort for our bombers from the UK into Germany.[18]

Giles went to Requirements Division for a recommendation of the most suitable fighter for accompanying the bombers, and was initially told that the P-38 offered the best possibilities. Accordingly, Lockheed was the first fighter manufacturer approached for recommendations to improve the P-38's long-range-flight capabilities.[19] As deliberations continued regarding the most suitable choice for the long-range escort fighter, Lockheed notified Materiel Command that a 110gal cone-shaped fuel tank installed aft of the P-38 pilot's seat was being tested.[20]

On June 19 NAA's Field Service News noted that improved self-sealing fuel cells would be installed in every P-51B. Essential features included pressure-molded aromatic fuel-resistant liners; six-ply materials bonded to each other, with two outer layers cross-laminated; neoprene impregnated rayon fabric; and third and fifth layers of vulcanized rubber. The inner layer was synthetic rubber, collectively half an inch thick, and sufficient to prevent leaks into the gun bay.[21]

On July 3 NAA announced that its proprietary High Shear Flush Rivets, which greatly improved the shear-load-bearing capability of both the fasteners and the aluminum panels, were being used for spar/exterior skins, longerons/exterior skins, engine mounts, and fuel tank compartment doors.[22]

Also on July 3, preceding the Lockheed report, Col Mervin Gross, Assistant Chief, Air Staff, OC&R, Requirements Division, submitted a report closing the loop from Gen Giles' "request for the most suitable fighter for accompanying the bombers." In his report Gross summarized the findings, saying "The P-51B is the most promising plane."[23]

On or about July 4 Gen Fairchild published the Fighter Airplane Range Extension Program (FAREP) report, which directed the fighter manufacturers to provide maximum fuel internally. In summary, the report and recommendations focused on extending the combat radius of fighters, contemplating that only remaining internal fuel was useful for combat and return home after external tanks had been jettisoned.

On July 5 Gen Giles sent a telex to NAA, Lockheed, and Republic stating, "Provide maximum combat range at earliest possible time."[24]

On July 7 Lockheed advised that two 55gal fuel tanks could be installed in the wing leading edges of the P-38J: "Estimate four months to complete installation in 100 aircraft."[25]

Between July 7 and 18 several actions were taken, and key exchanges were made, between NAA and Materiel Command at Wright Field. On the 7th, Materiel Command, Columbus, telexed Rice at NAA, "Request additional tankage for fighter airplane. Dimensions 54"x25"x16."[26] On the 8th NAA Representative Hellman sent a memo to Rice: "Telephone conversation with Col Bradley, Maj Price and Maj Towner. Action immediately on calculating the aft CG travel. They (MATL CMD) very desirous of having a test flight made, also desire feasibility of making changes to service airplanes."[27]

Also on the 8th, P-51B-1-NA 43-12113 was accepted by the USAAF and allocated serial number FX848 for the RAF. It was the first of the "FX series" to be flown to Newark for delivery to Britain. The earliest (recorded) serial number returned to the Ninth Air Force on December 31, 1943 following agreement between the USAAF and the RAF to augment escort fighter strength was 43-12226/FX851.[28] Also noted was the new design of the P-51B/C engine mount, which permitted the Merlin to be removed without detaching the engine mount from the firewall – a major maintenance time improvement.

On July 10 Col M. E. Bradley, Chief, Fighter Projects, called Gen Echols to report the dangerous flight characteristics of the XP-75 and recommend that the focus be directed to adding more fuel in the Mustang. Echols approved the project to add more internal fuel but decided to continue the XP-75 program for 2,200 airplanes.[29]

On July 13 Brig Gen Charles E. Branshaw sent a telex to NAA:

AAFRR NAA, Inc Inglewood, CA
PEST-T-1320, Fighter Airplanes, Extra Tankage Program Desired as Follows:

1. Prep one airplane for flight by Col M. E. Bradley on 17th July 1943, with one non-leak-proof fuselage tank holding 85 gallons temporarily installed and either the SCR 522 radio plus Detrola (sic) or the SCR 274N radio.

2. Begin immediately the necessary engineering so that the fuselage tank described in NAA typ-MC-38731, dated 7 July 1943, to Mr Hellman be placed into production.

3. Have the Experimental Department make the installation on three P-51B-1 airplanes for delivery at earliest possible date. Letter follows through Requirements Division request.

Brig Gen Branshaw
MATR CMD[30]

That same day, NAA, per Materiel Command instructions, issued the following Change Orders to the P-51B-1 Specifications: "MCR C-326 Fuel Tank and Kits – 85-gallon Fuselage Tank, Rework P-51B-1 43-12212 to include 93-gallon steel tank for Flight Test. Rework three more P-51B (43-12388-390) with tanks per S.O. 16591 per MCR C-326 2 and 3."[31]

July 15 marked the release of Specifications for Combat Tanks, summarized as follows: "Aircraft equipped with combat tanks must be controllable on instruments, ratio of 75% capacity of combat tank to internal fuel capacity, must be able to extract 95% of combat tank fuel capacity at critical altitude of the fighter."[32]

On or about this time, NAA planned an installation of the 85gal tank into P-51B-1 43-12304 in the Experimental Department for three reasons. The first was to determine and document the modifications required to remove the existing radio, radio shelf, and oxygen supply, and then to install the support structure for the new tank and the increased oxygen supply, and install the plumbing and control switch, etc. The second reason was to coordinate the design changes between engineering and field services, additional parts fabrication, and the processes to assemble kits for future depot installation. The third reason was to document carefully, step by step, each stage of the modification work in Field Services Bulletin 73-95.

Also on the 15th, Col R. Kelly, Acting Chief Allocations and Programs Division, sent a memo to the Assistant Chief/Air Staff, OC&R, recommending 945 P-51Bs for Reconnaissance Aviation, beginning in October 1943, through June 1944.[33]

One week after the July 15 memo was issued to OC&R, there was no indication of any radical change of mind in the Air Staff, save for Gen Laurence Kuter, recently returned from Eighth and Twelfth Air Force senior command responsibilities. Despite the requests to add features relevant to the combat efficiency of the P-51B, there were no actions by Materiel Command, the Directorate of Military Requirements or the Directorate of Air Defense that pointed to using the P-51B in the long-range escort role. Only the next week, when Eaker and Emmons cabled Arnold from HQ Eighth Air Force during the beginning of "Blitz Week" in the ETO to "request P-51B this theater," was the first request received from top USAAF leadership to deploy the P-51B for escort duties.

The continued aversion to imagining the Mustang in the long-range escort role by various Air Staff departments at the Pentagon is mystifying to this day. The feedback from all pilots flying the Mustang outside the influence of Materiel Command, both in Washington, D.C., and at Wright Field, was uniform in the view that handling, maneuverability, and range were simply "superior" from low to medium altitudes, and "astonishing" at high altitude to those few who were able to fly the P-51B, notably Col Mark Bradley, Chief, Fighter Projects at Wright Field. That said, Bradley was the first USAAF officer positioned to be heard at a sufficiently senior level in Echols' own staff who possibly altered the latter's attitudes regarding the Mustang. It was at the beginning of July that Bradley became so thoroughly alarmed at the flight characteristics of the XP-75 that he convinced Echols the P-51B was the best chance for an effective single-engined, high-altitude escort fighter.

P-51B-1-NA 43-12112 was the first to have installed and flight test the fuselage tank on July 17, 1943. (Artwork by Jim Laurier, © Osprey Publishing)

In mid-July Chilton tested 43-12112 with both the new internal fuel tank and 75gal combat tanks during a 1hr 20min functional test. On the 17th he made a long-range 1,200-mile cruise test at 30,000ft with full internal fuel, simulating combat for 20 minutes at military power. Total flight time was 4hrs 45min.

The next day Bradley flew 43-12112 with a full load of fuel, including 75gal combat tanks and the 93gal steel fuselage tank, plus a full load of ammunition, from Muroc Field to Albuquerque, New Mexico. "I took off and flew to Albuquerque at 25,000ft, simulated full power over that city for 15 minutes, and then flew back to Edwards [as Muroc Field was renamed in December 1949] with plenty of gas left. The mission to Berlin had been accomplished."[34]

From the 21st Chilton commenced functionally testing 43-12305 in a series of rigorous flights to obtain a full set of speed and climb data versus throttle settings and altitude.[35]

NAA Engineering began production design tasks for a self-sealing 85gal-capacity fuel tank, the removal and rearrangement of existing radio, battery, and IFF to accommodate the fuel tank, a new fuel line, a five-position fuel tank cockpit selector switch, the fuel filler system, fuel gage, and extra oxygen capacity for longer range.

During the flight testing of P-51B-1-NA 43-12112, Materiel Command issued Change Order MCR C-348 to have the 85gal tank also installed in the NA-106 and NA-109 P-51D. That Change Order also influenced the bubble canopy project in Experimental Hangar 9, namely, to install the fuselage fuel tank "when available" into P-51D 42-106539 and P-51D-1 42-106540.[36]

VIII BOMBER COMMAND/ETO/LUFTWAFFE FROM JANUARY THROUGH JULY 1943

On January 5 Gen Frank "Monk" Hunter, Commanding General VIII Fighter Command, requested that the Commanding General of VIII Air Force Service Command seek local British manufacturing sources for 75gal and 110gal external fuel tanks.[37]

On the 12th the 56th FG arrived at Kings Cliffe, equipped with the new P-47C-2-RE. Two days later VIII Bomber Command attacked Wilhelmshaven – the first time its units had targeted Germany.[38]

On the same day, Gen Gordon Saville, Commanding General Air Defense, directed Requirements "Distribution of Aircraft" to prioritize *all* P-51s (A and B) to replace P-39s and P-40s by May 1943 (this was the order that directed future P-51B production to the Ninth Air Force in the ETO).[39] This order did not cause a delay to P-51B operations in the ETO. From September onward most of the production allocations of the P-51B were to the ETO, as the Mustang III for the RAF and the P-51B-1-NA for the 354th FG. The pipeline directed some to the CBI for assignment to the 23rd FG in December, but most of the balance of P-51B-1-NAs and new P-51B-5-NAs were also destined for Ninth Air Force fighter groups, including the new 357th and 363rd FGs, as well as for the 67th Tactical Reconnaissance Group (TRG) as F-6Cs.

In mid-January perhaps the most important series of events occurred in the Moroccan city of Casablanca during the Casablanca Conference. Gen Eaker was alerted that Prime Minister Churchill was adamant that the Americans join the RAF for night-bombing operations. Eaker was informed by Gen Arnold that not only was Churchill opposed to "wasting Allied assets" for a strategy that could not work, but he had also discussed the matter with President Roosevelt, who in turn met with Secretary of War Stinson and Chief of Staff, Gen Marshall. Eaker's reaction, when informed by Arnold, was:

> That is absurd. It represents complete disaster. It will permit the Luftwaffe to escape. The cross-Channel invasion will then fail. Our planes are not equipped for night bombing and our crews are not trained for it. We'll lose more planes landing in that fog-shrouded darkness than we lose over German targets. If our leaders are that stupid, count me out. I don't want any part of that nonsense![40]

Following two days of preparation for the meeting with Churchill, Eaker briefed Gen Spaatz on both the one-page summary for Churchill and the 16-page document for Arnold to present at the Combined Chiefs of Staff meeting on January 20–21. It was during Eaker's meeting with Churchill that the phrase "bomb them around the clock" was coined. At the end of the briefing Churchill responded, saying:

> Young man, you have not convinced me that you are right, but you have persuaded me that you should have further opportunity to prove your contention. How fortuitous it would be if we could, as you say, bomb the devils around the clock. When I see your President today, I shall tell him that I withdraw my suggestion that US bombers join the RAF in night bombing, and that I recommend that we continue our joint effort, day and night bombing for a time.[41]

Arnold later remarked of Eaker's meeting with Churchill:

A P-47D-2-RE leads four P-47C-2/5s and a second D-model of the 62nd FS/56th FG in echelon down formation past a B-24 full of press photographers on May 25, 1943. These aircraft were some of the first Thunderbolts to see combat with VIII Fighter Command. (*Tony Holmes Collection*)

> We had won a major victory, for we would bomb in accordance with American principles, using the methods for which our aircraft were designed. After that I had a meeting with the President and Gen Marshall on the same subject and, as far as they were concerned, the matter was settled. Everyone said, "Go ahead with your daylight bombing."[42]

During January the only operational fighter unit within VIII Fighter Command was the 4th FG, and it continued to fly a mixture of patrols to protect coastal shipping and undertake strafing attacks on French coastal airfields until the 13th. On the latter date the group flew escort for the 1st BW's attack on Lille, then another to escort RAF Bostons against St Omer airfield.

In the last week of January, Lt Col Cass Hough, CO of VIII Fighter Command's Air Technical Section, flew to the British Reassembly Depot at Speke to pick up one of the first P-47C-2-REs to arrive in the ETO. Over the next two weeks he performed various controlled speed and climb tests, culminating in a dive from 38,000ft.[43] The dive brought on severe compressibility, with a decidedly powerful "nose-down" tuck requiring much denser air to recover. While not as severe as it was in the P-38, it was a serious issue. The introduction of mid-wing dive flaps in mid-1944 solved the problem. Lt Col Hough arranged for several P-47Cs to be delivered to the AFDU at RAF Wittering, in Cambridgeshire, to begin the tactical trials that had not been conducted at Wright Field.[44] At the AFDU multiple problems were discovered, such as extreme flare from supercharger waste gates and faulty engine wiring harnesses affecting spark plug ignition, as well as causing radio interference.[45]

On January 27 the Bf 110 nightfighters of IV./NJG 1 were deployed against Eighth Air Force B-17s attacking Wilhelmshaven.[46] That the scarce and valuable nightfighter was introduced shows the alarm within Luftwaffe high command

Lt Col Cass Hough commanded VIII Fighter Command's Air Technical Section. His organization was instrumental in identifying and solving technical issues with inbound fighters delivered from the US for operations in the ETO. Hough also supplied myriad reports on his section's work to Materiel Command, and these were in turn distributed to US aircraft manufacturers. (*NARA, sourced by Jack Cook*)

regarding the difficulty of shooting down the Flying Fortress. As more Bf 110s were deployed as day fighters to complement the Bf 109s and Fw 190s, their armament was increased to four 20mm cannon plus underwing 210cm rockets. Although slower and less maneuverable than the single-engined fighters, the Bf 110 was lethally efficient until compromised by the P-38, P-47, and, finally, the P-51B.

On or about February 16 several Fw 190 fighters were seen to drop "bomb-like" objects onto the 91st BG's aircraft during attacks on the St Nazaire submarine pens. Approximately 50 air bursts were observed, and were believed to be a first attempt by the Luftwaffe to drop bombs on Eighth Air Force formations.[47]

The last Spitfire mission undertaken by the 4th FG (and VIII Fighter Command) was flown on April 1. One week later the first P-47C missions were flown by a combined but small force of 23 aircraft comprising the 4th, 56th, and 78th FGs on a "Rodeo" along the northwest French coast.[48] VIII Fighter Command P-47s achieved their first recorded victory credits when Maj Don Blakeslee, CO of the 335th FS/4th FG, destroyed an enemy aircraft on April 15 near Knocke – the 4th FG claimed four Fw 190s for the loss of three P-47s. One claimant of a victory was the group CO, Col Chesley Peterson, who was in turn forced to bail out of his P-47 due to engine failure 30 miles short of the British coast. He was rescued by RAF Air Sea Rescue.[49] After flying the Spitfire in combat, the veteran pilots of the Eagle Squadrons and 4th FG were not very happy with the Thunderbolt.

Combat operations for VIII Bomber Command for January 27 through April 17, 1943 included attacks on only three German targets: Wilhelmshaven, Vegesack, and Bremen. The Eighth Air Force was still very small by future standards, with only four B-17 bomb groups in the 1st BW and two B-24 bomb groups in the 2nd BW.

The April 17 attack on Bremen by the 1st BW marked a huge success for the Luftwaffe and, to a lesser degree, VIII Bomber Command. A well-coordinated strike by Fw 190s, Bf 109s, and Bf 110s hit the lead bomb group, the 91st, and took out a total of six B-17s. The trailing groups lost another ten during the one-hour air battle. The Luftwaffe fighter units credited with the attacks included I./JG 1, I. *Nachtjagdgeschwader* (NJG) 3, I. and II./JG 11, and III./JG 54. In context, the raid was equally successful in that 50 percent of the Focke-Wulf factory was destroyed and another 30 Fw 190s were destroyed around the plant.[50] The fall-out, other than the extraordinary high losses suffered by the attacking force, extended to a noticeable drop in the morale of VIII Bomber Command crews.[51]

To put this April 17 mission into context, the first P-51B-1 airframe was completed two weeks earlier, awaiting delivery of the now late Packard Merlin 1650-3 engine production deliveries. The P-47Cs now in-theater did not yet have centerline shackles and fuel feed to attach even ferry tanks. The current P-38H was not equipped with the leading-edge fuel cells that would become standard in late 1943. None of the US fighters in production were yet modified to carry pressurized external fuel tanks at high altitude. Lt Col Hough's study of a pressurization scheme in the ETO, leading to slaving the external tank fuel system to the instrument system vacuum pump, was just beginning.

In April the Warton Base Air Depot (BAD2) opened for business to both repair and/or modify inbound aircraft (initially B-24s, then P-51s from November).

In early May Gen Arnold became increasingly ill, leading to a second heart attack and an uncertain return to his post following recovery. His Assistant Chief of Air Staff, Operations, Maj Gen Barney Giles, took over during Arnold's recovery.

The rhythm of combat operations for VIII Fighter Command continued to increase during May and June 1943.

Early May also saw the first P-47D-1-REs emerge from BAD1 Burtonwood with all the necessary modifications required for ETO combat operations, these aircraft being immediately issued to the fighter groups. Although the first blocks of P-47D-1s through D-4s were delivered to the ETO without factory-installed bulged keels and bomb racks, they were so modified at Burtonwood. They were also delivered with provision to take the water injection system, deliveries of which would begin later.

In mid-May the 4th CBW was formed with the addition of the new 92nd, 94th, 95th, and 96th BGs, while the equally new 351st BG joined the 1st BW. For two weeks the 351st flew with the 2nd BW to balance the striking force of the two separate wings until the 379th went operational with the 1st BW. Finally, the long-awaited delivery stream of bombers was beginning to exceed attrition.

The 322nd BG, the first operational Martin B-26 Marauder-equipped combat unit in the ETO, flew a low-level attack against Ijmuiden power station on May 14. The medium bombers arriving in Great Britain were assigned to the 3rd BW. Three days later the 322nd returned along the same route and again targeted the Ijmuiden power station, this time with disastrous losses. Of the 11 attacking B-26s, only the aircraft that had aborted the mission before reaching the target returned home.

Following these disastrous losses, Eaker and the Air Inspector General, Col Harold A. McGinnis, visited the 322nd BG to gain a better understanding of what had caused such heavy attrition. Following the briefings, Eaker halted low-level missions and redirected the squadrons to medium-altitude attacks with fighter escort. In the fall the medium bomber units would be reassigned to the Ninth Air Force, but for the next several months they flew escorted missions at medium altitude, attacking airfields, power stations, and diversion targets, etc. in Holland, Belgium, and France. Their loss rates dropped precipitously.

On May 27 Eaker wrote to Maj Gen Barney Giles, Assistant Chief, Air Staff, Operations, with the following observations:

> I am going to put the medium bombers in the Air Support Command and give them maximum training as part of the tactical air force to support ground forces invading the continent. We have five new groups here with both air and

> ground echelons and they have already executed five or six missions. *Their operational use is severely restricted, however, because their organizational equipment has not arrived. We have raked and scraped from every source, including the British, all the tools, the bomb handling equipment, gas trucks and so forth which we could lay our hands on. Obviously, however, these units will not be at maximum operating efficiency until their equipment arrives.* The P-47s are doing all right. We are well pleased with their performance in combat and are having much less engine trouble. *The P-47 is, of course, of little more use than the Spitfire IX to accompany long-range bombers until the long-range tanks are provided. The tanks we have are of no use until they are perfected to the point where they will be usable at high altitude.*[52]

The authors have italicized two specific statements by Eaker to illustrate the failure of Materiel Command, Air Force Service Command, and Air Training Command to adequately support the Eighth Air Force mission arising from Casablanca.

First, the necessary planning, organization, and execution to train new bomber crews, mechanics, service groups, and ground echelons was inadequate. The bomb groups arriving in the ETO were also poorly equipped to deal with the existing facilities and the weather over Britain and the Continent. Eaker addressed those issues in prior correspondence, but the point about the new bomb groups arriving without necessary equipment to carry bombs and ammunition from storage areas to the flightline, or even refuel bombers from a full complement of truck/lorries, pointed to severe restrictions to operational efficiencies. The issues were further compounded by slow replacements for lost crew, to the point that there were more bombers available for missions than sufficiently trained replacement crews.

Second, the slow response by Materiel Command to initiate, manage, and issue contracts for external combat tanks, and the technical innovations to pressurize them, for more than a year after they were issued a "top priority" instruction from HQ-AAF following Arnold's February 1942 Fighter Conference, is mystifying. Gen Hunter, Lt Col Cass Hough, and Ambassador Harriman applied considerable energy to getting local British industry to make 110gal impregnated-paper tanks for VIII Fighter Command P-47s. The first production deliveries were scheduled for late September 1943. Additionally, Hough's Air Technical Section was already modifying metal 75gal tanks designed for the P-39 and coordinating a supply of valves from the British Thermostat Company to attach to the engine vacuum pumps. The latter still supplied pressure for the instrumentation, but now could also provide pressure for the external tanks to meter fuel as altitudes increased above 18,000–20,000ft.[53]

In mid-May the 2nd BW B-24 bomb groups, the 44th and 93rd, began low-level formation flying over the British countryside, provoking widespread speculation. They departed in late May to join the Twelfth Air Force B-24 bomb groups at Benghazi to begin unified training for the low-level attack on the oil refineries at Ploesti, in Rumania, on August 1.

The departure of the B-24 bomb groups was significant for two reasons. First, it represented a 20 percent loss of effective combat operations strength available to Eaker. Second, the crews and ground echelon had much higher levels of combat experience and efficiency than the recently activated B-17 groups. Once again, HQ-AAF interfered with Eaker's ability to grow the Eighth Air Force's striking capability to the level he required (and which Arnold had promised him at Casablanca) to prosecute the American role in the Combined Bomber Offensive. The earlier stripping of all long-range escort P-38 groups in the fall of 1942 was even more damaging to the fortunes of the Eighth Air Force in the summer of 1943.

Operational loss averages during May and June steadily increased to 5–6 percent, mostly due to Luftwaffe fighters.[54]

The events of June and July prepared the groundwork for the tumultuous crisis experienced in both the Doctrine and Command of the Eighth Air Force. June operations against targets in Germany were met with increasing resistance and intensity by the Luftwaffe's day fighter arm. That month saw the first redeployment of various Luftwaffe units from the Ost (Russia) and Süd (South – Vienna, Italy, Greece, Rumania) fronts to the west for Defense of the Reich. The current training programs were inadequate to replace the losses experienced in the west, so the only near-term alternative seemed to be the transfer of experienced units, rather than to feed in newly trained pilots.

Upon his return from convalescence, Arnold was increasingly critical of the performance of VIII Bomber Command and, by inference, of Gen Eaker. On June 11 Arnold cabled Eaker with specific and sharp criticism. This included the perception that Eaker's Chief of Staff (Col Newton Longfellow) was an ineffective leader, and pointed to the poor number of operational raids flown by the Eighth Air Force in contrast to the number of days the RAF was able to attack during the spring. He was also critical of the number of effective bombers launched on any particular day in contrast to the total number based in Britain, and followed this with the suggestion that the Eighth Air Force was perhaps "not capable of handling the supply and maintenance problems which will greatly increase with the large number of airplanes being assigned to your theater within the next several months."[55]

During these increasingly sharp exchanges between Arnold and Eaker, Assistant Secretary of War Robert A. Lovett was in Britain. He toured many Eighth Air Force bases, frequently accompanied by Ambassador Winant and Gens Eaker, Jacob L. Devers (who commanded the 6th Army in the ETO), Hunter, and Idwal H. Edwards (the USAAF's chief of staff in the ETO). Lovett devoted his time and energy toward a better understanding of the issues encountered by the Eighth Air Force in developing full capability. He sent a letter to Arnold following the latest in the sharp exchanges between Arnold and Eaker. Among his comments was the part that Arnold forwarded to Barney Giles, previously detailed in this book, concerning the mandatory delivery of a long-range fighter solution.

When Lovett returned to Washington, D.C. he met with Arnold. In the meeting he supported Eaker and his comments about the situation in Britain, highlighting

Gen Frank "Monk" Hunter, Commanding General VIII Fighter Command, briefs John G. Winant, American Ambassador in London, on the cockpit layout of a 4th FG P-47 at the fighter group's Debden home in the summer of 1943. (*NARA*)

several more issues, including "more replacement crews," "better trained crews," "delivery of equipment and ground echelons prior to arrival of combat groups," "planes arriving with necessary equipment in Great Britain (too many depot-required modifications dramatically slowed delivery to combat units), particularly with respect to forward firing guns." "If these urgent needs are met promptly," he added, "the operational efficiencies of the Eighth Air Force will, in my opinion, increase by 50 per cent."

Lovett's push on Arnold had an immediate effect on the flow of replacement crews and aircraft, and the incorporation of more improvements stateside for B-17s, B-24s, B-26s, and P-47s. However, his chief point to Arnold was his insistence on the "immediate need for long-range fighters." "This may be met by proper tanks for P-47s, but ultimately P-38s and P-51s will be needed," he said, and in addition:

> Fighter escort will have to be provided, particularly to get them through the first wave of German fighter defense, which is now put up in depth so that B-17s are forced to run the gauntlet both in to the target and out from it. The P-47s can serve as top cover if satisfactory tanks can be developed for them. The ideal plane, however, now in production is the P-38. It has been used in over-water escort duty on operations with a radius of 400 miles. However, the moment it drops its wing tanks it must turn back. High hopes are felt for the P-51 with wing tanks.[56]

The increasing sense of urgency to engage and destroy the Luftwaffe was driven by two primary fears. The first was that Germany's technological capabilities could develop a bomber destroyer aircraft capable of denying air supremacy to the Allied air forces over the Continent. In this context, the Messerschmitt Me 262 jet fighter made its first flight on April 18, 1941, and the first with "only jet engines" on July 18, 1942. The second fear was that the combined strategic forces of the RAF and USAAF would fail to neutralize the Luftwaffe over the landing beaches planned for *Overlord* and cause failure of the invasion.

On June 13 Brig Gen Nathan Bedford Forrest, chief of staff of the Second Air Force, was killed in action while flying as an observer in a B-17 of the 95th BG, which lost ten of 24 aircraft attacking the Kiel U-boat facility. Overall, the Eighth Air Force lost 22 of 76 4th BW aircraft dispatched on this date. Unusually, most losses were inflicted by Bf 109G-6s of JGs 11 and 26 in perhaps the first successful use of the underwing 20mm cannon gondolas.[57] This loss triggered a cable from Eaker to Arnold requesting "more bombers, replacement crews and long-range tanks for P-47s."[58]

By then the first examples of both the YB-40 and P-47D-1-RE had arrived in-theater and were prepared for their first combat operations. The YB-40 was the first example of a B-17 variant fitted with the very-high-priority twin 0.50cal chin turret. Eight YB-40s were assigned to escort the 94th BG for its operational debut on June 22, but the mission was aborted due to adverse weather.[59]

The June 25 raid to Hüls, in Germany, was a tactical success, causing a complete shutdown of synthetic rubber production for more than 30 days. Conversely, Hüls cost the Eighth Air Force one YB-40 to flak and 19 more B-17s to flak and fighters – nine percent of the attacking force. Additionally, the raid was an example of Eighth Air Force planners failing to schedule another follow-on strike on an important target.

Three days earlier, the first Mustang IAs were received for introduction into operational service by No. 268 Sqn, based at RAF Odiham, in Hampshire. It was not until August 13 that the new aircraft were deemed to be reliable enough to commence operations over enemy-occupied territory.[60]

The obvious shock in June–July 1943 was the growing realization that the long-held mantra of the senior leadership of the USAAF had been changed to, "The Bomber May NOT Always Get Through – unless escorted." The effect on HQ-AAF was immediate and intense, as evidenced by Gen Giles' instructions to Lockheed, Republic, and NAA to increase internal fuel for their respective fighters, and became even more obvious when NAA was assigned A1 Priority for Packard Merlin 1650-3 engines. Curtiss, Bell, and Lockheed were denied 1650-3 engines for any current or future aircraft development. As noted earlier, Packard was never able to meet delivery commitments for combined USAAF/RAF orders.

Operations for the Eighth Air Force from July 1 to 16 included more short-range missions to airfields, aircraft industry factories, ports, and marshaling yards – all within the escort range of RAF Spitfires and VIII Fighter Command P-47s. While

The YB-40 was a B-17F "upgunned" at the Lockheed-Vega plant. The chin turret fitted to the aircraft was deemed extremely high priority because of the effectiveness of the success enjoyed by the Luftwaffe with its "Company Front" attacks on both the B-17 and B-24. This particular aircraft (41-24341) came off the production line as the second B-17F Flying Fortress, and it was then modified to become the XB-40. The subsequent YB-40 went into combat in the ETO with VIII Bomber Command in a slightly different configuration, with the cockpit fairing cut short of the mid-dorsal position. The introduction of the heavily armed escort bomber followed such proposals voiced in 1941. Totally ineffective, the aircraft proved to be too slow to keep up with bomb-free B-17s and B-24s on the return leg of the mission. They were eventually returned to the US to revert back to B-17F configuration. The chin turret, however, was fitted to very late production B-17Fs and continued into the B-17G series. (*NARA*)

the pressure was on Eaker to begin large-scale attacks on Germany's aircraft industry, he balanced the need to train the replacement crews while he rebuilt the Eighth Air Force's bomber inventory after losing his entire complement of 2nd BW B-24s to execute the *Tidal Wave* attack on the Ploesti refineries. In addition, he was waiting for the P-47s to gain increased escort range after being converted to carry the 205gal "tub" ferry tank.

On or about July 7 the 352nd and the 355th FGs arrived in the Firth of Clyde and traveled by train to Bodney and Steeple Morden airfields, respectively.[61] July 7 also saw the arrival of the 13th Photographic Squadron (PS)/7th Photographic Group (PG) at Mount Farm, Oxfordshire, equipped with F-5A Lightnings. All of the latter were unarmed P-38G-1/3/10-LOs modified with camera noses.

In addition to the daily operations, actions at VIII Air Technical Section under Lt Col Hough's guidance secured the vacuum pressure fittings for both the P-38 and P-47, directed installation of the P-47 centerline rack kits initially performed at BAD1 Burtonwood, and began the testing of higher-altitude tank pressurization capability for the 75gal and 150gal tanks (P-38). Following Gen "Monk" Hunter's approval of the British-made 108gal impregnated paper fuel tanks, the first Bowater-Lloyd fuel tanks were delivered to the VIII Air Technical Section at Bovingdon, Hertfordshire, on July 12 to begin testing with the new pressure valves.[62]

In mid-July Lt Gen Delos Emmons arrived as a designated observer from HQ-AAF to review the status of Eighth Air Force operations following the June exchanges between Eaker and Arnold. On July 17 Eaker cabled Arnold, "Request P-51 groups to limit of availability for September–November. Expect these airplanes will be very effective to complement P-47s in support of the bomber effort." Five days later Emmons also cabled Arnold, "Request that all P-51s with Merlin engine be supplied this theater."[63]

July 24 was noteworthy for the very-long-range attack mounted on the aluminum plant at Heroya in Norway. For the first time in the ETO, long-range fuel tanks were installed in the B-17s. Even with these tanks, the strike force flew at low altitude to further conserve fuel. "Blitz Week" ended on July 31 after a series of attacks on Hamburg, Hannover, Kassel, Oschersleben, and Warnemünde.

Kassel is approximately 415 miles from London in a straight line – approximately double the combat radius of the P-47 with the 205gal ferry tank to be introduced on July 28. Furthermore, Stuttgart, Schweinfurt, Brunswick, and Bordeaux are approximately 450-plus miles from the fighter bases in East Anglia. Bombers attacking those targets would not receive escort from VIII Fighter Command until the deployment of P-51Bs and P-38Js during "Big Week" in February 1944.

The Hamburg attacks were particularly noteworthy as a combined series of raids by RAF and USAAF bombers. They were also remarkable for the introduction of Chaff – aluminum strips tuned in length to known German radar frequencies to cause complete signal confusion and totally disrupt German radar. The devastation caused at Hamburg severely shocked Speer, Goebbels, Hitler, and Göring. The Luftwaffe's effectiveness was also badly affected while it struggled to solve the

Lt Col Cass Hough's Air Technical Section modified the P-47C/D to carry unpressurized 205gal ferry tanks, with limited success. Not only prone to leaking, they also occasionally failed to release in flight. This aircraft, P-47C-2 41-6192, was assigned to 1Lt Robert Wehrman of the 336th FS/4th FG. (*NARA, sourced by Peter Randall*)

interference of its entire radar network – particularly the defensive net aimed at detecting RAF night attacks.

Despite the success of Chaff, VIII Bomber Command had already begun to realize that there were serious problems surrounding the employment of the YB-40. The airplane was simply too slow, particularly after the strike force dropped its bombs and increased speed on the return leg of the mission. With its enormous quantity of ammunition, extra 0.50cal guns, and two additional turrets, the YB-40 also struggled to climb with the aircraft it was supposed to be escorting.

The July 28 mission resulted in one significant VIII Fighter Command victory. The 4th FG fitted the ungainly 205gal ferry tanks and departed for a rendezvous with the 1st BW returning from Kassel. The 4th was tasked with providing withdrawal support, beginning at Emmerich in Germany. Although the actual usable fuel was reduced to 100gal owing to the tank being unpressurized, the 4th surprised the fighters of I./JG 3 and I./JG 26 by attacking them 40 miles further inland than was believed possible by the Luftwaffe. The 4th claimed nine fighters destroyed for the loss of one P-47 in the ensuing fight.[64]

July 28 also marked the first use of WGr. 21cm mortar shells, with aircraft from both JGs 1 and 11 deploying them that day.

ABOVE The Bf 110G was the mainstay of the *Zerstörergruppen* in 1943–44 during the Defense of the Reich. Here, a Bf 110G from III./ZG 26 awaits the reloading of its WGr. 21cm mortar tubes. The Mustang's long range was the downfall of the Luftwaffe's deployment of the twin-engined *Zerstörer* against US bomber formations in the spring and summer of 1944. (*EN Archive*)

RIGHT Both the Fw 190A and Bf 109G were first modified in 1943 to employ 152kg WGr. 21cm mortar shells fired from single-tube underwing launchers. Here, armorers load a shell into a tube fitted beneath the wing of an Fw 190A-8/R6 from *Stab*/JG 26 in the summer of 1944. (*EN Archive*)

Heavy bomber operations in July 1943 ended on the 30th with a strike by 134 B-17s against the Waldau and Bettenhausen Fieseler Works in Kassel. Twelve B-17s were listed as missing in action and a further 82 suffered varying degrees of damage – the former represented a nine percent loss. The attacks by Luftwaffe day fighters increased significantly during "Blitz Week," resulting in the loss of 84 B-17s and one

P-47. Additionally, 531 B-17s were damaged and 18 written off.[65] The total losses for July were 33 percent greater than in June.

During this period in the battle of Germany the Luftwaffe reacted by introducing several changes to capabilities and tactics. First, the armament of single-engined fighters was upgraded, both internally and with kits, to augment their firepower. Examples included attaching gondolas under the wings outboard of the landing gear to carry single and multiple MG 151 20mm cannon and, later, 30mm Mk 108 cannon, as well as launch tubes for 152kg WGr. 21cm mortar shells. Such weapons were regularly used by Bf 109s, Fw 190s, Bf 110s, and Messerschmitt Me 410s.

In addition to armament enhancements, the Bf 109G series upgraded to the DB 605A engine giving 1,455hp at 1.42ata (atmospheric pressure) boost at the full-throttle height of 23,000ft. At first, in mid-1942, the boost was reduced to 1.32ata, but it was restored to the original figure in June 1943. The Fw 190A-4 and A-5 were both equipped with the BMW 801D engine, upgraded to 1,740hp take-off power.[66] Although the P-51B-1 being delivered to the USAAF in June 1943 had less horsepower with the Packard Merlin 1650-3 than the Bf 109G with the DB 605A at the same full-throttle height of 22,000ft, it was 30mph faster at that altitude.

Both the Bf 109G and Fw 190A series were equipped with centerline rack kits to carry an external 300-liter (79gal) combat fuel tank to extend operational range. Additionally, several variations of the Fw 190A-4/5 with extremely powerful armament emerged. The latter included two wing-root-mounted Mk 108 30mm

Pristine Me 410B-1/U4s of 5./ZG 26 gathered at Königsberg Neumark in the spring of 1944. The aircraft are fitted with long-barrelled Rheinmetall Bordkanone 5 50mm cannon, a weapon adapted from a tank gun. The Me 410 also boasted two MG 151 20mm cannon in the nose. Although potentially a formidable bomber destroyer, the Me 410 proved very vulnerable to USAAF long-range fighter escorts. ZG 26 was badly mauled by Mustangs in May, June and July 1944, forcing it to convert to the Fw 190A-8 in *Sturm* configuration. (EN Archive)

cannon inboard, two MG 151/20 cannon outboard, and the U12 gondola packs containing two 20mm MG 151/20 each.

Next, the Luftwaffe reorganized its defense sectors, with local control of fighters to respond to attacks but with the latter coming under more centralized overall control. Given information provided by the intelligence sources feeding the command center, they could direct each or all of the sectors to assemble and attack under planned circumstances. In particular, the intelligence sources included radar, coast-based watchers using optics to identify the strength, altitude, and heading of USAAF bombers, and listening posts for radio traffic on all important frequencies, even bomber to control tower or squadron leader to group leader during take-off and assembly. The Luftwaffe always knew when American bombers were preparing to attack, from the time the engines were started, through assembly of squadrons into groups and wings, and into position within the bomber stream as the armada set course over the coast of Britain.

Based on lessons learned, the Luftwaffe developed tactics to break up formations with rocket-firing Bf 110s and Junkers Ju 88s (and later Me 410s) to cause individual bombers in the targeted formations to evade, whereupon the single-engined Bf 109s and Fw 190s would close on separated bombers. The Luftwaffe learned to intercept the formations but not to immediately engage them, instead flying parallel to them, out of the range of the bomber gunners. The attackers would then radio speed, course, and altitude information to central fighter controllers and flak batteries. The aircraft most used for "stalking" were Ju 88s.

The Luftwaffe controllers presented a "layered defense," with the first assembly of German fighters beginning over the North Sea and just inland of the French coast,

The Fw 190A-7 was the first example of the Focke-Wulf fighter to be fitted with two MG 131 13mm machine guns in the upper forward fuselage weapons station ahead of the windscreen. The A-7 also featured four wing-mounted MG 151 cannon, as introduced by the Fw 190A-6. (*Tony Holmes Collection*)

beyond the range "most of the time" of escorting RAF and USAAF fighters. Following the first series of attacks, the various fighter units landed, refueled, and reloaded ammunition as the bomber forces proceeded inland, leaving the second layer, including twin-engined *Zerstörergruppen*, to take up the defense. As the Eighth Air Force dropped its bombs to return home, the first wave was refueled, rearmed, and in the air along the predicted course for Britain, ready to attack the escaping bombers.

Next, the Luftwaffe command continued transferring experienced combat units from the Ost and Süd to reinforce the Defense of the Reich fighter force – both single- and twin-engined day fighters. In concert with the fighter squadron migration, Hitler finally approved the plan submitted by Milch in early 1943, namely to concentrate industry and networks to achieve more and faster production of aircraft, as well as to increase the percentage of Bf 109, Fw 190, and Me 410 fighters.[67] As Luftwaffe operations closed for July 1943, they also recorded the highest number of sorties against the Eighth Air Force (2,420, compared with 1,303 in June), which remained the highest until the sorties doubled in October. Additionally, Luftwaffe claims rose to 108 destroyed, compared with 59 in June.[68]

The Fw 190A-5/U11 was one of several variants designed to be bomber destroyers through the addition of extra weaponry. This trials aircraft has been fitted with two MK 103 30mm cannon in pods in place of the MG FF 20mm weapons previously housed in the outer wings. The fighter retains a single MG 151 20mm cannon within either wing root. (*EN Archive*)

CHAPTER 6

THE MISSION OF LONG-RANGE ESCORT REACHES CRISIS POINT

Future Eighth Air Force commanding officer Brig Gen Jimmy Doolittle (right) converses with "Dutch" Kindelberger during a tour of NAA's B-25 line at Inglewood in the fall of 1942. Construction of the medium bomber was moved to Kansas City in 1943 to make room for increased Mustang production in Inglewood. Doolittle's famous order to VIII Fighter Command, "Seek the Luftwaffe and destroy them in the air and on the ground", would effectively unleash the Merlin Mustang on the Luftwaffe in early 1944. (© *The Boeing Company*)

CHRONOLOGY FOR NAA/HQ-AAF/MATERIEL COMMAND FROM AUGUST THROUGH OCTOBER 1943

Events overseas in both the ETO and MTO greatly concerned Gen Arnold and his staff. First, "Blitz Week," ending July 30, recorded a major spike in B-17 losses to Luftwaffe day fighters. Then the *Tidal Wave* low-level attack on Ploesti on August 1 resulted in more than 50 B-24s being listed as missing in action to flak and fighters, including large numbers of the 44th, 93rd, and 389th BG aircraft loaned to the Twelfth Air Force. All three groups eventually limped back to Britain to refit and train new replacement crews, but did not commence attacks on the Continent until September 7, 1943. Then, on August 17, the loss of 20 percent of the 315 B-17s attacking Schweinfurt and Regensburg escalated the pressure on HQ-AAF to "do something" to accelerate the deployment of the P-51B to the ETO and field more examples of the P-38H in-theater. The pressure and urgency to bring the P-51B and P-38J to operational status was intense.

On August 5 Col Bradley's NAA Report of the flight tests of P-51B-1-NA 43-12304 fitted with fuselage and combat tanks was extremely positive. The performance was detailed and summarized in the report, and its date of publication coincided with the first flight of the P-51C-1-NT.[1] The test flight by the Materiel Command Chief, Fighter Projects, solidified uniform impressions that the P-51B must be deployed as soon as possible. The first P-51C-1-NT, 42-102979, was delivered from the Dallas plant to the USAAF on August 17. It remained there for flight testing until November 1.[2]

On August 9 Chilton flew 43-12112 with the production Firestone 85gal self-sealing fuselage tank in place of the prototype steel test tank.

Work continued to also install a production Firestone 85gal fuselage tank (per NA-104 production design) into 43-12304, for planned stability test flights to begin on September 9. The test series was planned to include flights with full fuselage tanks plus external long-range combat and ferry tanks to evaluate stability and control characteristics with full fuel loading. Additionally, Field Services was closely engaged to be able to draft the future release of Field Services Bulletin (FSB) 73-95, which would accompany all 85gal fuselage tank modifications for all P-51B-1, B-5, and C-1 Mustangs dispatched to the ETO prior to the tanks being installed during production.

On or about the first week in August, NAA Field Services, the Experimental Department, and Production Engineering began detail preparation of FSB 73-95. Engineering initiated a complete set of drawings covering installation of the production 85gal fuselage tank, the necessary parts and assemblies to incorporate the tank, the fuel supply plumbing and tank selector switch changes to add the fifth tank (two 92gal main wing tanks, two external combat tanks, and the new fuselage tank)

F-6Cs, P-51B-1s and Mustang IIIs sit side-by-side within Hangar No. 2 at Mines Field. In the background is P-51B-1 43-12304, which was the second Mustang modified in the Experimental Department to incorporate the prototype 85gal self-sealing fuselage tank and added oxygen supply. In the foreground is P-51B-1-NA 43-12388. Per Materiel Command MCR to the P-51B-1 specification, it was the first of three Mustangs to install the production Firestone 85gal fuselage tank plus all necessary changes per NAA Field Service Bulletin 73-95. All three aircraft were delivered to Eglin Field in October 1943 for suitability testing. (© *The Boeing Company*)

RESTRICTED

Weekly

SERVICE NEWS

NORTH AMERICAN AVIATION, INC.

FIELD SERVICE DEPT. INGLEWOOD, CALIF.

VOL. 2—NUMBER 11 OCTOBER 30, 1943

ADDITIONAL FUEL FOR FIGHTER AIRPLANES

An urgent military need has brought about the incorporation of provisions for additional fuel capacity for fighter airplanes. An 85-gallon self-sealing auxiliary tank is to be installed in the fuselage, aft of the pilot's compartment. FIGURE 1 shows the bulletproof cell installed in a test ship at the factory. The tank is 54 inches long, 25 inches wide, and 16 inches deep (FIGURE 2).

A booster pump, fitted with a self-draining outlet, is attached to the bottom of the tank, which is independently

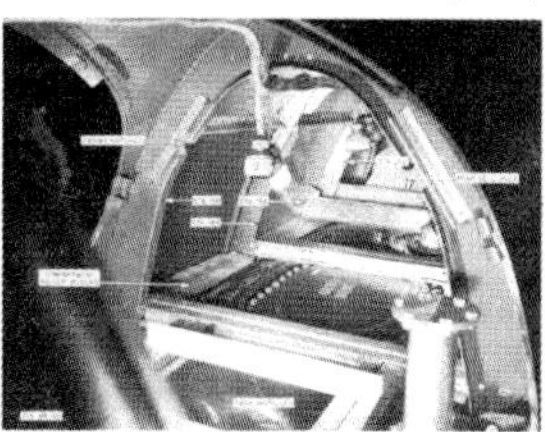

Figure 1

vented (FIGURE 3). The direct-reading gage is goosenecked, so it may be seen from the pilot's seat. The drain line ends in a petcock on the left underside of the fuselage, just forward of the radiator; a Dzus-fastened door covers the opening. The filler neck cap is located on the left side of the fuselage, just forward of the insignia on the side of the airplane. The vent outlets are located on the right side of the fuselage immediately below the insignia. An access door is built into the top of the tank.

Airplanes Affected

The 85-gallon fuel cell is to be installed in the following service airplanes at the earliest possible date:

P-51B-1 AAF43-12093/12492, inclusive
P-51B-5 AAF43-6313/7112, inclusive
P-51C-1 AC42-102979/103378, inclusive

Production installation begins with P-51B-10 Airplane AAF43-7113 and P-51C Airplane AC42-103379.

Figure 2

Field Service Requirements

When the 85-gallon fuel cells are available in sufficient quantity, the following Field Service program is contemplated:

NAA is to fabricate kits containing all necessary parts. These are to be shipped with the tanks to Modification Centers and theaters of operations designated by the AAF. The first shipment of kits is leaving the factory this week. NAA Field Service Bulletin (Special Instructions NA No.

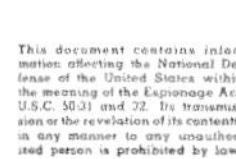

This document contains information affecting the National Defense of the United States within the meaning of the Espionage Act. U.S.C. 50:31 and 32. Its transmission or the revelation of its contents in any manner to any unauthorized person is prohibited by law.

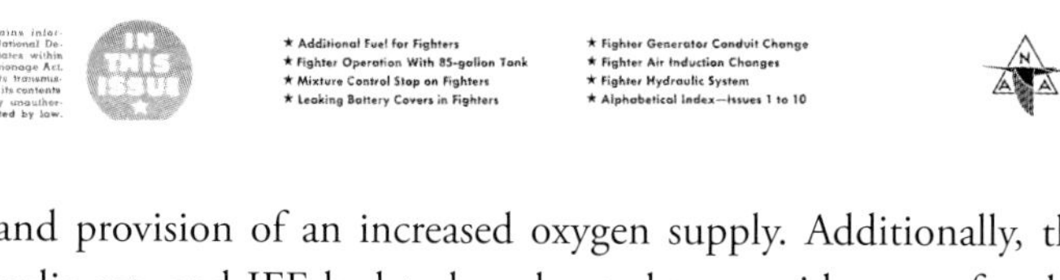

RESTRICTED

PAGE 2 WEEKLY SERVICE NEWS

Figure 3

16) has been issued with full details concerning Field Service installation. Later, the Special Instruction Bulletin will be superseded by Field Service Bulletin (NA 73-95) and an AAF Technical Order.

Rework Involved

To install the new 85-gallon fuel cell, extensive revisions have to be made in the airplane. The oxygen system and radio equipment are relocated, electrical installations modified, and major rework is required to change the aft fuselage structure. Details of the tank installation are shown in FIGURE 4.

Field Service rework of the above airplanes is to be accomplished by the 4th Echelon Maintenance. It is estimated that 450 man-hours will be required to install the 85-gallon tank.

The 522 radio is to be used when the 85-gallon auxiliary tank is installed. The radio is mounted on a metal shelf above the aft end of tank. To make possible the use of the SCR-695 (IFF) radio as alternate equipment, NAA is to install group "A" parts for SCR-695 radio in production airplanes; this installation does not interfere with the installation of the tanks. Further, the group "A" parts which cannot be installed in production are to be furnished in kit form for each airplane. This action is being taken because the SCR-695 (IFF) radio set and the 85-gallon tank cannot be installed in the fuselage due to space and C.G. limitations.

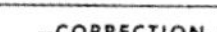

—CORRECTION—

The factory change point for P-51B Airplanes, as given in the article "Elimination of Vibration of Gun Camera" on Page 3 of Issue No. 9 of Weekly Service News, dated October 16, 1943, is incorrect. The correct change point for P-51B Airplanes is AAF43-6813 and subsequent.

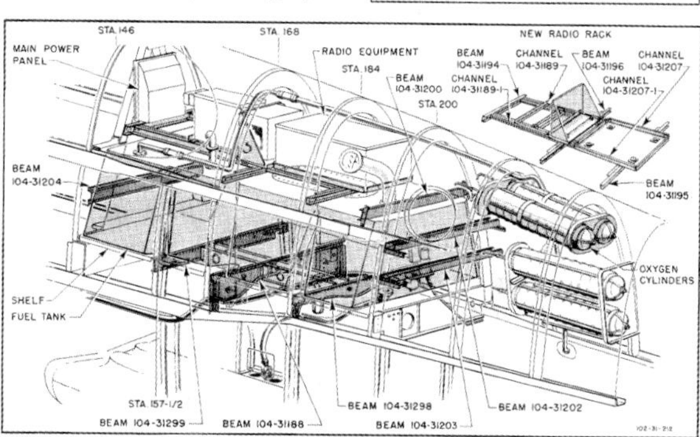

Figure 4

RESTRICTED

ABOVE LEFT Page one of the NAA *Weekly Service News* dated October 30, 1943 explaining the introduction of the 85gal fuselage tank kits for the P-51B. (*© The Boeing Company*)

ABOVE Page two of the NAA *Weekly Service News* dated October 30, 1943 detailing some of the changes and requirements needed to allow the installation of the 85gal tank. (*© The Boeing Company*)

and provision of an increased oxygen supply. Additionally, the battery, command radio set, and IFF had to be relocated to provide space for the tank. The target to define the parts and process to assemble and package the kit installation was late August, with an initial order for 800 kits to be produced (later increased to 1,200 and finally 1,600).

Materiel Command contacted NAA to request an "immediate" change point for early P-51B-5-NA production, but this was deemed to be impossible by the company without significant delay in the construction of the P-51B-5 and C-5 Mustangs. Accordingly, the change point was set for the first P-51B-10, and was the major reason for the block change. Materiel Command also requested that the V-1650-7 be introduced in the P-51B-5 and C-1. That said, even this proved to be too ambitious. The actual introduction of the Packard Merlin 1650-7 to the Mustang series were made in block change P-51B-15-NA 42-106739, P-51C-5-NT 42-103329 and P-51D-5-NA 44-13253.[3]

The August 10 order NA-117 for 3,500 P-51Hs was executed by Materiel Command, based on performance projections for the XP-51G with the R.M. 14 S.M. engine – an extension of the Rolls-Royce Merlin 100. Packard was also developing the V-1610-9 to roughly parallel Rolls-Royce development for the Merlin 100 and R.M. 14 S.M. With 150-octane fuel, combined with water injection to suppress detonation of the fuel-air charge at 90inHg manifold pressure, the engine

TOP RIGHT Page four of the NAA Field Service Bulletin's last update for January 1944 details both the serial number block and the quantity of the aircraft to be modified. Note that provisions to supply complete kits were made for all P-51B-1s, 800 P-51B-5s and the first 400 P-51C-1s. This 108-page document detailed every step required in the modification process for the fitting of the 85gal fuselage tank into existing P-51B/Cs in the field. (*© The Boeing Company*)

RESTRICTED

Page 4 of 107 FIELD SERVICE BULLETIN No. 73-95 January 12, 1944

Reason for Change:

This modification is made in accordance with the dictates of urgent military requirements.

Airplanes Affected:

This modification may be accomplished on any of the following airplanes:

P-51B-1-NA 43-12093 to 43-12492, incl. 400
P-51B-5-NA 43-6313 to 43-7112, incl. 800

P-51B Airplanes, Serial Nos. 43-7113 and subsequent and P-51C Airplanes, Serial Nos. 42-103779 and subsequent will be completely provisioned with the 85-gallon fuselage fuel cell at the factory prior to delivery. Three (3) P-51B Airplanes, Serial Nos. 43-12388, 43-12389, and 43-12390, of the above group have been completely provisioned at the factory prior to delivery.

NOTE: *The parts kits contract was negotiated for 1600 kits. The additional 400 parts kits are to be used on the 800 P-51C Airplanes as designated by the AAF.*

Maintenance Parts Affected:

None.

Accomplishment:

This change shall be made *as soon as possible.*

Echelon Recommended:

Fourth echelon.

Man-Hours Required:

Approximately 450 man-hours for complete modification. Approximately 150 to 300 man-hours for later airplanes with partial provisions incorporated at the factory.

Weight Change:

This modification causes a maximum net weight increase of approximately 25 pounds and basic weight C.G. moves approximately 0.7 inch forward. (See Section XV for further data.)

Size and Weight of Parts Kit:

SIZE: Approximately 55" x 46" x 20".
WEIGHT: Approximately 290 pounds.

RIGHT A view looking aft behind the cockpit of a P-51B-7 during the equipment installation process. Visible in this photograph are the battery holder and racks for the radio transmitter and receiver, the black rubber 85gal fuselage fuel tank and its standing fuel gauge. The external filler cap (proof that the Mustang has indeed been modified with the 85gal tank) can also be seen to the left of the "star and bar", with the ADF loop on the fuselage spine. The loop points to the aircraft's scheduled deployment to the CBI. (*© The Boeing Company*)

horsepower was projected at 2,200hp at 22,000ft. This order would be canceled in April 1944 and transferred to NA-126.

A flurry of commands and instructions emanated from HQ-AAF in August and September. First, Gen Fairchild's issuance of the update to the FAREP was approved in mid-August. The only amendment to the FAREP was the requirement that changes accepted as post-production kits were to be made production items in the existing and future aircraft "as soon as practicable." To give specific examples, the P-38 had to incorporate the 55gal leading-edge tank (the P-38H already included bomb rack and shackle/sway braces for external tanks, as well as pressurization for high-altitude operations); the P-47 was to be delivered with external rack/sway braces and a pressurization system, the wings had to be modified for the attachment of bomb racks, sway braces, and plumbing for external combat tanks, and an increase to internal fuel was to be developed as soon as possible; and the P-51, which already included wing fuel, bomb racks, and sway braces via the A-36, had to have the 85gal tank installed in the production deliveries, along with factory-supplied tank pressurization for the external combat tanks.

On August 17 the Fighter Branch Engineering Section recommended that NAA not continue seeking additional fuel capacity in the P-51B wing, specifying "Fuselage tank – only."[4]

The issue arising from completed aircraft being released without new equipment installed was that they had to be sent to Depots for modification before they could be ready for combat operations.

On September 3 two orders of significance were released. First, Gen Arnold cabled Gen Marshall, pointing out that "Recent events indicate need for Long Range fighters to accompany bombers. Request that priority assignments of P-38 to MTO be denied and sent to ETO."[5] The actual arrival of the 20th FG at Kings Cliffe on August 26, followed by the 55th FG at Nuthampstead on September 16, indicate that Arnold was keeping his boss informed, rather than asking for permission.[6]

On the same day, Gen A. E. Jones, Chief, Procurement Division, Materiel Command, by order of Brig Gen Branshaw, issued instructions to "provide three P-51B aircraft with hand-made 85gal fuselage tanks to AAFSAT [AAF School of Applied Tactics] for Flight Testing," plus "install 55gal tank for P-51D-1 aircraft at the factory prior to delivery" – the latter instruction was amended to 85gal tank. The order also confirmed previously issued Materiel Change Request C-348 for NA-102 for P-51B-1-NAs 43-12388, -12389, and -12390. The three completed P-51Bs were delivered to the Experimental or Advanced Production Department in early August for modification, and delivered to the AAFSAT in Orlando, Florida, in or about October 1943. The instructions also provided for a "Purchase Order for fabrication of 800 kits to be furnished for P-51B-1, P-51B-5, and P-51C-1 airplanes." It also expressed the desire "that NAA make every possible effort to provide the 55-gallon tanks for the P-51D-1-NA and P-51D-1-NT and subsequent in all airplanes prior to delivery."[7]

As noted earlier, NAA's Field Services used information gained from the modification of P-51B 43-12304 using the production Firestone fuselage tank, and to prepare the first draft of the instruction manual and training program for Air Depot center personnel, NAA FSB 73-95. The field kits not only supplied the components required to fit the 85gal tank, but also the new oxygen bottle installations for longer-range operations. NAA brought in modification service supervisors from the Buffalo Air Depot for training before release of the kits in October 1943.

NAA's Field Services team worked in close coordination to assist in designing the kit packaging and preparing instructions for retrofitting the P-51B-1, P-51B-5, and P-51C-1 production blocks that would not have all the new features when they were completed and accepted by the USAAF. Field Services also began preparation of the 108-page FSB 73-95. The first draft emerged in late August, as designs for fabrication of the parts necessary for the installation of the kits were completed. As all the changes were not introduced simultaneously into production, FSB 73-95 was revised several times to

P-51B-1-NA 43-12102, Mines Field, California, November 1943. (*Artwork by Jim Laurier, © Osprey Publishing*)

reflect the progressive reduction in total project labor requirements from 450hrs to 150hrs, as the last block of P-51B-5s and C-1s rolled off the assembly line with most of the infrastructure for incorporation of the fuselage fuel tank already included.[8]

Ultimately, 1,600 kits were contracted to provide for all P-51B-1s and P-51B-5-NAs, P-51C-1s, and the first 50 P-51C-5-NTs.[9]

On September 10 Chilton flew 43-12304 with an 85gal production self-sealing fuselage tank installed to begin stability testing before 43-12388, -12389, and -12390 were scheduled to arrive at Eglin. None of these aircraft was yet fitted with internal baffles to prevent the fore-and-aft and side-to-side "sloshing" of fuel in a partly filled tank.

Within the next two weeks several events occurred. Namely, the first P-51B-1-NAs arrived in the ETO,[10] and then some were diverted to the RAF, beginning with FZ100.

In concert with the recent update to the FAREP, and events pointing to increased pressure from Arnold, Materiel Command issued a series of orders relating to combat-worthiness enhancements concerning P-51B/D series aircraft, as well as the P-38 and P-47.

On September 17 Brig Gen Branshaw sent another cable to NAA ordering "convert Packard Merlin 1650-3 to -7 as soon as possible. Packard to produce supercharger kits as required in the field."[11] His memo also included the request that testing of a P-51 with a Packard 1650-7 be expedited to evaluate performance differences. Two days later the Experimental Department project logs note "C-258-1 (P-51D-1) and C-258-2 (P-51B-1) reworked to prepare for flight tests. Adv. Engineering 10% complete for add. of 85gal fuse Tank."[12]

At this point in the bubble canopy modification project, P-51B-1 43-12102 (C-258-2) was closer to completion than P-51D-1 42-106539 (C-258-1) because the 85gal fuselage tank installation had just begun for the D-model Mustang but was not necessary for 43-12102. The second NA-102 P-51B-1 fuselage assembly was also in the Advanced Production area, undergoing modification with the bubble canopy cockpit enclosure for NA-106 static tests. Important Change Orders incorporated on the NA-102 fuselages included dropping the firewall slightly to accommodate the new P-51D windscreen assembly, as well as modifying the leading edge of the wing between wing station 61 and the fuselage with a new sub-spar to accommodate the new landing gear well and wheel door. Additionally, the six 0.50cal AN/M2 machine guns were installed in the upright position, rather than using the slanted design originated in the A-36 and continuing through the P-51B/C.[13]

On September 21, Col W. M. Morgan, Acting Chief, Production, Materiel Command, approved funding for the internal pressurization system to support combat tank pressurization independent of "B-12 Vacuum Pump" if "possible." He also instructed NAA to assemble kits and incorporate into the production of all Mustangs the external fuel tank pressurization system "per NAA Drawing 102-948008."[14] As previously noted, Materiel Command initially requested immediate insertion, but was persuaded that such an order, if followed, would shut down P-51B production for a period unacceptable to the War Production Board. The planned insertion point for production was P-51B-5 (No. 400) 43-6713, but this was changed to 43-6913. The temporary expedient of linking the B-12 vacuum pump installation to sustain the feed operation of external combat tanks for the P-51B-1s now arriving in the ETO was accomplished via NAA's Legarra with Hough at VIII Air Technical Section.

Following Col Morgan's memo to NAA regarding the pressurization system's approval, Materiel Command issued a memo on the 23rd "requesting fuselage self-sealing tanks in as many P-51 aircraft as possible."[15]

During the flurry of Materiel Command instructions, NAA completed engineering for the 104-48013 "Equipment Installation – Fuse. Fuel Tank," and released the system for insertion into P-51B-10 No. 1 (43-7113) block. Engineering on the NA-106 P-51D-1-NA's "Installation Cockpit Enclosure" for the bubble canopy was also released to both the Production and Experimental Departments. The latter initiated the final bubble canopy fabrication for both the P-51D-1 and P-51B-1 as per MCR C-258-1 and -2, respectively. Also recorded in the C-258 project logs for the 22nd was the note, "C-258-3 – Another P-51B-1-NA Fus Being Rewk'd in Adv. Prod. for Static Tests," and "C-258-3 – 5 E.O.'s (Engineering Change Orders) Rel. to accommodate fuselage fuel cell. Adv. Prod. is only about 10% Comp."

On September 23 Allison, NAA, and Materiel Command concluded a meeting at Wright Field to discuss and agree to build the XP-51J with the new Allison V-1710-119F27 two-speed/two-stage supercharger.

LATE SEPTEMBER THROUGH OCTOBER – HQ-AAF "CRISIS MONTH"

During Arnold's visit to Britain in September he discussed several major requests with Sir Charles Portal, including naming one single leader to command both RAF Bomber Command and the Eighth Air Force, and deploying more RAF assets, particularly the Mustang IIIs arriving in Britain, to escort operations in support of the Eighth Air Force.[16]

P-51D-NA 42-106539, Mines Field, California, November 1943. (*Artwork by Jim Laurier, © Osprey Publishing*)

7th Photographic Group (Reconnaissance) F-6C 43-12425 had cameras installed but no 85gal tank. The tank and camera could not exist simultaneously in the early F-6C. (*USAF, sourced by Jack Cook*)

On September 29 Gen Arnold ordered that all P-38s and Merlin Mustangs be directed to the ETO. Planned deployments of P-38s and P-51Bs to the MTO and CBI were suspended – the MTO never received another P-38-equipped fighter group for the rest of the war.[17]

The day after the October 14 disaster of 60 B-17s missing in action on the Schweinfurt mission, Eaker urgently cabled Arnold, "Highest Priority – early arrival of P-51B and P-38s 'imperative'." He also requested 5,000 110gal and 3,000 150gal combat tanks "Soonest."[18] Arnold cabled Portal, requesting that all Mustang IIIs in Britain, as well as those en route from the US, be loaned to the Eighth Air Force or used by the RAF to provide escort to the Eighth Air Force "temporarily."[19] Two days later, on the 16th, Gen Orvil Anderson, Chief of Staff, Eighth Air Force, admitted in a meeting with Eighth Air Force wing and group commanders that attacking targets beyond fighter escort was "no longer feasible."[20]

Portal replied in a letter that the British Air Staff was contemplating the possibility of using all RAF Mustangs equipped with Merlin engines to support Eighth Air Force bombers. He agreed that the success of *Overlord* depended upon "the extent to

43-12102's P-51B wing, with its "smaller" leading edge angle from the fuselage, is clearly visible from this elevated angle. (© *The Boeing Company*)

which, by the date of the operation, we have been able to achieve a reasonable reduction of enemy fighter forces." He also accepted the contention that "the success of *Pointblank* equally depends on our ability to check the growth and reduce the strength of the day and nightfighter forces which the enemy can concentrate against us in this theatre." But Portal tried to show that it was one thing to express these necessities in directives, and quite another to achieve them in operations.[21]

What remains a complete mystery is that when the first P-51B-1-NAs arrived in September, Eaker did not resist when they were assigned to tactical duties with the Ninth Air Force.

On October 24 Gen Laurence Kuter reported to Arnold from Air Staff that a complete reappraisal must be made of *Pointblank*'s probability of succeeding in the "destruction of the Luftwaffe prior to D-Day," given the crisis in the ETO. He urged that the highest priority be assigned to destruction of German fighter factories, and that deployment of escort fighters to the ETO was called for. This report was the foundation for planning and execution of "Big Week" strikes on the German aircraft industry during February 20–25, 1944.[22]

On October 26 Arnold cabled Brig Gen George Kenney, commander of Allied Air Forces in the South West Pacific, and Lt Gen Carl Spaatz, commander of the Twelfth Air Force in the MTO, informing them that only P-47s would be delivered to those theaters. All P-51s and P-38s were to be directed to the ETO. He also instructed that Depot modifications for F-5 and F-6C reconnaissance aircraft be suspended until further notice.[23]

On the 29th Lt Gen Spaatz ordered that all Eighth and Ninth Air Force fighter groups should prioritize the support and protection of heavy bombers engaged in *Pointblank*.[24]

Maj Gen Jimmy Doolittle was named commander of the Fifteenth Air Force, which was activated on October 31. The Eighth and Fifteenth Air Forces would subsequently comprise the United States Strategic Air Forces (USSTAF), under the command of Spaatz, when it was activated on February 22, 1944.[25]

NAA AND MATERIEL COMMAND FROM LATE SEPTEMBER THROUGH DECEMBER

On October 5 Allison's General Manager, K. B. Newell, wrote to Brig Gen Branshaw, informing him of the availability of the two-speed/two-stage Allison for spring 1944, and noting that the projected capacity for Allison engines was greater than the projected production orders.[26] The last Allison Mustang, P-51A-10-NA 43-6312, was completed in June 1943. The P-51A contract was originally for 1,200 aircraft, but this was changed after P-51A No. 350 so that funds could be shifted to 400 NA-102 P-51B-1-NAs in October 1942, and then the remainder into NA-104 P-51B-5-NAs. Newell was aware of the drop-off for 1943, forecast in late 1942, as P-39 and P-40 production was coming to an end. Still available for Allison, however, were orders for the P-63 and P-38.

On October 27 the cockpit enclosures for both P-51B-1-NA 43-12102 and P-51D-NA 42-106539 were complete. The P-51D was 90 percent complete regarding the 85gal tank installation. The P-51B-1 was in the Flight Test Department, being readied for its first test flight the next week. All three bubble canopy conversions were from the same NA-106 design cockpit enclosures.

The first bubble canopy-modified Mustang, P-51B-1 43-12102 completed its maiden flight in this configuration on November 6, 1943, while P-51D-NA 42-106539 flew for the first time 11 days later. Both 43-12102 and 42-106539 endured severe buffeting during a test dive later that same month. 43-12102 suffered the destruction of its left horizontal stabilizer, and the unpainted replacement is clearly visible in this publicity photograph. Note also the aircraft's unmodified four 0.50cal-equipped "B" wing. (© *The Boeing Company*)

Several milestones were reached in November. First, Chilton took P-51B-1-NA 43-12102 with the bubble canopy modifications for its maiden flight on the 6th. During the first two weeks of tests all went well. On the 17th Chilton made the first flight of P-51D-NA 42-106539, and the following day the structural dive testing began, both P-51s being flown by Chilton and a Maj West from Materiel Command. The dive tests for both aircraft were uneventful until speeds exceeded 450–505mph true airspeed. Chilton noted severe buffeting of the left elevator, including signs of the fabric covering ballooning. Also noted were fogging of the windscreen and the "drafty cockpit." The left elevator fabric on 43-12102 was ruptured and had to be replaced to enable flight tests to continue. There are also vague references to the fabrication processes for the new -2 canopies introduced into the P-51D-5-NA production series first flown in January 1944, from draping over a mold to a vacuum-forming process.[27]

The results from these tests initiated a series of design and wind tunnel projects to solve the problems, which turned out not to be solely due to the bubble canopy changing the airflow over the top deck. The solutions necessitated both a change of the horizontal stabilizer's angle of incidence (down) and replacement of the elevator fabric covering with thin aluminum sheet. The changes were tested by Materiel Command in the fall of 1944 and approved for production insertion in the P-51D-20 block. Later, the extended horizontal stabilizer designed for the XP-51F/G/H and P-51H, combined with the lower incidence angle, improved longitudinal stability at both low and high speed. The final solution of extending the fuselage about 13in further aft from the P-51H's main spar reference line was the best of all.

On November 9 P-51 production project engineer George Gehrkens, at a Ninth Air Force HQ meeting, confirmed the decision that "1st 75 P-51Bs will go operational without 85gal tank, but kits are being installed at US- and UK-based Depots retroactively." He also reported that "1st UK inst'l due 1st week Dec. Sliding Balloon Hoods being manufactured for all P-51B/C in ETO." Gehrkens also noted in his report that the "first 85-gallon fuselage tank kits and combat tank pressurization kits were shipped to Depots on 9-15-43."[28] The first (tentative) P-51B-5 was sent to Buffalo, New York, for Depot installation of an 85gal fuselage tank kit. All previous P-51B-1s and -5s that had already departed for Britain were modified at BAD1 Burtonwood.[29] Because of the massive stream of B-17s and P-47s arriving in the ETO, the new P-51B/C deliveries from Liverpool/Speke were moved to BAD2 Warton for all future Mustang variants.

On or about November 20 NAA issued kits for combat tank pressurization for all P-51As, all P-51Bs through 43-6712, and all P-51Cs through 42-103378. All subsequent Mustangs departing Inglewood and Dallas had the pressurization modification installed as a production feature.[30]

On the 23rd USAAF Air Service Command formally requested that NAA incorporate "quick change" designs in future fighter aircraft, beginning specifically in the P-51F series, to reduce engine change labor and elapsed time significantly.

The following day Brig Gen Branshaw directed that all Depots installing the 85gal fuselage kits also denote the existence of the kits by placing a white 6in. x 6in.

ABOVE The Depot-applied six-inch white cross that denoted the installation of an 85gal fuel tank in a P-51B/C is clearly visible on the fuselage of B-7 43-6913, assigned to high-scoring 4th FG ace Capt Don Gentile. Materiel Command also decreed that all Mustangs fitted with the 85gal tank be re-designated from B-1, B-5 and C-1 to B-7 or C-7. (*Association of the 4th Fighter Group*)

ABOVE RIGHT P-51B-1 43-12388 was modified into a B-7 at Inglewood before NAA received the Materiel Command directive to apply a six-inch white cross below the data block to denote the installation of an 85gal fuel tank. It was photographed at Eglin Field during fall 1943 while undertaking trials to explore stability issues related to the newly-installed 85gal tank. (*NARA*)

cross beneath the data block on the left side of the fuselage. The marking of such Mustangs was primarily to identify the so-modified P-51B/Cs as aircraft to be flown with care when fully fueled due to the aft movement of the CG limit. Some aircraft were identified by the designation P-51B-7 and C-7, but this practice was not consistent.[31] NAA incorporated the requested identification in the top 102-000010 drawing for the P-51B-10-NA 43-7113 and subsequent P-51C-5-NT 42-103379. In addition to the fuselage tank stencil, the first P-51B/Cs to be specified to have natural metal finish were P-51B-5-NA 43-7082 and P-51C-1-NT 42-103179, but in actual practice the olive drab/gray camouflage was continued past January 1944.

Five days later 43-6913 (the 4th FG's future "VF-T," destined to be flown by high-scoring ace Capt Don Gentile) emerged from the Buffalo Depot. It had the 85gal fuselage tank modification, and was also the first P-51B-5-NA with the production combat tank pressurization system.[32] This B-5 was the first of the last 200-ship P-51B-5 block, and was also re-identified at Buffalo as a "P-51B-7-NA."[33]

At Inglewood in December 1943, fabrication of XP-51F 43-43332 began in the Experimental Department. The first P-51B-10-NA, 43-7313, was accepted by the USAAF but stayed at Inglewood for flight testing by Chilton until the end of the month. During December more dive tests and six gun-firing trials were flown with 43-12102 and 42-106539. Bob Chilton flew to Sarasota to participate in familiarization and mock-combat testing of the P-47C, P-47G, P-38H, P-39Q, P-40N, P-51A, and P-51B, including aerial gunnery, dive-bombing, and mock aerial combat.

On December 26 Materiel Command instructed all aircraft companies that camouflage paint should no longer be applied, effective January 1, 1944. Six days later NAA provided specific details as follows:

> Both aircraft and spares to cease application of camouflage paint. External surfaces, fabric, plywood, magnesium and Dural shall require protective primers and aluminized coating.

> Alclad and stainless steel shall require no covering. Anti-glare paint shall be applied on top of fuselage forward vision areas. Wing leading edges will be smoothed as outlined on P-51B/C Series Maintenance Repair Manual, Report No. NA-5742 except camouflage replaced with aluminized lacquer applied. Estimated 16 pounds weight reduction.[34]

Evidence shows that, while the practice of eliminating camouflage may have been instituted, it was about a week before 100 percent natural metal finish for fuselage and empennage emerged (apart from the anti-glare panel).

The preparation and finish process for the Mustang changed only with respect to paint versus aluminized lacquer applied as a final coat. The top and bottom surface of each wing, from the leading edge to approximately 40 percent chord (just past maximum thickness/chord location) was still puttied, sanded, and sealed to smooth the wing over all rivets and butt joints. This feature of the Mustang significantly reduced drag caused by friction and surface irregularities/gaps for the NACA/NAA 45-100 wing. Future experiments with polishing the wing surface and/or applying smoother finishes did not increase speed to any measurable extent.

On December 29–30, the P-51D-1 was completed in Advanced Production. It comprised an NA-102 P-51B-1-NA fuselage modified with an NA-106 cockpit enclosure and bubble canopy, a revised firewall, and a six-gun wing. Chilton did not fly 42-106540, and last flew 42-106539 on December 24. Presumably, both were then turned over to the USAAF in the last week of December.[35]

OPERATIONS – USSTAF AND THE LUFTWAFFE FROM AUGUST THROUGH DECEMBER 1943

The fortunes of the Eighth Air Force in late July during "Blitz Week," through the major losses to the "loaned" 2nd BW B-24s at Ploesti on August 1, pointed to two obvious facts. First, the cherished belief held by Arnold, Spaatz, and Eaker that "the bomber will always get through" was shattered. Second, the losses of aircraft and trained bomber crews was nearly greater than the replacements arriving in Britain. As seen in the previous chapter, the exchanges between Arnold and Eaker grew increasingly tense.

The issuance of Gen Kuter's assessment that *Pointblank* would fail to achieve the desired impact on the Luftwaffe in time for *Overlord* confirmed Arnold's opinion that changes had to be made. The report from Kuter dictated that, as well as attacking the critical aircraft industries, there was an even more urgent need for the USAAF in the ETO and MTO to seek out the Luftwaffe in the air and on the ground. It was equally obvious that the Eighth Air Force would not succeed in these objectives without escort fighters accompanying the bombers all the way to the targets.

That said, Eaker continued to believe that the Eighth Air Force could win a war of attrition, basing his conclusion on erroneous USAAF intelligence reports and vast overclaiming regarding the destruction of German fighters by the defensive firepower from B-17s and B-24s. His appeal to Arnold during June was, "Get me the bomber inventory (600) that you promised at Casablanca." The Eaker and Emmons cable to Arnold in July, requesting all available Mustangs, reflected a definite change of perspective by the former, but the scheduled dates for operational deployment of long-range escort fighters were mid-fall for P-38s and December for the P-51B. Eaker and the Eighth Air Force could not afford the luxury of waiting.

From June to the end of September more than 12 *Gruppen*, comprising three *Staffeln* each, of both single-engined day fighters and a combination of twin-engined *Zerstörergruppen*, had reinforced Luftwaffe defenses against attacks from the Eighth Air Force. Specifically, the establishment (paper) strength for *LwBfhMitte* and *Luftlotte* 3 increased from 916 to 1,416 day fighters. The operational strength (allocated) increased from 740 to 1,204 day fighters, and the serviceable (flyable) strength from 553 to 712 day fighters. During that quarter no new Luftwaffe *Jagdgeschwader* were organized, the growth being achieved by stripping other theaters. In the last three months of 1943 the combined serviceable strength of day fighters remained about the same due to increased attrition, primarily from VIII Fighter Command.[36]

The movement of such key forces from the Ost and Süd fronts placed severe burdens on the remaining fighter units in those theaters. These reinforcements were effectively a substitute for a non-existent robust fighter training program similar to that of the Allies. Although replacements from the fighter training schools also compensated for attrition in existing squadrons, the *Gruppen* returning to defend Germany were manned by seasoned veterans.

The missions flown by VIII Bomber Command during August 1–9 were all P-47-escorted 3rd BW B-26 strikes to airfields in France. The replacement heavy bombers, and refurbished Flying Fortresses damaged earlier, combined to enable the launching of 330 B-17s to attack Gelsenkirchen and Bonn with unimpressive results and the heavy loss of 25 B-17s, plus 172 damaged. Gunners from the 1st and 4th BWs claimed 29-7-13 German fighters destroyed/probably destroyed/damaged, once again illustrating severe overclaiming, as the Luftwaffe lost only 11 fighters, including those downed by the 4th FG, which claimed 4-0-1. The Luftwaffe was able to undertake 210 sorties with single-engined fighter units from JGs 2 and 26 on the coast and JGs 3 and 27 from Holland-Ruhr airfields. The most noteworthy feature of these missions during this period was that all the P-47s from the 4th, 56th, and 78th FGs were equipped with the new 108gal pressurized combat tanks. On August 12 the 353rd FG flew its first operational mission by sweeping the Dutch coast in the Ostend area.[37]

The following day, Eighth Air Force B-24s returning from Twelfth Air Force control for the Ploesti mission bombed the Bf 109 plant at Weiner-Neustadt, in Austria, from the south. The attack destroyed more than 50 completed Bf 109s and put the plant out of full operation until October. It was the most successful *Pointblank* attack on the German aircraft industry to date, surpassing the July 26 attack on the Fw 190 factory at Kassel. It also exposed the very weak Luftwaffe defensive force assigned to defend attacks from the south.

On August 15–16 attacks by the Eighth Air Force were launched to make the German High Command believe that the invasion was imminent. Medium bombers from the RAF's 2nd Tactical Air Force and heavy bombers from the Eighth Air Force targeted airfields, bridges, and petroleum storage centers around the Pas de Calais area. The 16th also marked the best day in respect to the fortunes of P-47s against experienced Luftwaffe fighter pilots. The 4th claimed 18-1-6 for one loss. Luftwaffe records show 17 lost, with nine pilots killed in action and two missing in action, mostly from JG 2. For the second time in two weeks, US-trained and equipped fighter pilots had proved that the P-47C/D could not only compete but prevail in aerial combat against equal or greater numbers of Luftwaffe fighters.

August 17 brought the twin strike at Regensburg and Schweinfurt in the southeast corner of Germany. The mission was characterized by bad luck, with adverse weather delaying the launch of the 1st BW by three hours. What was planned as a carefully timed attack to dilute the combined Luftwaffe force, and thereby reduce the Luftwaffe's ability to land after the first defense, refuel, and rearm, and scramble to achieve a second series of attacks on the bombers' return route, was defeated by British fog.

The 1st BW fought its way to and from Schweinfurt, literally from the Dutch coast to the target and back, losing 36-3-118 (missing in action/written off/damaged) while claiming 148-18-63 Luftwaffe fighters. The earlier Regensburg attack had better fortune, but only because the Luftwaffe ground controllers were taken by surprise when the bombers set course for Africa after dropping their bombs. VIII Fighter Command P-47s provided a somewhat effective escort, but concentrated on the penetration escort for the lead boxes of B-17s. Most of the defending fighter units were directed toward the rear of the bomber stream by the *Jagdfliegerführer* Holland-Ruhr controllers. As they engaged over Holland, the Luftwaffe continuously attacked the 4th BW all the way to Regensburg, then landed to refuel and rearm, awaiting a return that never happened.

The final totals for the Eighth Air Force that day were, for VIII Bomber Command, 60-4-168, while claiming 288-37-72 German fighters, and, for VIII Fighter Command, 19-3-4 for the loss of three P-47s. Spitfires and Hawker Typhoons of RAF Fighter Command performing withdrawal support claimed 14-2-1 while losing two. The overclaiming by the bomber groups was completely beyond belief, even for VIII Bomber Command. The Luftwaffe recorded the loss of 38 single-engined fighters and 21 twin-engined Bf 110s. The latter were from very important nightfighter units, critical for defending the Reich from RAF night attacks. They were used for both direct attacks on the bomber boxes and for attacks on stragglers separated from their formations. The 59 fighters lost mostly fell to the P-47s, Spitfires, and Typhoons (33-5-5 claims). The 56th FG claimed 16-1-9 after over-running their assigned bomber withdrawal support rendezvous, and returned to bounce II./JG 26 and NJG 1 – neither Luftwaffe force was expecting to be attacked from behind. During this battle, II./JG 26 *Kommandeur* Wilhelm-Ferdinand Galland, brother of Generalmajor Adolph Galland, was killed in action west of Maastricht.[38]

The authors have devoted more attention to this battle to illustrate several points. First, the very heavy radio traffic arising from the bomber bases was a tip-off to the Luftwaffe that a large-scale attack was imminent. Second, based on past experience, from the time that the radio traffic dwindled (approximately take-off time), the Luftwaffe controllers had an excellent estimate of elapsed time required for the bombers to form up, climb over Britain, set course for Germany, and reach the French or Dutch coast.

Next, the coastal network would spot the incoming bomber stream to assess the coast crossing point and heading, providing the Luftwaffe controllers with better information about where to direct fighter attacks and from which bases. Third, long-range fighters such as the Ju 88 were dispatched to intercept and shadow the inbound formation, radioing course, and altitude information. Fourth, the central coordination of attacks from different air defense sectors in Germany, combined with the introduction of heavily armed twin-engined nightfighters, enabled heavier firepower to be deployed against the Eighth Air Force bombers. Tactics evolved in which the twin-engined Bf 110s were directed to attack a crippled B-17 out of formation, beyond the range of fighter escort. When mistakes were made, positioning the Bf 110s inside the P-47's combat radius, the big, slow, German fighter suffered severe losses.

The shock of the day's losses not only spread within the Eighth Air Force, but also rippled to HQ-AAF stateside. It was abundantly clear that the cost of raids deep into Germany, beyond escort fighter range, was prohibitive. The Eighth Air Force was nearly losing more bombers and crews than could be compensated for by replacements from the US and damaged aircraft returned from repair facilities at Base Air Depots, and there was no solution on the near horizon. Eaker was not granted permission to suspend attacks on the German aircraft industry while awaiting redirected P-38 and P-51 fighter groups to arrive, train, and begin combat operations.

The limitation of only 305 gallons of internal fuel for the P-47C/Ds severely restricted combat radius owing to the much higher fuel consumption of the Pratt & Whitney R-2800 radial engine compared with the in-line Allisons and Merlins. Only when the bubble canopy P-47D-25-RE, with 370-gallon capacity, arrived in squadron-level numbers after D-Day did the Thunderbolt have sufficient range to conduct deep escort flights into Germany. More external fuel, plus racks and plumbing, would extend the P-47D's range to Kassel and Frankfurt in the spring of 1944, but the aircraft was unable to perform the role of long-range escort fighter in the ETO until well after June 6, 1944.

Albert Speer made the following observation on the Regensburg and Schweinfurt raid on August 17 in his memoir post-war:

> Ball bearings had already become a bottleneck in our efforts to increase armament production. But in this case the other side committed a crucial mistake by dividing up the attacking force to also attack Regensburg, but with only minor consequences. The production of ball bearings dropped by 38 percent, and we could do nothing but repair the facilities, for an attempt to relocate our ball-bearing industry would have held up production for three

> or four months. In those days we anxiously asked ourselves how soon the enemy would realize that he could paralyze the production of thousands of armaments plants merely by destroying five or six relatively small targets. The second attack on October 17 cost 67 percent of ball-bearing production, and we had used all of our spare parts reserves to sustain armaments production – and could not adequately increase supply with purchases from Sweden and Switzerland. What really saved us was that the enemy, to our astonishment once again, ceased attacks on our ball-bearing industry.[39]

What Speer could not know was that the constant draining of Eighth Air Force assets to other theaters, and the slow replacement of bombers and crews that Eaker required to meet his Combined Bomber Offensive commitments to Arnold, kept the force strength far under the desired inventory of 600 operational heavy bombers. After the raids of August 17 and October 14, the Eighth Air Force could not mount equivalent attacks for at least 60 days.

Following the great success of the Luftwaffe day fighters against VIII Bomber Command on August 17, the RAF wrought havoc on the Peenemünde V2 rocket testing facility that night, setting the program back by months. After a violent haranguing from Hitler in the aftermath of this attack, Generaloberst Hans Jeschonnek committed suicide. Following his death, Milch persuaded Göring to permit the transfer of many fighter units from the Eastern Front and the Mediterranean to the Reich. The tactically brilliant Generalfeldmarschall Wolfram von Richthofen was nominated as Jeschonnek's replacement, but Göring rejected the strong leader and chose the capable but not well-known General Günther Korten. His two immediate key contributions were to reorganize the Luftwaffe toward fewer, but critical missions. Next, he expanded the ground-support arm for the Eastern Front. Finally, he ordered the transfer of more single- and twin-engined fighter units from the Ost and Süd fronts and added them to the *Reichs-Luftverteidigung* (RLV).

Although German fighter production increased significantly in the last two quarters of 1943, training hours for new pilots continued to be scaled back owing to the lack of abundant aviation stocks and the pressure to increase replacement pilot numbers. This attempt to maintain average graduation rates by scaling back training hours would prove disastrous.[40]

The factors limiting the combat radius of available escort fighters forced Eaker and the Eighth Air Force to confront a grim future – one in which the USAAF strategic daylight bombardment doctrine had to be abandoned to join with the RAF in the night bombing campaign. With respect to planning for air supremacy over the Luftwaffe by D-Day, there was no possibility that Germany's day fighter arm could be neutralized in time for the Normandy invasion.

For the rest of the month of August the Eighth Air Force conserved experienced crews and aircraft, including the recently returned B-24-equipped 44th, 93rd, and 389th BGs and the new 392nd BG, limiting operations to raids on airfields in France, Belgium, and Holland.

A 328th FS/352nd FG P-47D-2, fitted with a locally-made 108gal impregnated paper centerline tank, is serviced between flights at Bodney in 1944. *(NARA, sourced by Peter Randall)*

During a raid on August 31, Col William Gross, CO of the 1st BW, demonstrated the value of very high frequency radios as standard bomber equipment to provide air-to-air communication between bombers, bomb groups and different bomb wings. While acting as mission commander in the lead bomb group, he noted that cloud covered the target and radioed the information to the trailing wings, permitting them to divert to the secondary target with ample time for the lead crews to plot a course and communicate the Initial Point (IP) for the bomb run to the rest of the group.[41]

During September and through to October 13, the following significant events occurred. New 108gal pressurized steel combat tanks, and the locally made 108gal impregnated paper tanks, were now available in sufficient quantity and enabled the P-47C/D to achieve a combat radius of 250-plus miles. The 75gal tanks were also in good supply. The first P-51B-1 arrived in the ETO for the Ninth Air Force, followed by several more for the RAF as the Mustang III. The Ninth Air Force intended to use its P-51B-1-NAs in the Army Co-Operation/CAS and Tactical Reconnaissance roles, the aircraft being issued to the soon-to-arrive 354th FG as replacements for the P-39s that the group had previously flown in California and Oregon. The 357th and 363rd FGs were scheduled to follow suit in short order.[42] Additionally, several more P-47D-equipped fighter groups were inbound from the US, with more scheduled for early 1944.

As previously noted in this chapter, on September 3 Arnold cabled Marshall that "the recent losses during July through mid-August demonstrated the critical need for Long-Range fighters to accompany the bombers." He further requested "that priority assignment to MTO for new P-38 FGs be denied and sent to ETO." As the new P-38H-equipped 20th FG had already arrived a week earlier, and the 55th FG reached Britain on September 16, one can conjecture that Arnold issued those instructions before he notified Gen Marshall.

September 6 brought another disastrous loss when VIII Bomber Command went back to Germany for an attack on the Stuttgart industrial area. The largest mission to date (338 dispatched/262 effective), it was defeated primarily by very poor weather into and over the target, which caused the formations to scatter and resulted in many aborts and uncoordinated attacks on targets of opportunity. Twelve crews, out of fuel, ditched on the return leg, and four landed in Switzerland. The Luftwaffe claimed nine B-17s, two P-47s, and a Spitfire for the loss of 22 fighters and nine damaged, compared with B-17 claims of 98-20-50. Actual losses for the Eighth Air Force were 45-10-116 B-17s and one P-47.[43]

The 352nd and 355th FGs went operational on September 9 and 14, respectively, as the fourth and fifth VIII Fighter Command P-47 fighter groups.

To conserve forces while training new replacement crews, the Eighth Air Force returned to attacking French airfields until the night of September 22–23, when five B-17s from the 422nd BS bombed Hannover with the RAF. There were no losses.

On the 27th the Eighth Air Force attacked Emden with the first Pathfinder Force (PFF), using the British-developed H2S radar for target acquisition through the undercast. The 95th, 96th, and 385th BGs had been equipped and trained for night operations and designated to train the other Eighth Air Force bomb groups if and when a decision might be made to abandon daylight attacks. On the night of the 27th, the 96th and 385th participated in their first RAF *Bulls Eye* night practice missions.[44]

On October 3 and 8, the Eighth Air Force went back to German targets, attacking Frankfurt and then Bremen and Vegesack. Losses for the Bremen/Vegesack mission totaled 30 B-17s and B-24s – approximately 19 percent of the attacking force.

"Black Thursday," October 14, 1943, marked the high point of Luftwaffe success in the battle of Germany. Due to the incredible loss of 60-7-138 B-17s, after losing 22-1-62 at Anklam/Marienburg/Danzig on the 9th and 30-3-102 at Münster on the 10th, the deep penetrations into Germany ceased. Those three days represented 110 bombers and more than 1,000 crewmen missing in action, plus major-to-light damage to 300 B-17s requiring repairs. This meant that less than half of the Eighth Air Force inventory that existed on October 8 was available one week later.

Once again, the Eighth Air Force reverted to undertaking short-range missions, for which more fighter escort was available all the way to and from the assigned targets. The only benefit of the shorter-range targets was the relatively low-intensity combat training now required by new VIII Fighter and Bomber Command pilots and crews as the inventory of fighters and bombers increased. On the other hand, the Luftwaffe was also able to increase its strength following the sudden cessation of the long-range daylight bombing campaign.

On October 15 Eighth Air Force crews enjoyed the last visual bombing conditions of the year. For the next several days only VIII Fighter Command was operational as fog shut down most of East Anglia. From the October 15 mission onward all bombing

Col Jack Jenkins was CO of the 55th FG, which was the first operational P-38 group to return to the ETO. The unit undertook its first combat mission on October 15, 1943 – just one day after the "Black Thursday" disaster. The order to re-direct the P-38 deployments to the ETO was given by Gen Arnold after pleas from Gen Eaker following heavy losses experienced during the end of "Blitz Week" in July 1943. (*USAF, sourced by Jack Cook*)

was performed using *Oboe*- (a precision navigation and bombing aid) or PFF-led bomb groups, beginning with a force of 114 B-17s and B-24s. The mission started with 282 bombers assigned to attack Duren, but most turned back, facing thunderstorms and cumulus clouds topping 30,000ft.

On the 15th both the 55th and 356th FGs performed their first combat operations, making sweeps along the French and Belgian coast.

On October 21 BAD2 Warton was designated the primary Eighth Air Force Air Depot for the

RIGHT P-51B-5 43-6457 (closest to the camera) and two other Merlin Mustangs are off-loaded at Liverpool Docks. After a ferry flight to BAD2 Warton in early December 1943, 43-6457 was fitted with all the ETO-required modifications, including the 85gal fuselage tank kit and Malcolm Hood. It arrived at the 355th FG's Steeple Morden base in late February 1944, where it was coded WR-G and assigned to the 354th FS. Remaining with the 355th through to war's end, the fighter was salvaged in September 1945. (*NARA, sourced by Peter Randall*)

BOTTOM RIGHT A P-47D is carefully craned onto a trailer attached to an RAF truck on the dock at Princess Landing, Liverpool, in November 1943. (*NARA*)

TOP LEFT From Liverpool, the fighters were dispatched to several depots for reassembly and cleaning. These B-10s were photographed at USAAF Station 803 at Filton, near Bristol, on April 18, 1944. Airmen set about stripping them of spray-on Par-Al-Ketone (a blend of controlled oxidized petroleum fractions in a solvent solution) corrosion inhibitor applied to protect the aircraft against salt water on their voyage across the Atlantic. (*NARA*)

BELOW LEFT A recently stripped and cleaned P-51B has its engine run up prior to being transported from Speke to BAD2 for final ETO-specific modifications. Following BAD2-applied changes, each Mustang would then be flown to its operational base. (*NARA*)

P-51 and B-24, BAD1 Burtonwood as primary Air Depot for the B-17 and P-47, and BAD3 Langford Lodge (formerly operated by Lockheed on contract) was allocated for the P-38. All early P-51Bs arrivals were initially sent to Burtonwood BAD1, but soon after this decision the P-51Bs delivered to Liverpool docks via ship transport were transported to nearby Speke for assembly and then to BAD2 for the necessary ETO modifications.

On October 29, as related in the previous chapter, Spaatz directed that all Eighth and Ninth Air Force fighter units "will be used for the support and protection of heavy bombers engaged in *Pointblank*."[45]

November 1, 1943, marked the activation of the Fifteenth Air Force, with headquarters in Tunis. Maj Gen James Doolittle took command of six heavy bomber groups, five medium bomber groups, and four fighter groups, plus the 68th Reconnaissance Group and a partial squadron from the 5th Photographic Reconnaissance Group. The five medium bomber groups were soon returned to the Twelfth Air Force. The reason for activating the Fifteenth Air Force and placing it under USSTAF control, commanded by Spaatz, was to create a "second front" to attack Axis strategic targets from bases that benefited from much better weather than was often experienced in Britain. On the first day of its activation the Fifteenth sent four B-17 groups of the 5th BW to attack the Spezia naval base and the Vezanno marshaling yards.[46] On November 2 the Fifteenth Air Force conducted the first *Pointblank* mission, attacking the Messerschmitt plant at Wiener Neustadt in Austria.

Col Ken Martin was the first CO of the 354th FG, and he was also the group's second ace with five Luftwaffe aircraft destroyed. Martin became a PoW after a head-on mid-air collision with a Bf 109 over Frankfurt on February 11, 1944. (*NARA*)

The 354th FG reached Liverpool on November 1 and traveled to Greenham Common as the first IX Fighter Command fighter group and the "pioneer" Mustang combat unit for the P-51B. Col Ken Martin was the CO – a position he had held since its activation in November 1942. The group's first experience with any Mustang was with the only A-36 in Britain (on trial with the RAF). Further exposure came on "loaners" in the form of F-6Bs (P-51As) initially provided by the 67th TRG from Membury on November 7. The group's first P-51B-1-NAs arrived on the 11th, then the 354th moved again, to Boxted. By November 30, 54 B-1s and three B-5s had been delivered and prepared for operations. None had yet been modified for either the 85gal kit installation or the Malcolm Hood.

Of significant note was the attachment of the 421st Service Squadron to the 354th, which was crucial for supporting the multiple actions necessary to keep the new Merlin Mustangs operational. The myriad problems included a total lack of P-51-specific tools, jigs, and stands customized for Mustang engine and wing changes, gun jams for the canted Browning 0.50cal AN/M2s, American-made plugs fouling too soon, boost control failures reducing power settings, leaking propeller shaft lubrication, cooling system plumbing leaks at joints under cowlings causing spray on windscreens, and an inadequate oxygen supply (until the 85gal kits arrived).

356th FS/354th FG P-51B-5-NA (possibly 43-6358) returns to Boxted from BAD2 following depot-level modifications. Barely noticeable is the white "cross" below the data block and the fuel filler cap on the upper fuselage for the newly-installed 85gal fuselage tank. (*NARA*)

P-51B-5 43-6431 *MAN o'WAR* of the 355th FG's 354th FS was assigned to squadron CO Lt Col Claiborne "Clay" Kinnard Jr. The fighter was photographed during a visit by Kinnard to the 4th FG base at Debden. (*USAF, sourced by William Marshall Collection*)

The 421st solved the gun jam by designing a servo from a B-26 top-turret drive motor with splines to feed the machine gun breeches. It also designed a carb adjustment wrench which served until the correct tools arrived from the US and solved the spark plug problem by procuring Merlin spark plugs from the RAF. The 421st was also the first fighter base service squadron to perform the Malcolm Hood installation with kits supplied by R. Malcolm Ltd. Previously, all such modifications were undertaken at BAD1. Its early "adapt" attitude led to processes that were passed on to both the Base Air Depots to correct problems before aircraft were sent to operational units as well as to other fighter group service squadrons.[47]

In November the Luftwaffe formed *Sturmstaffel* 1. Originally equipped with the more heavily armored and armed Fw 190A-7, it comprised pilots and leaders sworn to press home attacks at close range. It would morph into the feared *Sturmgruppen* of Fw 190A-8s that were even more heavily armored and armed, having both 20mm and 30mm cannon. The latter weapon could take out a B-17 or B-24 with one hit to a vital spot, such as a main wing spar. Also during late October and into November, the westernmost-based *Jagdgeschwader* commanders of the *LwBfhMitte* adopted the tactic of sending one or two flights to find and attack escorts to force them to drop their combat tanks early, but losses became so prohibitive that this was soon discontinued.[48]

The RLV formation leaders' school was established at this time and attached to I./JG 27 in Austria, offering successful combat pilots the bare minimum of instruction for leading formations against US bombers. The recently formed *Wilde Sau* single-engined nightfighter force was also expanded, with the original JG 300 being joined by JGs 301 and 302. They remained engaged against the RAF at night, but converted to daytime operations beginning with I./JG 300 in December.[49]

The P-38J-10 was the first Lightning variant capable of escorting heavy bombers all the way to Berlin after two 55gal leading edge kits were installed in the wings. The production insertion for the 55gal leading edge tanks was made on the P-38J-15-LO series. Even with a full internal load of 410gal, plus two 300gal external tanks, the P-38J-15's combat radius was still less than the P-51B/D with 110gal combat tanks. The primary discriminant between the P-38J-15 and the P-51B/C with an 85gal fuselage tank was internal fuel remaining per engine when external tanks were dropped at the commencement of combat with enemy aircraft. (*USAF*)

The flood of replacement crews from the US brought the inventory to an all-time high for the November 3 mission to Wilhelmshaven. For that mission 566 B-17s were dispatched. In addition, 333 P-47s from all seven of the Eighth Air Force's operational P-47 groups (4th, 56th, 78th, 352nd, 353rd, 355th, and 356th FGs), plus 45 P-38s from the 55th FG, provided a maximum-effort escort. The relatively short range of the Wilhelmshaven strike, despite having the largest bomber inventory to date, demonstrated the acknowledgment by Gens Eaker and Anderson that the Luftwaffe had achieved air superiority over Germany.

On November 3 a notation in a II./JG 1 diary stated that the Luftwaffe pilots noticed for the first time that the P-47s were pursuing German fighters to medium altitudes, rather than breaking away to return to escort.

Six days later, a conference was held at Ninth Air Force HQ to discuss P-51B status. The following memo by E. C. Walton from the US Mission for Economic Affairs to the Ninth Air Force Technical File noted, in summary:

> 130 AAF P-51B, 60 RAF Mustang III in ETO, 30 en route; ASC [Air Services Command] completed assembly and delivered 25 to 354FG for training; 354FG will provide escort to 8AF until tactical ops begin; 85-gallon kits arrived Sept 15 – 41 in ETO to date, 1st conversion complete next week; excessive oil consumption problems were identified, but NAA Gehrkens reported 1,450 miles with 20 min combat for only 3gal consumed. R-R to design smaller breather vents for engine rocker box, NAA to study better oil tank design. Sliding Balloon Hood to be installed in all P-51B/ Mustang III.[50]

On November 13 only the 55th FG reached Bremen. By this time the Luftwaffe pilots had a sense of the P-38's weaknesses in both dive and maneuver, and were able to exploit them.[51] During the fight near the target area the 55th was gradually broken up into flights and elements, unable to turn back the inbound JG 11, which downed seven B-24s and four P-38s.

63rd FS/56th FG P-47D-21-RE 42-26258 is seen here at Boxted with factory-installed underwing racks and a centerline rack for a combat tank. This aircraft was one of the last production P-47Ds built without a bubble canopy and 370gal internal fuel tank. With the earlier P-47D-15-RE and -16-RE, the April–May 1944 combat radius for the P-47D was past Brunswick and Ulm when furbished with two 150gal wing tanks. (*NARA, sourced by Peter Randall*)

During this period many more Merlin Mustangs arrived, including P-51B-5s and Mustang IIIs. The first P-38Js were also delivered, these being dispatched to Langford Lodge for the necessary ETO modifications. Early P-47D-11-REs with factory-installed water injection as well as internal plumbing for external wing-rack modifications also arrived. None of the P-51B-1/5s had yet been factory modified with the 85gal tank kits (including extra oxygen supply), nor had the early P-38J-10s arrived equipped with the leading-edge tanks. More than 200 P-51B fuselage tank installation kits and 100 P-38J 55gal leading edge kits were on hand at the end of November.

On November 29 the 357th FG reached Scotland's Firth of Clyde, and it was subsequently transported to the newly constructed Raydon airfield on December 1. The 357th was the second assigned Mustang fighter group for IX Fighter Command, and it began training with the new P-51B in the last week of December.

NAA P-51 Project Manager George Gehrkens provided the following update to the November 9 meeting at Ninth Air Force HQ:

> First 75 P-51Bs to go operational without 85gal fuselage kits installed; carburetor mixture for best cruise set to "auto-lean" requiring NAA to update range data and tables. Boost control to receive stronger spring to enable smooth advance from MP [military power] to WEP [war emergency power] and 61inHg to 67inHg manifold pressure. Gate set to 61in.; recommended change to 1in. internal diameter fittings between Nos. 3 and 4 cylinders on inboard side of rocker covers; R-R building new oil tank discussed in Nov 9 meeting; some outboard rows of tubes in Harrison radiator found to be crushed – pointing to damage at Harrison prior to delivery to NAA; re: N3B 100mil gunsight replacement by 70mil MKII Star – British developing a gyro corrected gunsight. Recommend discontinue installing/shipping N3B gunsight to save labor and unit cost; first Malcolm hood for 9th AF should be completed by end of December; 14SM engines for XP-51G two months late – revised delivery 1 February 1944. SU-type fuel pump working well.[52]

Fitted with a Malcolm Hood, Mustang III FX893 undertook Rocket Projectile 3 firing trials for the RAF. Most British Mustang IIIs were fitted with Malcolm Hoods upon arriving in Britain. (*Philip Jarrett Collection*)

On November 30 the 354th FG's CO, Col Martin, informed both Gen E. R. Quesada (CO IX Fighter Command) and Maj Gen Brereton, Commanding General of the Ninth Air Force, that his group was ready for operations.

On or about November 30 at least two P-51B-5-NA/Mustang IIIs (FZ100 and FZ101) assigned to the RAF were dispatched to R. Malcolm to have the hood installed. These are the first two so identified on their individual aircraft record cards, but it is probable that earlier P-51B-1-NA/Mustang III FX893 was modified with the Malcolm Hood by the RAF for service acceptance trials.

On December 1 Lt Col Don Blakeslee, Operations Officer for the 4th FG, led the first 354th FG combat mission – a standard "introductory" sweep from Knocke to St Omer. He also led the next mission on the 5th – a penetration escort to Paris.[53]

IX Fighter Command and the RAF received the first P-51B-1/5s to arrive in Britain, then more were gradually absorbed by the 357th and 363rd FGs as they trained for operations in February 1944.

Foul weather plagued Eighth Air Force operations during December. The P-38-equipped 55th FG, followed by the 20th FG, experienced the highest number of aborts in VIII Fighter Command, averaging 35 percent returns, although this improved slightly during the last week. Curiously, VIII Bomber Command's effective dispatch ratio, compared with the summer, increased, possibly due to far better navigation aids and the improved navigation capabilities of bomber crews. Additionally, most of the targets were to areas defined by water signatures detected by H2X radar in the Pathfinders.

On December 13 the 359th FG became the seventh operational P-47 fighter group. Between the 15th and 18th the leadership roles of Eaker and Doolittle changed. On the 18th Eaker was informed by the Army Adjutant General that he was relieved of command of the Eighth Air Force and reassigned to command the Mediterranean Allied Air Forces (MAAF), including the Twelfth and Fifteenth Air Forces and the RAF Desert and Balkans Air Forces. By the end of the month Spaatz had been transferred from North Africa to Britain, bringing Doolittle with him to command the Eighth Air Force and directing Maj Gen Nathan Twining to replace the latter as CO of the Fifteenth Air Force.[54] The Ninth Air Force's 354th FG was placed under operational control of the Eighth Air Force at this time. Further command decisions over the next 60 days included trading the P-51B-equipped 357th FG to the Eighth Air Force in return for the newly operational P-47D-equipped 358th FG, as well as assigning the new IX FC 363rd FG to the temporary control of the Eighth Air Force.

Gens Carl Spaatz (Commander, USSTAF), Jimmy Doolittle (Commander, Eighth Air Force) and William Kepner (Commander, VIII Fighter Command) at Debden in April 1944. (*NARA*)

On December 14 the 325th FG of the Fifteenth Air Force flew its first operational mission in P-47s after converting from P-40s. By this date all of the Fifteenth Air Force fighter groups (1st, 14th, 31st, 52nd, 82nd, 332nd, and 325th FGs) were based in the general area of Foggia, in Italy, in preparation for escort assignments north and east. On the 15th, and again on the 19th, the Fifteenth Air Force was finally tasked to bomb important *Pointblank* targets at Innsbruck, in Austria, and Augsburg, in Germany. The latter raid was deemed an unqualified success, wrecking the Augsburg plant and costing the Germans 200 Bf 109s a month for two months before partial production was restored.[55]

On the 20th the 358th FG became the ninth operational P-47 fighter group.[56] On the 22nd the 20th FG went combat operational as VIII Fighter Command's second P-38 group. Curiously, it had taken the 20th two more months to do so after the 55th went operational on October 15.

Also on the 22nd, Army Air Force Proving Ground Command Eglin Field released Report 4-43-23-1 "Test to Determine the Effect of an Additional 85 Gallons of Internal Fuel on Performance and Handling of the P-51B Airplane." The flight trials on P-51B-1-NA 43-12388, -12389, and -12390 had commenced on November 22 and concluded on December 8. NAA received preliminary results and USAAF recommendations in early December, and began work to design internal baffles for the 85gal fuselage tank. The essential conclusions were:

a) The 85gal tank is desirable as a production item because of the additional range it affords.
b) When filled with 85 gallons of fuel the airplane is unstable longitudinally – violent pull-outs and tight turns must be executed with caution, as stick loads rapidly reverse; with the fuselage tank half empty these maneuvers may be executed in practically normal manner.
c) When the airplane is to be used with full internal tank for long-range missions, it is best to use the tank for warm-up, take-off and partial climb, before drawing fuel from the drop tanks.
d) Additional time in the airplane is required to become accustomed to the handling qualities of the airplane before violent maneuvers are attempted.

e) Lack of internal baffle bulkheads resulted in shifting of airplane balance.
f) The present location of the fuel gage is unsatisfactory – requires pilot to crane neck and look full to the rear to read it.
g) The weight and location of the full tank has no measurable effect on maximum speed of the airplane.
h) The weight of the fuel reduces military power climb time to 30,000ft by approximately one minute.
i) The turning circle of the P-51B with the fuselage tank half full is about the same as the P-38J and is smaller than the P-47D-15. (This is a slight increase over the airplane with empty tank.)

Recommendations:

a) Internal, self-sealing fuel tanks of 85 gallons capacity be installed in production P-51B type airplanes.
b) Missions should be planned so that the greatest possibility of entering combat with fuselage tank not more than half full.
c) Fuel to be used for long-range combat missions in the following order:
  1.) Fuselage Tank – Approximately 20 gallons for warm-up, take-off and climb, leaving 65 gallons in fuselage tank.
  2.) Droppable tanks – Expended in cruise toward destination.
  3.) Fuselage Tank – Continue cruise (approximately 30 more gallons.) At this point the airplane is ready for combat.
  4.) Main Wing Tanks – Combat and return to base.
  5.) Fuselage Tank – Reserve (35 gallons).
d) Pilots should be given extra time to become accustomed to the handling qualities of the airplane with full fuselage tanks before engaging in tight turns or similar maneuvers.
e) An Internal Baffle system be installed in fuselage tank to prevent fuel movement in both directions.
f) The present fuel gage should be moved forward so pilot can read it by glancing over his shoulder, or a remote indicating gauge be installed on the instrument panel.

On December 27 Arnold sent a Christmas greeting to the commanding generals of the Eighth and Fifteenth Air Forces. "My personal message to you – this is a MUST – is to 'Destroy the Enemy Air Force Wherever you find them, in the air, on the ground, in the factories.'"[57] This message echoed what he told Spaatz at an HQ-AAF Staff meeting at the end of November, stating, "The primary role of all US fighters in the UK until further notice will be to support and escort heavy bombers engaged in *Pointblank*."[58]

On the 30th the 376th BG was hit hard during a Fifteenth Air Force mission to the marshaling yard at Vincenza in Italy. On the 30th both the 376th and the 98th

BGs were withdrawn from combat to re-equip and train replacement crews owing to attrition – they would not return until February 1944.[59]

Also on December 30, VIII Bomber Command targeted the chemical works at Ludwigshafen, due south of Frankfurt. The bomber force lost 23 aircraft to Luftwaffe day fighters, while VIII Fighter Command claimed 8-3-6, with 13 losses. Luftwaffe losses were 15 fighters and 15 pilots killed in action, including some to RAF Spitfires near the French coast.

On the last day of the year the Eighth Air Force went to Bordeaux, Cognac, and Paris. The Bordeaux strike was accompanied by the two P-38 fighter groups, the 20th and 55th. The mission, of more than five hours' duration, was actually well beyond the combat radius of P-38H/Js without leading-edge fuel tanks. One of them ditched, the pilot being picked up by Air Sea Rescue, and the rest landed at the closest RAF emergency fields along Britain's south coast. While attacking Bordeaux and Cognac airfields, aircraft of the 1st Bomb Division (BD) were hit hard by the Luftwaffe, losing 23-10-108 while claiming 17-13-27. The 55th FG claimed 3-0-1 for one loss. The P-47 groups scored 4-1-0 for two losses, while the 354th P-51s scored 2-0-0 for one loss. The Luftwaffe actually lost 32 fighters (ten pilots killed in action), plus 20 damaged/destroyed on the ground.[60] [61]

SUMMARY – 1943

Beginning in December 1942, NAA introduced a series of designs to improve the Merlin-equipped Mustang for delivery in 1943. First, the wing was strengthened to enable increases in the new aileron throw angles. The P-51B aileron deflection angle was increased from +/-10 degrees to +/-10, 12, and 15 degrees. With 12 degrees recommended in the manual, the new ailerons improved roll rate from 20 to 40 percent. Next, after the discovery of the "rumble" in the radiator/intercooler ducting, a series of flight test/scoop modification/wind tunnel testing iterations were conducted to develop the "scoop and boundary-layer gutter" design applicable to all production P-51B/C/D/K Mustangs.

Second, a serious redesign was initiated, with a view to major weight reductions. This led to the XP-51F/G/J, which resulted in the ultimate production version, the future P-51H Mustang re-engined with the Packard Merlin 1650-9, equivalent in horsepower to the Merlin 100 series.

In parallel with the lightweight series design effort, NAA created new cockpit enclosures for the P-51D, popularly referred to as the bubble canopy, to improve the pilot's view rearwards. In addition, the wing armament was increased to six AN/M2 Browning 0.50cal machine guns, placed upright in the gun bay. Contrary to some opinions, there was no need to increase the thickness of the wing to accommodate this change. The original purpose behind designing the canted armament mount was to permit the installation of a 20mm cannon with belt feed, and to enable ammunition to pass over the top of one cannon to supply the other.

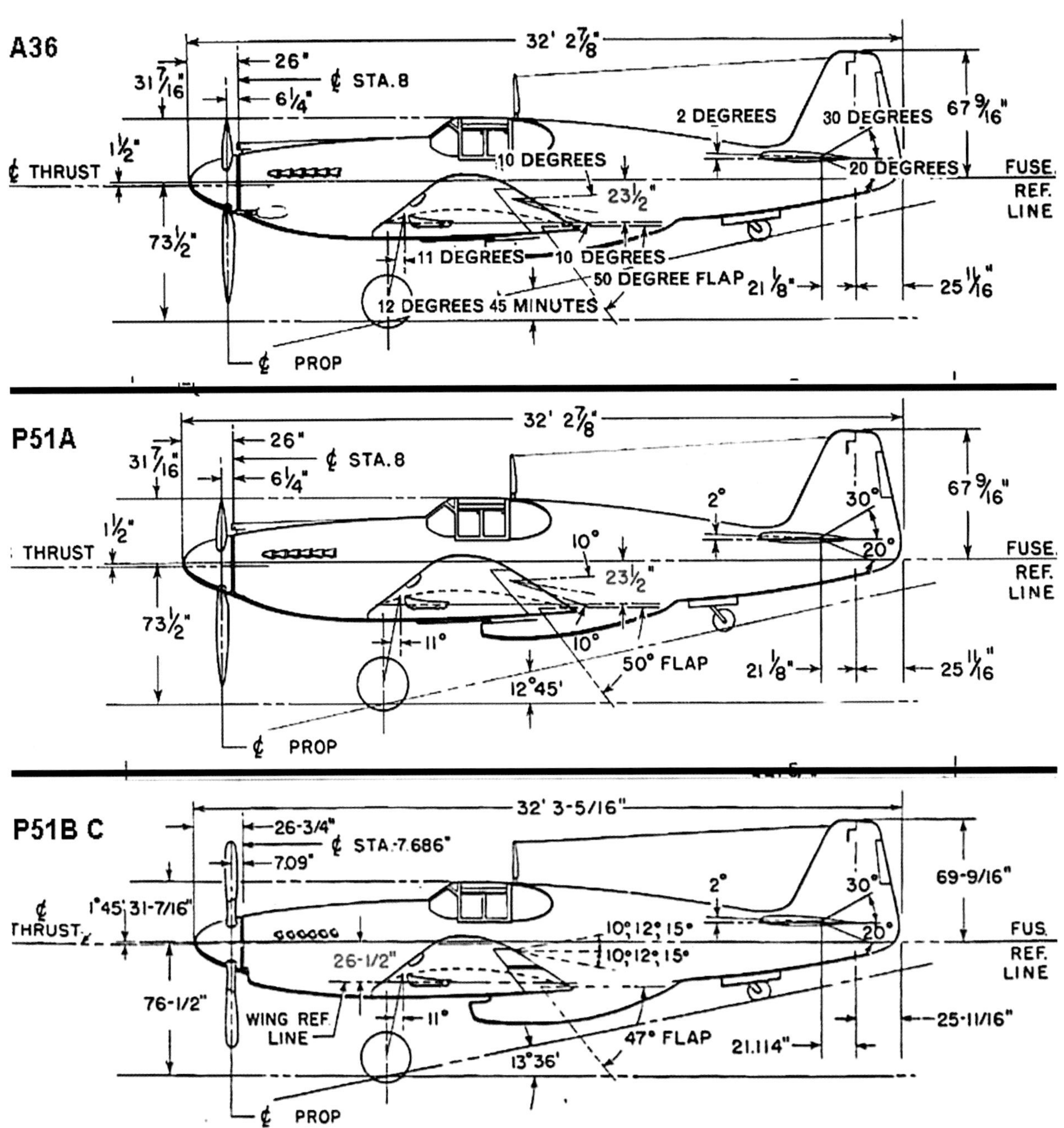

This major dimensions diagram of the A-36, P-51A and P-51B reveals the differing aileron throw angles of the first two aircraft to the Merlin Mustang. (© *The Boeing Company*)

For the first bubble canopy conversions, NAA pulled one completed NA-102 P-51B-1-NA and two NA-102 P-51B-1 spare fuselage (only) assemblies to begin work to convert the birdcage cockpit enclosure (sometimes incorrectly described as a "razorback") to the new NA-106 P-51D bubble canopy design. The first conversion, 43-12102, remained a basic P-51B-1-NA with unchanged wing planform and four-gun wing armament. The other two (P-51D-NA 42-106539 and P-51D-1-NT 42-106540) were not only modified with the NA-106 P-51D bubble canopy cockpit and lower aft deck but were also given the new six-gun P-51D wing and the production 85gal fuselage fuel tank for testing.

The first P-51B-10-NA completed, 43-7113 was also the first Mustang to be built at Inglewood with the 85gal fuselage tank installed during production operations in the factory. It also included all the essential long-range production engineering changes such as combat tank pressurization and extra oxygen supplies. (© *The Boeing Company*)

Finally, NAA responded to the USAAF FAREP directive to increase internal fuel by incorporating the 85gal fuselage fuel tank and increased oxygen supply and combat fuel tank pressurization in the P-51B/C and subsequent Mustangs. The company also produced 1,600 complete kits for installation into P-51B/Cs that had left Inglewood and Dallas before the required changes were introduced into production. At the end of 1943 more than 1,200 P-51B-1s, B-5-NAs and C-1-NT Mustangs were delivered to the USAAF, and the first production P-51D-5-NA and the XP-51F were nearing completion.

The first NA-104 P-51B-10-NA, 43-7113, was accepted and flew in December 1943. It was the very first complete long-range escort production Mustang to feature all the necessary change orders covering the installation of the 85gal fuselage tank, extra oxygen, new external fuel tank pressurization, etc. – production features that eliminated the need for future P-51Bs to go to Depots for installation of the FSB 73-95 modification kits.

MUSTANG RIVAL NOTES – 1943

During February 1943 Lockheed designed and tested the underwing dive flap developed to control the compressibility effects encountered by the P-38 when it entered a dive above 20,000ft. The boosted ailerons were also tested, but neither the flaps nor the ailerons were introduced into production until the P-38J-25-LO, which did not arrive in time for service in the Eighth Air Force. Although the first 200 kits for dive flaps were packaged and flown to Britain in November 1943, the USAAF Douglas C-54 carrying the shipment was intercepted and shot down in error by the RAF before reaching Ireland.[62]

Lockheed also redesigned the turbo-supercharger aftercooler radiator embedded in the wing leading edge to supplement a "P-40-style" radiator in front of each engine. This change was stimulated by multiple engine failures experienced in the extremely cold temperatures encountered in the ETO from April 1943. As soon as the P-38Gs and F-5s flew their first operational missions in the cold northern European skies, engine and turbo-supercharger problems arose. The primary issue was inadequate cooling of very-high-temperature air generated by the turbo-supercharger, via the leading-edge intercooler/aftercooler, which, when mixed with fuel supplied by the carburetor, caused an excessively high-temperature fuel/air charge to be introduced into the engine manifold.

On the last day of July Lockheed flew P-38E 41-1983 with a modified "J" radiator and new intercooler, combined with two leading-edge 55gal tanks that increased total internal fuel from 300gal to 410gal. The initial modifications to the P-38E/F/G/H and most early P-38Js slaved the external fuel tank pressurization to the Allisons. Later, in 1944, separate electrically driven booster pumps were provided.

From late September through October 1943, Lockheed Drawing 201601 "Installation – LE Fuel Tank Kit" was released for the installation of the leading-edge tanks in mid-block P-38J-LOs. Additionally, Lockheed provided 55gal leading-edge fuel tank kits for P-38Js that were en route to, or already in, the ETO – Lockheed Field Services shipped 108 kits to Langford Lodge for installation in the early P-38J-10s.[63]

Although the new designs offered long-range internal tanks to augment external tanks, superior maneuverability, and the potential to improve both available horsepower and engine reliability, the revised intercooler design cooled the compressed fuel charge too much at high altitude. Consequently, engine failures at high altitude continued to occur when the P-38J was introduced into the ETO in December.[64] An additional problem encountered with the new J-model was over-cooling of oil, causing a sludge-like composition to form. As the tempo of operations increased in November, more issues surfaced, pointing directly to the extreme effect of cold air on the General Electric turbo-superchargers. The oil in the turbo-supercharger's regulating turbo congealed and the unit failed to regulate the manifold pressure. When the throttle was advanced to maximum power, the engine manifold pressure surged, causing engine failure or explosion. When the "surge" to maximum power was detected, retarding the throttle slightly reduced maximum power below cruise settings, leaving the P-38 at the mercy of an attacking fighter.

The "surge" problem was primarily caused by the ETO-required directives (from VIII Air Force Service Command) to maximize cruise range by throttling down to low manifold pressure and low rpm, in direct opposition to Allison- and Lockheed-stated recommendations. When rpm and throttle were suddenly increased, as in air-to-air combat, the correct procedure was to adjust fuel from lean to rich, increase rpm, and *then* increase manifold pressure/boost to maximum power. Failure to following this procedure led to combinations of factors that caused the engines to fail or blow up. Additionally, the USAAF stated that the maximum cruise settings described above, while slightly more efficient in range, caused the P-38 to enter combat zones at significantly lower speeds than was prudent in a high threat environment.

When the standard process was changed to increase manifold pressure, with higher rpm in cruise, the turbo-supercharger operated at higher temperatures, which in turn heated up the air more to mix with fuel from the carburetor. The consequences of higher temperatures in the manifold were that they prevented fuel additive separation, and also stopped raw fuel from "puddling." The other benefit was a lower safe response time to spool up the turbo-supercharger to meet the maximum power demands on the engine.

The above summary points to the failure of Materiel Command to test the early-production P-38s at operational altitudes in full-throttle horsepower, and in environments that even remotely approached the cold ETO temperatures at 30,000ft. As a result of pulling the first operational P-38 fighter groups from the Eighth Air Force for *Torch* in late 1942, none of these issues surfaced until the 7th PG went operational in July 1943.

Republic also responded to the call for better engine power delivery, an increase in internal fuel capacity and changes to improve operational capabilities as feedback from war zones was prioritized. In early 1943 the company introduced a lower fuselage "keel" modification on the P-47 to provide for a centerline bomb and combat fuel tank rack and redesigned the nose from the firewall forward to allow faster engine changes. In May work started on the installation of a bubble canopy to replace the "razorback" sliding canopy. The XP-47K, a P-47D-5-RE modified with a Hawker Typhoon IB sliding Perspex bubble canopy, was completed and delivered in July.

The XP-47K, seen here in July 1943, was created from the last D-5-RE built by Republic. The aircraft had cut down fuselage decking and a Typhoon IB sliding hood. Unaware that NAA was already well on the way with installing its own bubble canopy on the P-51B-1 and P-51D-NA, Col Mark Bradley, Chief, Fighter Projects at Wright Field, flew this aircraft to Inglewood in July 1943. The first production P-47D-25-RE so equipped would not see combat until mid-May 1944 in limited quantities. (*USAF*)

The future P-47D-25-RE was also modified to take an additional 65 gallons of internal fuel. Because of the major modifications required to accommodate the extra internal fuel, Republic embarked on a redesign of the P-47D. At the least, the cockpit and firewall sections needed to be altered to take the additional fuselage fuel – changes that were too extensive for depot kits and rework.

When the P-47D-5-REs were rolling out of Farmingdale in May, in addition to the bulged keel kits, the factories were developing kits for the installation of the new General Electric C-21 turbo-supercharger. In June, 12 P-47D-5-REs were modified with external wing racks and plumbing to carry 165gal ferry tanks for a transatlantic flight in August.

In June 1943 VIII Fighter Command was equipped with a mix of only P-47C and D Thunderbolts that had yet to penetrate German airspace. On the last day of "Blitz Week" the P-47s of the 4th FG did so with the assistance of external fuel ferry tanks that were not even a production feature at the time. They were so equipped only because of herculean efforts by VIII Fighter Command's Air Technical Section, led by Lt Col Cass Hough. His organization was instrumental in identifying and solving technical issues with inbound fighters and reporting them back to Materiel Command.[65] However, VIII Air Force Service Command was designated the primary technical support service for the Eighth and Ninth Air Force, and it frequently clashed with the Air Technical Section regarding authority and responsibility.

The Air Technical Section researched and solved pressing operational issues related to VIII Fighter Command but fitting the external fuel tank to the P-47 to extend its range was a number one priority. Curiously, however, it was not on VIII Air Force Service Command's priority list. Hough and his team designed a modification to the 205gal ferry tank, with a front-mounted "wedge" to ensure that it would separate safely from the P-47 in flight. The ungainly looking belly tank was very "draggy," and because it was unpressurized it would not continue to feed unused fuel at 18,000 to 20,000ft, leaving more than half of the available contents unused at escort altitudes. The Air Technical Section solved the problem of external tank fuel feed at altitude by installing a locally sourced valve to enable the external tank to be pressurized by using air from the instrument vacuum system. Combat tanks of 108gal capacity were eventually subcontracted from British sources, as US production had not yet ramped up to meet demand.

Many design features to strengthen the wing for the new 1,000lb loads were incorporated into the D-6 (42-74615), which was accepted by the USAAF in July 1943 and arrived in the ETO in late September.[66] The first factory-produced water injection-equipped Pratt & Whitney R-2800-63 engine was installed in the P-47D-11-RE, which rolled out of the Farmingdale plant from October 1943.[67] Based on the modifications made to the 12 P-47D-5s to equip them with external wing racks and plumbing to feed fuel from them to the engine, the Field Service instructions for this lengthy process were dispatched to both the ETO and Southwest Pacific Base Depots in the fall of 1943. The new 150gal "flat" tank was first used on the modified centerline rack in the December 1943 time frame to further increase combat radius.

The kits to modify the P-47C-2 into the D-11 arrived at BAD1 Burtonwood to enable work to begin on the conversions to install wing pylons, plumb for fuel lines from external tanks, and provide tank selector capability – a long and labor-intensive process. The Depot-modified P-47s did not reach squadron strength until March 1944. The P-47D-16-RE with factory plumbing and external wing pylons started leaving the Evansville plant in December. When they finally flowed through BAD1 Burtonwood for other ETO-specific modifications, the remaining operational VIII FC Thunderbolt fighter groups (56th, 78th, 353rd, 356th, 359th, and 361st FGs) obtained enough P-47D-16s and -21-REs to equip them for longer-range penetration and withdrawal support missions from late March/early April 1944.

The P-47D-10-RE, with strengthened wings capable of carrying the pylons and 150gal fuel tanks, entered production in September. This was first variant to have the R-2800-63 with the General Electric Type C-23 turbo-supercharger, and to be equipped to enable the water injection kit to be installed.

On October 21 Republic completed, and released for production, the engineering design for the P-47D fuel pressurization system. Also in October 1943, the first P-47D-11-RE arrived at Speke with both centerline and wing-rack capability for B-10 shackles. The -11 was remarkable for several reasons. It could carry a 75/108 or 150gal centerline combat tank, or depot modified, a 108gal combat tank under each wing; it was field-modified to pressurize each tank up to the critical altitude of 30,000ft; and it was factory-equipped with the R-2800-63 and water injection. When it was fully operational in squadron strength, in February 1944, the -11 extended the P-47's combat radius to nearly 400 miles.[68]

At the end of December Republic completed, and released for production, drawing 93F65003 "Main Fuel Tank, Installation" for the P-47D-25-RE, which was to also be the first production bubble canopy version of the P-47D. The modifications required to previously completed P-47D versions through the P-47D-22-RE to increase internal fuel to 370gal were extensive, affecting both the center and aft fuselage sections. Accordingly, Depot modifications were deemed too prolonged and labor intensive to be of value. As a result of the post-D-Day introduction of the D-25 in squadron strength, the P-47D was relegated to penetration and withdrawal escort during Operation *Overlord*, deferring target escort responsibilities to the P-38J and P-51B/C. The Eighth Air Force developed a "relay"-type escort tactic to capitalize on the abilities of the P-38 and P-51 to fly deep into Germany to rendezvous with the bombers, leaving the P-47D-equipped fighter groups the task of penetrating the defenses arrayed from the coast to targets approximately the radius of Bonn and Hannover from East Anglia at the end of 1943/January 1944.

With increased performance via the addition of water injection for the Pratt & Whitney R-2800 engine, the P-47D-11-RE had commenced operations in the ETO by the end of 1943. In early 1944, increased external fuel tank capability started to be introduced by the addition of shackles and fuel feed from wings. Until the P-47D-25 started arriving just before D-Day, with internal fuel capacity increased from 305 to 370gal, the P-47D was still incapable of providing bomber escort beyond mid-Germany.

175

CHAPTER 7

"DESTROY THE LUFTWAFFE – IN THE AIR AND ON THE GROUND"

JANUARY – USSTAF AND LUFTWAFFE OPERATIONS

Future USAF general James Howard began his aviation career as a US Naval Aviator who served with the American Volunteer Group, where he learned combat leadership and fighter pilot skills. When the AVG disbanded, Howard joined the USAAF, and he transferred to the 354th FG when it was activated. On January 11, 1944, Lt Col James Howard, CO of the 354th FG's 356th FS, became the first Merlin Mustang fighter ace. (*NARA*)

On January 1, 1944, Lt Gen Spaatz was officially named commander of the USSTAF, and Maj Gen Eaker departed for Tunis to take command of the MAAF.

On the 5th the Eighth Air Force resumed deep penetration missions beyond the escort range of the P-47D. The Bordeaux strike was unescorted for the last 200-plus miles, and losses totaled 11-2-49. The 78th FG had five more P-47s shot down near Rennes and Caen. The longer-range strike to the Kiel shipyards (450 miles) was escorted by the two P-38 fighter groups, plus the 354th FG. The 20th and 55th FGs, flying P-38s, claimed 5-1-4 for the loss of seven (two to engine issues), and the P-51s of the 354th FG claimed 15-4-5 for no losses. This mission illustrated two points. First, the combat radius for the raid was the maximum (as per the planning guidelines) for the P-38J with 300gal wing tanks and no leading-edge tanks – it was also the extreme combat radius for the P-51B with 75gal wing tanks but no 85gal fuselage tank. Second, although the combat experience levels of the P-38 pilots were greater, they suffered a less than 1:1 victory credit-to-loss ratio versus the Fw 190 and Bf 109. The 354th FG pilots downed five Fw 190s and one Bf 109 when attacked by them, and also downed nine twin-engined fighters.

The Luftwaffe's missions against VIII Bomber Command over Kiel were eventful owing to the shocking loss of twin-engined fighters, which had been positioned well beyond previously believed maximum escort ranges.

On the 6th and 7th Spaatz appointed Maj Gens Doolittle and Nathan Twining as the new Eighth Air Force and Fifteenth Air Force commanders, respectively. Maj Gen Anderson was retained as Deputy CO for Operations for the Eighth Air Force.[1] Planning began for the forthcoming Operation *Argument* ("Big Week") to coordinate simultaneous strikes into Germany from Italy and Britain.

On January 7 a Fifteenth Air Force attack on Wiener Neustadt turned back early due to adverse weather. The 1st and 14th FGs continued past the rendezvous point and engaged the Luftwaffe south of the target, claiming 5-1-6 for the loss of six P-38s.

Four days later Doolittle first advanced and defined VIII Fighter Command's official mission under his command in his meeting with VIII Bomber and Fighter Command wing commanders. During this gathering he changed the motto of VIII Fighter Command from "Protect the Bombers" to "Destroy the Luftwaffe in the air and on the ground."[2] The bomb wing commanders were angry, but the fighter wing commanders were elated by the new directive to aggressively seek out the Luftwaffe fighters.

January 11 also saw the first mission flown by the heavily armed Fw 190s of *Sturmstaffel* 1 from the unit's base at Rheine, pilots targeting the 1st BD's attack on Oschersleben and Halberstadt. Those two raids marked the first renewal of the *Pointblank* directives against Germany's aircraft industry. Flying their modified Fw 190A-6s and -7s, equipped with four MG 151 20mm cannon plus two MG 131 machine guns and protected by reinforced cowling armor and canopy side panels, the pilots of *Sturmstaffel* 1 closed on the rear of one of the boxes and downed three B-17s. Oberstleutnant Hans-Günter von Kornatzki led the attack.

Also, during the Oschersleben strike, Lt Col James Howard, CO of the 354th FG's 356th FS, led his unit in an attack on the German fighters swarming around the 401st BG, which was leading the 94th BW. During the course of the engagement he became separated from his wingman and the rest of his squadron but remained to do battle with an estimated 40-plus German single- and twin-engined fighters. Over the next 20 minutes while flying above the target area, Howard shot down three fighters and damaged another, thus becoming the 354th FG's first ace. He was awarded the Medal of Honor and was the only fighter pilot to receive this decoration while serving with the Eighth or Ninth Air Force.

The 354th's Mustangs scored more victory credits (16-9-20) than all the rest of the Eighth and Ninth Air Force escort fighters (592 sorties, two P-38 and twelve

During the Oschersleben raid on January 11, 1944, Lt Col James Howard, a veteran of combat in China, led the 356th FS in an attack on German fighters swarming around the 401st BG. Although he soon became separated from his wingman and the rest of his squadron, Howard was confident in the ability of his P-51B to hold its own against an overwhelming number of German fighters (more than 40 were reportedly seen in the area). He engaged the enemy for 20 minutes while flying above the target area, downing three and damaging a fourth to become the 354th FG's first ace. Awarded the Medal of Honor for his exploits that day, Howard was the only Eighth/Ninth Air Force fighter pilot to receive America's highest and most prestigious personal military decoration. (*USAF, sourced by Jack Cook*)

P-47 groups) combined, which claimed 14-4-5. Despite the ferocity of the 354th FG's attacks near the target, the Luftwaffe day fighters still brought down 43-2-15 bombers, plus one P-38 and two P-47s.

Although they had provided long-range escort in a target-rich environment, no P-38s engaged in combat. This was probably because the Lightning was easy for Luftwaffe pilots to spot and identify early, whereas the Mustang was nearly impossible to distinguish from the Bf 109 until the white ETO bands became visible, by which time it was often too late to avoid combat.

On the 21st, VIII Fighter Command's Air Technical Section was reorganized by Doolittle as the Operational Engineering Section, with Col Ben Kelsey as commanding officer. Lt Cols Cass Hough and Algene Key were tasked to head up fighter and bomber projects, respectively. Two hangars were set aside at Bovington, along with a staff that grew to 200. The 361st FG became the ninth operational P-47 FG of the Eighth Air Force.

The Operational Engineering Section would duly become the first to modify the P-38 nose to accommodate a bombardier and bombsight – dubbed the "Droop Snoot" – to give tactical level-bombing capability. Cass Hough and Ben Kelsey also recommended that a P-38J be set aside and sent to Rolls-Royce for Merlin 65 installation. Although this was approved in June, the project was killed at HQ-AAF. Various rumors suggested that Lt Gen William Knudsen, former Chairman of GMC, was the "culprit," but the truth was probably far simpler and more benign. The Packard Merlin 1650-3, -7, and -9 (in development to parallel features of the Merlin 100) had been prioritized A1 for P-51 production. Neither Curtiss nor Lockheed had a hope of competing for Packard Merlins when Packard was unable to meet existing committed demand. Furthermore, cooler heads recognized that installing the Packard

Generalmajor Josef Schmid led I. *Jagdkorps*, which was probably the most important command and control center for Germany in 1944. He was highly regarded for his leadership in the Defense of the Reich. (*Donald Caldwell Collection*)

1650-7 two-speed/two-stage engine into the P-38, eliminating the General Electric turbo-supercharger, and changing the aftercooler radiator design was no less daunting than the design/fabrication process from Allison/P-51 airframe to Merlin/XP-51B to P-51B-1. Other authors have been quoted as saying that the change was relatively simple, but this was not so.

On January 24 Maj Gen Kepner, who had taken command of VIII Fighter Command four months earlier, "officially" untethered his groups from strict close escort, enabling them to pursue the Luftwaffe fighters away from the bombers. Previously, under the leadership of Eaker and Hunter, the directive was "repel and return," thus giving the Luftwaffe the freedom to attack and disengage nearly at will. The command also had the effect of unleashing VIII Fighter Command to drop to the deck and shoot up targets of opportunity on the way home.

The fighter group commanders also brought new tactics into battle. Some groups were now to provide area coverage along the bomber track, giving squadron COs more latitude to assign sections and flights rather than remain as an intact unit. At their discretion, fighter group commanders were to designate an attacking or "bouncing squadron" to meet incoming German forces, while the other squadrons remained in loose protective cover for the bomber boxes. The tactics evolved as more fighter groups were equipped with Mustangs. In addition to the penetration escort, target escort, and withdrawal escort relay system, a fourth role was implemented, namely a fighter sweep 50–75 miles in front of the bomber stream. The sweep mission was tasked with surprising Luftwaffe formations as they were either taking off or in the process of assembling, and attack them. In March and April the sweeps frequently extended beyond Berlin, and no airfield or assembly area was safe.

Finally, Doolittle pronounced that a German aircraft destroyed on the ground counted toward "ace" status. The award process was unique to the Eighth Air Force, and it activated the most destructive airfield attacks launched by any combatant in any theater – namely strafing attacks everywhere in German-occupied territory within the range of long-ranging escort fighters. However, it cost the Eighth Air Force far more pilots and fighters than the Luftwaffe downed in aerial combat by a large margin.

Later, Generalmajors Adolph Galland and Joseph Schmid, commander of I. *Jagdkorps* (probably the most important command in the RLV), remarked that these directives by Doolittle and Kepner, and subsequent actions by VIII Fighter Command, were the turning points in the air war over Germany.[3 4]

Spaatz convened a meeting on January 24 with Maj Gens Doolittle (Eighth Air Force) and Brereton (Ninth Air Force) to "undo" the mistakes made by both HQ-AAF and Eaker in permitting the preferred assignment of all Merlin Mustangs destined for the ETO to the Ninth Air Force. Brereton objected to the transfer of the 354th, 357th, and 363rd FGs to the Eighth Air Force, but compromised. He agreed to the continued temporary assignment of the 354th and 363rd to the Eighth Air Force until D-Day invasion operations by the Ninth Air Force were due to start, in late May, and also agreed to swap the inexperienced Mustang-equipped 357th FG for the P-47D-equipped 358th FG, effective on January 31.[5]

On the 24th, I. *Jagdkorps* commander Generalmajor Schmid wrote a memo to the *Reichsluftfahrtministerium*, copied to Generalmajor Hans-Jürgen Stumpff, commander of the new *Luftflotte Reich*:

> In order to assure successful air-defense measures within the territory of the Reich, the following conditions must be met:
>
> 1. One central agency should be given the responsibility of preparing the "mission picture"
>
> 2. All the remaining agencies engaged in RLV activity (radio reconnaissance, radar and ground reporting stations) should be made subordinate to this agency.
>
> 3. A central commanding unit should be set up to direct the commitments of day- and night-fighter units in home air-defense activity.[6]

When the Eighth Air Force attacked aviation industry and marshaling yard targets at Frankfurt on January 24, terrible weather forced the 2nd BD's B-24s to turn back. However, the fighter escort notably shocked German fighter pilots by aggressively pursuing them, in many cases down to the deck. The two P-38 groups scored 2-2-1 for the loss of four missing in action, while the ten P-47 groups claimed 17-1-6 for the loss of three. The sole P-51-equipped unit, the 354th FG, was stalked between cloud decks by Fw 190s of 4./JG 1 and lost two for credits of 2-0-2. The Luftwaffe lost 21 fighters and had eight pilots listed as missing in action.

The attacks on Frankfurt and Ludwigshafen on the 29th brought a significant Luftwaffe response. The German fighter attacks began over southern Belgium and continued all the way to both Frankfurt and Ludwigshafen. VIII Bomber Command lost 29-5-135. The P-47D penetration escort, notably the 4th and 352nd FGs, separated sections to attack the inbound fighters near Maastricht. Together, they were credited with nine (with one missing in action) and six (with two missing in action), respectively, of the total of 32 claimed by the P-47s. The 56th bounced and claimed 6-1-0 for one missing in action near Koblenz on the Frankfurt escort penetration leg. The two P-38 groups, the 20th and 55th FGs, respectively claimed 10-1-1 for four missing in action, and 1-0-0 for no loss. The 354th FG scored 4-2-4 for no losses.

The Brunswick mission the next day was also fiercely defended, the Luftwaffe forces including several *Staffeln* of Bf 110 and Ju 88 nightfighters. In all, the Luftwaffe put up 480 sorties, causing 20-3-115 bomber losses, while losing 75 single- and twin-engined fighters, including 66 pilots killed in action and 16 missing. The 56th FG encountered several nightfighter units and escorts from Lingen to Quackenbruck on penetration, being credited with 18-1-3. The 354th scored heavily against the twin-engined fighters with 3-2-5 Bf 110s plus 2-5-0 Bf 109s and Fw 190s near Brunswick. The 20th FG, also providing target escort, scored 4-0-1 for two missing in action, while the other P-38 fighter group did not engage.

January 30 was a big day for the Fifteenth Air Force's 325th FG. XV Bomber Command planned to target four key airfields in support of the stalemate at the Anzio beachhead to prevent strengthened forces of Luftwaffe long-range bombers in northern Italy from attacking Anzio harbor. The plan also called for a low-level surprise attack below the radar coverage against Villaorba airfield approximately 15 minutes before the Fifteenth Air Force bombers arrived. The 325th caught the Luftwaffe trying to evacuate the airfield, and shot down 16 aircraft, Capt Herschel Green being credited with six. Overall, the mission was a success, destroying approximately 60 aircraft on the ground at Udine, Aviano, Villaorba, and Levariano airfields, for the loss of one B-17 and two B-24s. XV Bomber Command followed up the attacks on the 31st and added Klagenfurt airfield to the target list. The two raids contributed to the destruction not only of aircraft, but of the harder-to-replace maintenance and repair facilities required to repair those aircraft damaged in the attacks.

January 31 marked an uneventful VIII Bomber Command attack on St Pol/Siracourt targets, with no losses. VIII Fighter Command launched the first series of dive-bombing attacks by the 4th and 355th FGs against the airfield at Gilze-Rijen. The 55th swept Eindhoven/Venlo/Arnhem and engaged units from JGs 1 and 3, claiming seven for six losses.

JANUARY – P-51/P-38/P-47 PROBLEMS AND SOLUTIONS

On January 4, details of a P-51B-5 empennage failure during a high-speed slow roll were relayed from Maj Charles Krouse of VIII Air Force Service Command to Frank Lyons, NAA Field Services manager. During January a variety of other problems experienced by 354th FG Mustangs were reported. They included (1) external combat tanks failing to feed at various altitudes above 20,000ft, (2) propellers throwing oil, (3) glycol reserve tank leaks spraying windshields and freezing, (4) cooling system overheating due to radiator corrosion, combined with leaks in the system, (5) radios failing, (6) alarming control response issues due to sloshing fuel in the 85gal tank, (7) poor spark plug performance, (8) excessive oil loss, and (9) ammunition feed failures causing gun jams.[7]

As NAA Field Services manager, Frank Lyons was a key figure as his team proved instrumental in the acceleration of the new P-51B into combat operations in the ETO as well as the coordination of operational improvements with NAA engineering at Inglewood. (© *The Boeing Company*)

In early January P-51B-1 43-12102, modified with a bubble canopy for tests in November 1943, was fitted with the new canopy design intended for the production P-51D-5-NA and the first example of the metal-covered elevator modifications, as yet without incidence change, to "fix" the problems discovered during dive tests two months earlier.

Notable NAA developments in January included the loss of the first P-51D-NA, 42-106539, in an accident due to a structural failure at Redondo Beach, California, on the 11th. Maj Augustus Pitcairn was killed.

The kits to install baffles into the 85gal fuselage tanks were shipped to the ETO in January, arriving at BAD2 Warton and 4th Air Depot Charmy Down later that same month. The first production P-51D-5-NA, 44-13253, was flown by Chilton on January 27. Ongoing testing of different dorsal fin fillet modifications in an attempt to mitigate the Merlin Mustang yaw issues identified by Rolls-Royce continued at NAA.

The NA-73 quarter-scale model, constructed from different types of wood and fitted with various dorsal fin fillet designs, was exhaustively tested in the NAA wind tunnel in late 1943. This model was instrumental in the development of Parasite drag values for various Mustang airframes and changes. Full-scale wind tunnel tests of P-51Bs improved correlations between predicted and actual drag. (© *The Boeing Company*)

On January 4 contract NA-120 was executed for the XP-82 Twin Mustang very-long-range escort fighter, also designed to have Packard Merlin 1650 engines and intended for the Pacific theater in 1945.

P-38 operations from October 1943 to date were dogged by continued engine failures; much higher abort rates, limiting the number of P-38s actually performing escort; an inability to pursue Bf 109s and Fw 190s in dives owing to compressibility issues; frigid cockpit conditions leading to early fatigue; complex flight training requirements compared with the P-47 or P-51; and much more complex maintenance requirements. Already Eighth Air Force leaders were cognizant that, while they needed the Lightning for long-range critical mass in the near future, its effectiveness in the "destroy the Luftwaffe" mission for VIII Fighter Command was seriously below that of the P-47D and P-51B. The P-38's single-mission highest victory credit to date was 10-1-1, by the 20th FG on January 29, but this was somewhat balanced by four losses. The next highest mission total for either of the P-38 fighter groups was 7-3-1 for January 31, for six missing in action (55th FG), and 6-4-6 for seven missing in action (55th FG) on November 13, 1943. From the time both units began operations in October and December 1943, through January 31, 1944, their combined record was 62-14-50 for 54 missing in action. By contrast, the P-51B-equipped 354th FG record from December 1, 1943 through January 31 was 51-18-57 for 11 missing in action.[8]

The obvious questions for Eighth Air Force planners regarding the P-38 were: why was the air-to-air combat ratio of credits to losses so much better for the P-51B-equipped fighter groups versus the P-38 fighter groups?; why did the single P-51B fighter group score 14 and then 15 victory credits in the span of one week, when the two P-38 fighter groups were providing target escort for the same bombers to the same targets (January 4 and 11), but scored only 1-0-1 credits, in total, for the same period?; why was there such a high percentage of mission aborts for a theoretically mature P-38-type airplane in combat operations since April 1942, in contrast to the first deployment of the brand new P-51B type with early-production cycle airframe and engine "bugs" to shake out?; and, last, would the operational performance against the Luftwaffe ever improve? The near-term answer to the last question, developed from the forthcoming Operation *Argument*, beginning February 20 through to the end of May, was "not enough."

The engineering for the P-47D-25-RE long-range fuselage fuel tank was completed and released on January 1. Drawing 93F65003, "Installation, Main Fuel Tank," showed main fuel tank capacity increased by 65 gallons for a total of

370 gallons of internal fuel. When the first production P-47D-25 arrived in mid-May, with two 150gal tanks, it finally enabled the Thunderbolt to achieve the same escort combat radius as the P-51B with external two 75gal combat tanks.

Gen K. B. Wolfe notified Maj Gen Echols that 100 water injection kits to retrofit pre-P-47D-11s had been dispatched from Republic to BAD1 Burtonwood.

FEBRUARY – ETO/MTO USSTAF OPERATIONS

The operational rhythm of the Eighth Air Force intensified with several returns to German aircraft industry targets at Frankfurt (February 4 and 11) and Brunswick (February 10). The 354th FG continued to provide strong fighter escort, claiming 8-1-7 and 14-0-10 on the 10th and 11th, outscoring the two P-38 fighter groups that claimed 13-2-12 for those three operations.

On the 5th the 364th FG arrived at Honington and was deemed nearly ready for combat operations in its P-38J-5/10s. Over the next three weeks many more modifications to install the 55gal leading-edge tanks in P-38J-10-LOs were completed, and the aircraft were distributed to the 20th, 55th, and 364th FGs.

On February 8 1Lt James Morris, a P-38 pilot with the 77th FS/20th FG, destroyed two Bf 109s and two Fw 190s to set an ETO record for the most Luftwaffe aircraft shot down in one mission. He also became the second Eighth Air Force P-38 ace.

On the 12th the 357th FG made its operational debut as the first Eighth Air Force Mustang fighter group. It would finish ops in the ETO with a higher tally of aerial victories than any other fighter group in both the ETO and MTO apart from the 354th and 56th FGs. New P-51B-5s, and some P-51B-1s and C-1s, arrived at Steeple Morden on or about February 15, enabling the men of the P-47D-equipped 355th FG to familiarize themselves with the new fighter. The 4th FG's CO, Col Don Blakeslee, met with Gen Kepner to plead his case to equip his group with Mustangs before the 355th, stating that the 4th would train and fly combat missions by the end of the month. His argument that many of the group's pilots and crew chiefs were very well prepared for the Merlin Mustang, based on two years of Spitfire experience in both RAF and early VIII Fighter Command operations, was convincing. The 355th began to transfer its "trainer" P-51Bs to the 4th on February 26.

77th FS/20th FG ace 1Lt James Morris was the first Eighth Air Force pilot to down four enemy aircraft in one mission, on February 8, 1944. He downed 5.333 German fighters in his P-38J-10-LO between February 3 and 24, 1944. (*USAF, sourced by Jack Cook*)

The strength of VIII Bomber Command had increased to the level of being able to launch 600-plus B-17s and B-24s on most missions before "Big Week," scheduled to start on February 20 – a far cry from post-Schweinfurt operations in the fall of 1943. The careful management of strikes with accompanying fighter escort in November through January was beneficial, not only for training new crews but also for the development of doctrine and tactics for VIII Fighter Command. The Luftwaffe was a co-conspirator in the development of skills and experience of VIII Fighter Command pilots. The imposed Rules of Engagement for the day fighter commands and pilots arrayed against the Eighth Air Force – "strike the bombers and avoid the escort" – was a key factor. It had the effect of neutering the previously aggressive posture of the Luftwaffe fighter pilots and, by contrast, enabled their American opponents to gain experience and skills. Perhaps the most important outcome was that Luftwaffe passiveness encouraged an aggressive "attack mind-set" in US fighter pilots for the air battles to come.

During mid-February, from the 14th to the 19th, most missions were scrubbed. Finally, the weather forecast improved on the evening of the 19th, pointing to a week of decent weather over northern Europe. Operation *Argument*, otherwise referred to as "Big Week," commenced the next day.

On February 20 the Eighth Air Force launched five days of maximum-effort attacks on German aircraft and related industries. The targets ranged from Tutow, Poznan, and Rostok to Leipzig, Bernburg, and Oschersleben, and from Hannover, Brunswick, and Magdeburg to Schweinfurt, Regensburg, and Augsburg. The attacking strength of VIII Bomber Command ranged from 500 to 1,000 bombers, accompanied by 650 to 767 VIII Fighter Command fighters each day. Poor weather in southern Germany on the 22nd forced 333 B-24s to abort the Schweinfurt attack, but otherwise a high percentage of the bombers made it to the targets and back. This short week of deep penetration strikes also included significant airfield strafing – VIII Fighter Command destroyed five and damaged 17 aircraft on the ground, all after being relieved from escort duty.

The Fifteenth Air Force also joined the offensive against aircraft industry targets, attacking the Regensburg and Steyr factories. Even though the Fifteenth did not fly nearly as many sorties into Austria and southern Germany, the mere launching of bombers from Foggia and other airfields placed Luftwaffe assets on alert for an incursion from Italian-based heavy bombers. During "Big Week" and through April, the Fifteenth Air Force also continued to bomb airfields and rail networks to support the Anzio beachhead crisis and the Allied push toward Rome.

The contrast between the P-51B and the P-38J as long-range escorts became even more pronounced during "Big Week." In the five days of combat operations, providing the target escort for deep strikes, the two P-38 fighter groups (20th and 55th) scored 9-2-45 for the loss of four. The two P-51 fighter groups (354th and the new 357th) scored 66.5-8-32 for nine losses. The 11 P-47 fighter groups scored 137.5-14-29 for 17 losses.

Notably, for the future narrative, this was the first time that VIII Bomber Command had one long-range target escort fighter group for each of its three bomb divisions. In the case of the February 25 strike to Augsburg, Stuttgart, Regensburg, and Fürth, the two P-51 groups went deep to the latter two cities. The 357th escorted nearly 270 B-17s in five boxes to Regensburg, while the 354th took 170 B-24s in four boxes to Fürth. The two P-38 groups went to Stuttgart and Augsburg, each escorting four boxes of B-17s to their targets. Until late summer 1944 there were never enough long-range escorts (either P-51s or P-38s) to provide more than two fighter groups to escort an entire bomb division of 300-plus bombers.

It should also be noted that the RAF was operating in support of the Eighth Air Force during this period. Fighter Command squadrons equipped with Spitfire IXs, plus some Mustang IIIs (without 85gal tanks) augmented penetration and withdrawal support tasks. Portal imposed on Air Chief Marshal Sir Trafford Leigh-Mallory, Commander-in-Chief, Allied Expeditionary Air Force, to make Mustang IIIs from the Second Tactical Air Force available until late May, when all Mustang units in the Ninth Air Force were released from operational control by the Eighth Air Force.

Both the 355th FG and the 4th FG started receiving Mustangs at this time, with VIII Fighter Command planning to equip the former group first for early March operations. However, as mentioned earlier, Blakeslee convinced Kepner that the 4th should precede the 355th because of his group's Spitfire/Merlin experience. Accordingly, he put the 4th on a crash schedule to continue to fly missions in the P-47s while devoting time to convert onto the new P-51B and be ready for ops on February 26. When the mission on that date was scrubbed, the 4th had to wait 48 hours to make its operational debut with the Mustang. The group duly claimed one victory without any losses.[9]

The inexperienced and under-trained 363rd FG was assigned to the Eighth Air Force for escort duty on February 24, providing a total of three P-51B-equipped groups to complement the two P-38J-equipped groups.

February 1944 marked a crucial month in the struggle for air supremacy over Germany between the USAAF and the Luftwaffe. The *LwBfhMitte* was dissolved and replaced by the *Luftflotte Reich* to improve I. *Jagdkorps*' command and control of the various *Jagddivisionen* (1, 2, 3, and 7) defending Germany, while *Luftflotte* 3 retained control of II. *Jagdkorps*, comprising *Jagddivisionen* 4 and 5, protecting the coastal routes into Germany from Britain. The programs for pilot training were meeting student-pilot objectives for the fighter pilot replacement pool, but because of reductions in fuel reservation allocations, the training hours were reduced below 1941–42 standards.

The recent disasters inflicted on the twin-engined day fighter force by the Mustangs on January 4 and 11 over targets previously thought to be safe from US fighter escort was particularly disturbing. Rethinking both deployment and protection of the Bf 110 and Ju 88 units was now considered necessary, as it was clear that no attack by twin-engined fighters on Eighth Air Force bombers inside a 450-mile radius was considered safe from P-51 interceptions. Following the attacks on January 4 and 11, Generalmajor Schmid was called to Berlin to explain the forced necessity of providing top-cover escorts of Bf 109G-5/6s with GM-1 equipment for twin-engined fighters. As it became clear that the P-51B's performance at 30,000ft was better in rate of climb and far superior in top speed over the G-5/6, the Bf 109G-6AS, with the new Daimler-Benz DB 605 AS(M) engine for better high-altitude performance, was designated for *Hohengruppen* (high-altitude *Gruppen*) to provide escort protection against US fighters.

Generalmajor Schmid's notes for an April 18 I. *Jagdkorps* staff meeting, summarizing February 1944, included:

1. The geographical concentration of day fighters was carried out in north-western German, eastern Holland and the area between Bremen and Hannover.
2. The technique of combat by mixed units in close formation proved effective when weather conditions were favorable. Assembly was rarely possible in poor weather.
3. The technique of attack from the front had not been mastered by all fighter units.
4. There was no numerical reinforcement of the RLV day fighter units, although they had been requested by I. *Jagdkorps* commander in December.
5. The use of day fighters by the Herrmann-*Jager* [*Wilde Sau* nightfighters], and the high losses of the latter during January 1944, hurt the operation of the day fighter forces.
6. Supply of reinforcement day fighters was, for the most part, satisfactory.
7. The total striking power of I. *Jagdkorps* was greater in January [1944] than late 1943. The successes on January 11 did much to increase the confidence of the line units in an ultimately successful defense, although the tactical and numerical superiority had not been fully demonstrated.
8. During January, the average daily operational strength of I. *Jagdkorps* was: 400 single-engined fighters, 80 twin-engined fighters and 100 nightfighters available for day use.
9. January sorties by I. *Jagdkorps* = 2,306; Losses = 122 or 3.5 percent.[10]

FEBRUARY – P-51 ISSUES AND RESOLUTIONS

On February 3 the Office of the Assistant Chief of the Air Staff, Materiel, Maintenance and Distribution forwarded a memo dated January 27 from Materiel Command to the Technical Executive. It noted that, in response to the recommendations of the December 22 report from Eglin Field that "lateral baffles" be installed in the 85gal tank to prevent fore-and-aft movement of fuel, these had indeed been fitted in all production tanks. The memo further stated that, in the opinion of Materiel Command, this installation sufficiently retarded the motion of fuel, and that the fitment of a longitudinal baffle would be a waste of labor and materials.

On February 11 the new P-51B dorsal fin fillet was tested by Chilton on 43-12095, which was then sent to NACA Langley Field for further testing. While at Langley, 43-12095 was also used to test a modification for the new rudder fin cap.

44-13253 was the first P-51D-5-NA to fly in January 1944. Shown here is 44-13255 (No. 3) with the first D-model dorsal fin fillet in late March of that same year. *(© The Boeing Company)*

Various dorsal fin fillets and fin caps were also tested on the early P-51D-5s. The "tall fin" was a further experiment by NAA to try to solve adverse yaw instability, particularly in dives and sideslips, and was later used on the P-51H to yield the best Mustang yaw characteristics. Three days later, on the 14th, Chilton took XP-51F 43-33332 for its first flight. He later remarked that it may have been the best version of the Mustang that he ever flew for pure exhilaration, recording climb rates exceeding 5,500ft/min and a ceiling of 45,000ft, "only limited by zero cockpit pressurization."

MARCH – USSTAF AND LUFTWAFFE OPERATIONS

Operations in March 1944 could be summarized as "Mustangs turned loose by the Eighth Air Force" in the ETO. The extremely long range of the P-51B/C, its excellent performance attributes from high altitude to sea level, and the encouragement of airfield strafing by Eighth Air Force commanders led to a change of tactics to provide group and squadron COs more latitude to "attack." The changes resulted in soaring

RIGHT P-51B-1-NA 43-12105 is seen on the Mines Field ramp before the dorsal fin fillet and tall fin modifications had taken place. (*© The Boeing Company*)

BOTTOM RIGHT P-51B-1-NA 43-12105 was the first NAA Mustang modified with the dorsal fin fillet. This photograph was taken after the latter was fitted and after the aircraft was flown to Langley Field in December 1943 for flight testing with NACA. The dorsal fin fillet was added in April 1944. Note the wing "sleeve" designed to test different low drag wing sections for the XP-51F and G. (*© The Boeing Company*)

NA-105 XP-51F prototype 43-43332 shown before its first flight on February 14, 1944. Note the aircraft's distinctive small wheels, enlarged canopy and long lower cowl. The fastest-climbing Mustang until the even more impressive XP-51G, the XP-51F's rate of climb approached 5,500ft per minute at full internal combat weight. (© *The Boeing Company*)

destruction totals of German aircraft in the air and on the ground. The P-47D-equipped fighter groups performed well too, but continued to operate in regions more sparsely populated by German aircraft.

Curiously, the twin-engined P-38s demonstrated more vulnerability to anti-aircraft flak while strafing airfields than either the Mustang or the Thunderbolt. The Lightning's relative "approximate" ratio of losses to strafing to German aircraft destroyed was just less than 1:1.5. The same ratio for P-47s was 1:3.7, while the P-51B ratio of losses to aircraft destroyed was approximately 1:5.3.[11]

The ratios of losses to victories for airfield strafing presented above are not engraved in stone. The results were calculated by collecting and tabulating victory credits for ground scores compiled in the Eighth Air Force Victory Credits Board published in June 1945, and further modified by USAF Study 85 and Dr. Frank Olynyk's research into air victory credits. Analysis has also been made of thousands of Missing Aircrew Reports contained on the Fold3.com National Records Database for eyewitness accounts of losses due to German fighters and light flak, and judgment calls made on the cause of the loss for category "Unknown" by asking the question "was the aircraft last seen strafing – or flying at medium to high altitude?"

With March 1944 came the first USAAF attacks on Berlin, enabled by a critical mass of three P-38 and four P-51B fighter groups. The leaders of the Eighth Air Force, particularly Doolittle and Anderson, understood that an attack on Berlin would elicit a major response from all available Luftwaffe resources, including those based east of Berlin. Furthermore, even with the critical mass of seven long-range escort fighter groups to cover the last 150–180 miles (beyond the greatest P-47D range) for the planned 30–31 bomb groups attacking Berlin, it was difficult to protect a very long bomber stream under the most favorable formation conditions. Imagine one fighter group out in front and four others perfectly situated 20 miles apart to defend against concentrations of 200-plus German fighters striking anywhere along the 100-mile-long bomber stream. When successfully planned by Luftwaffe controllers, a concentrated attack by one or two *Jagdgeschwader* overloaded the available local US escorts, forcing the fighter group commander to dispatch flights and sections against multiple *Staffeln* and *Gruppen* at the point of attack.

The raid on March 3 was the first attempt to attack Berlin-area targets at Oranienburg (50-plus miles north of Berlin) and the Berlin-Erkner ball-bearing factories. The planned route was straight through Berlin, then south, and then west near Leipzig to return home. Despite the foul weather that caused most of VIII Bomber Command's aircraft to turn back, some 3rd BD B-17s pressed onward. The 20th, 364th and 357th FGs heard the recall order and also aborted the mission. Several elements of each of the four remaining target escort fighter groups, unaware that a recall order had been sent, continued toward the rendezvous for the bombers attacking Berlin. The 55th FG P-38s and 4th, 354th, and 363rd FG P-51s all pressed eastward, with the 4th first encountering Luftwaffe fighters northeast of Wittenburg. Chasing them northwest of Berlin, the group claimed five victories for no losses. The 354th FG engaged northeast of Wittenburg and west of Berlin, scoring two for one loss (due to magneto/engine failure on the way in). The 55th flew over and around Berlin. The new Mustang-equipped 363rd FG flew a target support mission, its pilots being led by 356th FS/354th FG squadron leader Lt Col James Howard. The group engaged and shot down several Me 410s at the rendezvous point over Grabow (26 miles northeast of central Berlin), before proceeding around Berlin with its assigned bombers.

Following the mission, Howard reported to IX Fighter Command's 70th Fighter Wing commander Col J. W. McCauley that the 363rd FG pilots "were not ready," and should be grounded indefinitely until such time as their weather flying was up to ETO standards. Howard also commented that the leadership was sub-par, flight and radio discipline was poor, and the group was experiencing too many aborts. McCauley refused to stand the 363rd down, however, probably because the Eighth Air Force so desperately needed escort fighters with the range to reach Berlin.

The very next day, scheduled for a return trip to Berlin, the 363rd FG encountered huge thunderstorms and low visibility over the North Sea and lost 11 Mustangs – five from the 381st FS and six from the 382nd FS. Despite 11 aborts and the 11 lost, several 363rd FG aircraft escorted their assigned bombers to Berlin, around to Magdeburg and part way home before breaking escort. This day marked the highest single group loss of any P-51 fighter group in either the ETO or the MTO, and dramatically illustrated the requirement for more in-theater instrument training for newly arrived pilots. The 363rd stood down for several days of re-equipping and training from the 10th through the 16th, before resuming combat operations.[12]

On March 6 the Eighth Air Force finally got the weather conditions required to launch 31 bomb groups, with 730 bombers tasked to attack targets in and around Berlin. The Luftwaffe was ready, well organized, and motivated for what turned out to be the greatest aerial battle fought up to that point in World War II. The overall documented statistics show the loss of 69-6-347 of the 672 "effectives" from the bomber force, plus 11 losses from the Eighth and Ninth Air Force escorts. The victory credits were P-38 3-0-1 for three losses, P-47 37-7-12 for five losses, and P-51 43-1-20 for five losses. The Luftwaffe put up 463 sorties, including landing/rearming and taking off again to intercept the returning bombers. The Luftwaffe recorded losses of 75 fighters, 37 aircrew killed in action, and 32 wounded. More importantly,

35 percent of the twin-engined day fighters and 50 percent of the twin-engined nightfighters that engaged were lost. The continued attrition of the once very effective "bomber destroyers" by escort fighters would soon negate their threat.[13]

Noteworthy features of these statistics are, (1) the P-38s were able to perform escort in high threat target areas, but engagements and multiple victory credits eluded the fighter groups flying them; (2) although the number of P-47D-equipped fighter groups outnumbered the Mustang fighter groups by a factor of 2:1, the P-51B/C units scored much higher victory credits for similar losses; (3) I. and II. *Jagdkorps* coordinated both inbound attacks, as well as the second wave, which landed to rearm and then re-engaged the Eighth Air Force on its way home. Without the escort relay system, which enabled the 100 launched P-51B/Cs to meet the Berlin-area attacks, the bomber losses could easily have exceeded 100.

The reasons for the lack of P-38 victories compared with the P-47D and P-51 became clearer. First, it was obvious that the Lightning's large size and twin-engined signature made it easily identifiable by Luftwaffe pilots. The choice to avoid a fight, or to position in advance to gain a favorable tactical advantage to attack, gave the advantage to the much smaller (and harder to see) Luftwaffe single-engined fighters. Second, the issues arising in changing from forced low-speed cruise engine management to full military power in the P-38 (before procedures were adopted to take account of extreme high-altitude conditions in the ETO) made the Lightning even more vulnerable to a surprise bounce at escort altitudes. Many engines failed in those moments of crisis. Last, the compressibility issues experienced when entering dives above 20,000ft made the P-38 less effective in both pursuit and defense. Specifically, an Fw 190 pilot, when pursued, could easily out-roll the P-38 and either split-S to escape in a dive or maneuver to a better tactical position. Both the Fw 190 and Bf 109 could easily out-dive the P-38.

On March 8 the third Eighth Air Force Mustang-equipped fighter group, the 355th FG, dispatched the 357th FS to perform its first target escort to Berlin – the unit had borrowed eight P-51s from the 4th FG in February in order to start the conversion to the Mustang. The 357th FS scored 2-0-1 for the loss of one P-51. As an example of the positive impact the P-51B had on the fortunes of former P-47-equipped groups in respect to the number of German aircraft destroyed, by mid-April the 355th had risen from the middle of the ETO-based fighter groups to third place in the unofficial victory table. After the 352nd FG converted from the P-47 to the P-51B/C in April, the two fighter groups would "trade" this spot in the overall total of aircraft destroyed (air and ground) behind the 4th and 56th FGs until the 355th permanently nudged the 352nd into fourth spot in March–April 1945.

While returning, the 354th FS/355th FG dropped to the deck at Hesepe airfield and destroyed seven Bf 110s and damaged two, for the loss of one pilot killed in action – 2Lt Charles Sweat was the 355th FG's first strafing casualty. The group strafing loss total would reach 90 casualties by VE Day, the highest in the USAAF. While earlier ground scores had been achieved, this attack perhaps represented the beginning of the premeditated strafing attacks that returning escort fighters would undertake for the rest of the war. The 354th FS/355th FG would emerge as the top USAAF airfield-strafing fighter squadron of World War II.[14]

On March 15 the 56th FG claimed 24 aircraft shot down for one loss. This was also the last day on which the P-47D (Eighth and Ninth Air Force combined) had more cumulative aerial victory credits than the P-51B between January 1 and March 15, 1944. By D-Day, the P-51B would have more aerial victory credits than all the cumulative ETO aerial victory credits of the P-47C/D from the beginning of ETO operations in April 1943, and twice as many "ground credits" as the P-47 and P-38 combined.

Beginning on March 16, the Eighth Air Force returned to southeast Germany for the first time since "Big Week." VIII Bomber Command's results were mixed due to layered cloud cover obscuring most of the targets, and the PFF crews had difficulty in picking up the radar target markers.

The Luftwaffe reacted strongly, dispatching 375 sorties. VIII Bomber Command "only" lost 23-1-79, primarily due to good escort coverage both inbound (P-47 penetration escort) and over the targets (P-38s and P-51s). The Luftwaffe lost 67 fighters shot down, with perhaps the most serious losses being inflicted on *Zerstörergeschwader* (ZG) 76, which in turn claimed 18 B-17 victories. This Bf 110-equipped unit had 19 aircraft destroyed and four badly damaged out of 43 when it was engaged by the 4th and 357th FGs. ZG 76 flew one more mission and was then disbanded to provide replacements for other units. The 355th FG destroyed 16-2-12 of the escorting Bf 109s, largely from JGs 3, 5, and 101, between Ulm and Augsburg.

The Eighth Air Force returned to southeast Germany to bomb targets from Friedrichshafen to Munich on the 18th. The Fifteenth Air Force attacked Udine airfield in northern Italy, tying up many of the Luftwaffe's southern defense forces arrayed in Austria and far southern Germany. Two of the P-38 fighter groups, the 20th and 55th, escorting B-24s attacking targets in the Friedrichshafen area, scored 12-2-2 for five losses. This P-38 daily total remained the highest combined P-38 FGs' aerial victory tally until July 7.

The well-planned two-pronged, staged attack by the Fifteenth Air Force on March 18 was noteworthy for its spectacular successes. The 1st Task Force (TF) drew Luftwaffe fighter reaction from Graz and Klagenfurt by feinting up the Yugoslavian coast before breaking west to force the interceptors to chase them. The Fifteenth Air Force escort engaged, and claimed seven for no losses, while the 1st TF proceeded to drop 20lb fragmentation bombs on Villaorba and Udine airfields. The 2nd, 3rd, and 4th TFs bombed Goriza, Levariano, and Maniago airfields. Intelligence reports cited 56 aircraft as damaged or destroyed on the ground, as well as maintenance and repair facilities, for the loss of seven bombers. XV Fighter Command claimed 33-3-3 for the loss of two P-47s and two P-38s.

On the 21st the 4th FG performed a lone group fighter sweep, looking for targets of opportunity all the way to Bordeaux. The group split up to cover a greater area and destroyed 9-1-0 in the air and 11 on the ground, but paid a huge price to airfield flak with seven aircraft being lost. One pilot evaded and returned in July. This day's results for airfield strafing, combined with four losses to flak for three additional victory credits on the ground by the P-47D-equipped 353rd FG on March 22, pointed to a sobering conclusion for VIII Fighter Command – strafing airfields was now more hazardous than aerial combat.

The following day the 4th and 354th FGs collaborated near Brunswick to destroy 12 and 17, respectively, for three losses.

Missions on March 27, 28, and 29 resulted in major spikes to victory credits for the destruction of parked aircraft in southern France and distant east-southeast Germany. On the 27th the 4th FG shot down three aircraft and destroyed 23 on the ground at Cayaux airfield for two losses during a freelance sweep to Bordeaux. On the 28th the 355th FG destroyed 24 and damaged 34 on the ground at Dijon airfield for zero losses. The following day those two groups, along with the 354th FG, destroyed 24 and 14 in the air, respectively, for the loss of three to German fighters.[15]

The P-51B aerial victory credits in March for the ETO for Luftwaffe aircraft destroyed totaled 251, compared with 175 for the P-47 and 26 for the P-38.[16]

MARCH – P-51, P-47, AND P-38 ISSUES AND RESOLUTIONS

In mid-March several significant problems were encountered with the P-51B. The most serious were structural failures of the empennage, wing, and engine mounts. All aircraft were grounded between March 10 and 15.

The engine mount failures were quickly traced (initially) to improper heat treatment of the high-tensile-strength bolts used to attach the Merlin to the engine mounts. All of the bolts were removed and inspected, tested, and either returned as satisfactory or discarded while local sources were scoured to find properly heat-treated

P-51D NACA 102 44-13017 has its gun bay instrumented prior to undertaking dive-testing at NACA Langley in 1944 following return from carrier trials by the USN. *(NASA)*

The P-51D's wing load test in early 1944 showed "deformation of ammo door at 66% of Design Limit load – indicating need to strengthen the ammo door for Mach critical dives." (© *The Boeing Company*)

bolts. When the accidents persisted, the failed bolts (previously tested and passed) were found to not contain enough nickel to provide the required high-tensile strength, and all engine bolts were inspected again. The substandard bolts were replaced. NAA traced the defective bolts to a specific contractor, and all P-51s on the line and in the field were tested. Remedial steps were taken at the contractor site, and NAA established test processes in-house as new bolts were received.

The empennage issues were more complicated. The elevator failures were ultimately traced to the differential vertical loads on the horizontal stabilizer imposed by a combination of pull-out loads and the propeller vortex, which added another vertical load to the left elevator. The empennage failures due to torsion were traced to both the elevator and fin/rudder, and were due to a combination of the propeller vortex and increased yaw input caused when performing high-speed sideslips and slow rolls, and excessive rudder input during high-speed diving maneuvers. The solution included installation of the dorsal fin fillet to improve flow over the empennage during sideslip, beefing up the elevator support structure, and adding a reverse rudder boost tab. Following acceptance by the USAAF, work was started to fabricate kits and prepare a Technical Order covering the installation of both the new fin fillet and the reverse rudder boost tab.

The last issues causing wing failures began with the problem identified by Rolls-Royce during the late 1942/early 1943 Mustang X dive tests, when the tendency for the main landing gear to "unlock and drop" during high-G (in dive pull-outs or violent turn maneuvers, for example) forced the main-wheel cover fairings to open – which in turn let the gear partially extend into the very-high-velocity slipstream. Additional issues were caused when the door fairing latches failed, releasing the doors and causing an immediate change in the pressure distribution over the wing. The instantaneous result was a sharp change in yaw and roll at high speed. The resultant violent forces on the wing caused by such high and instantaneous drag and lift forces resulted in catastrophic failure. Door up-lock kits were dispatched to the ETO and in-theater by late April. The wheel door fairing latches were modified and introduced in July.

The structural failures at Eglin Field during A-36 trials earlier in 1943 had been traced to the violent change of aerodynamic flow and forces when the dive brakes were opened *after* initiation of the dive-bombing run – similar in cause and effect to the wheel door fairing opening during a dive.

The least obvious root cause for wing failure was only discovered during the terminal-dive testing for the P-51D, begun in November 1943. The ammunition/ gun bay doors were found to "bulge" owing to aerodynamic loads imposed during the formation of shock waves in the transonic region. The ammunition/gun access doors were stiffened to prevent a catastrophic failure of the wing during extremely high-speed dives.

It was also during this period that the elevator bob-weight designs were modified to improve control stick authority when the Mustang approached control reversal during high-G maneuvers.

Chilton made several important test flights in 43-12105 and 43-12102. P-51B-1 43-12095 had been modified with a wind tunnel-tested dorsal fin fillet and reverse rudder boost tab for flight tests beginning February 11 through March 7. After deeming the combination beneficial, and with no attendant maneuverability issues, NAA turned 43-12095 over to the USAAF for acceptance testing. The metal elevator tests, plus the first changes to elevator incidence, were made with the bubble canopy-converted P-51B 43-12102. After March 11 this aircraft ceased to be the initial test bed for the future modification of the horizontal stabilizer and metal elevator.

Continued testing for the horizontal stabilizer/elevator introduced in late 1944 (kits and production) was initiated with P-51D-5-NA 44-13256 (NA-109 No. 4). Later, the final configurations were installed on 44-14314, which was delivered to the USAAF for acceptance testing.

On March 24 USAAF test pilot Maj Ritchie submitted "AAF Memo Report ENG-47-FR-TC2 re: Stability Tests on P-51B-1 43-12095 equipped with new DFF [dorsal fin fillet] and Reverse Rudder Boost." In summary, the dorsal fin fillet and reverse rudder boost reduced yaw oscillation dampening with improved stability due to hard rudder input, and improved dive stability. The NAA engineering drawings 104-25001 (P-51B/C) and 109-25001 (P-51D) for the dorsal fin fillet were released for production that week (March 31 and March 25, 1944, respectively). The P-51B dorsal fin fillet and reverse rudder boost tab were fabricated and installed on 43-12105 in early February.

On March 25 Chilton began initial trials of 100/150-octane fuel in P-51B-10-NA 43-7113. Performance testing was undertaken to determine the effects of boosting manifold pressure to 75inHg for the Packard Merlin 1650-7. As expected, the full-throttle horsepower for the engine/fuel combination was reduced, but the top sea-level speed and overall rate of climb at 75in. improved dramatically.[17]

On the 29th Chilton made a run with a P-51A modified with the V-1710-F20R engine equipped with water injection. On the 31st he flew 43-7113 to test 100/150-octane fuel, and the aircraft was found to have exceptional climb rates. At 75inHg of manifold pressure in clean condition (no racks) and only half load of fuel, the P-51B's rate of climb exceeded 5,000ft/min. During this same period P-51D-5-NAs 44-13255 (No. 3) and 44-13258 continued testing of the dorsal fin fillet design which was just released for production insertion at 44-13903 in July.[18]

During mid-March the Eighth and Ninth Air Forces received large quantities of impregnated-paper 108gal "non-reusable" combat tanks. The 108gal tanks enabled the P-51B and newly arrived P-51C-1-NTs to perform target escort deep into Poland and Czechoslovakia (average 700-plus miles from East Anglia).

P-51B-10-NA 42-106950 of the 354th FS/355th FG, Steeple Morden, Hertfordshire, May 1944. *(Artwork by Jim Laurier, © Osprey Publishing)*

During late March and early April, the combat radius of the production "as built" P-47D was extended by an influx of P-47D-16-REs with factory wing pylons and combat tank fuel lines, plus tank pressurization and increased oxygen capacity. In addition, many existing ETO-based earlier P-47D series Thunderbolts emerged from BAD1 Burtonwood with the modifications to use the 75gal, 108gal, or 150gal combat tanks. With two 150gal tanks, the combat radius of the P-47D-16 (or equivalent) was extended past 425 miles from East Anglia; roughly to Hamburg, Brunswick, and Stuttgart. By this time, however, there were enough P-38Js with 550-mile capability (Berlin, Leipzig, Munich) and P-51Bs with 750-mile-radius capability (Stettin, Poznan, Prague) to render the P-47D more useful for penetration and withdrawal escort for deep targets. The new P-47D combat radius, however, had the effect of permitting the P-51B and P-38J to "fast cruise" directly to target escort RV to permit more escort time with the bombers around the target and back.

APRIL – USSTAF AND LUFTWAFFE OPERATIONS

On April 1 the Combined Bomber Offensive was officially concluded with the transfer of control of USSTAF to the Supreme Commander, Allied Expeditionary Forces, Gen Dwight Eisenhower.

In April the 352nd FG received its first complement of Mustangs to begin training for complete conversion from the P-47D.

On the 4th and 5th the Fifteenth Air Force sent bombers to Bucharest and Ploesti, beyond the range of their P-38 escorts for target support. They met with heavy resistance near the targets, losing seven and 13, respectively.

April 5 also saw the 4th FG sent to the Berlin area, while the 355th FG went to strafe Munich-area airfields in a snowstorm. During the mission one of the 4th FG's top aces, Capt Duane Beeson, was shot down by flak. The 4th set a new daily record with credits of 43 destroyed on the ground and two in the air over Berlin-area airfields, notably Brandenburg-Briest, only for the 355th to better it later that same day. After making landfall over Ostend, the 355th dropped to the deck and navigated 470 miles under low-altitude ten-tenths cloud cover to strike four airfields in a snowstorm, claiming 59-2-81, all around Munich. The 355th credits were reduced to 8-0-0 air/40 destroyed and 81 damaged on the ground – nevertheless, a record for a one-day mission total until it was broken by the 479th FG in September. The 355th was awarded a Distinguished Unit Citation for this mission. An unintended benefit was the destruction of many specialized Ju 88s and Bf 110s equipped for night fighting.

The air battles intensified as the Luftwaffe improved the planning and execution of its defense system. *Gruppen* and *Staffeln* were distributed along the primary ingress routes used by the Eighth Air Force to strike northeast, east, and southeast German targets, and command and control directed Luftwaffe fighters along the bomber stream to find bomb wings least protected by fighter escort, then sent large concentrations to those locations. In addition, experienced combat units from the Ost and Süd operating areas continued to reinforce *Luftflotte Reich*.

Gruppen and *Staffeln* leaders became more adept at stalking bomber formations when cloud cover and escorts were present, striking when opportunities arose. During the spring, poor weather conditions frequently blighted Europe, often making timely planned formation assembly by VIII Bomber Command problematic. Positioning 1,000 bombers over East Anglia, then assembling 30-plus bomb groups in their proper place within the different task forces to attack various targets was often only partially successful. On many occasions situations occurred when bomb divisions were off course and off-time for planned waypoints along the inbound routes. These failures to achieve planned routes and times often caused missed rendezvous with the fighter escort, creating great opportunities for the Luftwaffe controllers and fighter leaders to attack isolated bomb wings lacking any escort, or perhaps with one strung-out fighter group trying to cover an entire bomb division.

The oft-repeated testimony of some Luftwaffe day fighter pilots in the spring and summer of 1944 was "We were greatly outnumbered by Mustangs, often ten-to-one." In fact that was impossible. During the period prior to D-Day, there was never a circumstance in which Eighth Air Force planners could direct more than one or two fighter groups of P-51s (and P-38s in combination) to provide target escort to each of three or more task forces attacking targets out of P-47 range. At best, perhaps two groups of 40–45 Mustangs each (after aborts) or Lightnings would be tasked to escort ten bomb groups along a 20–25-mile distance from lead to trail bomb groups. When cloud cover also obscured visibility, there were often no forewarnings of the presence of German fighters until they were attacking, and the bombers sent radio calls for help over the common command channel to the fighter group that was tasked to be in that area.

On April 8 the 4th FG had another spectacular day. Flying an Area Support to the Ulzen-Brunswick area, the group spotted 75–100 German fighters from Celle heading for 2nd BD B-24s. In the ensuing fight, the 4th FG was credited with 33-1-8 in the Celle/Ulzen area for the loss of four. The 354th attacked another

50–75 and scored 20-2-15 in the Wittingen area northeast of Brunswick, also for the loss of four. The Luftwaffe lost 77 fighters plus 43 aircrew killed in action, mostly in the vicious aerial battle around Brunswick that cost the Eighth Air Force 32 B-24s.

April also marked the last two missions in which VIII Bomber Command lost more than 60 bombers in one day. Leading up to April 11 the Eighth Air Force lost 34-2-347 bombers on April 8 while attacking Brunswick and Oschersleben, then 32-10-167 over Marienburg, Poznan, and Tutow on the 9th. Escort fighters claimed 83-3-46 air and 49-6-38 ground victories for 23 pilots missing in action on the 8th and 20-1-6 air/19-0-8 ground victories on the 9th. After losing 77 day fighters and 43 pilots killed in action on the 8th, the Luftwaffe lost another 27 fighters and 14 pilots during the fighting on the 9th.

On April 10 the 352nd FG's 428th FS flew Mustangs for its first mission, while the rest of the group was still equipped with P-47s. The 352nd and 355th were virtual "sister" fighter groups, both arriving in Britain at the same time and both beginning operations in the second week of September 1943. The 355th FG surged ahead of the 352nd for third place in Eighth Air Force's victory credits tally, but the 352nd recaptured this spot in May 1944. The two would trade places until the 355th secured third spot behind the 4th and 56th FGs in March–April 1945.

On April 11 the Eighth Air Force went to Schweinfurt and Munich, provoking a very heavy reaction from the Luftwaffe and losing 64-5-406 bombers and 16 fighters. The Luftwaffe flew 356 sorties, losing 53 fighters and 37 killed in action. The Luftwaffe discovered the 3rd BD unescorted, and took out 33-1-153 B-17s attacking Politz and Rostock. The Eighth and Ninth Air Force escorts accounted for 51-5-25 in the air and 65-0-67 on the ground. The aerial victory credits were as follows – P-38 (1-1-1 air credits, 0 losses), P-47 (3-1-2 air credits, 6 losses (4 to flak)), P-51 (47-4-22, 6 losses). The 357th FG scored 23 of the 47 victories credited to the P-51.

On the 12th the Eighth Air Force attacked Schweinfurt, Zwikau, and Bernburg with 455 bombers, losing 6-22-26. The escort fighters claimed 18-1-3 for five losses, P-38 groups losing three and the P-51 groups two. The Luftwaffe defended against the Eighth Air Force with 205 fighters, losing 24 plus 12 killed in action. The Fifteenth Air Force also attacked Vienna, losing 11 bombers. Its three P-38 and one P-47 fighter groups claimed 17-2-8 for one loss. *Jagddivision* 7 put up 170 fighters from southern Germany, Austria, and Hungary against the attack from the south and lost 17 fighters and 12 killed in action.

On the 13th the Eighth Air Force attacked Schweinfurt, Oberphaffenhofen, and Augsburg with a force of 566 bombers, losing 38-3-350 to an attacking force of 434 single- and twin-engined fighters. Escorts claimed 42-8-10 (plus 35 destroyed and 21 damaged on the ground), while the Luftwaffe lost 45 fighters and 11 killed in action. Once again, despite an action-packed target escort to Augsburg, the P-38-equipped 20th, 55th, and 364th FGs managed to shoot down just one German fighter, and lost two Lightnings to engine failures.

On April 21, 1944 the Fifteenth Air Force targeted the oilfields at Bucharest and Ploesti, with the bombers being accompanied over the target for the first time by XV Fighter Command. The veteran 31st FG, recently equipped with Mustangs, provided escort. No bombers were lost to enemy fighters during the raid on the 21st, and the 31st FG destroyed 17-7-10 for the loss of two Mustangs. These were the only fighter victories credited to the Fifteenth Air Force that day. (*NARA*)

That same day the Fifteenth Air Force attacked Budapest and Gyor, in Hungary, and the Luftwaffe responded with most of *Jagddivision* 7, including the two available Hungarian fighter squadrons, comprising one Me 210 nightfighter unit and a Bf 109G day fighter squadron. The former lost all 13 of its Me 210s, causing a recall of all Hungarian air force units on the Eastern Front for home defense. The losses in the south were 21 aircraft plus eight killed in action. The Fifteenth Air Force lost 13-7-7. The three P-38 fighter groups and one P-47 fighter group claimed 18-3-7 for the loss of one Thunderbolt.

On April 15 the Eighth Air Force sent 700 VIII and IX Fighter Command fighters to sweep 26 German airfields. The 20th, 78th, and 353rd FGs were recalled because of bad weather, and conditions remained marginal across the Continent. Nevertheless, the Luftwaffe launched fighters to defend its airfields, losing 19 plus five pilots killed in action. Eleven fighters were lost by III./JG 11, forcing it off operations to rebuild. USAAF losses consisted of 11 P-38s from the 55th and 364th FGs for claims of 3-1-1 air and 2-2 ground. In all, the categories of US fighter losses were 19 to weather, four to engine failure (three P-51s and one P-38), and ten to airfield flak.

April 18 marked a significant success for the first operational *Sturmguppen*, IV./JG 3, which found a hole in the clouds through which to attack the 3rd BD undetected by escorts and shoot down 14 B-17s near Berlin. That same day Lt Col Thomas Hitchcock perished in a P-51B crash near Salisbury while making practice dive-bombing runs. Hitchcock was arguably one of the most, if not *the* most, important figures in pushing the hybrid NAA/Rolls-Royce Mustang into the USAAF inventory in the nick of time.

The mission on the 19th was notable for continuing problems with the paper tanks, causing some aborts. The 352nd FG provided continuous penetration-target-

withdrawal support to Kassel-area targets and back to the coast. The 4th, 352nd, 355th, and 357th FGs sent flights and sections to attack different gaggles of 25-plus Luftwaffe fighters between Kassel and Eschwege. Collectively, they destroyed 16 German fighters, for two losses. Overall, the Luftwaffe lost 24 fighters and 14 killed in action during 208 sorties, destroying 5-0-119 B-17s of the 1st BD.

On April 21 the 31st FG flew its fourth P-51B/C mission – a target escort to a Fifteenth Air Force strike against Ploesti. It surprised a large gaggle of fighters near Bucharest, being credited with 17-7-10 for the loss of two. It was the first time that the Fifteenth Air Force had been escorted all the way to Bucharest/Ploesti and back.

The 22nd marked another major contribution from the 4th FG during a freelance sweep in front of the Hamm strike – an attack by all three VIII Bomber Command bomb divisions with 779 bombers. The 4th sighted a gaggle (probably III./JG 1) assembling at 6,000ft southwest of Kassel and all three squadrons bounced the Bf 109s, scattering them from Warburg and south to Lake Eder, where they encountered more Bf 109s possibly from I. and II./JG 1. Capt Willard Millikan downed four to match the ETO record held by 20th FG ace 1Lt James Morris. The 4th was credited with 17-0-0 for one loss.

ABOVE On April 22, 1944, P-51B pilot Capt Willard Millikan of the 336th FS/4th FG matched 1Lt James Morris's score of February 8 that same year when he too claimed four aerial victories. (*USAF, sourced by Jack Cook*)

During the course of the Hamm raid Luftwaffe *Experten* Major Heinz Bär, *Gruppenkommandeur* of II./JG 1, shot down a B-24 near Ahlen, Germany, for his

200th victory. As the 2nd BD B-24s returned home, they were unaware that Me 410s from II./KG 51 had shadowed them in the waning light. The Me 410s destroyed seven, caused seven more to be written off due to crash landings and damaged another 50-plus. The Eighth Air Force never again permitted a late take-off for VIII Bomber Command that would necessitate the bombers returning after dark.

On the 23rd VIII Fighter Command performed a fighter-bomber sweep against enemy airfields in Belgium, France, and Germany. The 20th and 55th FGs flew their first mission with the "Droop Snoot" P-38 as lead bomber for a horizontal bombing attack on Laon airfield. This was the first example of tactical use of the Cass Hough-modified Lightnings. P-38 units claimed 0 air/2-3 ground credits for two losses to airfield flak, P-47 squadrons were credited with 9-25 ground for five losses to airfield flak, and P-51 pilots scored 3-1 ground for no losses.

That same day, the Fifteenth Air Force went to the Austrian airfields at Schwechat, Bad Voslau, and Wiener Neustadt. The Luftwaffe reacted by scrambling 174 fighters from subordinate commands in Austria, Hungary, and southern Germany, shooting down two B-24s. The strong escort of three P-38 fighter groups, one with P-47s and one with P-51s, engaged German aircraft at different locations, claiming 26-6-16 for the loss of three P-38s and two P-51s. The P-38-equipped 1st, 14th, and 82nd FGs were eventually credited with 12, the 325th FG (P-47s) claimed none and the 31st FG (P-51s) was also credited with 12.

On the 24th the 1st BD experimented with a new formation, splitting the 41st BW into two forces – with 41A leading and 41B placed alongside on the right – to direct a greater concentration of fire at anticipated head-on attacks around Munich-area targets. The rest of the 1st BD bomb wings flew the normal formation, in trail to the lead 41A wing. The concept was a disaster because the B-17s in 41B could not keep up during a course change to the left, which caused them to be isolated on the far right-hand side of the lead 41A, while slowly losing position further aft. The rest of the 1st BD stayed in trail, in excellent formation, as the task force proceeded southeast past Paris, then made a left turn to the east-southeast toward Stuttgart. It then turned due east at Stuttgart to attack targets at Erding airfield, before heading south past Munich and then west to the IP southwest of the city. From the IP, 41A and 41B diverged course to their respective targets to strike Oberphaffenhoffen and Landsberg. The other two task forces (2nd and 3rd TFs) split from the 1st TF stream as its passed Stuttgart to attack Friedrichshafen and Leipheim/Gablingen, respectively. The P-38 escort went to Friedrichshafen, while the 4th FG, sweeping in front of the 1st TF, engaged JG 11 east of Stuttgart, near Worms, and destroyed 16 for the loss of three. The rest of the Mustang escort groups, save the 355th and 357th FGs, covered the 3rd TF attacking Leipheim and Gablingen.

The Luftwaffe controllers deduced the relative weakness of two fighter groups tasked to protect the now lone task force striking Munich targets, and dispatched approximately 200 single- and twin-engined fighters to Munich. The 355th and 357th arrived at the rendezvous point near Augsburg on time, but the 1st TF had already been under attack for 15 minutes when the other Mustang groups split to

OPPOSITE The Air Technical Section led by Lt Col Cass Hough developed the P-38 "Droop Snoot" that could carry a bombardier in a glazed nose section who would guide Lightning formations in level bombing attacks over western Europe from May 1944. This "Droop Snoot" P-38J was assigned to the 402nd FS/370th FG in April 1945 (*USAF, sourced by Jack Cook*)

354th FS/355th FG ace Capt Robert Woody was the first Eighth Air Force pilot to destroy more than four aircraft in the air during the course of a single mission, being credited with 4.5-0-2 (one shared) victories over the Munich area on April 24, 1944. (*USAF, sourced by William Marshall Collection*)

cover the departed 2nd and 3rd TFs. In the ensuing battle the 355th claimed 22 and the 357th 23, but the final review awarded credits of 20-1-6 and 22-6-6, respectively. Each fighter group lost three aircraft in aerial combat, plus one to flak while strafing on the return. Capt Bob Woody of the 354th FS became the new ETO single-mission highest scorer after he was credited with 4.5-1-2 (one shared), while leading his flight to break up an attack by a *Staffel* of Bf 109s on 41B immediately upon rendezvous.

The Luftwaffe had dispatched 318 single- and 48 twin-engined fighters that day, and they were credited with 40-1-257 bombers (of which 14 were forced by battle damage to divert to Switzerland, one being shot down by the Swiss air force on final approach to land). Approximately 176 single- and 41 twin-engined fighters engaged the 1st TF from Ulm to Munich, the German aircraft being unmolested by escort fighter until the formation reached Augsburg. The 1st TF lost 27 of the 40 bombers downed that day, including nine that diverted to Switzerland. As previously noted, one was shot down by a Swiss Bf 109 and crashed into a lake. The Luftwaffe lost 66 fighters plus 43 aircrew killed in action. Again, the Bf 110Gs of II. and III./ZG 26 suffered heavily. For the day, VIII Fighter Command was credited with 60-5-21 air and 56-42 ground. Three P-38 fighter groups were credited with 4-0-1 air/0 ground for one loss, the seven P-47 fighter groups were credited with 1-1-0 air/20-20 ground for two losses, and the five P-51 fighter groups were credited 55-2-20 air/36-22 ground for 12 losses.

The Fw 190A-7 was fitted with 13mm MG 131 machine guns and armor plating for the cockpit area to serve with *Sturmstaffel* 1, formed and led on anti-bomber operations by Oberstleutnant Hans-Günter von Kornatzki from October 1943. (*Tony Holmes Collection*)

Relatively uneventful missions in respect to Luftwaffe day fighter reaction were flown in bad weather to Brunswick and multiple V-weapon sites along the French coast through the 28th. During this period the Luftwaffe re-equipped and integrated replacement pilots for the losses incurred through the 24th. Losses for VIII Bomber Command during those four days were 23-11-654. The Luftwaffe claimed two of the 23, with the rest being lost to flak and weather-related collisions.

April 29 marked the last loss of more than 50 VIII Bomber Command aircraft on a single day. In fact, after the 29th, only three missions cost VIII Bomber Command between 45 and 50 bombers for the rest of the war. The dominant factors for the future losses were combinations of bomber wings off course, deviating from the planned routes and times for rendezvous. May 12, June 20, and June 21 were specific examples. These same factors cost VIII Bomber Command dearly on April 29.

For the raid to Berlin, 679 bombers were dispatched on a route obscured by towering clouds and ten-tenths undercast for most of the mission. The 4th BW/3rd BD, comprising the 385th and 447th BGs, strayed off course and was unescorted when hit hard near Magdeburg, losing 18 near the target. One of the attacking units was *Sturmstaffel* 1, flying its last mission before being absorbed into IV./JG 3. Their Fw 190A-7s, armed with two 13mm machines guns and two 20mm and two 30mm cannon, were especially lethal, and effectively carved out eight of the 18 losses for the 4th BW and caused five more bombers to drop from the protection of the formations. The Eighth Air Force losses for the day were 63-2-432 bombers and three P-51s (one air-to-air, two to flak) and three P-38s (three air-to-air). VIII Fighter Command victory credits were P-38, 0-4-4 air-to-air, no ground; P-47, 3-1-0 air-to-air, no ground; and P-51, 3-0-1 air-to-air, 7-4 ground. The Luftwaffe lost 27 fighters and 12 killed in action, mostly to bomber gunners and bad weather.

As April closed, the 339th FG commenced P-51 combat operations by sweeping in front of VIII and IX Fighter Command fighter-bomber attacks. The 4th, 78th, 352nd, and 357th FGs, flying top cover for the dive-bombing Thunderbolt fighter groups, had aerial victory credits of 13-0-0 for the P-51s and 4-1-3 for the P-47s (of the 78th FG).[19]

APRIL – P-51, P-47, AND P-38 PROBLEMS AND RESOLUTIONS

During April the new P-51B-10s and C-5s in natural metal finish began arriving in quantity from BAD2 Warton after receiving the necessary ETO-related modifications as directed by Air Force Service Command. The cycle time from docking at Liverpool, through the BAD2 Depot, was much shorter due to the applied NAA production insertions for the 85gal tank, the external fuel tank pressurization, and increased oxygen supply. The 357th FG was not thrilled with the lack of camouflage and scoured local British sources for a suitable dark green substitute for the USAAF proscribed Olive Drab.

In April NAA released kits to be applied in concert with Tech Order 01-60J-18 and Field Service News, dated April 8, 1944, to install the dorsal fin fillet and the

PAGE 284 The Field Service Bulletin released on April 1, 1944 explained why NAA had chosen to fit the P-51D with a dorsal fin fillet and reverse rudder boost tab. (© *The Boeing Company*)

PAGE 285 Page two of The Field Service Bulletin from April 1, 1944 shows the dorsal fin fillet kit fabricated specifically for the P-51B and C. The reverse rudder boost installation was the same as that fitted to the D-model Mustang, however. (© *The Boeing Company*)

RESTRICTED

Weekly
SERVICE NEWS
NORTH AMERICAN AVIATION, INC.
FIELD SERVICE DEPT. INGLEWOOD, CALIF.

APRIL 1, 1944 VOLUME 2—NUMBER 33

New Dorsal Fin and Rudder Reverse Boost Tab Installation

To improve the flying characteristics of P-51B horizontal tail surfaces, the following action has been taken:

In a few instances, flight discrepancies have been observed in slow rolls and yawed flight. From an analysis of the load encountered under these conditions, it was concluded that the asymmetric horizontal tail loads responsible were caused by rudder reversals. These reversals were found to exist for angles of sideslip in the vicinity of approximately fifteen degrees left or right. Such characteristics may contribute to inadvertent snap rolls occurring during slow rolls made with large angles of yaw.

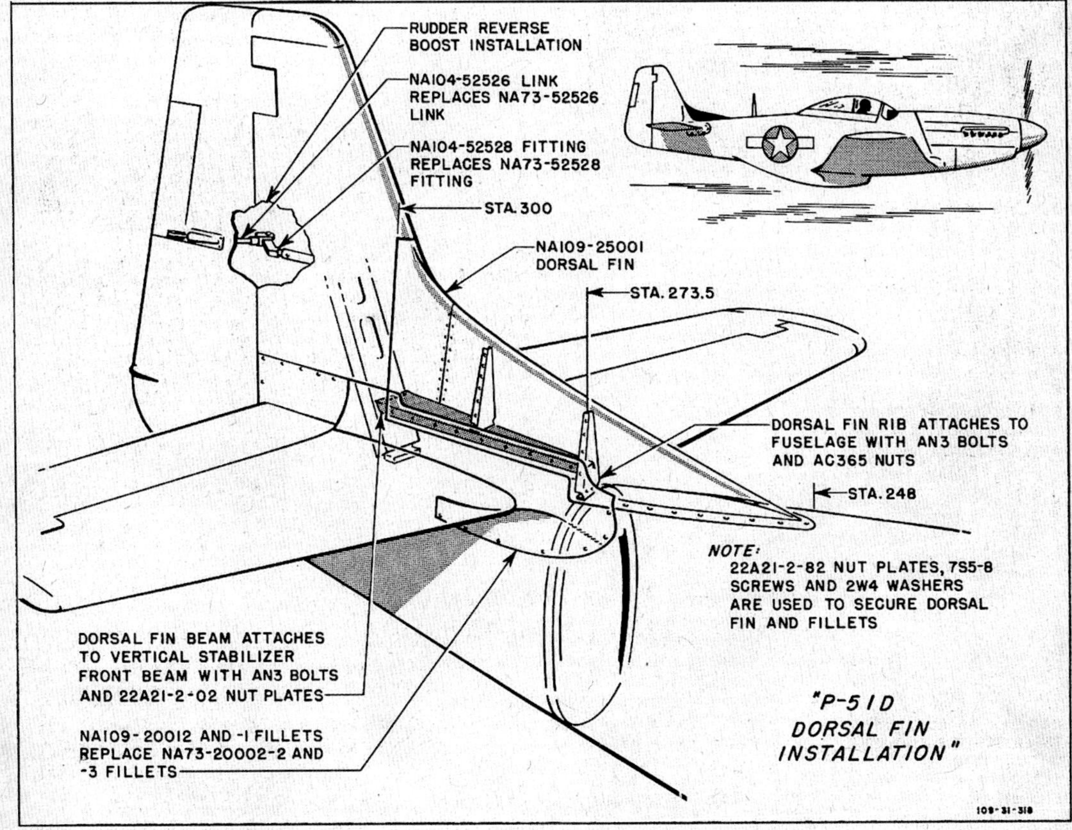

Figure 1

New Dorsal Fin and Rudder Reverse Boost Tab Installation

To provide the desired directional stability, a dorsal fin, used in conjunction with a reverse boost tab motion of .6 to 1 when right rudder is fully applied and .4 to 1 when left rudder is fully applied, is to be installed on P-51B, P-51C and P-51D Series Airplanes.

On P-51D Airplanes, the dorsal fin is attached to the top of the fuselage from approximately station 248 to the point where fuselage station 297 intersects the vertical stabilizer's leading edge. The dorsal fin installation on P-51D Airplanes will be slightly different than on P-51B and P-51C Airplanes, due to the sliding blister-type canopy (FIGURE 1).

The rudder reverse boost installation used on P-51D Airplanes will be identical to the installation on P-51B and P-51C Airplanes. It will provide an increase in rudder forces, over and above that provided by the dorsal fin, lessening the possibility of overcontrolling the rudder at large angles of yaw. This is accomplished by exchanging the end fitting (NA 73-52528) with a new offset fitting (NA 104-52528). The present trim tab to push rod link assembly (NA 73-52526) will be replaced with a shorter link assembly (NA 104-52526). Refer to FIGURE 1.

These changes will be incorporated in production as soon as practical. All P-51B, P-51C and P-51D Airplanes that are now in service and all future production airplanes without this installation will be modified in accordance with Field Service Bulletin NA 51-134 which is now being prepared. A change notice has been submitted to the Air Service Command. The P-51B and P-51C Field Service installation is shown in FIGURE 2.

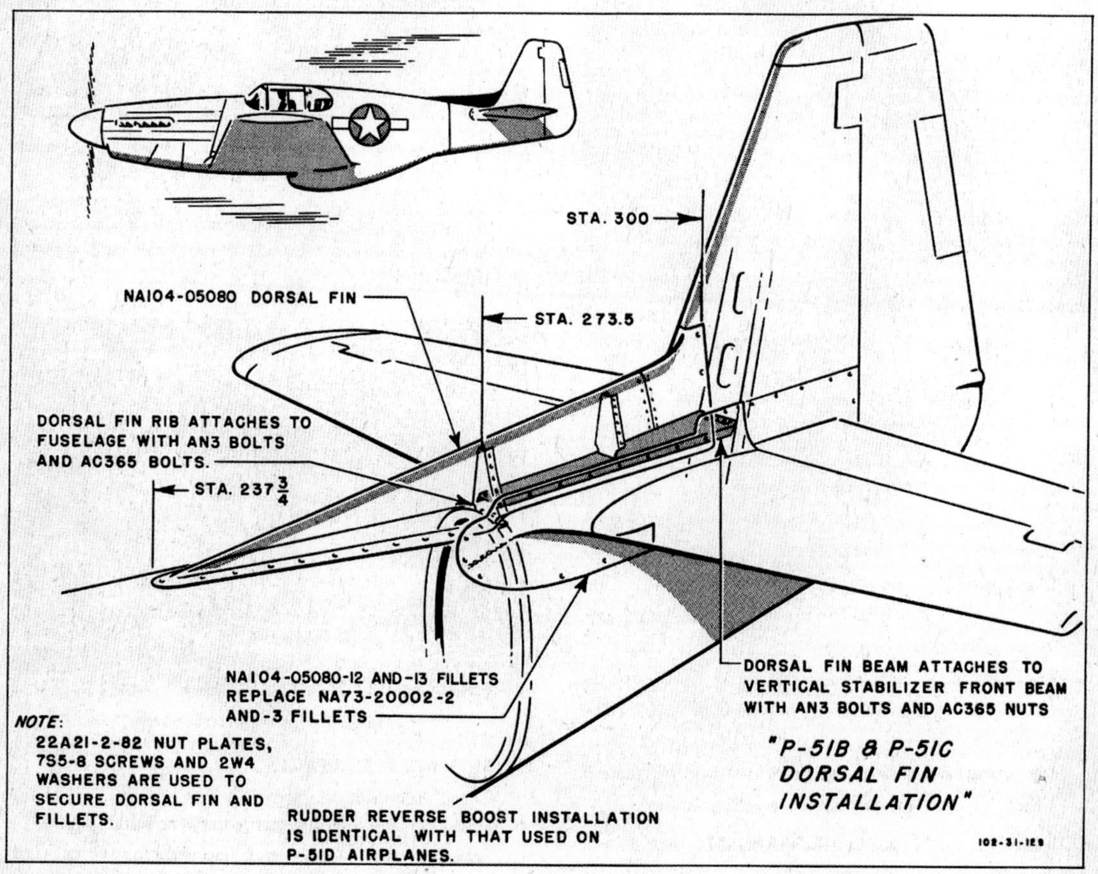

Figure 2

reverse rudder boost tab. These changes improved airflow past the empennage and increased rudder control input resistance, assisting the pilot in reducing rudder deflection under high loading (i.e., during a dive). Work to strengthen the horizontal stabilizer and the fin spar also began at this time, with more dive tests being conducted to evaluate reducing the angle of incidence to the horizontal stabilizer. The ultimate final "solution" for yaw stability, however, was designed into the P-51H – namely increasing the aft fuselage length from the main spar datum line by approximately 13in., incorporating a redesigned dorsal fin fillet and adding the "tall tail rudder cap extension" to reduce adverse yaw inputs to the airframe.

NAA Field Service released kits and a Field Service News Bulletin, dated April 1, 1944, to illustrate the installation of the dorsal fin fillet and reverse rudder boost tab kits in the field. The kits were deemed straightforward enough to be applied by fighter group base Service Groups.[20]

The dorsal fin fillet and reverse rudder boost tab kits began to arrive, along with the Technical Order 01-60J-18 specifications to install the former on the P-51B/C, as well as on all P-51Ds through 44-13902. NA-111 P-51C-10-NT dorsal fin fillets were installed in production. The first P-51D-5-NAs arrived at the Eighth Air Force's BAD2 Warton and the Ninth Air Force's 4th Tactical Air Depot Charmy Down in late April to undergo inspections and necessary modifications. A few would reach the 4th, 352nd, 354th, 355th, and 357th FGs before D-Day.

Both Materiel Command and Packard cleared the use of 44-1 100/150-octane fuel for 75inHg manifold pressure in the 1650-3 and 1650-7 engines.[21]

The P-51H contract under NA-117 was reduced from 3,500 aircraft and absorbed into the NA-126 contract execution on April 26. Although Materiel Command was very pleased with the results of the XP-51F flight tests, one glaring issue, based on current events in Europe, placed future production orders in jeopardy. Design of the XP-51F, based on then-current events in Europe, was begun months before the 85gal tank was installed in the P-51B. The XP-51F and the following XP-51G and J were not designed structurally to allow extra fuselage fuel to be accommodated to enable them to achieve nearly the same combat radius as either the P-51B or the new P-51D. The incorporation of the 50gal fuselage tank into the P-51H was the major reason for its weight increase over the XP-51F and G.

Additionally, the concept of the P-82 Twin Mustang, with even more range to provide escort distances for projected attacks against Japan, seemed to place the XP-51F/G into the category of interceptor or middle-range escort. Discussions the previous November, focused on four 20mm Oldsmobile cannon for P-51F production armament, tended to imply that the interceptor role was seen as the higher probability for the new NAA Lightweight Fighter. In the cold light of procurement, "Why buy a fighter whose primary highest value as an escort fighter was no more than that of a P-38 without 55gal leading-edge tanks?"

When design of the P-51H began, the critical specifications were (1) range and firepower equivalent to that of the P-51D, (2) better maneuverability and climb rate, (3) higher top speeds, pointing to a Packard 1650-9 or Merlin 100 equivalent horsepower, and (4) reducing yaw issues. Achieving those design goals led to increasing gross weight from that of the XP-51F fighter configurations to that of the P-51B – still approximately 600lb less than the equivalent combat load of the P-51D. Significantly, while the design limit and ultimate load factors of 7.3G and 11G at 9,600lb (full internal combat loading) were less than the Mustang I's 8G and 12G, respectively, the Mustang I's structural design factors were for a gross weight of 8,000lb. Consequently the P-51H was *stronger* than the P-51D for the same combat loading at 10,200lb.

April 29 marked the date that Air Force Service Command at Patterson Field released the P-51B for operations with 44-1 150-octane fuel at 75inHg manifold pressure, while indicating that both the P-38 and P-47 were experiencing continuing difficulties that prevented immediate clearance.[22] Eighth Air Force reduce the allowable boost to 72inHg.

MAY – USSTAF AND LUFTWAFFE OPERATIONS

For Germany, May 1944 marked the worst possible change to Eighth and Fifteenth Air Force strategy for the *Argument* offensive – bombers were now to target key refinery and chemical plants throughout Axis-held territory (including Poland), as well as in Germany, Czechoslovakia, Rumania, and Austria.

During the month of May, IX Fighter Command alternated between escort under Eighth Air Force control and tactical operations as directed by the Ninth Air Force in concert with the RAF's Second Tactical Air Force. By mid-May IX Fighter Command had two P-38J fighter groups (367th and 370th FGs), 12 P-47D fighter groups (36th, 358th, 362nd, 365th, 366th, 367th, 368th, 371st, 373rd, 404th, 405th, and 406th FGs) and two P-51 fighter groups (354th and 363rd FGs).

From the second week of May until the 479th FG began operations later that same month, VIII Fighter Command had three P-38J fighter groups (20th, 55th, and 364th FGs), four P-47D fighter groups (56th, 78th, 353rd and 356th FGs), and seven P-51B/C fighter groups (4th, 339th, 352nd, 355th, 357th, 359th, and 361st FGs). For the first time the Eighth Air Force could plan to position at least three fighter groups (a total of 80–100 escorts, depending on aborts) to escort any single bomb division/task force of ten to 12 bomb groups, with at least one long-range fighter group performing a freelance sweep in front of the task force leading the attack that day. The Ninth Air Force took operational control for the IX FC fighters.

The Fifteenth Air Force began May with three P-38 fighter groups (1st, 14th, and 82nd FGs), two P-47 fighter groups (325th and 332nd FGs) and two P-51 fighter groups (31st and 52nd FGs).

As IX Fighter Command's P-47 strength increased to maximum, they were assigned more penetration and withdrawal support missions. The primary Eighth Air Force P-47 groups with greater combat radius were increasingly assigned to medium-range target escort and sweeps (e.g., to Brunswick, Hannover, and Stuttgart,

1Lt Carl Luksic of the 487th FS/352nd FG was first Eighth Air Force pilot to shoot down more than 4.5 aircraft, the ace being credited with three Fw 190s and two Bf 109s destroyed over the Brunswick area on May 8, 1944. (*USAF, sourced by Jack Cook*)

all approximately 440 miles from East Anglian airfields). For this reason, the six combined P-38 fighter groups were more often assigned as target escort to intermediate "long-range" targets such as Augsburg, Kiel, Bordeaux, and Schweinfurt, approximately 460–490 miles from East Anglia. The nine combined P-51B/C FGs were generally assigned targets 570–700-plus miles from East Anglia, such as Berlin, Stettin, Poznan, Brux, Prague, Munich, and Leipzig. The strategic combat radius footprint of the Mustang's "arc" was 300 miles more than that of the long-range P-47D-16-RE (and equivalent upgrades) and approximately 100 miles more than that of the P-38J-15-LO (and equivalent upgrades).

During May and in future months, the Luftwaffe, despite vastly improved detection, tracking, and command/control of its day fighters, found it increasingly difficult to find unescorted bomber boxes within a bomb division. Significantly, the number of Eighth Air Force aircraft destroyed per sortie dispatched continued to drop rapidly, with exceptions when the rendezvous was missed between bomber groups and escort fighter groups. April 29 marked the end to the high percentage of losses inflicted on Eighth Air Force aircraft launched on missions to deep targets in Germany or Poland. The same applied for the Fifteenth Air Force during MTO operations.

May opened with attacks on V1 sites (Operation *Crossbow*). Fighter escort victories were sparse, as well as losses, as all the missions were to coastal France until the 4th, when the Eighth Air Force went to Brunswick and Berlin. Weather forced a recall of VIII Bomber Command, but the Luftwaffe dispatched 268 fighters, 87 of which made contact with the fighter escort. Two P-47s and one P-51 were lost by VIII Fighter Command, for nine victory credits. The Luftwaffe lost eight fighters plus five aircrew killed in action.

On the 7th the Eighth Air Force returned to Berlin. This was another very bad weather day, with ten-tenths undercast over the German capital, but the Pathfinders for each bomb division were able to mark the targets well and the 1,300-plus tons of bombs dropped caused heavy damage to the city center. The bomber losses were 8-2-265, seven of the eight being downed by flak. VIII Fighter Command lost two P-38s and a P-47 to engine failures, and one P-51 to flak.

The next trip to Berlin, on May 8, was a break-out day for the 352nd and 359th FGs. The former was "riding herd" on the lead boxes of the 1st TF/1st BD attacking Berlin. They picked up escort from the 359th FG, flying penetration escort for the 1st TF/1st BD in its first all-P-51 mission after converting from P-47s. The 359th scored 10-1-3 in a running fight from Steinhuder Lake to Bremen and Brunswick for two losses. When the 352nd FG commenced escort duties it was confronted by 100–150 new fighters inbound from the east. The 355th FG dispatched a squadron to cover the lead box to fill the vacuum. In the next 30 minutes the 352nd scored 26-2-7 for the loss of one. During the fight around Brunswick 1Lt Carl Luksic downed three Fw 190s and two Bf 109s to become the new ETO single-mission highest scorer.

Despite the efforts of the 359th, 352nd, and 355th FGs, the 1st BD lost 25 B-17s under the fierce assault by 358 German fighters of the 400 launched to defend the track to Berlin. Final losses for VIII Bomber Command were 36-8-197. VIII Fighter

Command was credited with 58-4-20 for five losses. The victory credits/losses were P-38s, 5-0-1 credits/four losses; P-47, 9-1-5 credits/four losses; and P-51, 39-4-11 credits/five losses. The Luftwaffe withheld its twin-engined *Zerstörer* from the battle, and suffered 51 fighters lost and 16 damaged, with 25 killed in action.

In May, the dominant fighter mix to defend the Reich comprised Fw 190A-7s plus new Fw 190A-8s, Bf 109G-6s, and G-6/ASs, and Bf 110Gs. The variation included the heavily armed Bf 109G-6/R6, with two 13mm machine guns, and one 30mm and two underwing MG 131 20mm cannon.

On May 5 and 6 the Fifteenth Air Force went to Ploesti. The attack on the 5th was the Fifteenth's first 1,500-ton day. It lost 19 bombers during the course of the mission, while the Mustangs of the 31st FG were credited with 13 for one loss. These were the only fighter victories credited to the Fifteenth Air Force.

On May 9 pre-invasion tactical strikes were launched against coastal France and inland objectives. The primary targets were marshaling yards and airfields. The RAF's Second Tactical Air Force also began tactical missions in concert with IX Fighter Command P-47s. Only JGs 2 and 26 were able to mount token defenses. By the time these strikes were undertaken on the 9th, the 359th and 361st FGs had fully converted to Mustangs for their first 100 percent P-51 mission.

On May 10 the Fifteenth Air Force sent 400 bombers to the Wiener Neustadt Bf 109 factory and airfield. XV Fighter Command claimed 15-1-20 Luftwaffe fighters, with credits issued for 15-0-18. The P-38 fighter groups scored 13 for the loss of three, with the P-51 fighter group claiming the remaining two for no losses. The Luftwaffe dispatched 175 fighters and caused nine bomber losses, largely by evading the escort fighters. It lost at least 12 fighters and had eight killed in action.

On the 11th the Luftwaffe lost JG 1 *Kommodore* Oberst Walter Oesau, shot down by Ninth Air Force P-38s from either the 367th or 370th FG. The Eighth Air Force lost 8-1-172 bombers and four fighters. The Luftwaffe lost 25 fighters and had nine pilots killed in action, but the death of Oesau was particularly significant, as he was one of the few successful leaders of *Gefechtsverband* (large force) assemblies.

On May 12 the campaign against the German oil industry commenced. The attacks that Albert Speer dreaded began in earnest when 886 Eighth Air Force bombers were dispatched in three task forces to attack synthetic oil centers at Merseburg, Lutzkendorf, Zwickau, Brux, and Bohlen. For the first time the RLV controllers managed to concentrate a large mass of I. *Jagdkorps* fighters in a single location – Frankfurt. In all, 475 day fighters were dispatched, including 22 *Jagdgruppen* and three *Zerstörergruppen*, plus another 40 twin-engined fighters. It was the largest defensive mission over Germany of the entire war.[23]

Unfortunately, the astute direction of Luftwaffe resources coincided with the wayward 2nd TF/3rd BD B-17s, which were 30 minutes behind schedule and 30 miles off course to the south – on track for Frankfurt rather than Koblenz. The three task forces were now widely separated, as in the April 29 raid on Berlin. At 1130hrs the 355th, 4th, and 357th FGs were staging from Bonn to Kassel to rendezvous with the 2nd TF to pick up escort as the 1st TF left Bonn. It was then that the 2nd TF

P-51B-1-NA 43-12375 *BONNIE "B" II* of the 353rd FS/354th FG, Lashenden, Kent, June 1944.
(*Artwork by Jim Laurier, © Osprey Publishing*)

radioed the fighters to let them know it was running 20 minutes late. The 56th FG was doing a freelance sweep in front of the 1st TF, utilizing the "Zemke Fan" formation (named after the group's CO and ace Col Hubert "Hub" Zemke), while the 78th and 353rd FGs were performing penetration escort for them. The 355th noticed that the last several boxes of the 1st TF were not escorted and moved up to cover them.

At approximately 1200hrs the Luftwaffe positioned 100-plus Fw 190s and Bf 109s from JGs 3 and 11 on an interception course with the 2nd TF and they duly converged on the 259 unescorted B-17s, engaging them west of Frankfurt. When the call for help was heard, the 56th, 4th, and 357th FGs headed southwest. The 78th and 353rd FGs also headed south and met the second wave just as one section from the 352nd FG broke escort and headed southwest too.

In the ensuing battle the 56th FG destroyed 19 for three losses, the 4th FG was credited with ten for no losses and the 357th downed 19 for two losses. 1Lt Robert "Shorty" Rankin of the 56th FG claimed five shot down near Marburg/Koblenz to match the total achieved by Luksic of the 352nd FG. During the second wave of attacks the 78th destroyed six for one loss, the 353rd four for no losses, and the 352nd six for one loss. More fights occurred near Chemnitz and nearby targets. The 2nd TF/3rd BD lost 41-3-152 in the melee. The 354th FG was credited with 7-1-4 while escorting the 1st TF to the Merseburg/Leipzig-area targets. The P-38s of the 20th and 55th FGs rounded-out the scoring with one victory credit each for no losses. The Luftwaffe losses were 88 fighters plus 29 killed in action.

Albert Speer remembered May 12, 1944 as "the day the end of the technological war was decided, with the attack of 900 daylight bombers of the American Eighth Air Force upon several fuel plants in central and eastern Germany. A new era in the air war began. It meant the end of German armaments production."[24]

May 13 brought another maximum-effort VIII Bomber Command attack aimed at oil refineries in western Poland, but weather restricted the raids to Stettin, Poznan and targets of opportunity along the Baltic coast for both the 1st BD and the 3rd BD.

The primary Luftwaffe attacks occurred from Kiel to the north and east of Berlin, including the Me 410s of ZG 26. Both the 355th and 357th FGs hit the Me 410 *Gruppen* east of Berlin and Grundberg, each destroying six-plus. The 355th went all the way to Poznan, flying the longest ETO/MTO escort mission to date – 1,470 miles from Steeple Morden. The Mustang-equipped 352nd, 354th, 355th, and 357th FGs were credited with a total of 36-1-9 for four losses.

Between May 15 and 27 the Eighth Air Force alternated attacks between *Noball* V1 sites, airfields, and marshaling yards in France and western Germany, as well as *Chatanooga* attacks against locomotives and rolling stock by VIII and IX Fighter Commands. In between those dates the Eighth Air Force returned to Brunswick and Berlin on the 19th and the 24th, getting a strong response from the Luftwaffe.

On May 18 the Fifteenth Air Force attacked Ploesti once again, as well as the marshaling yards in Nils and Belgrade, to support the Soviet Red Army advance from the east. Adverse weather forced most of the Ploesti strike to turn back, but 206 bombers fought their way to the refineries, reducing production by 60 percent. The Luftwaffe managed to avoid the initial fighter escort and brought down 14 B-17s and B-24s and accounted for three P-38s. The escorting P-38s were credited with 11 destroyed, while the 31st FG P-51s scored two for no losses.

On May 19 the Luftwaffe resisted the Eighth Air Force in considerable numbers, dispatching 447 single-engined fighters, all from *Luftflotte Reich. Luftflotte* 3 basically stayed on the ground to conserve resources for the known forthcoming invasion, but one JG 26 *Staffel* shot down a B-17 on the return route. Although the 2nd BD strike at Brunswick was within escort range of all VIII and IX Fighter Command P-38s and P-47s, it took the most casualties – 12-0-26. Most fell to IV.(*Sturm*)/JG 3 and III./JG 54. VIII Bomber Command lost 28-2-353, with VIII and IX Fighter Command losses totaling 19. The day's victory credits were 70-0-23 air-to-air and 7-10 ground. The P-38s recorded 0-0-2 air-to-air for two losses, the P-47s scored 29-1-11 for four losses, and the P-51s scored 41-2-6 for nine losses to all causes.

On May 24 the Eighth Air Force dispatched half of VIII Bomber Command to Berlin, losing 33-0-289 in the 520-strong bomber strike. The 100th BG was separated by weather and penetrated alone, losing nine B-17s. The Luftwaffe put up 238 sorties to oppose the Berlin attack, claiming most of its victories after the 3rd BD left the target. The Germans lost 34 fighters and 19 killed in action. VIII and IX Fighter Command credits were P-38, 4-0-3 for one loss; P-47, 0-0-0 for no losses; and P-51, 27-3-6 for seven losses. The fighter losses for the day were equally balanced between air combat, airfield flak, and mechanical problems.

On the 26th the 479th FG became the last operational VIII Fighter Command P-38 group, and the 15th and last fighter group assigned to the Eighth Air Force. From the beginning of operations it was principally equipped with the P-38J-15-LO, in which most of the bugs associated with the earlier J-model's turbo-supercharger and aftercooler had been resolved. Cockpit improvements included better fuel management on a single switch panel connected to the four mains, with submerged booster pumps and a fuselage-mounted booster pump for the auxiliary combat tanks.

A second generator for electrical system management and operations redundancy, including supporting a rheostat in the cockpit for flight suit heating, was added. The dive flaps and boosted ailerons were not included in the P-38J-15-LO, however.

Spaatz received authority from Eisenhower to send the Eighth and Fifteenth Air Forces back to strategic oil and aircraft related targets for three of the last four days of May. During this period the Ninth Air Force continued tactical, medium, and light bomber attacks in concert with IX Fighter Command and the Second Tactical Air Force, averaging 500-plus sorties a day and causing heavy damage to bridges, marshaling yards, and airfields expected to support attacks on the Normandy and Calais area beachheads following the invasion.

On the 27th the 52nd FG flew its first Mustang escort mission after converting from Spitfires in the MTO. The Fifteenth Air Force now had three P-38 fighter groups, three P-51 fighter groups, and one P-47 fighter group.

On May 28 the Eighth Air Force targeted most of the oil/fuel plants in eastern Germany, primarily via visual bombing. According to Speer, "a mere 400 bombers delivered a greater blow on May 28–29 than twice that in the first attack (May 12)." Concurrently, the Fifteenth Air Force struck Ploesti. Oil/fuel production was now reduced by half.[25]

Speer may have been misled regarding the strength of the attacks on May 28–29. The Eighth Air Force dispatched 864 "effectives" (out of 1,341) on the 28th, with 1,100-plus VIII and IX Fighter Command escorts. The P-47s and P-38s escorted as far as east of Gardelegen before the formations made rendezvous with Mustangs. The bomber losses on the 28th were 32-1-210, due primarily to the Luftwaffe dispatching 330 fighters and catching the 94th BW off course and unprotected near Magdeburg. The 351st, 401st, and 457th BGs were hit by JG 11 and lost 15 collectively, plus 33 written off – another bad day in comparison with May 12. VIII and IX Fighter Command escorts were credited with 39-5-9 for the loss of nine to all causes. The final tally was P-38, 0 credits for 0 losses; P-47, 0-0-1 credits for four losses; P-51, 46.5-5-9 credits for eight losses. IX Fighter Command's 354th FG scored 15.5 and the 363rd FG had its best day of the war with 11-4-5 aerial and 5-7 ground credits for three losses. The P-51B/Cs of the 363rd FG would be converted to F-6Cs when the group was re-designated the 363rd TRG in August. The Luftwaffe lost 50 fighters and 23 killed in action.

On the 29th the Eighth Air Force went back to eastern Germany, and also to Poland, to strike at oil targets and the aircraft industry. Of 993 bombers dispatched, 888 proceeded to their targets. The main 1st TF strike proceeded along the Baltic coast to attack Politz, Tutow, and Schwerin. The 2nd TF broke southeast north of Gardelegen and attacked targets in Magdeburg, Leipzig, and Zwickau. The 3rd TF continued along the Baltic course, trailing the 1st TF until they had passed Berlin and then branching off to attack Poznan, Krzesinki, and Sorau. *Jagddivision* 1 hit the B-24s of the 1st TF with Me 410s, Fw 190s, and Bf 109s from ZG 26 and JGs 3 and 26, respectively, near Rugen Island, pressing to Stettin. Escorts from the 359th and 361st FGs broke up the attack, but five B-24s were shot down, six landed in Sweden,

P-51D-5-NA 44-13303 of the 336th FS/4th FG, Debden, Essex, June 1944. (*Artwork by Jim Laurier, © Osprey Publishing*)

and one ditched on the way home. Three more were written off after returning. The Eighth Air Force lost, wrote off, or damaged 34-3-327. VIII and IX Fighter Command achieved 41-1-4 aerial credits as follows: P-38, 0 credits for 0 losses; P-47, 1-0-1 credits for three losses; P-51, 40-1-3 credits for seven losses. These daily losses continued to include a high percentage due to mechanical failures and flak.

The Fifteenth Air Force also hit a variety of targets, including Wiener Neustadt, on May 29 and caused heavy damage to the factories and airfield. The 52nd FG, flying its third straight day of operations in the new P-51s, destroyed 13, the 31st FG another 18, and the two P-38 fighter groups were credited with four between them.

On the 30th, as a prelude to hindering logistics to the invasion front, the Eighth Air Force went to eastern central Germany for aircraft industry targets, and to western Germany for marshaling yards and airfields. VIII Bomber Command losses were 12-3-201. The *Luftflotte Reich* was able to generate only 171 single- and 13 twin-engined sorties due to the attrition of the previous 18 days, incurring a loss of 41 plus 18 killed in action. Records for the missions flown on this date in both the ETO and MTO are sparse.

After attacking Ploesti on May 6 and 18, the Fifteenth Air Force returned to bombing tactical targets in support of the Allied push to take Rome. The primary focus until the 24th was on ports, marshaling yards, and airfields in Italy and Austria.

On the 24th, 25th, 28th, 30th, and 31st the Fifteenth Air Force had joined the Eighth Air Force to split Luftwaffe defenses in the south.

On the last day of May, neither the Eighth or Ninth Air Forces, or the Second Tactical Air Force, met any significant resistance from the Luftwaffe, which continued to hold forces in reserve while planning for the coming invasion. May 31 also saw the Fifteenth Air Force mount another maximum effort against Ploesti and Bucharest, attacking both refineries and marshaling yards. Mustang pilots from the 31st and 52nd FGs had a field day against the Luftwaffe and Rumanian fighters, being credited with a combined 16 destroyed, while 14th FG P-38s were credited with five more.

354th FS/357th FG ace Capt "Pete" Peterson chats with his groundcrew while sat in the cockpit of his P-51B-5 43-6935 *Hurry Home Honey* at Leiston. The aircraft was adorned with full Invasion stripes on the afternoon/evening of June 5, 1944. (*USAF, sourced by Jack Cook*)

During May, XV Fighter Command flew 122 missions (combined P-38, P-47 and P-51), of which 105 were escort, 14 were fighter-bomber sweeps, and three were Air Sea Rescue. The 306th FW now comprised the 1st, 14th, and 82nd FGs with P-38s, the 31st, 52nd, and 325th FGs with P-51s and the 332nd FG with P-47s. After the 332nd FG converted from P-47Ds to P-51B/Cs in late June 1944, it outscored each of the veteran Fifteenth Air Force P-38 fighter groups for the rest of the war.[26]

June brought a serious focus on beach-area airfields, bridges, rail centers, and marshaling yards from Caen to the Pas de Calais and Cherbourg by most of the Allied air forces in the ETO. VIII Fighter Command performed escort duties to several inland tactical targets, as well as fighter-bomber strikes to add to those undertaken by IX Fighter Command and the Second Tactical Air Force.

The Fifteenth Air Force flew one major historical mission on June 2, attacking the Debrecen marshaling yards in Hungary on the way to Poltava and Mirgorad, in the Ukraine, for the first *Frantic* shuttle mission. Seventy 325th FG Mustangs escorted them, but there was no enemy reaction other than flak along the route.

On the eve of June 5 all Britain-based airfields were locked down. Groundcrews received instructions to paint alternating white and black chord-wise stripes on the top and bottom of both wings and around the rear fuselage of their aircraft. Near midnight at all bases, pilots and crews were summoned to group Headquarters, noticing armed guards patrolling the base entrances, flightlines, and quarters. The group commanders were focused as they delivered the announcement that tomorrow was "The Day."

At midnight on June 5, 1944, the victory credits boards, proudly displayed above every mantle within fighter base officers' quarters for VIII and IX Fighter Command units, attested that the challenge that Eighth Air Force commander Gen Jimmy Doolittle had posed to his pilots in January – to attack and destroy the Luftwaffe's ability to resist *Overlord* – had been a resounding success. The following day's events would testify to this. As Gen Eisenhower proclaimed to the Allied Expeditionary Force, "If you see an airplane over the beach, it will be ours!" And it was so.

The summary of USSTAF VIII/IX and XV Fighter Command victory credits for the ETO/MTO are cited below by type of fighter, period, and totals through June 5, 1944:[27]

VIII/IX Fighter Command					
ETO 1943	**P-38**	**P-47**	**P-51B/C**	**Spitfire**	**Grand Total**
November	24	81	0	0	105
December	5	78	9	0	92
Total 1943	29	159	9	0	197
1944					
January	32	144	43	0	219
February	32.5	233	89.5	0	355
March	26	175	251	0	452
April	23	82	329	0	434
May	27.5	118	433.5	0	579
June 1–5	0	0	2	0	2
Total 1944	141	752	1,148	0	2,041
Total 11/43 to 6/5/44	170	911	1,157	0	2,238

XV Fighter Command					
MTO 1943	**P-38**	**P-47**	**P-51B/C**	**Spitfire**	**Grand Total**
November	14	0	0	7	21
December	41	3	0	14	58
Total 1943	55	3	0	21	79
1944					
January	49	58	0	42	149
February	16	8	0	57	81
March	45	38	0	19	102
April	126	35	53	2	216
May	74	13	87	0	174
June 1–5	0	0	0	0	0
Total 1944	310	152	140	120	722
Total 11/43 to 6/5/44	365	155	140	141	801

POSTSCRIPT TO *ARGUMENT*, NOVEMBER 1943 THROUGH JUNE 5, 1944

By D-Day, only seven VIII Fighter Command P-51B/C-equipped fighter groups were sustaining combat operations into the deepest reaches of Poland and Czechoslovakia, while four P-38-equipped fighter groups (the Ninth Air Force's fighter groups were now "tactical") were limited to the Berlin-Augsburg radius of action and relegated mostly to either middle-range target escort or deep penetration and withdrawal escort in the relay system. Similarly, the Fifteenth Air Force was operating three P-38J-, one P-47D-, and three P-51B/C-equipped fighter groups based in Italy.

What is not overstated is that Eisenhower, Spaatz, Doolittle, and Twining were going to launch the USSTAF part of Operation *Argument* to achieve daylight air superiority over the Luftwaffe regardless of bomber losses – independent of the hoped-for success of introducing the P-51B to combat operations. The Eighth Air Force and the newly formed Fifteenth Air Force were tasked with destroying the Luftwaffe, at any cost to bomber crews in a war of attrition, because of the Allied High Command's perception that Germany's undiluted western day fighter force constituted a grave danger to the success of the invasion. When the Fifteenth Air Force was formed from the Twelfth Air Force in November 1943 to be part of the planned USSTAF, there were serious political struggles as Eisenhower formulated his command staff and, by definition, key advisors for the Air Mission. When Eisenhower was named Supreme Allied Commander of SHAEF, both the Second Tactical Air Force and the Ninth Air Force were tasked with CAS and light/medium bomber tactical bombing to support the Allied armies after the invasion.

The political battle lines over control of Ninth Air Force fighters before the invasion were drawn by Air Chief Marshal Sir Trafford Leigh-Mallory and Lt Gen Carl Spaatz, the latter soon to be appointed commander of USSTAF. Spaatz was determined to use the fighter assets of the Ninth Air Force, and particularly the long-range P-51B, as escorts for the upcoming *Argument.* Leigh-Mallory was equally determined that the P-51B would remain in Brereton's Ninth Air Force and operate under his command, in full belief that the Luftwaffe would be defeated in a grand battle over the beaches during the invasion. Leigh-Mallory's plan, fully supported by Brereton, was that, after brief assignment temporarily under Eighth Air Force control, all IX Fighter Command units would rejoin the Second Tactical Air Force in joint training programs to prepare for *Overlord.* The root of this serious political maneuvering would have been avoided if Eaker had not foolishly agreed to relinquish the P-51B to Ninth Air Force control, ostensibly to consolidate base depots and personnel.

It could be assumed that Eaker thought he had a "gentleman's agreement" with Brereton that the Ninth Air Force would place IX Fighter Command under Eighth Air Force operational control until future deliveries of the P-51B could be directed to VIII Fighter Command. It can only be further assumed that he did not know that *all* future Mustang deliveries were assigned to tactical air units across the globe by Gen Saville until Arnold intervened and gave priority to the ETO. As recounted in the narrative for July 1943, Emmons and Eaker "begged for Mustangs," and then Eaker inexplicably gave control of them away to the Second Tactical Air Force. Based on the various post-war tomes written by Eaker, Arnold, and Spaatz, one should assume that this was one of several factors influencing Arnold to get Eaker out of control of the Eighth Air Force and "promote" him to "fly south" to assume command of the MAAF. Spaatz was clearly frustrated, not only by the truculence and obstinacy of Leigh-Mallory, with full knowledge of his views as potentially devastating to the success of *Argument*, but also because he had to engage Portal, Arnold, Eisenhower and Marshall, all bosses in his chain of command, to seek assistance in dealing with Leigh-Mallory.

Lt Col Francis "Gabby" Gabreski's P-47D-25-RE 42-26418 in full D-Day stripes. The first examples of the long-range D-25 Thunderbolt began to reach the ETO in very limited numbers from mid-May 1944. This aircraft was lost in a crash landing after bending the prop while avoiding flak on July 20, 1944. (*NARA*)

In the summer and fall of 1943 the Luftwaffe demonstrated that, beyond the range of a P-47D escort, they could inflict unacceptable losses on the B-17s and B-24s. The introduction of leading-edge fuel tanks and improved reliability of the intercooler radiators and turbo-supercharged Allisons in the P-38J-10 (kits) and J-15 (factory installed) meant that the Lightning had the combat range and performance to escort bombers to Berlin from March 1944. That said, the P-38J remained far less effective in aerial combat than either the P-47D or P-51B through D-Day and beyond.

By the time the P-47D-16s with factory external wing tanks and P-38J-15 with factory leading-edge tanks arrived in quantity in the ETO and MTO, the battle for control of German skies beyond the range of the earlier models was nearly over. When some P-47D-25s with 370 gallons of internal fuel and a bubble canopy reached the ETO pre-D-Day, there were only four Thunderbolt-equipped groups remaining in the Eighth Air Force. As VIII Fighter Command converted from the P-47D and P-38J to the Mustang, both the old and newer versions of the Republic and Lockheed fighters were directed to the Ninth Air Force in the ETO for tactical operations. The Fifteenth Air Force also received the newer P-38J-10 and -15, but too late to make a major contribution to the defeat of the Luftwaffe day fighter arm as a long-range escort prior to D-Day.

Aside from a brief experience with P-47Ds assigned to the 325th FG, the Fifteenth Air Force was committed to the P-51B/D and P-38J for long-range escort. All of the remaining inbound P-38Js would similarly be diverted to the ETO for tactical operations, and as replacements for the three existing MTO Fifteenth Air Force fighter groups.

The fighter that the USAAC/USAAF did not want in 1940, 1941, and early 1942 found the necessary sponsors and technology boosts in late 1942. Finally, the USAAF had the agile, long-range, high-altitude, single-engined fighter that it knew it needed but, according to the technology-aware "experts" of 1936 through 1942, was impossible to deliver. The overturning of bureaucrat fiats in early 1942 made all the difference in the world to possibly tens of thousands of Eighth Air Force bomber crews in 1944.

The bastard stepchild P-51B wrote its place in the history of air power in very bold letters indeed.

APPENDICES

APPENDIX A

AERODYNAMICS AND PERFORMANCE DISCUSSION FOR THE P-51B

I. Wing Development

Although of interest to only a few readers of this book, the hard work involved in developing a theoretical airfoil from the same family type as the NACA-125 laminar-flow airfoil required choosing a mathematical derivation approach described as Conformal Mapping in Complex Variable Space. The first step, based on the study of the NACA 45-100 low-drag/high-speed airfoil, was to specify a desirable pressure distribution as a function of the percentage of airfoil chord, from leading edge (0 percent) to trailing edge (100 percent). The first cut on the pressure distribution was one that would generate desired lift, drag, and moment characteristics (without knowing yet what the airfoil shape must be), as described by Millikan's principles of selecting a wing and then mapping the associated surface velocities to achieve the pressure distribution in a Complex Space. The conformal mapping process begins by distributing the velocity data along a rotating Circle in Complex Space, then by transformation, mapping the circle to an airfoil shape with a similar but not yet final desired velocity distribution in real space.

The lack of modern computational fluid dynamics methodologies and high-speed computers made the task manually intensive, requiring Friden Calculators to make the calculations, iterate, and repeat the process until complete.[1] The NAA team of ten engineers toiled approximately 14 days (and nights) to derive the initial airfoil root and tip sections. Ed Horkey, Chief Aerodynamicist, remembered Ashkenas, Mellinger, Davis, Hoag, and Palley, plus telephone conversations with NACA's Russ Robinson at Langley, as the key contributors.[2] Contrary to legend, NACA did not perform any design or calculation assistance in development of the NACA/NAA 45-100 airfoil, but did lend valuable telephone support to Horkey's team to discuss the design of the NACA 45-125 airfoil and test results.[3]

The primary goal for a laminar-flow airfoil/wing was to develop a smooth aerodynamic shape and surface that enabled attached flow for greater distance along the airfoil before boundary-layer separation (the trigger that causes a profile increase to the free stream, thus increasing pressure drag losses). This was achieved to a greater degree in wind tunnel tests of the NACA-125 laminar-flow airfoil. However, the NACA airfoil was too thick for high-speed applications. It was unique in that it gradually achieved maximum thickness at approximately 50 percent of chord, instead of the conventional 25–30 percent.

Another objective of laminar-flow airfoils was to extend the region of peak pressure distribution across a greater percentage of the chord to regions past the airfoil's maximum thickness. Accompanying such a shape, for the same thickness of chord (T/C) ratio, is a lower velocity gradient (rate of change of airflow velocity) from the airfoil nose to the point of maximum thickness, than a corresponding conventional airfoil with its maximum thickness closer to 25–30 percent of the chord. The shape of the wing was also more wedge-like than the conventional bulbous shape.

This meant that the rate of increase of the surface airflow from the leading edge to the 37 percent of chord location of the new NACA/NAA 45-100 airfoil (with 16 percent T/C ratio at the root) was less than such flow from the leading edge to the 25–30 percent chord location for the conventional NACA 23016 with the same maximum thickness. The "theory" proposed three benefits, namely (1) delayed boundary-layer separation to a point further aft of the conventional 25–30 percent chord point, where the "adverse pressure gradient" of the resultant turbulent wake disrupts lift and increases drag; (2) delayed transonic shock wave formation due to the reduced velocity gradient as the flow moves from the nose to 37 percent thickness (where the maximum air stream velocity over the airfoil occurred in the NAA airfoil); and (3) located the Center of Pressure further aft, thus reducing the pitching moment change (nose-down) when the onset of a transonic shockwave occurs. The latter phenomenon was a major problem with the P-38, P-47, Bf 109, and Fw 190 airfoil designs, which were the same or nearly the same as the NACA 23016. The P-51 was controllable at near-terminal velocities and did not require the dive flaps installed on the P-38 and P-47.

The advanced shape of the wing and the extreme care taken in its construction (butt joints, flush rivets, etc.), plus wing surface preparation (including the application of filler over the first 40 percent of the wing, from the leading edge past the spar, to smooth the surface, filling imperfect flush-rivet locations, then sanding, priming, and painting), did enable the NACA/NAA 45-100 wing to achieve some actual reductions in parasite drag. That said, while Horkey claimed that "some laminar flow" extension existed, the true benefits to the wing shape (a more "wedge"-type airfoil and gradual T/C ratio to the 37 percent chord position) were in fact lower pressure drag of the wing at low angles-of-attack (i.e., high-speed cruise) and delayed shockwave formation to near the 37 percent chord region. At low and high speeds the NACA/NAA 45-100 airfoil simply had less resistance of its cross-sectional area (profile or pressure drag) than other airfoils with conventional shapes and thickness, such as NACA 230xx series.

Wind tunnel testing of actual Mustangs did show slight laminar benefits, with the wing airfoil shape delaying boundary-layer separation somewhat, but never to the theoretical transition regions hoped for. Profile and other parasite drag items, however, were indeed reduced when compared with conventional (i.e., NACA 23016) high-speed airfoils with the same thickness and surface preparations. Transonic benefits, such as delayed shockwave formation and reduced nose-down pitching moments were achieved. These key characteristics enabled the Mustang to dive far faster than the P-38 with complete control for pull-out, faster than the Fw 190/Bf 109, and at about the same speed as the P-47D after dive flaps were installed in mid-1944.[4]

The P-63 used the NACA 662x-16 series wing, which had slightly lower profile drag than the P-51's NAA/NACA 45-100 but had some serious stall issues that made it a tricky airplane to control at slower speeds, such as for landing.

Airfoil Data

So, what are the official data for the NACA/NAA 45-100 airfoil and P-51 wing? NASA, post-World War II, published a paper entitled "NASA F-51D Airfoil Sections" (author Anon, date unknown – in NASA Archives) containing a description of the NACA/NAA 45-100 (the same airfoil for NA-73 through all P-51D/K models). It is summarized as follows:

> The basic root and tip stations which control the contours cannot be expressed exactly (in conventional description format for airfoils) in terms of thickness distributions and mean lines. The sections were derived from desired pressure distributions developed by Theodorsen.
> 1. Wing Stations [WS] 50 and 215 were used for root and tip stations for purposes of aerodynamic definition.
> 2. The thickness distribution at WS 50 is somewhat like NASA 64, and 64,2 series. The thickness distribution at WS 215 is somewhat like NASA 66 series.
> 3. The mean lines throughout bear some resemblance to NASA mean lines, producing uniform chord-wise loading over varying portions of the chord.
> 4. The wing is usually identified as NACA-NAA laminar-flow, low-drag type.
> 5. The NAA team E. Horkey, I. L. Ashkenas, C. L. Davis, and H. J. Hoge published NAA Report NAA-5041 "Aerodynamic Load Calculations for NA-73 Airplane," dated 3-3-41, which documents the aerodynamic characteristics of the wing.
> 6. The Master Dimensions Specification MD-102-100 for P-51B/D.
> 7. Tip chord WS = 225, chord = 50"; tip location = WS 233.
> 8. Root chord at WS = 0, chord = 103.988 (NA-73 through P-51D/K).
> 9. Quarter-chord WS 0 to WS 215 constant at FS 99 (perpendicular to fuselage plane)
>   a. 0 degree sweep of 25% chord.

Full-scale testing of the production P-51B-1 43-12095 in NACA Langley Field's wind tunnel allowed NAA to further refine base parasite drag values for the Mustang. The values for the aircraft derived by sealing gun ports, exhaust stacks, gaps and the radiator intake scoop and removing the propeller were very close to those extracted from the GALCIT scale model testing. Only the radiator intake scoop/duct and cowling drag were higher drag values in the wind tunnel – but that was without the Meredith effect, a running engine and passing heated flow through the exit scoop. The unsealed production P-51B as delivered yielded wind tunnel test values approximately five percent higher. (*NACA*)

b. Geometric twist – Total: 1 degree, 53 minutes, 6.43 seconds
c. +0 degree 59 minutes, 56.46 seconds at WS = 0
d. -0 degree, 53 minutes, 9.97 seconds at WS = 215

10. At centerline WS (0), max. thickness = 16.13% of local chord and at 37.21% from leading edge of the root chord.

11. At tip WS (215), max. thickness = 11.46% of local chord and at 48.01% from the leading edge of the tip chord.

12. Max. camber and leading-edge radius
a. WS = 0, 1.29%
b. WS = 215, 1.34%
c. Leading-edge radius at WS = 0, 2.09% of root chord
d. Leading-edge at WS = 215, 0.60% of tip chord

For the complete set of wing ordinates data for the P-51D (differing only from the X73 through P-51B/C by different root chord and angled leading-edge extension), see drawing NAA 106-00006, "Ordinates for P-51D Wing," on page 198.

II. Performance Calculation Drag Data for P-51B-1, D-5 and H-1

Supplementary Documentation for Drag Coefficient Validations

NACA Drag Tests – USAAF and US Navy Service Aircraft[5]

Table II – Index of Important Drag Results[6]

Airframe	P-40	P-38	F4F	F4U	F6F	P-63	P-51B
Airfoil series	NACA	NACA	NACA	NACA	NACA-Mod	NACA-Mod	NACA/ NAA-Mod
Specific airfoil-root	2415	23016	23015	23015	23015.6	66.2X-116	45-100
Thickness/chord %	15	16	15	15	15.6	16	16.1
Max T/C location	30%	30%	30%	30%	30%	60%	37.20%
Total drag – CDt service cond.	0.0257	0.0293	0.0328	0.0284	0.0293	0.221	0.0209
Total drag –CDt sealed cond.		0.222		0.0216	0.021	0.0171	0.0173
Wing area – sq. ft.	236	327.5	233.2	314	334	248	233.2
Mean aero chord	7.02	6.8	7.01	7.02	8.12	6.87	6.63
Gross Wt.	6,000	14,500	7,426	11,000	11,441	7,662	8,412
RN at 100mph	6,55E+06	6.35E+06	6.54E+06	6.55E+06	7.57E+06	6.41E+06	6.19E+06

Note 1: The total drag of the sealed P-51B-1-NA 43-12105 is especially noteworthy because the combined profile drag and parasite drag of the Mustang in service condition is only slightly higher (<10%) than the values extracted from a perfectly smooth quarter-scale model tested for drag values in the NAA wind tunnel.

NACA Drag Tests – USAAF and US Navy Service Aircraft[7]				
Table I – Summary of Drag Measurements for the P-51B[8]				
Test #	**Modifications from Reference Test Condition**	**Ref. Test#**	**Cd at CL=0.20**	**Delta Cd at CL=0.20**
1	Airplane completely faired and sealed		0.0173	
2	Underslung duct inlet unsealed	1	0.0184	0.0011
3	Prestone duct exit unsealed – (flush position)	2	0.0188	0.0004
4	Oil cooler exit unsealed	3	0.0190	0.0002
5	Gaps of underslung duct unsealed	4	0.0190	0.0000
6	Wing-flap hinge and wing fillet unsealed	5	0.0192	0.0002
7	Cockpit and cockpit ventilator unsealed	6	0.0191	-0.0001
8	Ejection and linkage slots unsealed	7	0.0194	0.0003
9	Carburetor duct inlet unsealed	8	0.0194	0.0000
10	Wing control surface gaps, ammunition and gun-access doors, wheel wells, mooring rings, jack holes, and miscellaneous wing gaps unsealed	9	0.0198	0.0004
11	Wing gun cover plates removed	10	0.0200	0.0002
12	Exhaust stacks unsealed	11	0.0208	0.0008
13	Antenna installed	12	0.0208	0.0000
14	Elevator gaps unsealed	13	0.0208	0.0000
15	Rudder gaps unsealed (aircraft now in service condition)	14	0.0208	0.0000

The individual drag coefficients used by the Aeronautical Engineering Department led by Ed Horkey are presented in the table opposite for each of the principal P-51 Mustangs powered by Packard Merlin engines. The table is organized to show that NAA set up its original performance calculations based on drag coefficients derived from test results using a smooth quarter-scale model in both the NAA and the GALCIT wind tunnels at low speeds slightly above 100mph.

The table, presented and used by NAA for both the P-51B-1 and the P-51D-5, contains data at 1.84 and 2.0 x 10^6 Reynolds Number (Re) values, respectively, for the quarter-scale NAA model. The table also shows the data for the P-51H at 9.00x10^6 Reynolds Number for the P-51H.

The table also presents wind tunnel data for the smooth scale model at 6.19x 0^6 to correspond to the RN for 100mph for the production P-51B-1 43-12105 at the NACA Langley wind tunnel, as well as corresponding Re values for the P-51D-5 and the P-51H-1.

The P-51H-1 performance calculations used parasite drag values based on multiple sources, including a wind tunnel, but also extensive flight test data reduction, and are presented in NAA Report 8284-A as values based on 9.0x10^6 Re versus 1.84 and 2.0x10^6 Re for the P-51B-1 and P-51D-5. The authors have normalized the respective values from Re=1.84 and Re=2.0x10^6 and Re=9.0x10^6 for all three Mustang models to Re=6.19x10^6 to help the technical reader understand the different airframe component drag reductions from previous models, as well as placing the drag values in context with the NACA full scale testing of the P-51B-1. Take particular note of the dramatic reduction of the wing parasite drag value when NAA changed the wing airfoil for the P-51H to NACA 66,2-18155 (a=.6) from the NA-73 through NA-111 NAA/NACA 45-100 Low Drag airfoil.

A close inspection of the table reveals that the parasite drag values presented by NAA for the radiator duct (external, including intake scoop, cowl, oil cooler exit and radiator exit) are less than reported by NACA following Langley production airframe wind tunnel testing, and are also less than equivalent values later used for the P-51D-5 and P-51H-1 performance calculations.

III. Drag table extracted from the three NAA performance calculations for the P-51B-1-NA (NA-102), the P-51D-5-NA (NA-109) and the P-51H (NA-126)[9]

For each Re, the following Coefficient of Parasite Drag (CDp) and the Delta Coefficient of Drag (CDp1) for the items not affected by Re are tabulated below. The values for Re=6.19x10^6 are extrapolated from the base Re contained in the NAA performance calculation reports to provide reference to the NACA full scale aircraft test Re at 100mph in the NACA Langley wind tunnel referenced previously.

	P-51B[10]		P-51D[11]		P-51H[12]		
Reynolds number (Re)	1.84x10^6	6.19x10^6	2.00x10^6	6.19x10^6	2.0x10^6	6.19x10^6	9x10^6
Airframe component	CDp1	CDp1	CDp1	CDp1	CDp1	CDp1	CDp1
Wing	0.00760	---------	0.00700	0.00681	0.00560	0.00460	0.00450
Fuselage	0.00560	---------	0.00500	0.00448	0.00560	0.00490	0.00478
Cockpit enclosure (incl in P-51B fuselage)	---------	---------	0.00040	0.00036	0.00030	0.00020	0.00020
Empennage/tail	0.00210	---------	0.00220	0.00188	0.00190	0.00182	0.00180
Exhaust stacks*	0.00040	0.00080	0.00050	0.00050	0.00070	0.00070	0.00070
Carburetor duct (external)	0.00070	---------	0.00040	0.00036	0.00030	0.00030	0.00032
Radiator duct incl oil cooler duct (external)	0.00100	0.00170	0.00190	0.00170	0.00220	0.00210	0.00209
CDp1	0.01740	0.01980	0.01740	0.01565	0.01660	0.01462	0.01439
Delta CDp1*							
Ports for 4 0.50cal guns	0.00020	0.00020	---------	---------	---------	---------	---------
Ports for 6 0.50cal guns	---------	---------	0.00030	0.00030	0.00030	0.00030	0.00030
Antenna/pitot tube (estimated)	0.00040	---------	0.00040	0.00040	0.00015	0.00015	0.00015
Surface irregularities (estimated), doors, gaps, leaks, friction	0.00100	0.00080	0.00120	0.00120	0.00060	0.00060	0.00060
Delta CDp1*	0.00160	0.00100	0.00190	0.00190	0.00105	0.00105	0.00105
Total Parasite Drag CDpt	0.01900	0.02080	0.01930	0.01755	0.01765	0.01567	0.01544

Note 1: CDp values for Carb duct, Gun ports, antenna/pitot tube, surface irregularities/gaps, leaks, etc. are assumed independent of Reynolds number and influenced primarily by angle of attack. Data obtained at CL=0.15 to 0.20.
Note 2: The NACA Drag Test – Table I values are extracted and placed in column 2 above. All other values are NAA.

TOP NA-73/XP-51 41-038 intake scoop, showing the NA-73 air deflector and barely perceptible flow vanes. (*Chris Henry/EAA Collection*)

ABOVE NA-73/XP-51 41-038 intake scoop, showing the joint for the variable-dimension front scoop. (*Chris Henry/EAA Collection*)

IV. Radiator, Oil Cooler, Intercooler and Aftercooler Design issues for XP-51B/P-51B

The unique features differentiating the Merlin 61 from the Allison V-1710 included:

The carburetor intake was moved from the upper cowl for Allison-powered Mustangs to below the spinner. The "under-engine" intake was required for the updraft carburetor on the Merlin.

The two-speed and two-stage supercharger section of the V-1650-3 featured two separate impellers on the same shaft, which were normally driven through a gear train at a speed of 6.391:1. A hydraulic gear change arrangement of oil operated clutches that could be engaged by an electric solenoid to increase this ratio to 8.095:1 in high-speed blower position. The high-speed gear ratio of the impellers was not as great as the ratio used in the Allison, but the speed of the impeller alone was not the factor that increased engine performance at altitude. The double-staging of the compressed fuel/air mixture provided the boost pressure through a diffuser to the intake manifolds, which increased the critical altitude of the powerplant. The ability of the supercharger to maintain sea-level atmosphere in the induction system to the cylinders allowed the Packard Merlin to develop more power at 26,000ft than the Allison V-1710-81 had available for take-off at full power settings.

The two-stage impeller created extreme heating of the fuel/air mixture during the compression process, and in order to prevent detonation of the compressed charge it was necessary to cool the mixture before it entered the cylinders. This cooling was accomplished by the casting of an intercooler passage into the wheel-case housing between the first and second stage impellers. Ethylene glycol coolant was circulated by a pump through this passage to carry off excess heat generated by the impellers. Without the intercooler the temperature of the charge could be as high as 400°F.

Merlin two stage supercharger

1. Carburetor elbow, fuel/air charge admitted to 1st stage impellor.
2. First stage diffuser.
3. Supercharger case housing guide vanes and intercooling jacket.
4. Intermediate volute housing entry to second stage impellor.
5. Second stage impellor.
6. Aftercooler radiator.

The Merlin aftercooler was incorporated between the second stage compressor and the intake manifold to further reduce the charge temperature to prevent fuel-air charge pre-detonation. (*USAAF, sourced by Robert Gruenhagen Collection*)

The first intercooler in itself was not adequate to reduce the high temperatures sufficiently, and an additional cooling fin and tube core was placed between the outlet of the blower and the induction manifold to the cylinders. This radiator was known as an aftercooler and served as a reservoir for the system. The glycol mixture used for supercharger cooling was independent of the main engine cooling system, and used a centrifugal pump driven by the engine to circulate the coolant through an aircraft radiator

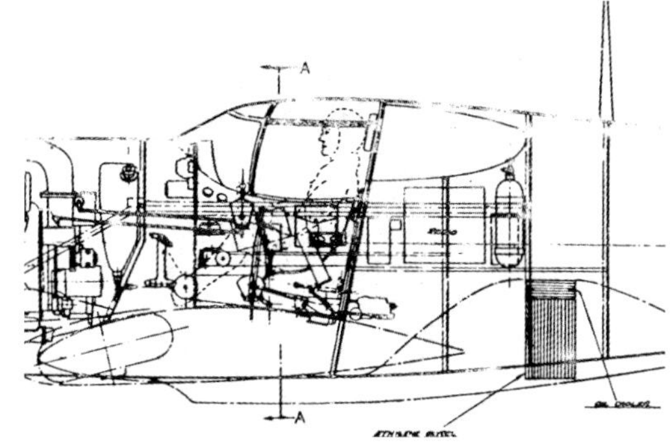

ABOVE This technical drawing of the X73 (the first iteration from the P-509 per Specification NA-1620) reveals the shape of the plenum and the location of the oil cooler, resting atop the rectangular radiator. This placement of the radiator for both the engine coolant system and the oil cooler would vary from the X73's initially square radiator to a round "donut" configuration, with the oil cooler in the center of the coolant radiator, by the time the X73 was completed. (© *The Boeing Company*)

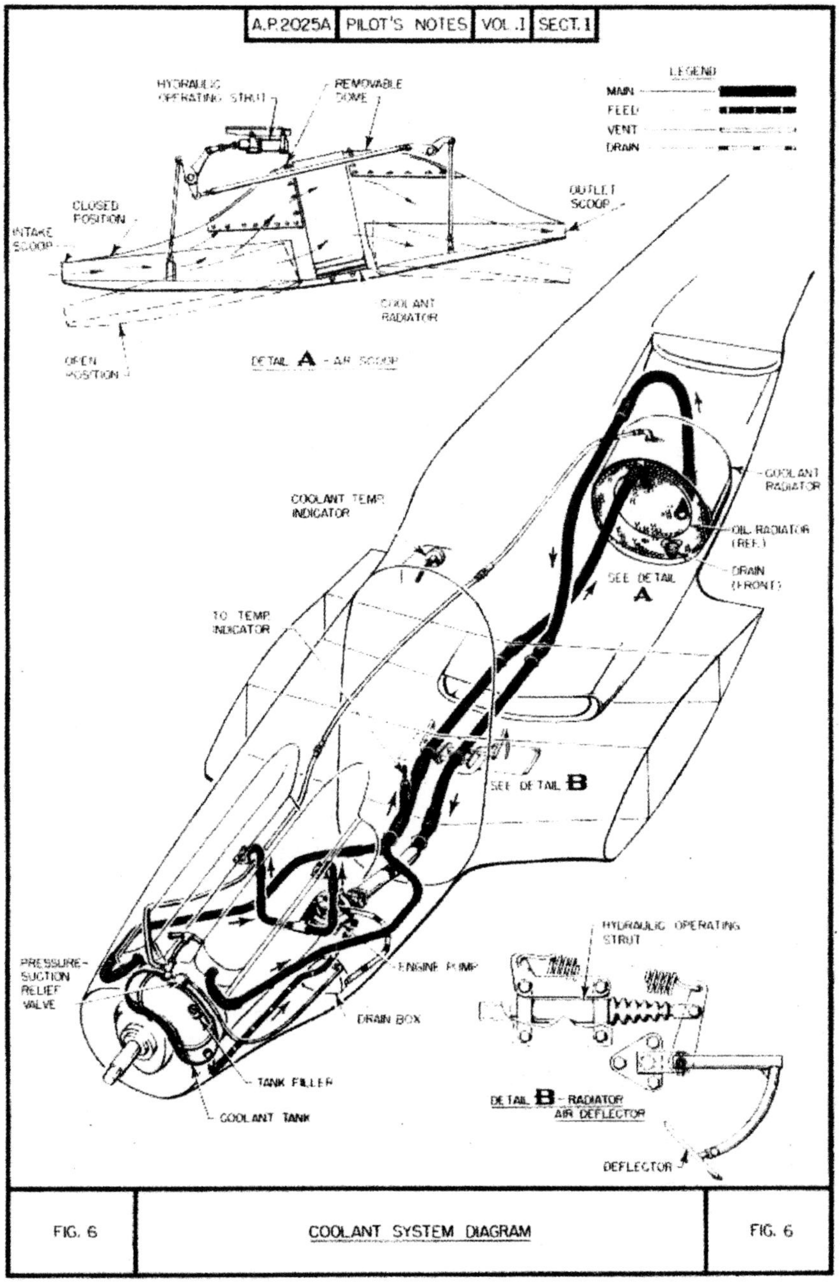

A.P.2025A PILOT'S NOTES VOL. I SECT. 1

LEGEND: MAIN, FEED, VENT, DRAIN

HYDRAULIC OPERATING STRUT, REMOVABLE DOME, CLOSED POSITION, INTAKE SCOOP, OUTLET SCOOP, COOLANT RADIATOR, OPEN POSITION, DETAIL A – AIR SCOOP

COOLANT RADIATOR, OIL RADIATOR (REF.), DRAIN (FRONT), SEE DETAIL A, COOLANT TEMP. INDICATOR, TO TEMP. INDICATOR, SEE DETAIL B, PRESSURE-SUCTION RELIEF VALVE, ENGINE PUMP, DRAIN BOX, TANK FILLER, COOLANT TANK

HYDRAULIC OPERATING STRUT, DETAIL B – RADIATOR AIR DEFLECTOR, DEFLECTOR

FIG. 6	COOLANT SYSTEM DIAGRAM	FIG. 6

LEFT The schematic of the NA-73's cooling system, with its circular "donut" radiator/oil cooler. The key difference between the NA-73 and the NA-81/91 was the deletion of the lower air deflector in front of the radiator scoop in the latter designs. (*The National Archives, ref. AIR10/2864*)

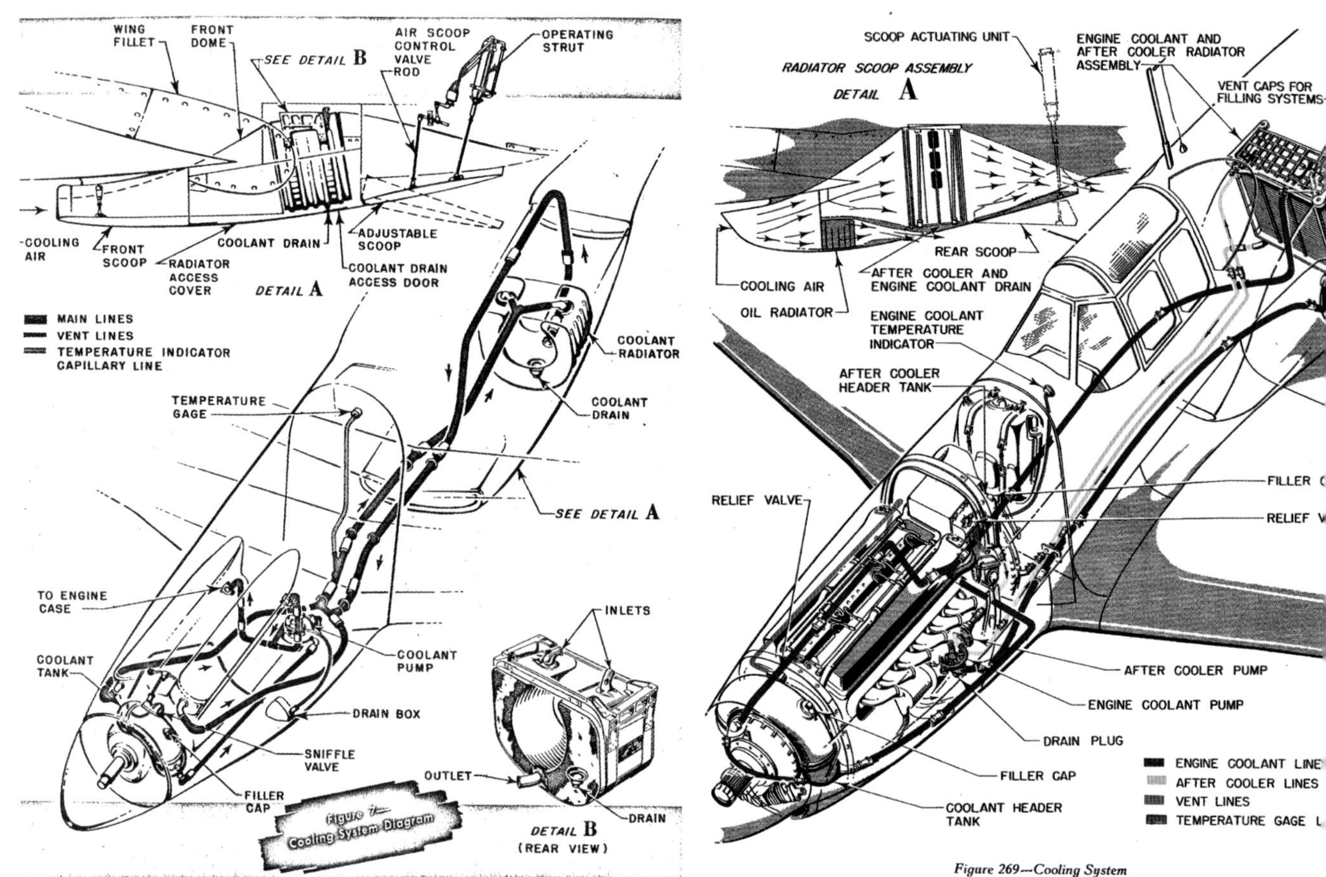

ABOVE The cooling systems for the A-36 and the P-51A were basically the same – both eliminated the adjustable front scoop. The P-51A's coolant radiator changed from "donut" to "horseshoe" shape but kept the oil cooler in the center of the radiator coolant matrix. (*© The Boeing Company, sourced by Robert Gruenhagen Collection*)

ABOVE RIGHT The cooling system for the B- and D-model P-51 were the same following the re-design in the wake of NACA's "rumble" testing of the XP-51B. Prior to the completion of the "rumble" tests at NACA Ames, the Harrison radiator was installed so that the aftercooler matrix occupied its top quarter. The production configuration changed by rotating the radiator 90 degrees to place the aftercooler section on its right hand side. (*© The Boeing Company, sourced by Robert Gruenhagen Collection*)

system at the rate of 30gal/min. This combined system reduced the charge temperature to suitable levels.

The throttle valves in the updraft carburetor throat were operated by an automatic boost control through the pilot's linkage to maintain the selected manifold pressure during changes in altitude. These valves were only partly open during ground- and low-level operation to prevent over-boosting of the engine. As air density decreased with an increase in altitude, the throttle valves were moved to an open position by boost pressure corresponding to aircraft altitude. This system provided full power within engine boost limitations up to the critical altitude of the engine.[13]

The introduction of the new Merlin 61/Packard 1650-3 to the NA-91 P-51-NA airframe imposed significant engineering analysis and design to provide the way forward on several key design issues. First, schematics to illustrate the cooling system migrations from NA-73 through the NA-99 P-51A are useful.

The added heat rejection requirements of the Merlin resulted in relocation of the oil cooler forward of the main radiator core, and provision of a co-residing aftercooler radiator core to augment cooling for the engine-mounted aftercooler.

A brief description of the Packard Merlin cooling system is as follows. The system capacity, including plumbing and radiator system, was 16.7gal of combined water and ethylene glycol, the latter providing anti-freeze. The ratio of ethylene glycol to water is based on the normal day temperatures on the ground, namely 30/70 for warm temperatures above 60°F/16°C and 70/30 when the temperatures were, on average, usually cooler. NaMBT was added to the glycol as a rust inhibitor. The system was pressurized to operate at 30psi, which raised the boiling point of the coolant.

The P-51B and C-1, plus the P-51D-5-NA and -5-NT, used the Harrison radiator, produced by a division of GMC. The 102-46005 Radiator Assembly drawing, released on October 23, 1942, details the assembly requirements. Drawing 106-46005, dated October 1, 1943, shows the effectivity and requirements for the United Aircraft Products, Inc. radiator, which was installed on all the later P-51Ds and P-51Ks through to the end of World War II.

Design Data for Harrison Radiator Division and United Aircraft Products Inc. Radiators

Specification	Engine coolant	Aftercooler coolant
Coolant (by volume)	70% water – 30% glycol	70% water – 30% glycol
Heat rejection	427 BTU/sec	100 BTU/sec
Flow	160gal/min	27gal/min
Temperature into radiator	260°F	160°F
Cooling air temperature at radiator face	+74°F	-2°F
Density at radiator face	0.0560lb/cu ft	0.0380lb/cu ft
Available cooling air static pressure across radiator	52lb/sq ft	40lb/sq ft
Operating water pressure	30lb/sq in.	30lb/sq in.
Test water pressure		
Coolant pressure drop	4lb/sq in.	3lb/sq in.
Available cooling airflow	13.3lb/sec	3.4lb/sec

The coolant was pumped through the system from the bottom of the engine, through the cylinder banks and heads, and then through two one-inch fittings and hose into an expansion tank. The exit temperature into the tank was regulated to 230°F or 110°C.

From the expansion tank, in two-inch lines, the flow continued to a "Y" fitting to converge to one 2½in. line and passed through the firewall into the fuselage section under the cockpit floor and then into the radiator. The Harrison radiator was a fin-and-tube design which fitted in the lower aft fuselage, with the top third devoted to the supercharger aftercooling system. Once installed, the Harrison radiator was rotated so that the aftercooling core now resided on the right-hand side (facing forward). The remaining 70 percent area and volume of the radiator was for the engine coolant flow, which flowed in the cooling tubes from top to bottom of the radiator.

The journey from the coolant tank was about 18ft, and contributed to dissipating the coolant temperature. A thermostat was installed in the radiator inlet line to measure coolant temperatures and control an electric actuator to vary the outlet

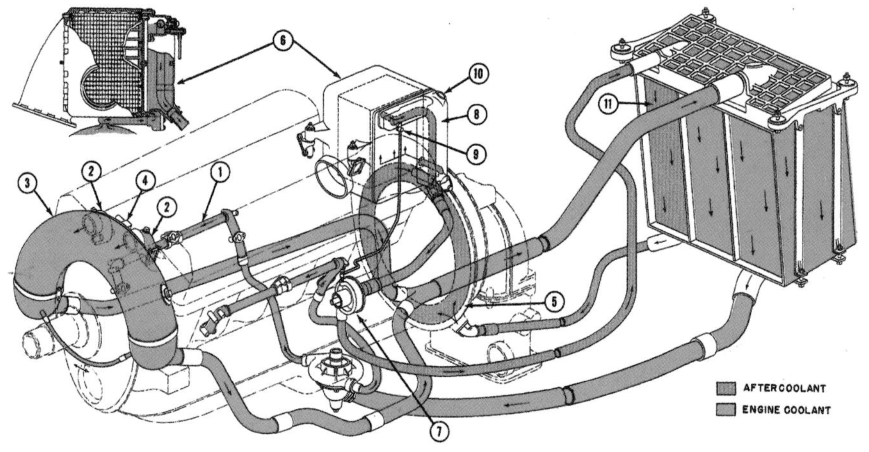

RIGHT Detailed schematic of the Harrison radiator showing the supply/return lines to and from the engine to the radiator/aftercooler matrix. (© *The Boeing Company, sourced by Robert Gruenhagen Collection*)

ENGINE COOLANT SYSTEM

1. CYLINDER BLOCK INLET PIPES
2. CYLINDER HEAD OUTLET CONNECTIONS
3. COOLANT HEADER TANK
4. HEADER TANK RELIEF VALVE

AFTERCOOLER SYSTEM

5. SUPERCHARGER INTERCOOLER
6. SUPERCHARGER AFTERCOOLER
7. AFTERCOOLER PUMP
8. AFTERCOOLER HEADER TANK
9. AFTERCOOLER HEADER TANK RELIEF VALVE
10. AFTERCOOLER HEADER TANK FILLER PLUG
11. AIRPLANE COOLANT RADIATOR

BELOW XP-51B schematic as drawn by NACA for its "rumble" test report. The drawing shows the louvers that were designed to bleed low energy boundary air from the top surface of the plenum. It also features the original, shallower, P-51A-based front scoop. (*NACA wartime report dated 8-1943*)

opening area of the aft radiator-duct system rear scoop to control the airflow through the radiator. From a "closed" position (1.3in.), this actuator started opening the rear scoop at 194°F/90°C. For taxi and climb the maximum opening of 14.5in. was set. The auto control could be overridden manually by the pilot.[14]

The duct system served to minimize major turbulence from the entrance scoop through both the oil cooler and radiator. Without the achieved efficiency of the designed intake duct/plenum, either the size of the radiator or the intake scoop area (and subsequent drag) would have increased. The aft plenum was designed to accept the airflow from passage through the radiator and gradually squeeze the airflow area until it exited the radiator to the area of the rear scoop, thus providing the jet effect.

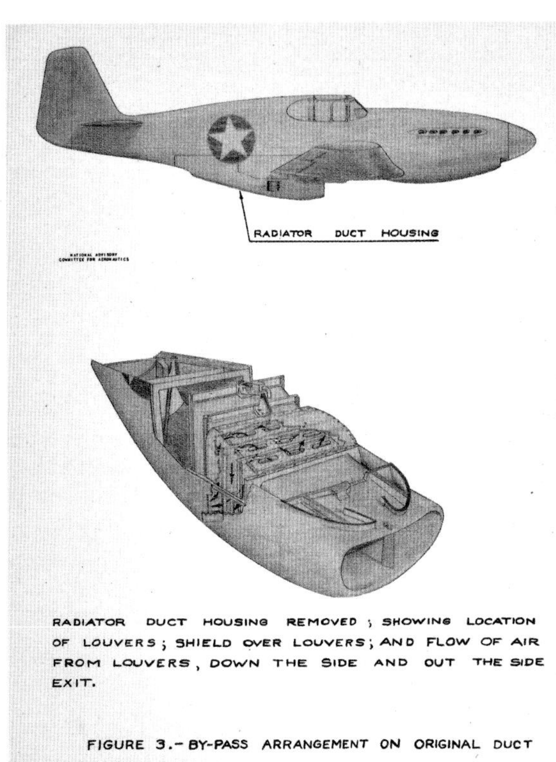

FIGURE 3.- BY-PASS ARRANGEMENT ON ORIGINAL DUCT

The XP-51B introduced major changes, as the cooling requirements for the engine and for aftercooling the fuel-air charge temperature due to the two-speed/two-stage Merlin supercharger were much greater than for the Allison.

The first major difference, aside from the deeper Harrison radiator with the aftercooler core residing in the left (facing aft) one-fourth of the radiator face, was to extract the oil cooler matrix from the radiator. This was necessary to enable approximately 33 percent more radiator/intercooler cooling in the primary matrix without having to drop an even larger radiator/aftercooler/oil cooler combination matrix into the fuselage and significantly alter the lower cowl lines of the P-51B from those of previous

Mustangs. Moving the oil cooler forward and then fairing over it to "smooth out" the flow to the Harrison radiator presented design issues, including (1) scheming a separate ducting and rear scoop to manage even temperatures for the oil, (2) continuing expanding the plenum aft of the oil cooler to introduce much lower velocity and pressure airflow to the entire front surface of the Harrison radiator, and, (3) reducing boundary-layer separation from the upper and lower ducts to achieve minimum momentum loss due to the airflow impinging on the radiator face. As previously noted, changing the inlet scoop geometry was required to prevent the boundary-layer from entering the plenum, and work also had to be done to reduce boundary-layer airflow from further development closer to the radiator face.

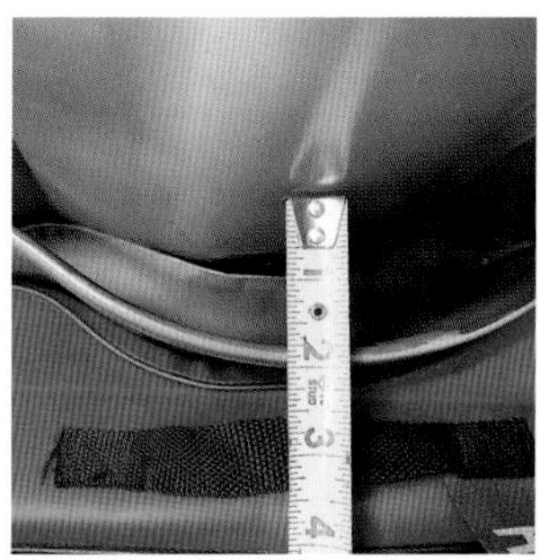

The A-36 and P-51A front scoop, which was a fixed, non-variable, opening. For the first time a gutter effect was created by lowering the upper surface of the intake scoop from the lower surface of the wing, thereby creating a mechanism for a natural bypass of lower energy airflow past the scoop. (*Chris Fahey/Planes of Fame*)

The Rolls-Royce team placed a separate aftercooler under the engine and used the Mustang I radiator/oil cooler basic design, with one major difference. The primary engine cooling radiator was still a circular/annular shape, but the oil cooler core was moved from within the center of the radiator to meet the larger cooling requirements for the Merlin. The oil cooler was placed on the front of the radiator. The Rolls-Royce team also experimented with greater fixed intake air scoop areas and rear scoop adjustable areas. To provide the necessary fuel-air charge intercooling/aftercooling, Rolls-Royce engineers positioned their aftercooler under the engine. To accommodate both the aftercooling matrix and carburetor intake duct airflow requirements, the lower front cowl had to be changed to more of a "P-40"-type system as used by the Merlin-powered P-40F.[15]

The NAA Horkey/Ashkenas team began with a modified P-51A scoop that was "larger in intake area and slightly bent, with the center radius removed," forming a shallow V conforming to the wing dihedral and close to the CL wing bolt fairing.

The first iteration was to provide a divider/splitter internally to separate the intake flow – upper to supply the radiator, lower to supply the oil cooler. The front face of the intake scoop was still perpendicular to the airflow. Through the first several iterations at NACA, NAA did not appreciably alter the plenum "cross-section." The top surface of the "V"-shaped upper scoop opening was "straightened," but not lowered.

The next iteration was to drop the upper intake scoop surface further below the wing centerline and straighten it (i.e. removed the shallow "V") so that an increased gutter was created at the edges. The suspected root cause for the continued "rumble" was believed to be

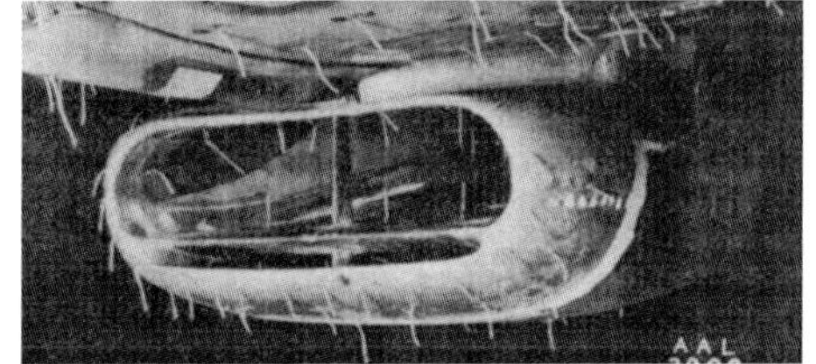

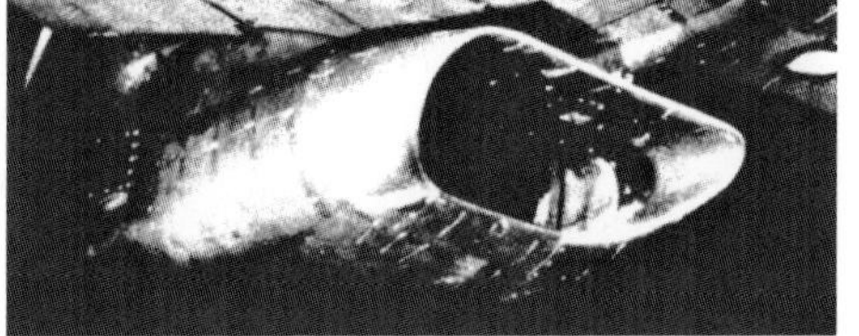

TOP LEFT The XP-51B changed its scoop configuration several times at NACA Ames Field. Note the new flat top, increased gutter and split horizontal duct to divide airflow to the oil cooler on the bottom and to the radiator/aftercooler above and behind the oil cooler. The front face of the intake scoop remained perpendicular to the wing's surface as with all previous Mustang designs. (*NACA, sourced by Robert Gruenhagen Collection*)

CENTRE LEFT The next change to the intake scoop configuration saw the addition of an angled front face from the lower wing surface, although the duct divider remained. (*NACA, sourced by Robert Gruenhagen Collection*)

BOTTOM LEFT The final P-51B/C/D intake scoop configuration. (*NACA, sourced by Robert Gruenhagen Collection*)

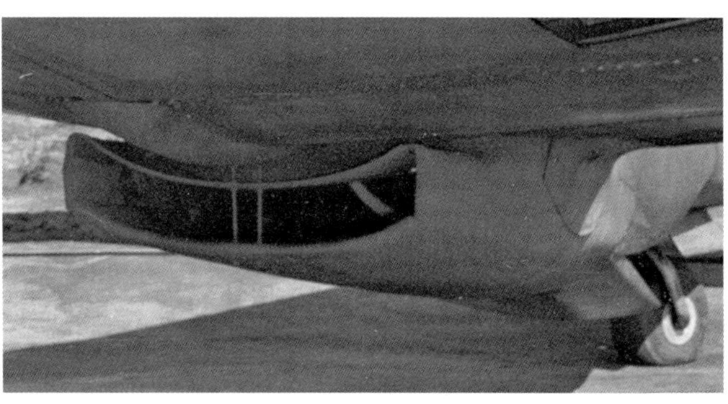

An experimental radius-based top front scoop was installed on P-51A 43-6007 as shown here. The authors do know the purpose of this one-off scoop, but suspect it was inserted between the original XP-51B design and the final configuration emerging from the NACA Ames tests. (© *The Boeing Company*)

multiple boundary-layer separations at both the upper and lower plenum surfaces. This was a slight improvement, but the duct rumble continued to be severe. The next iteration was to extend the upper lip forward but not change the geometry of the plenum, specifically the upper surface of the oil cooler duct. The loud rumble with the rear scoop in a closed position continued, but was much reduced at medium speed and with a wide-open rear scoop area.

The next two iterations for the XP-51B design first moved the upper surface of the oil cooler duct all the way forward, and then provided the upper oil cooler duct with a small gradual change in slope further aft. It then dropped to intersect at the base of the Harrison radiator. This iteration achieved a near-uniform pressure distribution for about 80 percent of the radiator front face, with eddies at the top of the radiator. Boundary-layer separation still occurred a little too far in front of the upper line of the Harrison radiator for optimal efficiency, but it was better than in the earlier Mustang designs. Left unchanged was the philosophy of a variable-dimension rear scoop controlled either manually or automatically, based on the coolant temperatures exiting the radiator.

Not shown in that NACA report was the final design iteration, in which the upper duct surface for the oil cooler was pushed back to the top front face of the oil cooler core, as shown. Ultimately the cause of the "rumble" was traced to alternating turbulent flows caused by boundary-layer separation which, when pushed by more inbound airflow, impacted the radiator with alternating greater forces than smooth airflows.

Design Area Data for Coolant System

Component	Frontal area	External area
Oil cooler		
Oil radiator face	174sq in.	
Exit shutter area – closed	26sq in.	
Exit shutter area – open	70sq in.	
Engine radiator		
Total coolant radiator area	545sq in.	
Aftercooler coolant area	150sq in.	
Engine coolant area	395sq in.	
Exit scoop area – closed	110sq in.	
Exit scoop area – open	318sq in.	
External surface area – system		55.47sq ft

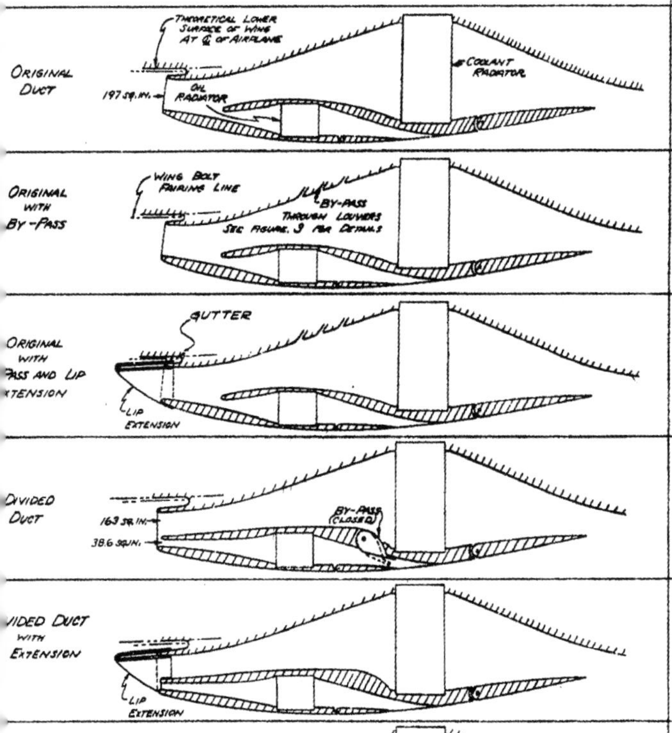

DUCT	FLAP OPENING - INCHES		RUMBLE $\alpha = -2°$		ΔC_D ($C_D - C_D$ WITH ORIGINAL DUCT) WING AREA = 233.19 SQ.FT. $\alpha = 0°$		MASS FLOW SLUGS PER SECOND q = 385 LB/SQ.FT. V = 430 M.P.H. MACH NO. = .570 $\alpha = -2°$	
	OIL	COOLANT	q = 254 LB/SQ.FT. V = 337 M.P.H. MACH NO. = .446	q = 487 LB/SQ.FT. V = 500 M.P.H. MACH NO. = .665	q = 63 LB/SQ.FT. V = 161.5 M.P.H. MACH NO. = .208	q = 127 LB/SQ.FT. V = 230.5 M.P.H. MACH NO. = .305	OIL RADIATOR DUCT	COOLANT RADIATOR DUCT
ORIGINAL DUCT	0.6	1.3	SEVERE	—	—	—	0.107	0.650
	0.6	5.6	STARTS	—	—	—	—	—
ORIGINAL WITH BY-PASS	0.6	1.3	HEAVY	—	—	—	—	—
	0.6	3.5	STARTS	—	—	—	—	—
ORIGINAL WITH …ASS AND LIP …TENSION	0.6	1.3	SLIGHT	MEDIUM	—	—	—	—
	0.6	5.6	NONE	STARTS	—	—	—	—
DIVIDED DUCT	0.6	1.3	MEDIUM	HEAVY	—	—	—	—
	0.6	1.9	STARTS	—	—	—	—	—
…VIDED DUCT WITH EXTENSION	0.6	1.3	NONE	NONE	.0003	.0000	0.103	0.520
	3.1	5.9	NONE	NONE	.0006	.0006	0.237	0.778
	8.0	14.5	NONE	NONE	.0005	.0006	0.306	1.250
…ED DIVIDED DUCT	0.6	1.3	NONE	NONE	.0000	.0000	0.093	0.412
	3.1	5.9	NONE	NONE	.0006	.0004	0.244	0.796
	8.0	14.5	NONE	NONE	.0003	.0005	0.299	1.220

NACA report summary table showing each intake scoop, boundary-layer bypass gutter and intake plenum configuration, along with wing tunnel results for both noise and temperature management efficiency. (*NACA, sourced by Robert Gruenhagen Collection*)

V. The Meredith Effect – what is it, really?

To quote from Meredith's paper:

> The Meredith Effect involved preventing excessive cooling air from flowing through the radiator at high speed by partly closing the outlet and developing a pressure behind the radiator, which, being less than on the forward face, created a jet of exhaust air. As with any pressure jet, this put a forward reaction force on the airplane which partly offset the drag of the radiator. The temperature increases in the exhaust air (from the air being heated by the radiator) expanded its volume and augmented this force appreciably because the size of the exit opening could be somewhat larger with the same internal pressure.[16]

What was implied, but not stated, was that the velocity increase of the emerging heated air in a contracting plenum with a small exit opening was significantly greater than the entrance velocity, and provided hoped-for thrust in the form of back pressure

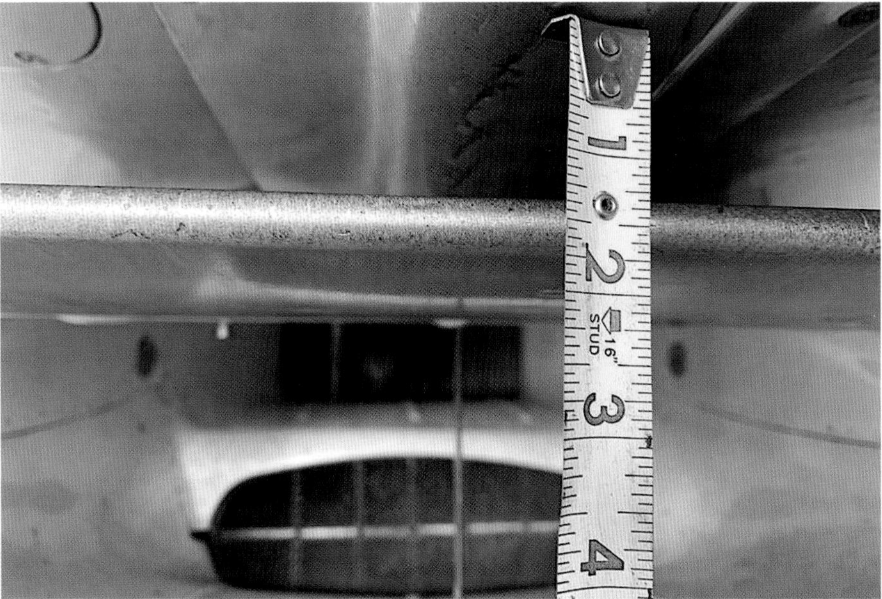

The depth of the final P-51B/C/D intake scoop configuration is seen here in a close-up view of an airworthy D-model Mustang owned and operated by the Planes of Fame Museum of Chino, California. (*Chris Fahey/Planes of Fame*)

against the radiator, offsetting the significant cooling-air pressure drag and friction drag from the intake scoop to the radiator. This cooling system was also known as a "minimum pressure drop" system.

Translating the theory into practical application took many iterations. The lowest cooling drag reductions were achieved in the XP-51F/G/J and P-51H/P-82. That said, the final designs for both the P-51B and D were very close in performance, and so are referenced in the performance analysis presented in the NAA Aerodynamics section. Both the P-51B (NA-5534) and P-51D (NA-8449) Performance Reports presented the parasite drag coefficients obtained initially by the GALCIT wind tunnel testing in 1940 and were well validated by the full-scale wind tunnel tests of the P-51B at Langley, and then the dive testing performed in the fall of 1944.

The consistent cooling drag of the combined pressure and friction drag of the losses in the plenum due to the radiator, as well as a small increment of profile drag for the open scoop, was stated above as CDp=0.0064 for the extreme condition of maximum climb. This value is an extraordinary increase over the total low-speed parasite/profile drag build-up of CDp=.0190 for all the major airframe components at zero lift minimum drag.

However, at top speed in level flight, "Net Zero Cooling Drag = zero" is cited on page 16 of the P-51B NAA Report NA-5534, and P-51D NAA Report NA-8284, referenced with endnotes in the Aerodynamics section. The importance of the differentiation between level flight and climb is that during climb, at approximately 160–170mph TAS, the total calculated parasite drag of the Mustang was approximately 125 percent of the parasite drag of the aircraft in level flight at the same flight speeds. However, when the authors applied the same analysis used by NAA for their performance calculations to explain a 25mph drop in airspeed when the aft radiator scoop was opened to Wide Open condition, the cooling drag CDpcool was 0.0042

– nearly two-thirds of the climb condition CDp=0.0064. For further details, see USAAF Flight Test for May 18, 1943 (No. FS-M-14-1587-A) found at www.spitfireperformance.com.

The process of design, wind tunnel testing, redesign, flight test, and redesign ultimately yielded the closest approach to achieve net zero internal pressure drag of the plenum/radiator/"exhaust" system designed in accordance with Meredith Effect principles. Personally, the authors believe that net zero internal cooling drag *was* nearly achieved at top speeds, as Horkey and Ashkenas stated in the P-51B/D and H Performance Analysis Reports. Well-known aerodynamicists David Lednicer and Ian Gilchrist postulated that 97–98 percent recovery of cooling drag thrust horsepower was required at Mach=0.5 (360mph TAS) at 15,000ft, with a rear scoop exit temperature assumed to be 170°F.[17] The importance of this statement is that Lednicer and Gilchrist determined from their model that CDp for cooling drag in high-speed level flight was approximately three percent loss of available power, whereas Horkey and Ashkenas reported zero loss. The authors believe the basic difference in conclusions are focused on assumed exit temperatures at the aft radiator scoop of 170°F. Lednicer extrapolates zero loss at approximately 183°F for exit temperature.

Lednicer, also a consultant regarding racing P-51s, performed sophisticated computer fluid dynamic modeling in the 1990s to show that the scoop, and plenum behind the scoop, still had room for improvement regarding the internal shape of the plenum. He specifically noted that the major expansion of the upper contour should be moved much closer to the radiator, thus moving the boundary-layer separation region in the plenum to a point closer to the radiator. Further, he noted that the external shape of the aft cowling needed modifications to reduce vortex drag aft of the wing.[18]

In summary, by assuming an exit temperature of the air at 170°F exiting the aft scoop in flush position, his modeling results pointed to a 97 percent drag reduction contribution at Mach=0.5 at 15,000ft, or approximately 29lb of net internal

NA-73/XP-51 41-038 intake scoop, showing the joint for the variable-dimension radiator/exhaust scoop. The front and rear scoop design did not vary much through the NA-91 series. (*Chris Henry/EAA Collection*)

duct friction and pressure cooling drag at that altitude and speed.[19] Note that if the assumed exit temperature of the radiator-heated air is greater than 170°F, then the pressure recovery approaches net zero drag, as claimed by the NAA Aero/Thermodynamics engineering team.

The primary questions that remain when comparing Lednicer's assumed exit temperature of 170°F and NAA's stated Zero Cooling Drag values for high speed are (1) how did NAA set up pressure and temperature sensors in the aft ducting/exit scoop to measure the exit velocity and temperatures, and (2) what were those values for Horkey and Ashkenas to pose "zero net cooling drag" at high-speed flush position in the respective P-51B, D and H performance analysis sections of the NAA performance reports?

Any reader seeking much more technical detail should obtain two specific documents, namely David Lednicer's paper "World War II Fighter Aerodynamics," Experimental Aircraft Association 135815, January 1999, and David Lednicer and Ian Gilchrist's paper "A Retrospective: Computational Aerodynamics Methods Applied to the P-51 Mustang," American Institute of Aeronautics and Aerospace, AIAA-91-32888.

The Ashkenas/Horkey claim that, at high speed, "Cooling drag=zero" is well supported by the following reasons:

- NAA's flight performance calculations using the parasite drag build-up had no provision for additional parasite and friction drag internal to the intake/plenum, radiator/plenum and aft scoop in the flush position, but:
- NAA's flight performance calculations yielded a *very close* predictive model for projected top speeds at all altitudes based on the BHP of the Merlin supplied by Packard, as demonstrated by the actual flight test data.
- As previously noted in the drag discussion, the NACA cumulative unsealed lower cowling, radiator intake scoop, oil cooler exit scoop and radiator exit scoop for the P-51B-1in full scale wind tunnel testing yielded a total CDp of 0.0017 without any radiator operating to heat the cooling air through the system.

VI. Conclusion

The USAAF flight tests of May 18, 1943 for the P-51B-1, during which high-speed level flight runs were made with recorded radiator coolant temperatures at 110°C (230°F), achieved 448mph but averaged 442mph TAS (approximately 0.65M) at 29,800ft. The coolant temperature at those speeds was controlled automatically by opening and closing the aft radiator scoop door, based on the exiting coolant temperatures from the radiator at a steady 110°C.

Although the exit temperature of the coolant-heated airflow was unknown during those speed runs, it is probable that the exit temperatures were above 170°F (used as the input value by Lednicer), given that the high-temperature airflow was contracted from the radiator face to the exit over approximately four feet.

VII. The Great Debate – Atwood versus Horkey on the Real Story of Superior Aerodynamics

It is a fact that the primary reasons for the superior speed and range attributes of the Mustang were not fully understood by either the British or the Germans during World War II. Both studied the Mustang in wind tunnels, but neither government installed sophisticated instrumentation to record exit velocities and temperatures through the rear scoop of the cooling system plenum in full-power flight mode.

Temperatures were recorded for the engine radiator coolant when the rear scoop was "closed" to the minimum area of 118sq in. for the flush position (compared with 318sq in. for the wide-open position) for high-speed runs, and adjusted accordingly to maintain the temperature point in the radiator and aftercooler matrix. The authors are not aware of NAA (or the British or Germans) recording and analyzing the air temperature of the "jet." For a sophisticated analysis, the exit temperature of the air passing through the radiator must be known, as well as the exit velocity and temperature through the small area (known) of the rear scoop.

That said, the debate between Lee Atwood and Edward Horkey/Edgar Schmued became sharp regarding the primary reason for the Mustang's superior performance. First, Horkey asserted that the airfoil/wing selected for the Mustang, the NACA/NAA 45-100 low-drag airfoil, had remarkably low-drag attributes, both at lower speeds and top speeds well into compressibility ranges of 0.6 to 0.8 Mach, and was the primary reason for low-drag. Second, the drag coefficient of the Mustang wing (CDo at zero lift angle-of-attack, representing the aircraft's minimum drag) was dramatically lower than that of the NACA 23016 airfoil of equivalent T/C ratio, used in the P-38, F4F, F6F, F4U, and Fw 190.

Lee Atwood maintained that the primary reason for low net drag was the Meredith Effect pressure recovery, leading to a reduction of horsepower required over conventional radiator designs of the time.

They were both correct. The superb drag coefficient of the Mustang in a low-speed wind tunnel, in which neither an engine running at full power nor heat transfer of the airflow through the radiator were accounted for, pointed to an outstandingly low coefficient of profile drag. At high speed, the mere fact that the aeronautical engineering team posited a "net zero cooling drag" implies that they were fully aware that, somehow, normal incremental pressure and friction drag of the Mustang's intake scoop/plenum/radiator combination in a wind tunnel, with no engine running, was reduced to little or zero net internal parasite and pressure drag in level flight with high coolant temperatures and airflow heat transfer exiting the radiator and then passing through the constricted exit area of the flush scoop.

The authors remain mystified regarding the intensity of the debate between Atwood and Horkey. The top speed of the Mustang must be attributed jointly to the wing/fuselage design, the very rigorous manufacturing standards, *and* the practical application of the Meredith Effect.

APPENDIX B

OPERATIONAL DATA, TABLES AND CHARTS – KEY FIGHTER AIRCRAFT FOR USSTAF EUROPE FROM NOVEMBER 1943 THROUGH JUNE 5, 1944

I. Range Tables

Notes regarding Range Table (on page 318) and map

The fuel consumption individual totals for warm-up, take-off and climb to cruise altitude were based on flight test averages in ideal weather for the P-47C/D, P-38H/J and P-51B at factory recommended RPM and manifold pressures for each stage. They were estimates derived during USAAF flight testing by skilled test pilots, and documented for purpose of combat operations planning.

The fuel consumption rates and totals for combat were based on dropping external combat fuel tanks at initiation of combat, and depending entirely on remaining internal fuel – less that consumed during warm up, taxi, take-off and initial climb before switching to external combat tanks (estimated at ten gallons for the P-47D, seven gallons for the P-51B and 12 gallons for P-38J). The specific charts and estimations do not account for mass element, flight, squadron and group formation loiter time while circling the airfield in marginal visibility. Nor does the Range Table on page 318 or the map data take into consideration winds aloft or weather conditions – both of which would be accounted for and entered into mission planning in the ETO.

Additionally, an important combat tank representation was not shown for lack of official data during research by the authors. There was no data found for the widely used single "flat profile" 150gal combat tank mounted on the center line rack of the P-47C/D. The tank was first introduced in December 1943 and was in wide service before "Big Week" (February 20, 1944). Repeated P-47 victory credits west of Hannover, Brunswick and Hamburg point to escort missions flown with a single 130gal tank as these engagements took place in excess of 375–400 miles from East Anglian fighter bases. As noted in the Range Table, a considerable volume of fuel is estimated for the Combat category so awareness of limiting combat time offered a significant extension in combat radius over the tabulated value assumptions detailed here.

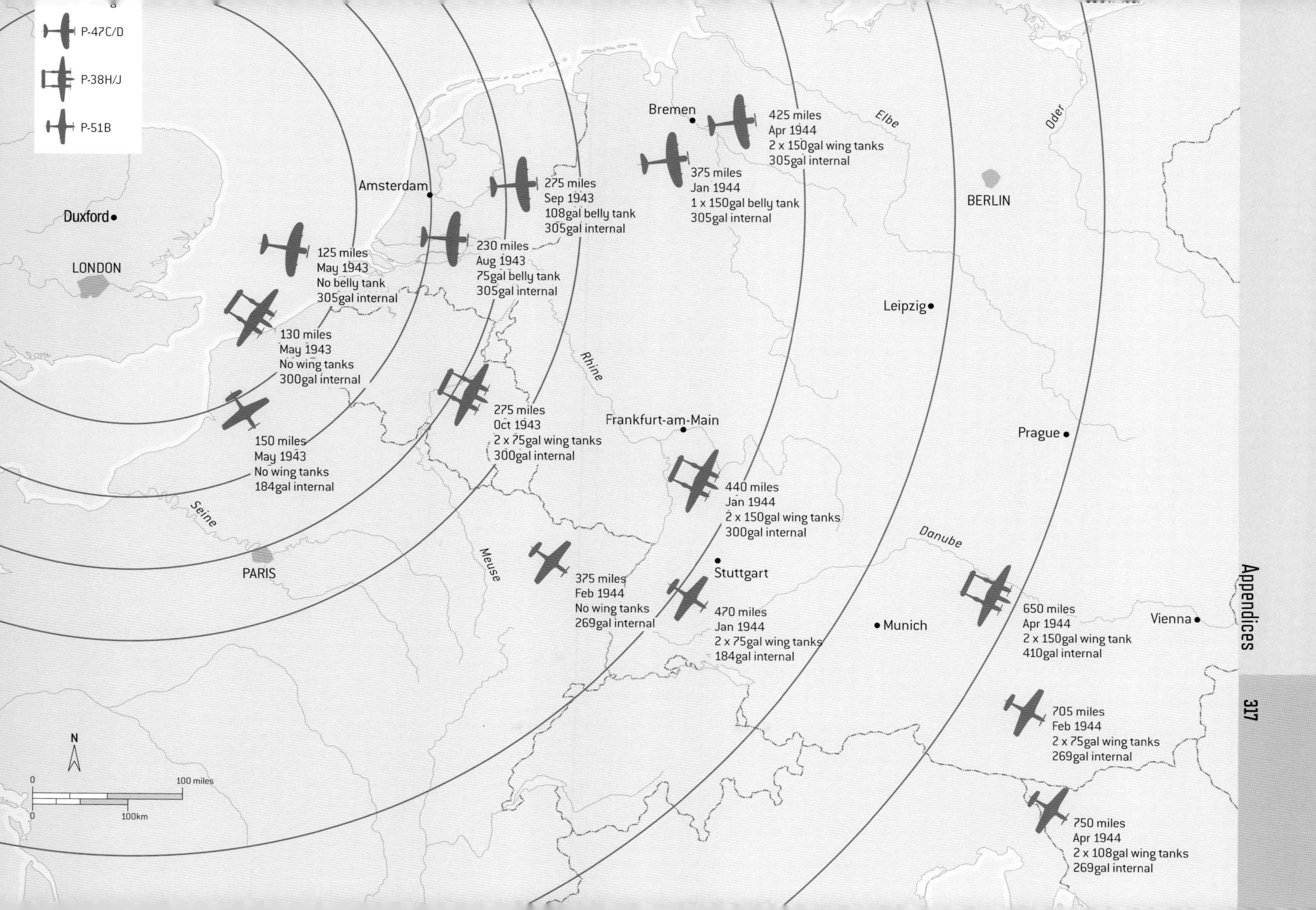
P-47C/D
P-38H/J
P-51B
Duxford
LONDON
PARIS
Amsterdam
Bremen
Frankfurt-am-Main
Stuttgart
Munich
Leipzig
BERLIN
Prague
Vienna
Oder
Elbe
Rhine
Danube
Meuse
Seine
125 miles
May 1943
No belly tank
305gal internal
130 miles
May 1943
No wing tanks
300gal internal
150 miles
May 1943
No wing tanks
184gal internal
230 miles
Aug 1943
75gal belly tank
305gal internal
275 miles
Sep 1943
108gal belly tank
305gal internal
275 miles
Oct 1943
2 x 75gal wing tanks
300gal internal
375 miles
Feb 1944
No wing tanks
269gal internal
375 miles
Jan 1944
1 x 150gal belly tank
305gal internal
425 miles
Apr 1944
2 x 150gal wing tanks
305gal internal
440 miles
Jan 1944
2 x 150gal wing tanks
300gal internal
470 miles
Jan 1944
2 x 75gal wing tanks
184gal internal
650 miles
Apr 1944
2 x 150gal wing tank
410gal internal
705 miles
Feb 1944
2 x 75gal wing tanks
269gal internal
750 miles
Apr 1944
2 x 108gal wing tanks
269gal internal
N
0
100 miles
0
100km

Fighter Model	Weight T.O.20 Weight (lb)	Fuel – gal Int gal	Ext gal	Total – gal	Fuel consumed – gal Combat	TO and Climb	Reserve 30 min	Max range – miles 21	Combat radius – miles 22	Internal fuel increase	External tanks
P-38H/J-5	17,000	300	-	300	111	86	50	800	130	None	
	18,980	300	300	600	111	98	50	1,600	440	None	2 x 150gal
P-38J-10 with leading edge (LE) tanks	17,700	410	-	410	111	90	50	1,175	275	2 x 55gal LE	
	19,850	410	330	740	111	105	50	1,910	650	2 x 55gal LE	2 x 165gal
P-47C/D-15	13,582	305	-	305	89	101	40	835	125	None	-
	14,082	305	75	380	89	113	40	925	230	None	1 x 75gal
	14,292	305	110	415	89	125	40	1,035	275	None	1 x 108gal
P-47D-16/-23	15,600	305	300	605	89	132	40	1,525	425+	None	2 x 150gal
P-51B-1/-5	9,320	184	-	184	58	46	26	835	150	None	-
	9,920	184	150	334	58	50	26	1,575	470	None	2 x 75gal
P-51B (all) with fuselage (fuse) tank	9,830	269	-	269	58	51	26	1,350	375	85gal fuse	-
	10,730	269	150	419	58	56	26	1,800	705	85gal fuse	2 x 75gal
	11,150	269	220	489	58	58	26	2,150	750	85gal fuse	2 x 108gal

II. Fighter performance results for both Top Speed and Rate of Climb

The three sets of Comparison Charts presented in this volume are, in order, Comparison I – for the period December 1943 through February 1944; Comparison II – for the period April 1944 through May 1944, and; Comparison III – the XP-51F.

All plots were derived from USAAF and Luftwaffe flight test results for unmodified factory-delivered fighters. Those that were tested "light" per full internal combat load will be noted accordingly so that the reader may mentally reduce rate of climb results for such comparisons as shown in the Performance Charts.

Notes regarding Comparison Charts test results versus actual ETO operations

All flight test results as presented were derived from aircraft flown without belly or wing racks to accommodate combat tanks to extend range. To this extent, top speeds and climb rates achievable in actual combat over Germany are therefore overstated. That said, the fuel rack drag values for all five fighters would have resulted in a 9mph to 15mph reduction of level speed and 200ft per minute rate of climb less than those shown in the performance comparisons – for both periods. It should also be noted that each of these fighters, particularly the American ones, had much better climb performance for combat engaged in which much internal fuel had already been consumed.

P-38J-5s, J-10s and early J-15s experienced severe performance issues related to engine unreliability above 20,000ft. Actual ETO average engine performance for early P-38Js compared to US-based flight tests was reduced to Military Power (MP) settings of 54" MP until the combination of carburetor, oil and fuel temperature issues could be sorted out. This means that the speed and climb plots for the P-38-10 as shown are very optimistic compared to actual experience through March 1944. It should also be noted that when operating as designed, the only difference with respect to performance values between the P-38J-10 and J-15 at full internal combat loading was the addition of two 55gal leading edge tanks to the P-38J-15 to increase fuel capacity to 410gal.

The type of fuel used also contributed to the average performance test and combat performance. The Bf 109G used 87 octane B4, while the Fw 190A series used 100 octane C-3. Although 150 octane fuel was tested and approved for the P-38, P-47 and P-51 before D-Day, the flight test results presented for Comparisons I and II were with 130 octane fuel used during the period covered by this publication.

The fighter aircraft compared for the two separate periods were:

Comparison I – December 1943 to February 1944

P-38J-10 with Allison V-1710-89/-91 engines at 60" MP WEP.

- Gross weight at take-off – 16,597lb, versus maximum internal combat gross weight of 17,009lb
- 300gal of internal fuel. No 55gal leading edge tanks installed
- No wing racks – clean

This P-38J-10 flight test was performed at 97 percent full combat load at take-off. Therefore, the maximum climb rate results were nearly 400ft per minute "optimistic/non-conservative" for 60" MP. Additionally, the V-1710-89/-91 could not achieve 60" above 20,000ft in the ETO until the carburetor/aftercooler/oil cooler issues were resolved in spring 1944.

P-47D-6 with Pratt & Whitney R-2800-21 engine at 52" MP (without water injection).

- Gross weight at take-off – 13,200lb, versus maximum internal combat gross weight of 13,582lb
- 305gal of internal fuel
- No wing racks – clean

This P-47D was tested 382lb under full combat load at take-off. The maximum climb rate results were perhaps 200ft per minute "optimistic/non-conservative".

P-51B-1/-5 with Packard Merlin V-1650-3 engine at 67" MP WEP.

- Gross weight at take-off – 9,205lb, versus maximum internal combat gross weight of 9,156lb
- 184gal of fuel, no 85gal fuselage fuel tank or 85gal additional fuel
- No wing racks – clean

This P-51B-5 was tested at 66lb over full combat load at take-off for a P-51B-1/-5 without the 85gal internal tank or fuel. The maximum climb rate results were perhaps "pessimistic/conservative".

Bf 109G-6 with DB 605A at maximum power 1.3ata

- Gross weight at take-off – 3,250kg, versus maximum internal combat gross weight of 3,129kg
- 106gal (approximately) internal fuel
- No Schloß 503 centerline rack – clean

This Bf 109G-6 flight test was at four percent above normal full internal combat load, and the presented test results are therefore pessimistic for rate of climb. The maximum climb rate achievement value for a nominally loaded Bf 109G without Schloß 503 should be closer to 3,300ft per minute at 1.3 ata.

Fw 190A-5/-6 with BMW 801D-2 at maximum power 1.42ata

- Gross weight at take-off – 4,000kg, versus maximum internal combat gross weight of 4,000kg
- 139gal (approximately) of internal fuel
- No ETC 501 rack – clean

This Fw 190A-5 was tested at full internal combat load and test results for rate of climb should be close to those expected.

Comparison II – April to May 1944

Changes from Comparison I

The P-38-10s had received Depot kit modifications to install the 55gal leading edge tanks that were factory delivered in the P-38J-15. So modified, J-10s were the same in respect to performance and range as the P-38J-15. Additionally, the engine problems – turbo over-speed, carburetor air temperature, oil cooling and fuel aftercooling issues – were largely sorted out, making 60" MP achievable up to Full Throttle Height.

The P-47D-25, which was the first "long-range" Thunderbolt with the new 370gal fuselage fuel tank and bubble canopy, is not illustrated in Comparison II for two reasons. Firstly, the P-47D-25 was operationally introduced in small numbers from mid-May 1944. Secondly, both the top speed and climb rates for the D-25 were less than the earlier models already in widespread service with the Eighth, Ninth and Fifteenth Air Forces. With two external 150gal external combat tanks, the D-25 had the largest combat radius of any P-47D – 670 miles at 25,000ft. The primary contributor for combat radius was the quantity of fuel remaining in the wings and fuselage tanks after external combat tanks had been dropped following the engagement of enemy aircraft.

From March 1944, production 85gal fuselage tank-equipped P-51B/Cs were available, and the P-51B-15 and C-5 were delivered with the Packard V-1650-7 engine with better low and most middle altitude engine performance than the V-1650-3. The P-51D-5 with the V-1650-7 also started arriving in mid-May but, like the P-47D-25, it was not available in squadron-size formations.

Comparison I (Dec 1943 to Feb 1944) – Level Speed Performance

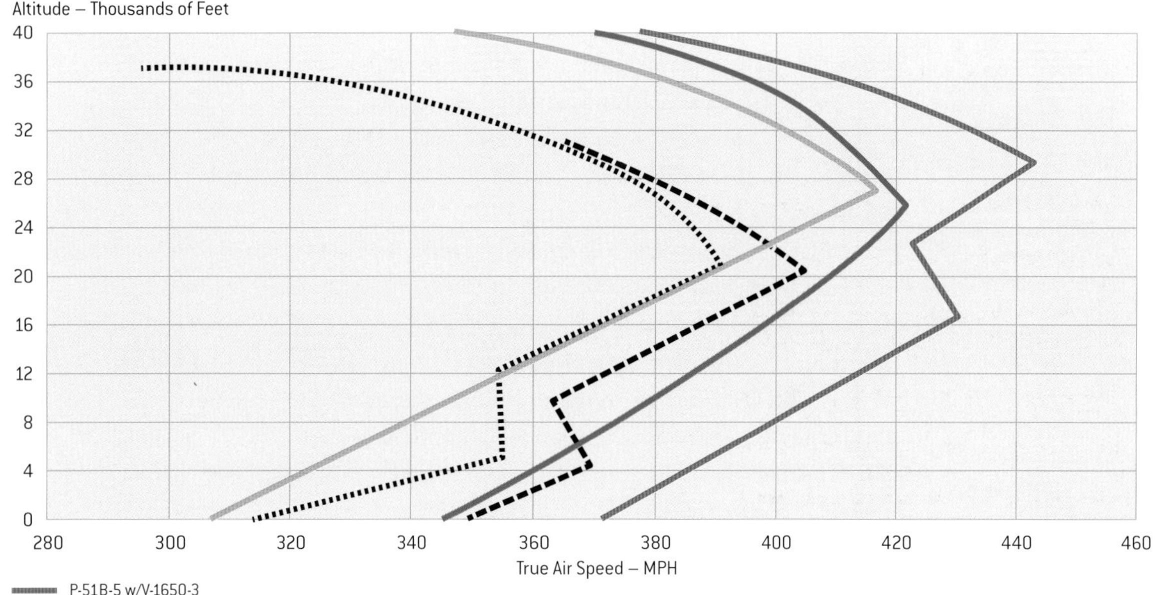

Comparison I (Dec 1943 to Feb 1944) – Rate of Climb Performance

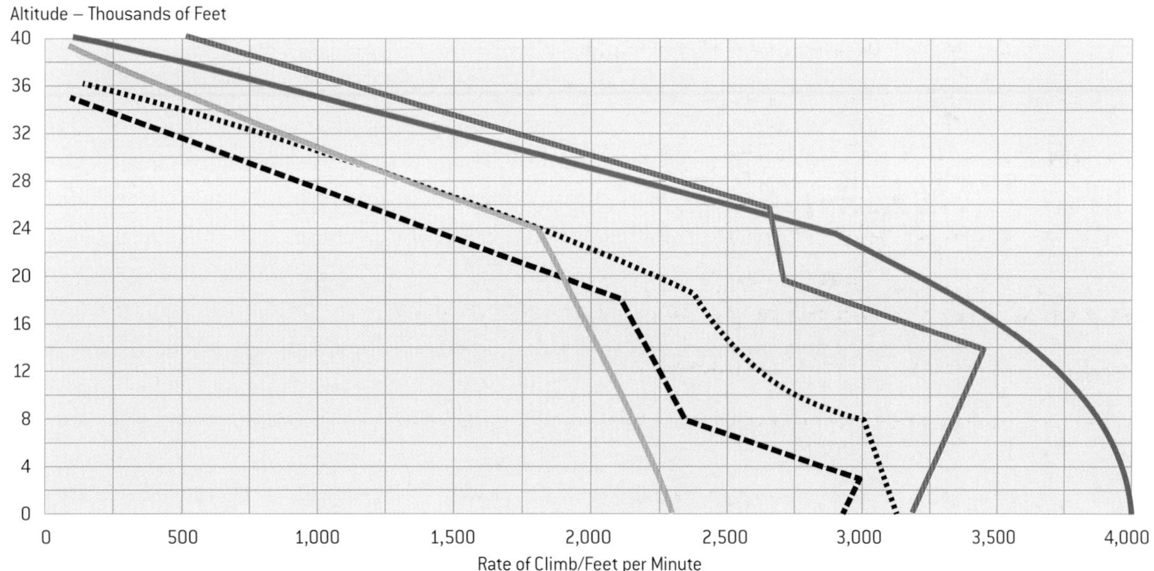

Published flight test results for the P-51B-15 and C-5 flown without racks and with the Packard V-1650-7 engine installed were not found. The test results from the lengthy flight testing of a P-51D-15 for range calibration with wing racks for external stores have been substituted for two reasons. Firstly, use of wing racks are more representative of actual performance of the P-51B/C/D in the ETO. Secondly, the flight tests were conducted with a take-off gross weight of 9,760lb. That gross weight was nearly identical to a fully loaded P-51B with maximum internal fuel (269gal, including the 85gal fuselage fuel tank), ammunition and oil. The fully loaded gross weight for such a P-51B was 9,679lb. The finding is fortuitous because the actual performance and drag values are the same for both types at the same gross weight and with the same engine type.

The Bf 109G-6's DB 605A engine was cleared for 1.42ata boost. Additionally, the DB 605AS engine was also installed to deliver 20mph greater speed at altitudes above 20,000ft. Collectively, the Bf 109G of early 1944 had a better rate of climb and a higher top speed than the G-model of 1943.

The new Fw 190A-8 became the most versatile and widely produced A-model variant. It was heavier, with more power available on take-off and widespread use of the MW 50 to increase maximum combat power. During 1944 the A-8 was deployed against the Eighth and Fifteenth Air Forces primarily as a "bomber destroyer", with heavy armor protection and widespread fitment of the Mk 108 cannon.

P-38J-15 with Allison V-1710-89/-91 engines at 60" MP WEP

- Gross weight at take-off – 17,363lb, versus maximum internal combat gross weight of 17,699lb
- 410gal of internal fuel. 55gal leading edge tanks installed
- No wing racks – clean

This P-38J-15 was tested at 98 percent full combat load at take-off. Therefore, the maximum climb rate results were nearly 200ft feet per minute "optimistic/non-conservative" for 60" MP. That said, the V-1710-89/-91 could achieve 60" in the ETO after the carburetor/aftercooler/oil cooler issues were resolved in spring 1944.

P-47D-10 with Pratt & Whitney R-2800-63 engine at 56" MP WEP with water injection

- Gross weight at take-off – 13,200lb, versus maximum internal combat gross weight of 13,582lb
- 305gal of internal fuel
- No wing racks – clean

This P-47D-10 was also tested 382lb under full combat load at take-off. The maximum climb rate results were perhaps 200ft per minute "optimistic/non-conservative". The primary difference from the earlier P-47C/D was the installation of the water injection kit to boost manifold pressure from 52" to 56" MP.

P-51B-15 and P-51D-15 with Packard Merlin V-1650-7 engine at 67" MP WEP

- Gross weight at take-off – 9,760lb (P-51D-15 tested), versus maximum internal combat gross weight of 9,720lb for P-51B-15
- 269gal of fuel including 85gal fuselage fuel tank
- Wing racks installed for P-51D-15 during flight test

This P-51D (substitution for P-51B-15 because no flight tests without racks were found for the P-51B-15)[23] was flight tested at nearly the exact gross weight as the fully loaded P-51B-15 without wing racks and full internal fuel. To achieve this reduction, the fuselage fuel tank for the P-51D was filled with only 25gal of 85gal capacity. The values for both top speed and rate of climb should be very close to each other, and representative of the April-May 1944 capabilities for both the P-51B-15 and P-51D-5.

Bf 109G-6 with DB 605AS at WEP 1.42ata boost

- Gross weight at take-off – 3,250kg, versus maximum internal combat gross weight of 3,129kg
- 106gal (approximately) internal fuel
- No Schloß 503 rack – clean

This Bf 109G-6/AS with DB 605AS and MW 50 boost was tested three percent above normal full internal combat load, and presented test results are therefore pessimistic for rate of climb. The climb rate achievement value for a normally loaded Bf 109G-6 without the Schloß 503 should be closer to 3,800ft per minute.

Fw 190A-8 with BMW 801D-2 at WEP 1.42ata

- Gross weight at take-off – 4,200kg, versus maximum internal combat gross weight of 4,200kg
- 162gal(approximately) of internal fuel
- No ETC 501 rack – clean

The Fw 190A-8 was flight tested at 100 percent of its fully loaded weight, with full internal fuel tanks and ammunition. As such, the performance values presented are as expected for normal operations without the ETC 501 rack.

Comparison III – P-51B versus the XP-51

The XP-51F Lightweight Mustang was first flown during the Comparison I period and extensively tested prior to D-Day. It was strongly considered as the future USAAF interceptor to replace the P-38J in late 1943. One of the two fatal deficiencies prohibiting a production contract, which became apparent during flight testing in early 1944, was the lack of necessary internal fuel capacity. By the time of its first flight, P-51B-1/-5 long-range escort Mustangs had been modified to an internal capacity of 269gal, compared to the XP-51F's maximum of 180gal in the wings. There was no room for an internal fuselage tank.

The second major issue was a deep distrust by Materiel Command of the structural integrity of the Lightweight Mustang, designed to RAF standards. That said, the structural integrity of a combat-loaded XP-51F at 7,550lb was better than

Comparison II (April–May 1944) – Level Speed Performance

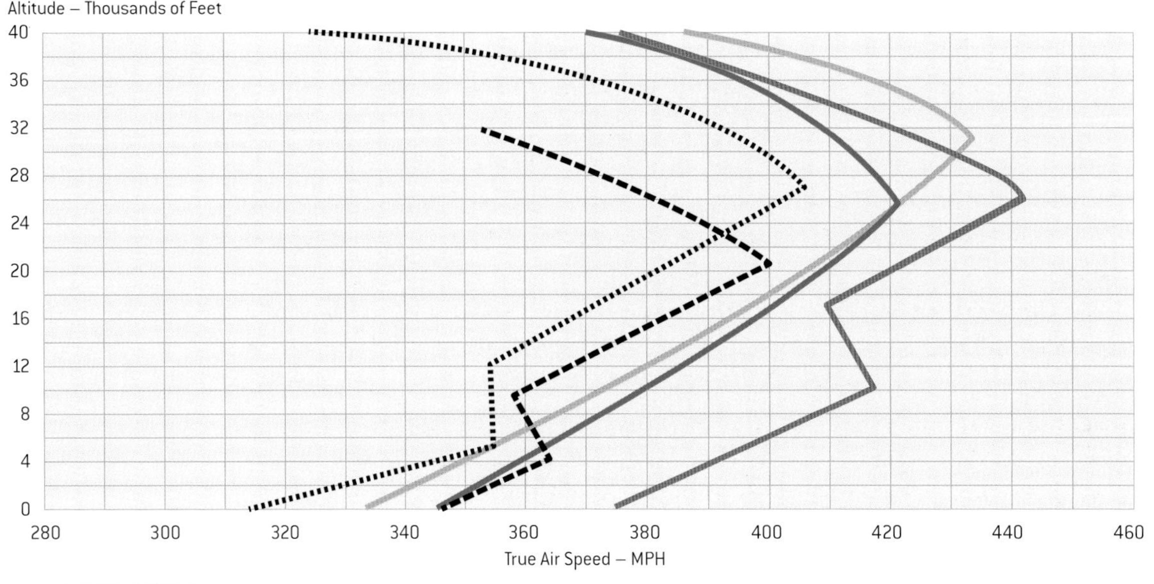

Comparison II (April–May 1944) – Rate of Climb Performance

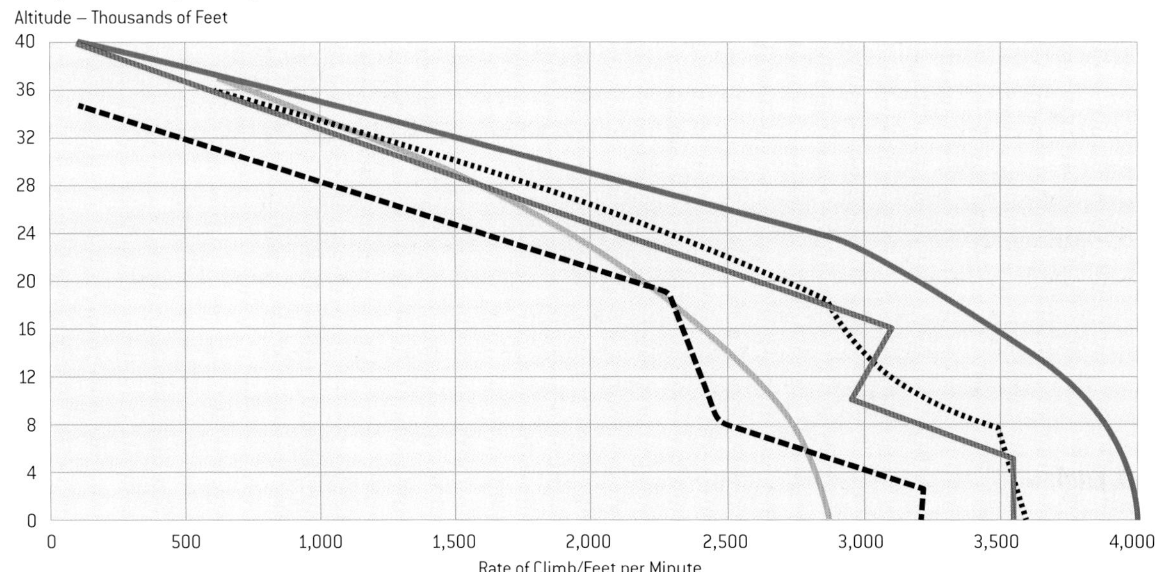

a P-51B (or D) at normal combat loading at 9,600lb. It was not, however, designed, nor adequately stressed, to add an additional 350lb to 550lb behind the cockpit. Additionally, the structural re-design requirements to add the extra weight for more internal fuel capacity was the primary reason for the creation of the P-51H, fitted with an additional 50gal internal fuselage fuel tank. That design, which began at about the same time as the completion of the XP-51F, required increasing the weight of the newer Mustang from 7,550lb (fully loaded combat weight) for the XP-51F to 9,600lb for the fully loaded (with internal fuel only) combat weight of the P-51H.

At the flight test weight of 6,286lb (minimum fuel, no guns or ammunition, especially prepared external surfaces and no wing racks), the XP-51F attained a maximum rate of climb of more than 5,500ft per minute.[24] For full internal combat weight of 7,550lb at 61" MP for the Packard Merlin V-1650-3 engine, with wing racks, the XP-51F achieved a rate of climb of 4,600ft per minute at 14,600ft and a top speed of 460mph at 31,000ft. The flight test comparisons shown in Comparison III are for the following conditions:[25]

P-51B-5 at 8,400lb (100gal fuel, no ammunition) with Packard Merlin V-1650-3, 61" Hg at 3,000rpm, clean – no racks
XP-51F at 6,930lb (105gal fuel, no ammunition) with Packard Merlin V-1650-3, 61" Hg at 3,000rpm, clean – no racks

Had the XP-51F moved to serial production, it would have entered combat in late 1944 with performance capabilities (top speed, climb, ceiling, dive and turn) approximate to the Bf 109G-10, Bf 109K, Ta 152H and Griffon-powered Spitfire XIV, but with a far greater range. As a reference, the fully loaded XP-51F had a wing loading of 32lb per square foot. As for the even higher performing XP-51G with the Rolls-Royce R.M.14 SM Merlin engine, it could not have entered production much earlier than the P-51H, the first of which was delivered in February 1945. By comparison, the XP-51G at 7,265lb (fighter condition with half fuel load of 105gal), with the R.M.14 SM engine at combat power of 72" Hg, had a rate of climb of 5,750ft per minute at 7,500ft and a top speed of 495mph at 22,800ft altitude. At 80" Hg, the maximum rate of climb at the same weight was nearly 6,500ft per minute at 4,000ft and a service ceiling of 46,000ft.

II. Engine Variations, Mustang Gross Weight Variations and Performance Charts – Allison and Packard Merlin[26]

The engine tables on pages 327 and 329 are for all the NAA-built Mustangs from 1940 through 1944 but do not include the Merlin R.M.14 SM (for XP-51G), the Merlin 65 and 66 (for Mustang I conversions to Mustang X), the Merlin 100 installed in the Mustang III by the RAF, the Packard Merlin V-1650-9 (for the P-51H), or the V-1650 -11 for the XP-82. Nor do they address the Allison V-1710-119 for the XP-51J.

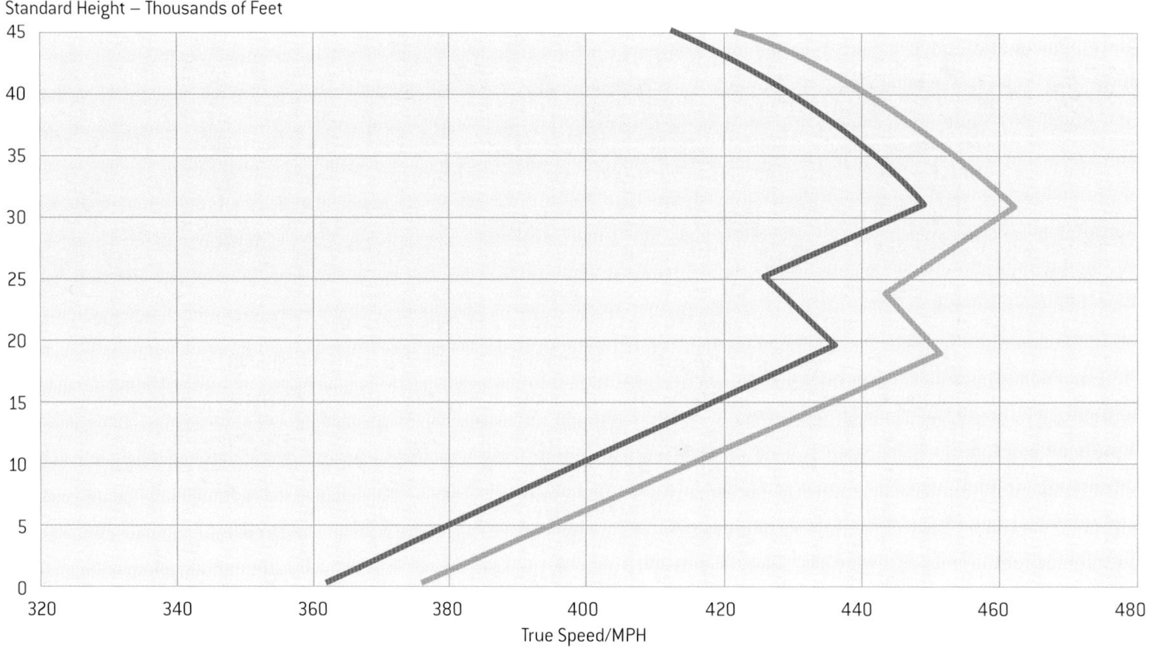
Comparison III (XP-51F vs P-51B-5) – Top Speed – Military Power
Standard Height – Thousands of Feet
45
40
35
30
25
20
15
10
5
0
320
340
360
380
400
420
440
460
480
True Speed/MPH
P-51B V-1650-3, 61" Hg, 3,000rpm, GW = 6,930lb
XP-51F V-1650-3, 61" Hg, 3,000rpm, GW = 6,930lb

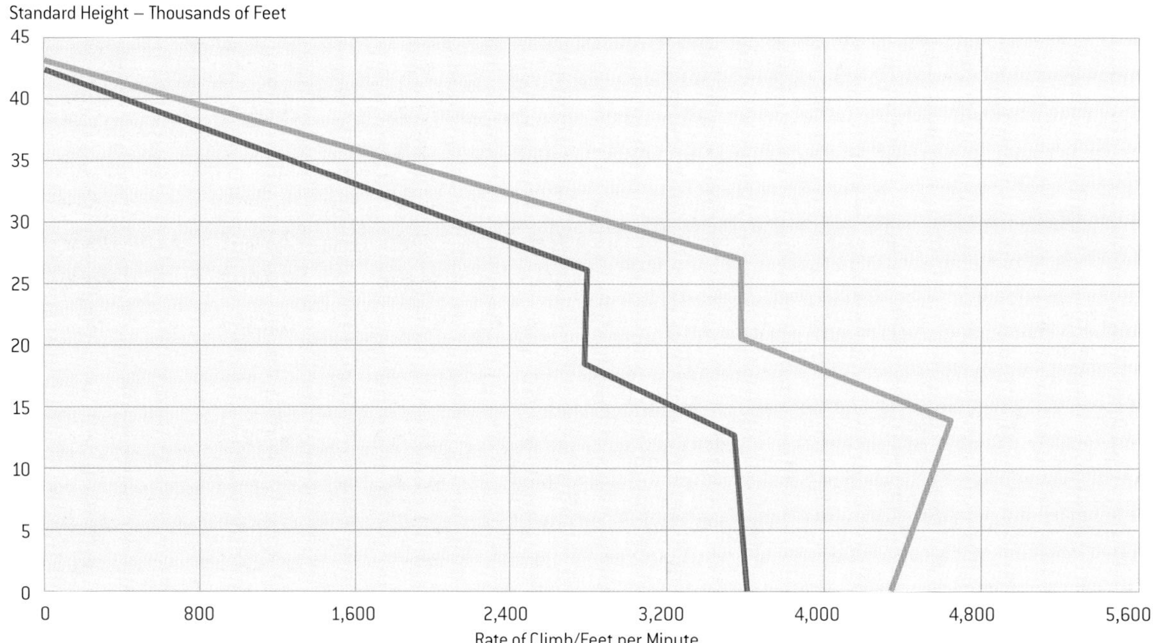
Comparison III (XP-51F vs P-51B-5) – Rate of Climb Performance – Military Power
Standard Height – Thousands of Feet
45
40
35
30
25
20
15
10
5
0
0
800
1,600
2,400
3,200
4,000
4,800
5,600
Rate of Climb/Feet per Minute
P-51B-5 V-1650-3, 61" Hg, 3,000rpm, GW = 6,930lb
XP-51F V-1650-3, 61" Hg, 3,000rpm, GW = 6,930lb

Mustang Engine Types and Ratings						
Mustang Model	Engine Type/No.	Power Rating	Brake HP*	Altitude - feet	RPM/MP ("Hg)	SC Type and Stage
	Allison V-1710 w GR= 0.5:1					1 Stage and 1 Speed
X73, XP-51 NA-73/-81, P-51	V-1710-39/F3R	T.O.	1,120	Sea Level (SL)	3,000/44.5	
		Mil.	1,220	10,500	3,000/44.5	
		Normal*	1,100	11,000	2,600/37.2	
P-51A	V-1710-81/F20R	T.O.	1,200	SL	3,000/52.0	
		Combat	1,330	11,800	3,000/57.0	
		Mil.	1,125	14,600	3,000/44.2	
		Normal*	1,000	13,800	2,600/38.3	
A-36	V-1710-87/F21R	T.O.	1,325	SL	3,000/47.0	
		Combat	1,500	2,500	3,000/52.0	
		Mil.	1,325	5,400	3,000/46.5	
		Normal*	1,100	6,600	2,600/41.0	
	Packard Merlin w GR= 0.479					2 Stage and 2 Speed
XP-51B, P-51D-NA, P-51B/C, XP-51F	V-1650-3	T.O.	1,380	SL	3,000/67	Low Bl.
		Combat	1,600	15,600	3,000/67	Low Bl.
		Combat	1,380	29,000	3,000/67	High B.
		Mil.	1,490	13,700	3,000/61	Low Bl.
		Mil.	1,210	25,800	3,000/61	High Bl.
		Normal*	1,110	17,400	2,700/46	Low Bl.
		Normal*	950	29,500	2,700/46	High Bl.
P-51B/C and P-51D/K	V-1650-7	T.O.	1,490	SL	3,000/67	Low Bl.
		Combat	1,720	6,250	3,000/67	Low Bl.
		Combat	1,505	19,250	3,000/67	High Bl.
		Mil.	1,590	8,500	3,000/61	Low Bl.
		Mil.	1,370	21,400	3,000/61	High Bl.
		Normal*	1,180	11,300	2,700/46	Low Bl.
		Normal*	1,065	23,400	2,700/46	High Bl.

Note: Maximum Continuous Power is expressed as Normal* in the chart above. This setting was most typically used for sustained climb and fast cruise.

For flight performance coupled with engine type and horsepower to be of important benefit for comparison purposes, the gross weight at take off or at the altitude of interest must be taken into context. For example, Mustangs in fighter condition typically have reduced fuel and ammunition load-outs when compared to maximum combat weight or overload weight. The most important weight condition for basis of comparisons is the fully loaded internal gross weight with full internal fuel load and full ammunition load – as might be expected when combat is initiated at the most vulnerable state when external tanks are dropped, and the Mustang must rely on the total quantity of fuel remaining to return to base after combat.

The table on page 329 has the maximum gross weight at take off for each Mustang produced at NAA for full internal load out. The table below should be used to place the following performance charts in context when presenting maximum rate of climb for each Mustang for the gross weights at take-off – and assuming climb is initiated from sea level with the gross weights as shown. You may note that some Mustangs are near maximum internal load, some less. To put the relative climb rate in context, rate of climb is proportional to the power available and inversely proportional to weight.

The three individual charts on pages 330 and 331 illustrate A.) the climb performance of the various Allison-powered Mustangs, B.) corresponding increases in climb performance for the Packard Merlin engines in the P-51B/C/D/K and H at max continuous power (2,700 RPM at 46" manifold pressure, and C.) The relative Merlin engine performance at maximum power combat settings available before 150 octane fuel was approved in the spring of 1944. The significant improvement between the climb rate at maximum continuous power to preserve the engine and War Emergency Power is shown only for the P-51A at 57" Hg for 1,330hp, as noted in the top graph on page 330 titled "Climb Performance of Allison Powered Mustangs at Typical Combat Weights." All the other climb rate plots are for max continuous power.

The gross weight for the P-51A at normal (max continuous power) of 8,500lb is 100lbs less than table value, so the rate of climb is as expected. The gross weight for the Mustang I is significantly higher from specifications (8,955 versus 8,670) to more closely evaluate the performance of the V-1710-39 versus the A-36 at the same weight (8,955 versus 8,955lb) with the V-1710-87. The A-36 gross weight as presented in the legend is very nearly 100 percent of the above table value of 8,905lb.

These charts were contributed by the Robert Gruenhagen Collection.

Mustang Variation Gross Weight Build Up (in pounds)						
	Mustang I	**Mustang IA, P-51**	**A-36**	**P-51A**	**P-51B/C w/85gal tank**	**P-51D/K w/85gal tank**
Empty Wt.	6,278	6,550	6,624	6,433	6,988	7,150
Trapped Fluids	61	61	61	61	65	65
Pyrotechnics	4	6	6	6	6	6
Gun Sight	4	4	4	4	6	6
85gal Tank	0	0	0	0	55	55
Guns						
0.30cal at 25 each	100	0	0	0	0	0
0.50cal at 69 each	276	0	414	276	276	414
20mm at 100 each	0	300	0	0	0	0
Bomb Racks	0	0	26	26	26	32
Basic Wt.	6,723	6,921	7,135	6,806	7,422	7,728
Useful Wt.						
pilot	200	200	200	200	200	200
Oil	60	60	90	90	90	90
Ammunition						
0.30cal at 1lb/5	400	0	0	0	0	0
0.50cal at 1lb/3	267	0	400	420	420	620
20mm at 3lb/5	0	300	0	0	0	0
Fuel						
Wings Tanks	1,020	1,080	1,080	1,080	1,104	1,104
Fus. Tank	0	0	0	0	510	510
Gross Wt.	8,670	8,561	8,905	8,596	9,746	10,252
Without 85gal Fuse.Tank					9,181	

TOP RIGHT To set a baseline for comparison of the climb performance between the Mustang I, the P-51, the A-36 and the P-51A, the three plots (P-51A, Mustang I and A-36) for normal climb power are at the gross weights cited in the body of the chart. Only the P-51A plot on the left is at full Emergency War Power of 57" Hg at full combat load-out weight. It adequately displays the difference between WEP climb rates from normal (maximum continuous-non combat) approximate gross weight.

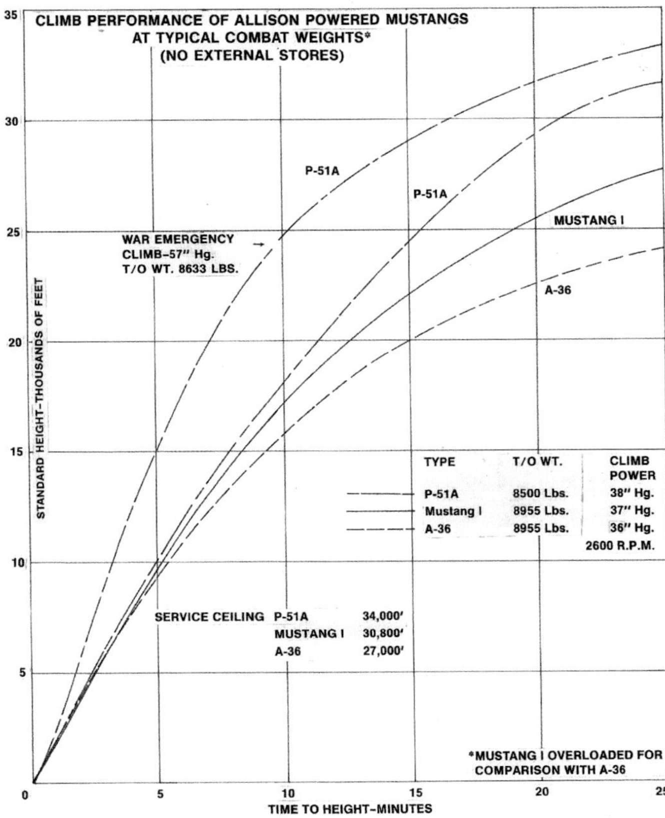

RIGHT The plots of rate of climb/time to altitude for the three major Packard Merlin powered production variants (P-51B, P-51D, P-51H) at maximum continuous (normal) power serves to show how little difference there is between each rate of climb at the same gross weight, with different V-1650 engine variants. The horsepower difference between the V-1650-3 and -7 and -9 at 46" Hg and 3,000hp is very small. Only when the significant boost (and rated horsepower) differences based on fuel rating and water injection at combat power come into effect does the rate of climb and time to climb significantly diverge.

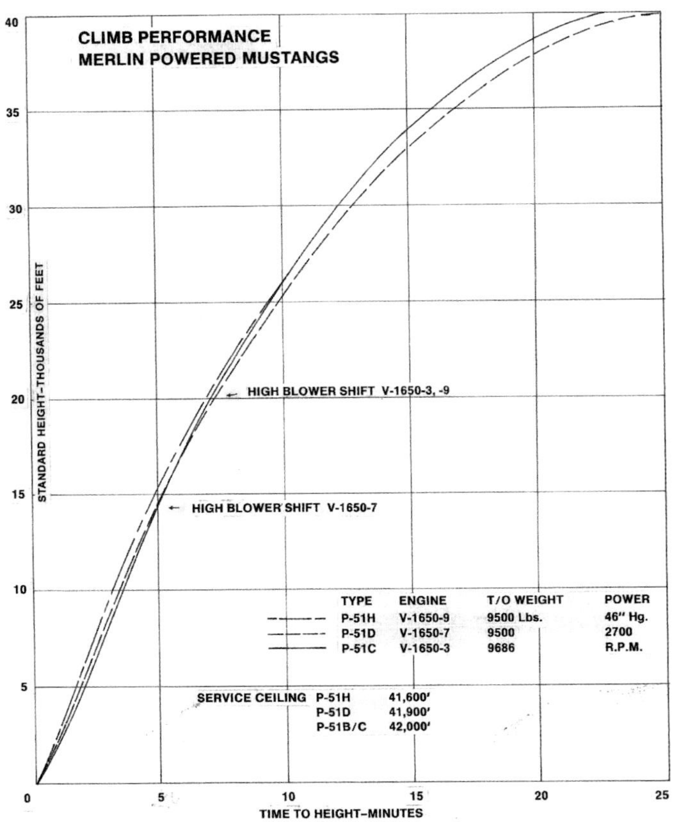

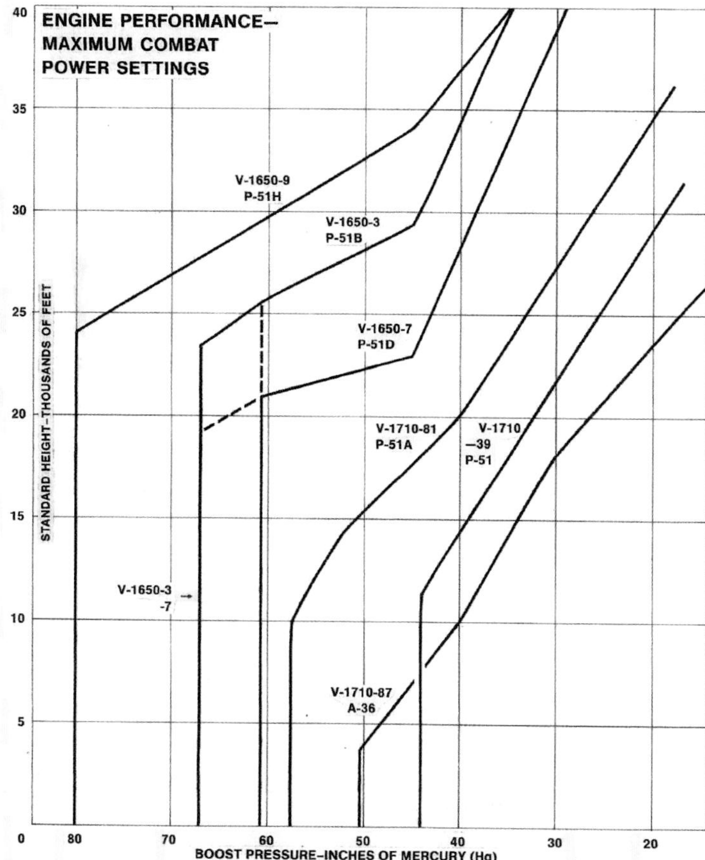

LEFT This graphic very well illustrates the difference in available manifold pressure available to each variant of the Allison V-1710 and Packard Merlin V-1650. It also serves to illustrate the shift in manifold pressure available from low blower to high blower as a function of altitude.

APPENDIX C

VICTORY CREDITS – USSTAF, NOVEMBER 1943 THROUGH JUNE 5, 1944

The official USAAF and RAF victory credit summations for all Mustang variants serving with the USSTAF and RAF ETO/MTO are presented here. The totals are derived from the exhaustive research of Dr. Frank Olynyk, Ph.D. All errors in manipulation of the database are solely the authors' responsibility.

A further explanation is in order based on dialogue with Colin Ford, historian for No. 268 Sqn, regarding the greater uncertainty surrounding RAF Mustang totals. Many early RAF Mustang claims were made when the aircraft were still serving with Army Co-operation Command. A number of questions pertaining to credited victories have surfaced as a result of ongoing research cross-referencing RAF claims against surviving Luftwaffe records, as well as other records from occupied countries. French Regional Gendarmerie, Belgian Gendarmerie, and Dutch Civil Defence all kept good local records of both Allied and Luftwaffe aircraft lost, often with accurate location, date and time references.[27]

In addition to the issues concerning the correlation of claims with eventual victory credits, the type of Mustang (I, IA or II) involved was less clear. This problem notwithstanding, the very fine work undertaken by Dr. Frank Olynyk and Christopher Shores in respect to RAF/Commonwealth Mustang victory credits is also presented here.

VIII/IX Fighter Command					
USSTAF ETO 1943	**P-38**	**P-47**	**P-51B/C**	**Spitfire**	**Grand Total**
November	24	81	0	0	105
December	5	78	9	0	92
Total 11–12/43	29	159	9	0	197
1944					
January	32	144	43	0	219
February	32.5	233	89.5	0	355
March	26	175	251	0	452
April	23	82	329	0	434
May	27.5	118	433.5	0	579
June 1–5	0	0	2	0	2
Total 1944	141	752	1,148	0	2,041
Total 11/43 to 6/5/44	170	911	1,157	0	2,238

XV Fighter Command					
USSTAF MTO 1943	**P-38**	**P-47**	**P-51B/C**	**Spitfire**	**Grand Total**
November	14	0	0	7	21
December	41	3	0	14	78
Total 1943	55	3	0	21	79
1944					
January	49	58	0	42	149
February	16	8	0	57	81
March	45	38	0	19	102
April	126	35	53	2	216
May	74	13	87	0	174
June 1–5	0	0	0	0	0
Total 1944	310	152	140	120	722
Total 11/43 to 6/5/44	365	155	140	141	801
USSTAF 11/43 to 6/5/44	535	1,066	1,297	141	3,039

Note: The tables above are cited for "USSTAF," which was conceptually initiated when the Fifteenth Air Force was activated in November 1943, although USSTAF was not an official organization in place until February 1944.

The total Mustang victory credits for commands other than the USSTAF, including the RAF, MAAF, and Tenth, Twelfth and Fourteenth Air Forces, are presented below.

	Twelfth Air Force			Tenth and Fourteenth Air Forces		
MTO 11/43 to 6/6/44	A-36	P-51/F-6	CBI 11/43 to 6/6/44	A-36	P-51/F-6	P-51B/C
1942	0			0	0	0
1943	2			2	0	0
1/1/44 to 6/6/44	0			0	53	4
Total MTO	2		Total CBI	2	53	4

	RAF MTO		RAF ETO	
MTO 8/42 to 6/6/44	Mustang I	ETO 8/42 to 6/6/44	Mustang I	Mustang III
1942	0	1942	3	0
1943	3	1943	28	0
1/1/44 to 6/6/44	0	1/1/44 to 6/6/44	4	27.75
Total MTO	3	Total ETO	35	27.75

APPENDIX D

TACTICAL ORDER OF BATTLE – USAAF, RAF, AND MAAF MUSTANG UNITS

I. USAAF – Tactical and Escort fighter groups that were assigned Mustangs for combat operations, 1943 through June 5, 1944

Groups – Eighth and Ninth Air Force – ETO	Mustang Type	First recorded Mustang operations date (approximate)	Tactical Assignment
4th FG	P-51B	February 28, 1944	Escort – Eighth Air Force
339th FG	P-51B	April 30, 1944	Escort – Eighth Air Force
352nd FG	P-51B	April 9, 1944	Escort – Eighth Air Force
354th FG	P-51B	December 1, 1943	Escort – Eighth Air Force/TDY Ninth Air Force
355th FG	P-51B	March 9, 1944	Escort – Eighth Air Force
357th FG	P-51B	February 12, 1944	Escort – Eighth Air Force
359th FG	P-51B	May 5, 1944	Escort – Eighth Air Force
361st FG	P-51B	May 13, 1944	Escort – Eighth Air Force
363rd FG	P-51B	February 24, 1944	Escort – Eighth Air Force/TDY Ninth Air Force
10th PG (Reconnaissance)	F-6C	January 1944	Reconnaissance
67th PG (Reconnaissance)	F-6B/C	November 1943	Reconnaissance
Groups – Twelfth Air Force – MTO			
27th FBG	A-36/P-40/P-47	August 1943	Tactical Support
68th TRG	P-51/F-6A	November 1942	Tactical Reconnaissance
86th FBG	A-36/P-47	June 1943	Tactical Support
Groups – Fifteenth Air Force – MTO			
31st FG	P-51B	April 1944	Escort – Fifteenth Air Force
52nd FG	P-51B	May 1944	Escort – Fifteenth Air Force
325th FG	P-51B	May 1944	Escort – Fifteenth Air Force
Groups – Tenth Air Force – CBI			
1st Air Commando Group	P-51A	March 1944	Tactical Support/Escort
8th TRG	F-6	March 1944	Tactical Reconnaissance
311th FG	A-36/P-51A	August 1943	Tactical Support/Escort
Group – Fourteenth Air Force – CBI			
23rd FG	P-51A/P-51B	November 1943	Tactical Support/Escort

II. RAF – Mustang squadrons assigned from January 1942 through June 5, 1944[28]

Squadron/Unit	Mustang type	First recorded date for Mustangs	Tactical assignment
No. 2 Sqn (AC) No. 2 Sqn (FR)	Mustang I Mustang IA	January 1942 February 1944	Army Co-operation/Tactical Reconnaissance
No. 4 Sqn (AC)	Mustang I	May 1942	Army Co-operation/Tactical Reconnaissance
No. 16 Sqn (AC)	Mustang I	April 1942	Army Co-operation/Tactical Reconnaissance
No. 19 Sqn (F)	Mustang III	January 1944	Escort – Fighter-Bomber
No. 26 Sqn (AC)	Mustang I	January 1942	Army Co-operation/Tactical Reconnaissance
No. 41 OTU	Mustang I	January 1942	Army Co-operation and Reconnaissance Training
No. 63 Sqn (AC) No. 63 Sqn (FR)	Mustang I Mustang IA	January 1942 November 1943	Army Co-operation/Tactical Reconnaissance
No. 65 Sqn (F)	Mustang III	December 1943	Escort – Fighter-Bomber
No. 122 Sqn (F)	Mustang III	January 1944	Escort – Fighter-Bomber
No. 129 Sqn (F)	Mustang III	March 1944	Escort – Fighter-Bomber
No. 168 Sqn (AC) No. 168 Sqn (FR)	Mustang I Mustang IA Mustang I	November 1942 August 1943 February 1944	Army Co-operation/Tactical Reconnaissance
No. 169 Sqn (AC)	Mustang I	June 1942	Army Co-operation/Tactical Reconnaissance
No. 170 Sqn (AC) No. 170 Sqn (FR)	Mustang I Mustang IA	June 1942 August 1943	Army Co-operation/Tactical Reconnaissance
No. 171 Sqn (FR)	Mustang IA	September 1942	Army Co-operation/Tactical Reconnaissance
No. 213 Sqn (F)	Mustang III	May 1944	Escort – Fighter-Bomber
No. 225 Sqn (AC)	Mustang I	May 1942	Army Co-operation/Tactical Reconnaissance
No. 231 Sqn (AC)	Mustang I	March 1943	Army Co-operation/Tactical Reconnaissance
No. 239 Sqn (AC)	Mustang I	May 1942	Army Co-operation/Tactical Reconnaissance
No. 241 Sqn (AC)	Mustang I	March 1942	Army Co-operation/Tactical Reconnaissance
No. 260 Sqn (F)	Mustang III	April 1944	Army Co-operation/Tactical Reconnaissance
No. 268 Sqn (AC) No. 268 Sqn (FR)	Mustang I Mustang IA	April 1942 July 1943	Army Co-operation/Tactical Reconnaissance
No. 306 Sqn (FS)	Mustang III	April 1944	Escort – Fighter-Bomber
No. 309 Sqn (AC)	Mustang I	August 1942	Army Co-operation/Tactical Reconnaissance
No. 315 Sqn (FS)	Mustang III	March 1944	Escort – Fighter-Bomber
No. 316 Sqn (FS)	Mustang III	April 1944	Escort – Fighter-Bomber
No. 400 Sqn (AC)	Mustang I	June 1942	Army Co-operation/Tactical Reconnaissance
No. 414 Sqn (AC) No. 414 Sqn (FR)	Mustang I	June 1942	Army Co-operation/Tactical Reconnaissance
No. 430 Sqn (AC) No. 430 Sqn (FR)	Mustang I	January 1943	Army Co-operation/Tactical Reconnaissance
No. 516 Sqn (AC)	Mustang I	April 1943	Combined Operations Training
No. 613 Sqn (AC)	Mustang I	April 1942	Army Co-operation/Tactical Reconnaissance

BIBLIOGRAPHY

PUBLICATIONS

Arnold, H. H., General of the Air Force, *Global Mission*, Harper & Brothers, New York, 1949

Atwood, Leland J., "The P-51. The Real Story Rebuttal," *Journal of the American Aviation Historical Society*, summer 1997

Blake, Steve, *The Pioneer Mustang Group: The 354th Fighter Group in World War II*, Schiffer Publishing, Ltd., Atglen, Pennsylvania, 2008

Bodie, Warren, *The Lockheed P-38 Lightning*, Widewing Publications, Hiawassee, Florida, 1991

Bodie, Warren, *Republic's P-47 Thunderbolt: From Seversky to Victory*, Widewing Publications, Hiawassee, Florida, 1994

Bowers, Peter M., *Curtiss Aircraft, 1907–1947*, Naval Institute Press, 1987

Caldwell, Donald, *The JG 26 War Diary – Volume Two 1943–1945*, Grub Street, London, 1998

Caldwell, Donald, *Day Fighters in Defense of the Reich – A War Diary, 1942–1945*, Frontline Books, an imprint of Pen & Sword Books Ltd., Barnsley, South Yorkshire, 2013

Caldwell, Donald, and Muller, Dr. Richard, *The Luftwaffe Over Germany: Defense of the Reich*, Greenhill Books/Lionel Leventhal Ltd., London, 2007

Carson, Col Leonard K., *Pursue and Destroy*, Sentry Books Inc., Granada Hills, California, 1978

Coningham, Arthur, "The Development of Tactical Air Forces," *Royal United Services Institute Journal* XCIII (May 1946)

Copp, Dewit S., *A Few Great Captains*, Doubleday, Garden City, New York, 1980

Copp, Dewit S., *Forged in Fire*, Doubleday, Garden City, New York, 1981

Craven, Wesley F. and Cate, James L., *The Army Air Forces in World War II, Volume II – Europe:* Torch *to* Pointblank *(August 1942 to December 1943)*, University of Chicago Press, Chicago, 1951

Davis, Richard G., *Carl A. Spaatz and the Air War in Europe*, Center for Air Force History, Washington, D.C., 1992

Dean, Francis H., *America's One Hundred Thousand: US Production Fighters of WWII*, Schiffer Publishing, Ltd., Atglen, Pennsylvania 2007

Delve, Ken, *The Mustang Story*, Arms & Armour, an imprint of Cassell & Co., London, 1999

Frederickson, John M., *Warbird Factory: North American Aviation in WWII*, Zenith Press, an imprint of Quarto Publishing Group USA, Minneapolis, Minnesota, 2015

Freeman, Roger A., *Mighty Eighth War Diary*, Jane's, New York, 1981

Freeman, Roger A., *Mighty Eighth War Manual*, Jane's, New York, 1984

Freeman, Roger A., *The Mighty Eighth: A History of the US 8th Army Air Force*, Doubleday & Company, New York, 1970

Fry, Garry L., and Ethell, Jeffrey L., *Escort to Berlin: The 4th Fighter Group in World War II*, Arco Publishing Inc., New York, New York, 1980

Greer, Thomas, *AHS Study 89: The Development of Air Doctrine in Army Air Corps, 1917–1941*, Office of Air Force History, Washington, D.C., 1985

Green, William, *Famous Fighters of the Second World War*, Hanover House, Garden City, New York, 1960

Greil, Manfred and Dressel, J., *Focke-Wulf Fw 190/Ta 152*, Motorbuch Verlag, Stuttgart, 1995

Gruenhagen, Robert W., *Mustang: The Story of the P-51 Fighter*, Arco Publishing Company, New York, 1969

Haight, John M., *American Aid to France: 1938–1940*, Athaneum, New York, 1970

Hazen, R. M., "The Allison Aircraft Engine," *SAE Journal*, 49:5 pp.498–500

Holmes, Harry, *The World's Greatest Air Depot: The US 8th AF at Warton 1942–1945*, Airlife Publishing, Ltd., Shrewsbury, Shropshire, 1998

Horkey, Edward J., "The P-51 – The Real Story," *Journal of the American Aviation Historical Society*, fall 1996

Horkey, Edward J., *The Real Stuff: The Story of the P-51 Mustang*, Olive Press Publications, Los Olivos, California, 1999

Jackson, Robert, *Mustang: The Operational Record*, Smithsonian Institution Press, Washington, D.C., 1993

LeMay, Curtis, and Cantor, McKinley, *Mission with LeMay: My Story*, Doubleday, Garden City, New York, 1965

Lloyd, Ian., *Rolls-Royce: The Merlin at War*, McMillan, London, 1978

Ludwig, Paul A., *P-51 Mustang: Development of the Long-Range Escort Fighter*, Chevron Publishing Ltd., Crowborough, East Sussex, 2003

Marshall, Bill, *Angels, Bulldogs and Dragons: The 355th Fighter Group in World War II*, Champlin Fighter Museum, Mesa, Arizona, 1984

Marshall, James William, *Our Might Always: The 355th Fighter Group in World War II*, Schiffer Publishing, Ltd., Atglen, Pennsylvania, 2014

McFarland, Stephan L., and Newton, Wesley P., *To Command the Sky: The Battle for Air Superiority Over Germany, 1942–1944*, Smithsonian Institution Press, Washington, D.C. and London, 1991

Meekoms, Ken J., *British Air Commission and Lend Lease*, Air-Britain Historians, Tonbridge, Kent, 2001

Meekoms, Ken J. and Morgan, E. B., *British Air Specifications File: British Military and Commercial Aircraft Specifications 1920–1949*, Air-Britain Historians, Tonbridge, Kent, 1994

Meyers, Robert, "The Packard Merlin Story," *Rolls-Royce Magazine*, September 1980

Miller, Kent D., *Fighter Units and Pilots of the 8th AF: September 1942–May 1945*, Schiffer Publishing, Ltd., Atglen, Pennsylvania, 2001

Miller, Kent D., *The 363rd Fighter Group in World War II: In Action over Europe with the P-51 Mustang*, Schiffer Publishing, Ltd., Atglen, Pennsylvania, 2002

Millikan, Clark B., Ph.D., *Aerodynamics of the Airplane*, GALCIT Aeronautical Series, John Wiley & Sons, Inc., 1941

Murray, Russ, *Kindelberger*, North American Rockwall Management Association of Southern California, 1972

Muir, David, Southern Cross Mustang – The P-51s of Australia and New Zealand, Glen Waverly Vic, Red Roo Models, 2009

Olmsted, Merle C., MSgt USAF (Ret), *To War With the Yoxford Boys: The Complete Story of the 357th Fighter Group*, Eagle Editions, Ltd., Hamilton, Montana, 2004

Olynyk, Dr. Frank, PhD, Stars and Bars, first published by Grub Street, London,1995

NAA Executive Staff, *Mustang Chronology*, North American Aviation, May 15, 1965

NAA Skywriter article, Vol. XI, No. 22, October 26, 1951

Neal, Robert, *Packard as and Aero Engine Builder*, Aircraft Engine Historical Society

Nowarra, Heinz, *Aircraft and Legend: Focke-Wulf Fw 190 & Ta 152*, First published by Motorbuch Verlag, 1987 (German language). English edition by Haynes Publishing Group, Sparkford, Somerset, 1989

Nowarra, Heinz J., *The Aircraft and Legend: Messerschmitt Bf 109*, First published by Motorbuch Verlag, 1986, (German language). English edition by Haynes Publishing Group, Sparkford, Somerset, 1989

Parton, James, *Air Force Spoken Here: General Ira Eaker and the Command of the Air*, Adler and Adler Publishers Inc., Bethesda, Maryland, 1986

Powell, Robert H. & Ivie, Thomas – 352nd Fighter Group Association, *The "Bluenosed Bastards" of Bodney: A Commemorative History*, Taylor Publishing Company, Dallas, Texas, 1990

Rust, Kenn C., *Fifteenth Air Force Story: in World War II*, Historical Aviation Album Publication, Temple City, California, 1976

Ruud, Ralph, "Horizontal Jigs Boost Aircraft Panel Production," article written for NAA, date unknown

Speer, Albert, *Inside the Third Reich*, Weidenfeld & Nicolson, London, 1970

Vincent, Col J. G., *Chronological Development of Packard Built Rolls-Royce Merlin Engine*, Packard Motor Car Company, Aircraft Engineering Division, Detroit, Michigan, 1945

Wagner, Ray, *Mustang Designer: Edgar Schmued and the Development of the P-51*, Orion Books, New York, 1990

NUMBERED NACA, NAA & USAF STUDIES

Primary Documents, including North American Aviation, Inc. and NACA Reports

NAA Report NA-1592, "Preliminary Design Data Single Place Pursuit - (Allison Engine)," R. H. Rice, March 11, 1940

NAA Report NA-1593, "High Speed of Allison – Powered Export Pursuit," Irving Ashkenas, Edward Horkey, March 18, 1940

NAA Report NA-1620, "Detail Specifications for XP-51 Airplane," Paul Anderson, April 24, 1940

NAA Report NA-1691, "Flight Test Report XP-51/Mustang I," August 26, 1941

NAA Report NA-1778-A, "Design Data Ground Attack Airplane (Modified NA-73) – Preliminary," Edgar Schmued, January 28, 1942

NAA Correspondence Report – "Production Differences Between NA-73 and NA-83," R. H. Rice, D. H. Dixon, March 20, 1942

NAA Correspondence Report – "Similarities of A-36 (NA-97) to Other Pursuit Models," R. N. Johnson, Engineering Planning, June 2, 1942

NAA Report NA-5534 "Performance Calculations for Model P-51B-1-NA," Edward J. Horkey, Louis L. Waite, October 19, 1943

NAA Report NA-5822, "Aerodynamic Dimensional Data P-51B/C Airplane," L. L. Waite, Chief Technical Section, August 6, 1943

NAA Report NA-8449 "Performance Calculations for Model P-51D-15-NA Airplane," Edward J. Horkey, Louis L. Waite, December 1, 1944

NAA Field Services Bulletin 73-95, "Modification of a P-51 Series Airplane for Long Range Operation," January 12, 1944

NAA Report, "Airfoil Development and Structure Within the Cambered Surface," Roy A. Liming, Head of Engineering-Lofting mathematics, North American Aviation, Aeronautical Digest Publishing Corporation, New York, 1948

NACA Advanced Confidential Report ACR No. L5A30, "Summary of Drag Results from Recent Langley Full-Scale Tunnel tests of Army and Navy Airplanes", by Roy H. Lange, February 1945 at Langley Memorial Aeronautics Laboratory, Langley, Virginia.

NACA Memorandum Report for the Army Air Forces Materiel Command "Tests of the North American P-51B airplane in the NACA full-scale tunnel", by Charles H. Kelly, December 1943, at Langley Memorial Aeronautics Laboratory, Langley, Virginia.

NACA Report ACR No. 4K02, "Correlation of the Drag Characteristics of the P-51B Airplane Obtained from High Speed Wind Tunnel and Dive Tests," James M. Mission and William T. Hamilton, August 1944

NACA Wartime Report by Howard F. Matthews, "Elimination of Rumble from the Cooling System of a Single-Engine Pursuit Airplane," Ames Aeronautical Laboratory, Moffett Field, California, August 1943.

USAAF Reports and Correspondence

(The great majority of USAAC/USAAF documents were retrieved from USAFHRC, Maxwell AFB, Alabama, and the US National Archives, Washington, D.C.)

AAF Report S.T. No. 4-43-23-1, "Program for Test to Determine the Effect of an Additional 85 gallons of Internal Fuel on the Performance and Handling of the P-51B Airplane," December 8, 1943

ACTS Intelligence Department, "The Use of Aviation in the Spanish War," USAF HD 248.501-79B

ACTS Report "Aerial Warfare in Spain, February 1937," p.5 in USAF HD 248.501-79

"Report of Inspection, Performance and Acceptance of North American Airplane Model XP-51," Captain Logan, A. C.

Report of the Army Air Forces Board, AAFSAT, Orlando, FL., "Report on P-51A-1," June 8, 1943, AFHRC 245.64

Report of the Army Air Forces Board, AAFSAT, Orlando, FL., "Report on Operational Suitability of the P-51A-1 Airplane," June 8, 1943, AFHRC 245.64

Proceedings of a Board of Officers for the Purpose of Evaluating Current Dive Bomber Now in Production, Army Air Corps Evaluation Board, March 22, 1943

Report of a Board of Officers, with Recommendations to the Future Development of Pursuit Aircraft, Its Accessory Equipment and Operational Equipment to C/AAF, Washington, D.C., October 27, 1941

Memorandum Report, "Pursuit Single Engine (XP-51) A.C. No. 41-038," dated December 27, 1941

Memorandum Report, "Pursuit Single Engine (P-51) A.C. No. 41-37320," dated June 16, 1942

Memorandum Report "Tactical Suitability of the P-51 Type Airplane," dated July 13, 1942

Memorandum Report for Army Air Forces, "Flight Tests of Modifications to Improve the Aileron Control Characteristics of a North American XP-51 Airplane, (A.C. No. 41-38)," NACA Langley Air Memorial Laboratory, Langley, Virginia, M. D., White and Herbert H. Hoover, June 20, 1942

USAF Historical Study 85 – U.S. Army Air Forces Victory Credits, World War II

MISCELLANEOUS DATABASES, PAPERS, TRANSCRIPTS, AND PRESENTATIONS

Atwood, Leland J, "Origins of the Mustang," August 8, 1973

Chilton, Robert C., Flight Logbooks – April 1940 to December 31, 1944

Collins, Martin, *Lee Atwood: An Oral History*, Recorded by Martin Collins, North American at El Segundo, California, January 19, 1989

Ford, Lowell F., "Allison Agony" (unpublished article)

Ford, Lowell F., "The Extended Range Mustang," NAA Retirees Bulletin, 2007 No. 4 Winter, pp.11–13

Lednicer, David, and Gilchrist, Ian, "A Retrospective: Computational Aerodynamics Methods Applied to the P-51 Mustang," American Institute of Aeronautics and Aerospace, AIAA-91-32888

Marshall, Bill, "Summary of Combat Operations – 355th FG and 8th AF FC 1943 through April 25th, 1945," Spitfireperformance.com, April 2006

Marshall, Bill, "Battle Over Munich – April 24, 1944," Spitfireperformance.com, September 2007

Olynyk, Dr. Frank, PhD, Victory Credits #5, AAF in Europe (ETO) – WW2; Victory Credits #6, AAF in Mediterranean (MTO) – WW2

Olynyk, Dr. Frank, PhD, Victory Credits – All Theatres During WW2, a comprehensive database provided by Dr.Olynyk

Neal, Robert, "Packard as an Aero Engine Builder," Aircraft Engine Historical Society

Schmued, Edgar, "The Preliminary Design of the Mustang," taped presentation at Long Beach City College Auditorium, Long Beach, California, January 30, 1970

Schmued, Edgar, "The Design of the P-51 Mustang," manuscript, 1985

Thornton, J. Kendall, and Beerer, Joseph G., "Method of Computing Dimensions of Airplane Engine Intercoolers," McDonnell Aircraft Corporation, date unknown

ENDNOTES

INTRODUCTION

1 Davis, Richard G., *Carl A. Spaatz and the Air War in Europe*, Center for Air Force History, Washington, D.C., 1992; Hereinafter Davis, *Spaatz*. Also Craven, Wesley, and Cates, James, *The Army Air Forces In World War II, Volume II – Europe:* Torch *to* Pointblank *(August 1942 to December 1943)*, University of Chicago Press, Chicago, 1951, p.715; Hereinafter Craven and Cates, *AAF–WWII, Vol II.*
2 Rust, Kenn, *Fifteenth Air Force Story*, Historical Aviation Album Publication, Temple City, CA, pp.5–6; Hereinafter Rust, *15th AF.*
3 USAAF Material Command instructions to Modification Centers, November 23–26, 1943.
4 Ibid.
5 NAA Drawing No. 102-000010.
6 Robert Chilton Logbook entries for both NA-102 P-51B-1 43-12102 and NA-106 P-51D 42-106539. Lowell Ford copy. Hereinafter Chilton

CHAPTER 1

1 Wagner, Ray, *Mustang Designer – Edgar Schmued and the Development of the P-51*, Orion Books, New York, 1990, p.31. Hereinafter Wagner, *Mustang Designer*.
2 Ibid, p.33.
3 Murray, Russ, *Kindelberger*, North American Rockwall Management Association of Southern California, 1972; Hereinafter Russ Murray, NARMA.
4 Schmued, Edgar, "The Preliminary Design of the Mustang," taped presentation at Long Beach City College Auditorium, 1970; Hereinafter Schmued, "PDM."
5 Murray, Russ, "J. Kindelberger," Presentation Data Group of Columbus Division of NAA, under direction of E. L. Foster, via interviews with J. H. Kindelberger, 1972. The Boeing Company.
6 Ibid.
7 Ibid.
8 "Lee Atwood: An Oral History": Recorded by Martin Collins, North American, at El Segundo, CA, January 19, 1989. Hereinafter Atwood, "Oral History" via The Boeing Company.
9 *NAA Skywriter* article, Vol. XI – No. 22, dated October 26, 1951. Also Ralph Ruud "Horizontal Jigs Boost Aircraft Panel Production," an article written for NAA, date unknown. The Boeing Company.
10 Gruenhagen, Robert W., *Mustang: The Story of the P-51 Fighter*, Arco Publishing Company, New York, 1969, p.39; Hereinafter Gruenhagen, *Mustang*.
11 Horkey, Edward, *The Real Stuff: The Story of the P-51 Mustang*, Olive Press Publications, Los Olivos, CA, 1999, p.11; Hereinafter Horkey, *The Real Stuff.*
12 Ibid, pp.97–100.
13 Ibid, pp.34–35.
14 Schmued, Edgar, *The Design of the P-51 Mustang*, manuscript dated 1985, pp.1–7; Hereinafter Schmued, *DM*.

CHAPTER 2

1 Wagner, *Mustang Designer*, p.5.
2 NAA – Atwood Drawing P-189 and Detail Specification 5-3 and 4-1-1935, respectively. The Boeing Company.
3 Wagner, *Mustang Designer*, pp.40–41.
4 Russ Murray, NARMA.
5 "J. H. Kindelberger" (Columbus, OH, 1972 collection of notes).
6 NAA "O" Report. The Boeing Company.
7 RAE Farnborough, Meredith, F. W., "Note on the Cooling of Aircraft Engines with Special Reference to Ethylene Glycol Radiators Enclosed in Ducts," Aeronautical Research Council R&M 1683, 1935.
8 Capon, R. S., "The Cowling of Cooling Systems," Aeronautical Research Council R&M 1702. 1936.
9 Nowarra, Heinz, *The Aircraft and Legend: Messerschmitt Bf 109*, p.14; Hereinafter Nowarra, *Bf 109.*
10 Schmued, *DM*, p.9.
11 Wagner, *Mustang Designer*, p.39.
12 Green, William, *Famous Fighters of the Second World War*, Hanover House, Garden City, New York, 1960, p.26.
13 Draft of article, "An Engineer's Perspective on the Mustang," by J. Leland Atwood, p.3. Patti Hyatt files via The Boeing Company.
14 Shamburger, Page and Christy, Joe, "The Curtiss Hawks," University of Michigan, 1971, p.112.
15 Bowers, Peter M., *Curtis Aircraft 1907–1947*, Naval Institute Press, 1979.
16 Daniel Whitney, *V For Victory: The Story of the V-1710.*
17 Hsiung, James and Levine, Steven, *China's Bitter Victory: the War with Japan 1937 to 1945*, M.E. Sharpe, 1992.
18 NAA "O" Report, and NA-44 project notes dated March 3, 1938. The Boeing Company.
19 NAA "O" Report. The Boeing Company.
20 Allison to NAA correspondence dated February 2, 1938 through February 8, 1938. The Boeing Company.
21 Arnold, H. H., General of the Air Force, *Global Mission*, Harper & Brothers, New York, 1949, pp.139 and 165; Hereinafter Arnold, *Global Mission*.

22 Millikan, Clark B., Ph.D., "Performance Estimate for Idealized 1938 Pursuit Airplane," p.7.
23 Millikan, Clark B., Ph.D., *Aerodynamics of the Airplane*, GALCIT Aeronautical Series, John Wiley & Sons, Inc., 1941.
24 NAA correspondence, letter from JHK to HHA, dated April 15, 1938. The Boeing Company.
25 Mustang Chronology, NAA Executive Staff, May 15, 1965. NAA via The Boeing Company. Hereinafter NAA Executive Staff, *Mustang Chronology*.
26 Allison to NAA, beginning July 20, 1938, NAA Memo dated July 20, 1938. The Boeing Company.
27 Gruenhagen, "Mustang," p.31.
28 Wagner, *Mustang Designer*, pp.40–41.
29 NAA Kindelberger letter to Ernest Breech dated February 1, 1940. The Boeing Company.
30 Arnold, *Global Mission*, p.169.
31 NAA Preliminary Design Data Report 1405 & Performance Calculations Report 1413 for Single Seat Pursuit, dated October 7, 1938. The Boeing Company.
32 Dean, Francis, *America's One Hundred Thousand: US Production Fighters of WWII*, Schiffer Publishing, Ltd., Atglen, Pennsylvania 2007, p.82; Hereinafter referred to as Dean, *AOHT*.
33 Ibid, p.237.
34 Kindelberger letter to Arnold, dated October 15, 1938. The Boeing Company.
35 Ford, Lowell, *Allison Agony*, p.2.
36 Arnold, *Global Mission*, pp.177–178.
37 NAA Executive Staff, "Mustang Chronology."
38 Meekoms, Ken. and Morgan, E. B., *British Air Specifications File: British Military and Commercial Aircraft Specifications 1920–1949*, Air-Britain Historians, Tonbridge, Kent, 1994.
39 Meekoms, Ken, *British Air Commission and Lend Lease*, Air-Britain Historians, Tonbridge, Kent, 2001; Hereinafter Meekoms, *British Air Commision and Lend Lease*.
40 Reitlinger, G., *The Final Solution*, Valentine, Mitchell & Co., 1953.
41 USAAC HQ Plans Division issued FM-1-15 "Tactical and Technology of Air Fighting" one year later, in September 1940, but conclusions drawn early in Emmons Board discussions. Greer, Thomas, AHS Study 89, "The Development of Air Doctrine in Army Air Corps, 1917–1941," pp.130–131; Hereinafter Greer, *AHS-89*.
42 Ludwig, Paul, *P-51 Mustang: Development of the Long-Range Escort Fighter*, Chevron Publishing, 2003, p.29; Hereinafter Ludwig, *LREF*.
43 NAA internal memos and correspondence dated March 1939 through April 1940. The Boeing Company.
44 Dean, *AOHT*, pp.80–82.
45 Meekoms, *British Air Commission and Lend Lease*.
46 The conclusion drawn by the authors is that the sketches and concepts evolved into P-509 in December 1939.
47 Wagner, *Mustang Designer*, p.20.
48 Ibid, p.20.
49 Greer, Thomas, *AHS Study 89 – The Development of Air Doctrine I Army Air Corps 1917-1941*, p.131. Hereinafter Greer, AHS-89
50 Bodie, Warren, *Republic's P-47 Thunderbolt: From Seversky to Victory*, Widewing Publications, Hiawassee, FL, 1994, pp.99–100; Hereinafter Bodie, *P-47*.
51 Horkey, Edward, "The P-51 – The Real Story," *Journal of the American Historical Society*, fall 1996, p.2; Hereinafter Horkey, *P-51*.
52 Meekoms, *British Air Commission and Lend Lease*.
53 NAA Files, Preliminary Designs including P-509. The Boeing Company.
54 NAA "O" Report. The Boeing Company.
55 Atwood letter to Horkey, dated September 1, 1994. Patti Hyatt files via The Boeing Company.
56 NAA Archive Microfiche Roll BD, Meter 43. The Boeing Company
57 ACTS Report "Aerial Warfare in Spain, February 1937," p.5 in USAF HD 248.501-79.
58 ACTS Intelligence Department, "The Use of Aviation in the Spanish War," p.16 in USAF HD 248.501-79B.
59 Arnold, *Global Mission*, pp.188–189.
60 McFarland, Stephan, and Newton, Wesley, *To Command the Sky: The Battle for Air Superiority Over Germany, 1942–1944*, Smithsonian Institution Press, Washington and London, 1991, p.37; Hereinafter McFarland and Newton, *TCTS*.
61 Greer, *AHS-89*, pp.116–117.
62 Ibid, p.117.
63 Ibid, p.123.
64 Ibid, p.125.
65 Arnold, *Global Mission*, p.74.
66 Dean, *AOHT*, p.146.
67 Ibid, p.237.
68 Ibid, p.197.
69 Greil, Manfred and Dressel, J, *Focke-Wulf Fw 190/Ta 152*, Motorbuch Verlag, Stuttgart, 1995; Hereinafter Greil and Dressel, *Fw 190*.
70 NAA Internal memos from Lowell Ford Collection.
71 Schmued, P-509 Preliminary Design, reference Reel no. AC133, circa February 1940. NAA Drawings from Boeing Archive.
72 Schmued, "Preliminary Design Data, Single Seat Pursuit (Allison Engine), General," circa mid-1939. The Boeing Company.
73 Kindelberger letter to Breech, dated January 2, 1940. The Boeing Company
74 Schmued, Edgar, combined references to "DM," pp.10–12, and "PDM"; Hereinafter Schmued, "PM&DM." The Boeing Company.
75 NAA Drawings for P-509, reference Reel no. AC 133 and 134, dated March 10, 1940. The Boeing Company
76 Schmued, NAA Report No. 1592 "Preliminary Design Data, Single Place Pursuit, (Allison Engine)," March 11, 1940. The Boeing Company
77 Horkey, Edward, Ashkenas, Irving, and Mellinger, G. R., NAA Report No. 1593 "High Speed of Allison-Powered

Export Pursuit," dated March 18, 1940. The Boeing Company.
78 Ibid, p.3.
79 Ibid, p.5.
80 Ibid, p.3.
81 Ibid, pp.8–13.
82 Haight, John M., "American Aid to France," pp.210–212, Athaneum, New York, 1970.
83 Ibid, p.222.
84 Draft notes "Origin and Evolution of the Mustang" by J. Leland Atwood, former Chairman, North American Aviation and Rockwell International; Hereinafter Atwood, *Origin and Evolution of the Mustang.*
85 NAA/NACA correspondence dated March 18, 1940, Lowell Ford Collection. The Boeing Company.
86 Atwood, *Origin and Evolution of the Mustang.*
87 NACA Letter to NAA, dated April 7, 1940. The Boeing Company.
88 Atwood, *Origin and Evolution of the Mustang.*
89 NAA Contract Files, dated April 11, 1940. The Boeing Company.
90 Atwood proposal draft for meeting with Burdette Curtiss, Patti Hyatt files, dated April 11, 1940. The Boeing Company.
91 Ibid.
92 Ibid. Page 5 of draft discussion points for Atwood-Wright meetings, Patti Hyatt files dated April 11, 1940. The Boeing Company.
93 NAA internal correspondence, Internal memo Atwood to Rice, May 1940, The Boeing Company.
94 Horkey, *The Real Stuff*, p.108.
95 Breech letter to Kindelberger, dated May 13, 1940. The Boeing Company.
96 Fogerty, Dr. Robert, "USAF Study 91 – Biographical Studies of General Officers, 1917–1952"; Hereinafter Fogerty, "USAF-91."
97 McFarland and Newton, *TCTS*, p.37.
98 Arnold, *Global Mission*, p.199.

CHAPTER 3

1 Schmued, *PM&DM.*
2 Reference future Atwood telex to B. Wright, Curtiss Wright GM, dated April 21, 1941. The Boeing Company.
3 NAA and BPC correspondence dated May 4, 1940. The Boeing Company.
4 Schmued, *PM&DM.* The Boeing Company.
5 NAA Engineering Organization Chart, Chief Engineer Office, dated July 2, 1941. The Boeing Company.
6 JHK to EB cable, dated April 17, 1940. The Boeing Company.
7 Ford, *Allison Agony*, p.3.
8 Ibid, p.3.
9 Ibid, p.4.
10 Drawing 73X-00002 before first revision, dated April 18, 1940. Boeing Archives.
11 NAA Design Data Report 1620, P. Anderson, NAA correspondence and enclosures, dated April 24, 1940. The Boeing Company.
12 JLA memo re Project Accounting NA-73, dated April 24, 1940. The Boeing Company.
13 NAA NA-73 project logs from PD, ED, and FD, dated August 15 through October 5, 1940. The Boeing Company.
14 NAA memo, Bowen to Rice dated May 1, 1940. The Boeing Company.
15 Drawing 73X-00002 and Report Design Data and Performance Reports, 1622 and 1623, dated April 29, 1940. The Boeing Company.
16 NAA memos and correspondence, dated March 1939 through May 4, 1940. The Boeing Company.
17 Collectively, memos drawn from NA-73 project files between May 3 and 18, 1941. The Boeing Company.
18 Ibid.
19 Ibid.
20 Vincent, J. G., "Chronological Development of Packard Built Rolls-Royce Merlin Engine"; Hereinafter Vincent, *Packard Merlin.*
21 Arnold, *Global Mission*, p.199.
22 Neal, Robert, "Packard as an Aero Engine Builder," Aircraft Engine Historical Society, pp.3–5; Hereinafter Neal, *Packard-Engine Builder.*
23 Vincent, *Packard Merlin.*
24 NAA NA-73X project logs and memos from PD, ED, and FD, dated May 13 through August 5, 1940. The Boeing Company.
25 Ibid.
26 The Boeing Company Also available via aircorpslibrary.com.
27 Arnold, *Global Mission*, p.197.
28 Horkey, *The Real Stuff*, p.37.
29 Vincent, "Packard Merlin," also Neal, *Packard Engine Builder*, pp.3–5.
30 Ford, *Allison Agony*, p.3.
31 Atwood to B. Wright, NA-73X/73 project files, dated March 22, 1941. Collection of Patti Hyatt, Exec. Sec'y LJA. The Boeing Company.
32 NAA NA-73 project logs from PD, ED, and FD, dated August 15 to October 5, 1940. The Boeing Company.
33 Series of letters and memorandums from Dutch Kindelberger re: NA-73 progress, Allison issues, and US Army interest, dated May 23, 1940 to May 23, 1941. The Boeing Company.
34 NAA "O" Report. The Boeing Company.
35 Fredrickson, John M., *Warbird Factory*, Zenith Press, an imprint of Quarto Publications, Minneapolis, MN, p.42.
36 Ford, *Allison Agony*, p.5.
37 Collectively from NAA NA-73X/NA-73 project logs and memos from PD, ED, and FD, dated August 19 through November 20, 1940. The Boeing Company.
38 Jackson, Robert, *Mustang: The Operational Record*, Smithsonian Institution Press, Washington, D.C., 1993, p.10; Hereinafter Jackson, *Mustang.*

39 Ibid.
40 Letter from R. F. Pyne of the BPC to NAA Noble Shropshire, Contact Administrator, dated December 9, 1940. The Boeing Company
41 Neal, "Packard Engine Builder," pp.3–5.
42 Davis, *Spaatz*, p.59.
43 Dean, *AOHT*, p.146.
44 Ibid, p.285.
45 Lowell Ford, "The Extended Range Mustang," p.3.
46 Ibid, pp.3–5.
47 E-mail exchange with Bob Gruenhagen regarding NAA factory serial number identities of the RAF "AG series."
48 Collectively from NAA NA-73X/NA-73 project logs and memos from PD, ED, and FD, dated January 1, 1941 through January 30, 1941. The Boeing Company.
49 Lednicer, David, and Gilchrist, Ian, "A Retrospective: Computational Aerodynamics Methods Applied to the P-51 Mustang," American Institute of Aeronautics and Aerospace paper AIAA-91-32888, pp.8–9; Hereinafter Lednicer and Gilchrist, *P-51*.
50 Collectively from NAA NA-73/83 project logs and memos from PD, ED, and FD, dated October 1, 1941 through June 30, 1942. The Boeing Company.
51 Wagner, *Mustang Designer*, p.84.
52 Kindelberger to BAC, dated March 11, 1941. The Boeing Company.
53 Ludwig, *LREF*, p.70.
54 Collectively from NAA NA-73X/NA-73 project logs and memos from PD, ED, and FD, dated February 1, 1941 through March 30, 1941. The Boeing Company.
55 Chilton logbook, Book 3, June 11, 1940 through April 4, 1941.
56 Horkey, *The Real Stuff*, pp.35–37.
57 NAA correspondence file, R-R Elor to Kindelberger, dated April 19, 1941. The Boeing Company.
58 Collectively from NAA NA-73X/NA-73 project logs and memos from PD, ED, and FD, dated January 1, 1941 through June 30, 1941. The Boeing Company.
59 Chilton logbook.
60 Collectively from NAA correspondence, Engineering, and NA-73 project logs and memos from PD, ED, and FD, dated December 9, 1940, through August 30, 1941. Via Lowell Ford.
61 NAA Correspondence log, May through July 1941. The Boeing Company.
62 BPC letter from T.B. Stebbings to NAA, dated August 6, 1941. The Boeing Company
63 Frederickson, John M., *Warbird Factory*, Zenith Press, an imprint of Quarto Publications, Minneapolis, MN 55401.
64 NAA "O" Report. The Boeing Company.
65 Vincent, *Packard Merlin*.
66 Copp, Dewit S., *Forged in Fire*, Doubleday, Garden City, New York, 1981, p.157; Hereinafter Copp, *Forged in Fire*.
67 Neal, *Packard Engine Builder*, pp.6–7.
68 Wagner, *Mustang Designer*, p.78.
69 NAA interoffice memo, Schleichter to Rice, dated October 23, 1941. The Boeing Company.
70 Boylon, "USAF Study 136 – Development Long Range Escort Fighter," p.51; Hereinafter Boylon, *USAF-136*.
71 Jackson, *Mustang*, p.8.
72 Ibid, p.8.
73 Interoffice memos from Kindelberger to Rice, Rice to JHK, dated November 19, 1941 and December 4, 1941. The Boeing Company.
74 Collectively from NAA NA-73 project logs and memos between AAC-MD and PD, ED, and FD, dated August 1, 1941 through December 30, 1941. The Boeing Company.
75 Materiel Command memo to NAA, dated January 1942. The Boeing Company.
76 Futrell, Robert, "USAF Study 24, A Study in the Control of Tactical Airpower and Command of Observation Aviation," 1952, pp.11–17; Hereinafter Futrell, *AHS-24*.
77 Ibid, p.15.
78 Ibid, pp.126–127.
79 Greer, *AHS-89*, pp.122–123.
80 Futrell, *AHS-24*, pp.15–17.
81 Ludwig, *LREF*, p.74.
82 Fogerty, *USAF-91*, Volume I.
83 Haight, John, *American Aid to France*, pp.210-222.
84 James Parton, *Eighth Air Force Spoken Here: General Ira Eaker and the Command of the Air*, p.126; Hereinafter Parton, *8th AF-Eaker*; Arnold, *Global Mission*, p.169; Copp, *Forged in Fire*, p.421.
85 Greer, *AHS-89*, p.122–124 and Appendix I.
86 Schmued, *PM&DM*.
87 Ludwig, *LREF*, p.130.
88 Dean, *AOHT*, p.330.
89 Greil and Dressel, *Fw 190*.
90 Bodie, Warren, *Lockheed P-38 Lightning*, Bookbuilders Ltd., Hong Kong, 1991, pp.71–72; Hereinafter Bodie, *P-38*.
91 Ibid, pp.207–208.
92 Caldwell, Donald, and Muller, Richard, *The Luftwaffe Over Germany: Defense of the Reich*, Greenhill Books/Lionel Leventhal Ltd., London, 2007, p.46; Hereinafter Caldwell and Muller, *TLWOG*.
93 Dean, *AOHT*, p.330.
94 Chilton logbook.
95 Kindelberger to Echols, dated January 28, 1942. The Boeing Company.
96 Project notes
97 Chilton logbook.
98 NAA Memo – Rice to Atwood, dated February 23, 1942. The Boeing Company.
99 Atwood letter to Hunt, dated February 26, 1942. The Boeing Company.
100 Gruenhagen, *Mustang*, p.71
101 NACA letter to Rice, dated March 10, 1942. The Boeing Company.
102 Memorandum Report for Army Air Forces "Flight Tests of Modifications to Improve the Aileron Control Characteristics

of a North American XP-51 Airplane" (A.C. No. 41-38), by M. D. White and Herbert H. Hoover, June 20, 1942.
103 NAA to USAAF-MD, Rice to Gen Branshaw, dated June 18, 1942. The Boeing Company.
104 Chilton logbook.
105 NAA Correspondence, Re: Production Differences Between NA-73 and NA-83 Airplane, dated March 20, 1942. The Boeing Company.
106 NAA Project logs and memos for NA-73 Long Range Tanks, from PD/ED. The Boeing Company.
107 Chilton logbook.
108 Correspondence from CO 4th Interceptor Command, Bryan to Chief Air Corps, dated January 8, 1942. NARA via Walter Burchell.
109 Parton, *8th AF-Eaker*, p.126.
110 Arnold, *Global Mission*, p.377.
111 Boylon, *USAF-136*, p.136.
112 Toole, Virginia and Ackerman, Robert, USAF Study 62 "The Modification of Army Aircraft 1939–1945," p.15.
113 Boylon, *USAF-136*, p.114.
114 Boylon, *USAF-136*, p.73; USAF HD 202.2-11.
115 Greer, *USAF Study-91*, pp.122–124; Futrell, *AHS-24*, pp.13–15.
116 Ibid, p.124.
117 Letter, Col. Patrick Timberlake. Chief Production, USAAF-MD, to Col. Howard Craig Asst. Chief, Air Staff, Plans Division, dated March 5, 1942. Ludwig, *LREF*, p.74–75.
118 Ludwig, *LREF*, p.75.
119 Memo "Procurement of 500 North American P-51," from Brig Gen Fairchild, A/CS Director Military Requirements, to CG Material Command, Maj Gen Echols, dated April 19, 1942.
120 Ludwig, *LREF*, p.75.
121 Ludwig, *LREF*, pp.98–100.

CHAPTER 4

1 Extract from Memorandum to Hives, Lovesy, Dorey, Lappin, et al., on May 1, 1942. From Birch, David, *Rolls-Royce and the Mustang*, Rolls-Royce Heritage Trust Historical Series No. 9, 1987, p.10; Hereinafter Birch, *R-R & Mustang*.
2 Birch, *R-R & Mustang*, pp.12–13.
3 Birch, *R-R & Mustang*, extracts from Lappin letters dated June 3, 1942, to Ray Dorsey and Ernst Hives, pp.13–14.
4 Birch, *R-R & Mustang*, pp.16–19.
5 Birch, *R-R & Mustang*, p.26,
6 Birch, *R-R & Mustang*, p.14.
7 Jackson, *Mustang*, p.12.
8 AFDU Report No. 43, Tactical and Armament Trials – Mustang I Aircraft (AFC 128,) May 5, 1942.
9 NAA Internal memo from Atwood and Rice, "Re: XP-78 Contract Negotiations," dated May 8, 1942. The Boeing Company.
10 Arnold, *Global Mission*, p.377.
11 Atwood, *Origin and Evolution of the Mustang*.
12 NAA Executive Staff, "Mustang Chronology". Also sourced via NAA Project notes and memos, Preliminary Design, dated May 29 through May 30, 1942. The Boeing Company
13 BAC to NAA, letters re: Malcolm Hood, dated June 1 and July 2, 1942. The Boeing Company.
14 Wagner, *Mustang Designer*, p.90.
15 Transcribed telephone call between Chidlaw and Wolfe dated June 8, 1942. The Boeing Company Also ref Lappin letter to Dorey, June 2, 1942 in reference to Arnold's London visit.
16 Chilton logbook.
17 Memo from Rice to BG Branshaw, Materiel Division, dated June 18, 1942. The Boeing Company'
18 NAA "O" Report. The Boeing Company; Gruenhagen, "Mustang," p.196.
19 NAA correspondence file, to Kindelberger, dated July 9, 1942. The Boeing Company.
20 NAA "O" Report. The Boeing Company.
21 NAA memos between Rice and Atwood and Kindelberger for NA-101, dated May 12 through July 2, 1942. The Boeing Company.
22 E-mail exchange with Colin Ford, historian.
23 Chilton logbook, dated May 29 through July 31, 1942. The Boeing Company.
24 Letter from Gates, Tech Office, BAC, to Rice, dated August 1, 1942. The Boeing Company.
25 NAA letter from Kindelberger to Branshaw, dated August 3, 1942. The Boeing Company.
26 Birch, *R-R & Mustang*, p.29.
27 Birch, *R-R & Mustang*, reference footnote 23, p.27.
28 NAA Drawing D-12009, dated August 8, 1942. The Boeing Company.
29 NAA Legarra to BAC Frank Wallace, dated August 14, 1942. The Boeing Company.
30 AAF Memorandum Report "Tactical Suitability of the P-51 Type Airplane," Eglin Field, FL, dated July 13, 1942.
31 Dean, *AOHT*, pp.143 (P-38), and 231 (P-47).
32 USAAF Flight test results for P-51B/D, P-38G/H/J, P-47B/C/D on "Spitfire Performance.com," Mike Williams webmaster.
33 Interoffice Memo, BG Franklin Carroll, Chief, Experimental Engineering Section, Material Division, Wright Field to Assistant Technical Executive, dated August 14, 1942. CC to NAA engineering, The Boeing Company.
34 Chilton logbook.
35 Ibid
36 Gruenhagen, *Mustang*, p.195.
37 Kindelberger to Chidlaw, A/C of Staff, Materiel Command, dated August 26, 1942. The Boeing Company.
38 Letter from BG A. J. Lyons – CG VIII ATS, summarizing Material Command reports, to Ernst Hives, Rolls-Royce, dated August 29, 1942. The Boeing Company.
39 AAF Memorandum Report "Tactical Employment of Mustang P-51," APG, Eglin Field, dated August 26, 1942.
40 NAA Files, Col Chidlaw, Asst. Chief of Staff, Materiel Command to Gen Lyons, CG VIII ATS, dated August 27, 1942.

41 Memo from Col James Phillips, Exec. Officer, Manufacturing Division, Materiel Command, HQ-AAF, to Col Chidlaw. Asst. Chief of Staff, Experimental Engineering Branch, Eng. Sec., Materiel Command, HQ-AAF.
42 Birch, *R-R & Mustang*, p.29.
43 Memo for CG Mat.Cmd. From Dir/Mil. Req.; Subj: Production of P-51 airplanes to follow completion of 500 A-36s. Dated August 31, 1942, in AGC Central Files, 452.1.
44 NAA Letter from Legarra to (illegible), dated September 1, 1942. The Boeing Company.
45 NAA files, Loening Report to Harold Talbot, dated September 29, 1942.
46 NAA memo, re: Project NA-101 log, dated October 1, 1942. The Boeing Company.
47 Report from Lt Col Hitchcock to Stettinius, Asst. Ambassador to Britain, dated October 8, 1942. The Boeing Company.
48 NAA memo, re: Project NA-101 log, dated October 1, 1942. The Boeing Company.
49 NAA inter-office correspondence re: Dallas Plant Requirements, dated October 8, 42. The Boeing Company.
50 Letter from Lt Col Hitchcock to Asst. Amb. Stettinius, London, dated October 10, 1942. Birch, *R-R & Mustang*, p.37.
51 Ibid, pp.40–43.
52 Letter exchanges between GM VP DuPont, Sloan (GM COB), Brown and Hunt (Allison) dated November 23 through December 5, 1942.
53 Boylon, *USAF-136*.
54 Chilton logbook, November 13 through November 29.
55 Allison E. C. Newill to Materiel Command C. G. Branshaw, dated November 5, 1943. NAA files – The Boeing Company.
56 Copp, *Forged in Fire*, p.422. Also, Memo to the President from Gen H. H. Arnold, Subj: P-51; November 12, 1942. ACG Central Files.
57 NAA Report NA-5567 "Weight Comparison between Spitfire IX and P-51B," dated November 23.1942.The Boeing Company.
58 Schmued, *PM & DM*. The Boeing Company
59 NAA "O" Report. The Boeing Company
60 USAAF "Conference to Prescribe New Military Characteristics for Fighter Type Airplane," remarks on second day, pp.2–3.
61 From Schmued, *PM & DM*.
62 NAA "Structural Repair Instructions for A-36, P-51, F6, and TF51," AN 01-60-3, dated March 15, 1952.
63 E-mail dialogue between the authors and author Steve Brooking, dated January 5 through January 17, 2019.
64 E-mail exchanges with Bob Gruenhagen, December 2018.
65 Chilton logbook
66 Gruenhagen, *Mustang*, p.178.
67 Birch, *R-R & Mustang*, pp.41–44.
68 Victory credits and loss statistical data were sourced primarily from the works of Roger Freeman, *The Mighty Eighth War Diary*; Dr. Frank Olynyk, *Victory List # 5 & 6 – USAAF (Europe) and USAAF (Mediterranean), During WW2*; Ken Rust, *15th Air Force Story*; Kent Miller *Fighter Units & Pilots of the 8th Air Force*; Donald Caldwell *Day Fighters in Defence of the Reich*; *8th AF Victory Credits Board*; plus works by various authors for AAF Unit Histories as cited.
69 Freeman, Roger, *The Mighty Eighth War Manual*, Cassel & Company, London, 1984, pp.137–139; Hereinafter Freeman, *TM8WM*.
70 Freeman, *TM8WM*, pp.238, 239, and 7,.
71 Caldwell, Donald, *Day Fighters in Defense of the Reich: A War Diary, 1942–1945*, Frontline Books, an imprint of Pen & Sword Books Ltd., Barnsley, South Yorkshire, 2013 p.13; Hereinafter Caldwell, *DFIDOR*.
72 Arnold, *Global Mission*,
73 Collectively, Freeman, *TM8WM*, pp.239 and 210; Dr. Frank Olynyk, *Stars and Bars*, p.338.
74 Caldwell, *DF-IDOR*, p.11.
75 Copp, *Forged in Fire*, p.299.
76 Caldwell and Muller, *TLWOG*, p.60; Freeman, *TM8WM*.
77 Colin Ford, Historian for RAF No. 268 Sqn 1940–1946, via e-mail exchange September 2019.
78 Freeman, *TM8WM*, p.213.
79 Fry, Garry, and Ethell, Jeffrey l., *Escort to Berlin: History of the 4th Fighter Group*, ARCO Publishing, New York, 1980; Hereinafter Fry and Ethell, *4th FG*.
80 Miller, Kent, *Fighter Pilots and Units of the Eighth Air Force: September 1942 to May 1945*, Schiffer Publishing, Ltd., Atglen PA, 2001, p.216; Hereinafter Miller, *8th FC*.
81 Freeman, Roger, *The Mighty Eighth War Diary*, Jane's Publishing Company Ltd., London 1981, p.16; Hereinafter Freeman, *TM8WD*.
82 Ibid, p.19.
83 Eaker to Spaatz – Spaatz Extract Diary; also, Boylon, *USAF-136*, p.67.
84 Colin Ford, Historian RAF No. 268 Sqn 1940–1946, via e-mail exchanges September 2019.
85 Caldwell, *DF-IDOR*, p.22.
86 Freeman, *TM8WD*, pp.28–30.
87 General Laurence Kuter, CG of 1st BW, is also credited for the joint development with LeMay of the combat box and wing. McFarland and Newton, *TCTS*, p.92.
88 Caldwell, Donald, *The JG 26 War Diary*, Grub Street, London, 1996, p.315.
89 Colin Ford, Historian for No. 268 Sqn, RAF, 1940-1946 via e-mail to author August 2019.
90 Colin Ford, Historian No. 268 Sqn 1940-1946, via e-mail exchanges during September 2019.
91 Colin Ford, Historian for No. 268 Sqn 1940-46 via e-mail to author August 2019.
92 Gen Curtis LeMay & MacKinley Cantor, *Mission with LeMay – My Story*, pp.256–258.
93 McFarland and Newton, *TCTS*, p.10.
94 Dean, *AOHT*, p.285.
95 Prien, Jochen and Rodieke, Peter, *Messerschmitt Bf 109F, G &K Series: An Illustrated Study*, pp.57–62; Hereinafter Prien and Rodieke, *Bf 109*.

96 Bodie, *P-38*, p.84 and 146.
97 Bodie, *P-47*, pp.123–125.
98 Memo from Myers to Robert Lovett, dated March 28, 1942. Boylon, *USAF-136*, p.114.
99 Caldwell and Muller, *TLWOG*, p.56.
100 Ibid, p.57.
101 Dean, *AOHT*, p.330.
102 Prien and Rodieke, *Bf 109*, pp.57–58.
103 Bodie, *P-47*, p.221.
104 Greil and Dressel, *Fw 190.*
105 Prien and Rodieke, *Bf 109*, p.62.
106 Bodie, *P-47*, p.390.
107 Caldwell, *DFIDOR*, p.24.
108 Caldwell and Muller, *TLWOG*, p.68 and p.66, respectively.
109 Greil and Dressel, *Fw 190.*
110 "GAF Training of a Fighter Pilot," USAFHRC 220.6093-1, p.10.

CHAPTER 5

1 Birch, *R-R & Mustang*, p.49.
2 Ibid, p.46.
3 Liming, Roy, "Master Dimensions Book, P-51D," dated February 10, 1943. The Boeing Company via Mike Gleichman.
4 McFarland and Newton, *TCTS*, p.104.
5 Birch, *R-R & Mustang*, p.45–47.
6 NACA Wartime Report by Howard F. Matthews, "Elimination of Rumble from the Cooling System of a Single-Engine Pursuit Airplane," Ames Aeronautical Laboratory, Moffett Field, California, August 1943, p.4.
7 NAA "O" Report. The Boeing Company.
8 Individual Aircraft Record Cards for 41-37352 and 41-37421. USAFHRC.
9 Chilton logbook and test notes, dated May 1 through May 24, 1942.
10 Internal Memo, "Packard Merlin Engine Production" – Col Sessums, A/CS (Fighter) to Maj Gen Echols, AC/AS and CO Materiel Command, dated March 17, 1942.
11 Ludwig, *LREF*, pp.65–68.
12 NAA "O" Report. The Boeing Company.
13 Muir, David, *Southern Cross Mustang*, details conveyed to B. Marshall in series of e-mails, 2016.
14 Telex to NAA from Materiel Command, Branshaw, reference P-51B Delivery Sequence, dated June 22, 1943. The Boeing Company.
15 War Department Field Manual FM 100 20, Command and Employment of Air Power, War Department, July 21, 1943.
16 USAAF Materiel Command telex to Rice, ref. Project Change Order C-258 to NA-102 P-51B Spec to provide Bubble Canopy. NAA NA-102 and NA-106 project logs March 1 through December 17, 1943. The Boeing Company.
17 NA-102 Project Logs for C-258, dated 3-16 through 7-19-1943 for C-258-1, -2, and -3. The Boeing Company via Lowell Ford.
18 Boylon, *USAF-136*, p.91. Arnold to Giles with attached report from Assistant Sec. War, Robert Lovett.
19 Ibid, p.93.
20 Ibid, p.132.
21 NAA WSN dated June 19, 1943. The Boeing Company.
22 NAA WSN dated July 3, 1943. The Boeing Company.
23 R&R, Assistant C/AS MM&D, Materiel Division from Assistant C/AS OC&R, Req. Div., July 3, 1943. USAF HD 202.2-11.
24 NAA files, TWX from Gen Giles, Chief Air Staff, forwarded by Col Branshaw, Chief, Materiel Command, Wright Field, dated July 5, 1943. The Boeing Company.
25 Boylon, *USAF-136*, p.132.
26 NAA files, telex from MAT CMD, Columbus to NAA - Rice, dated July 7, 1943. The Boeing Company.
27 NAA files, NAA- Hellman to Rice; Subj: 85 gallon Tank, dated July 8, 1942. The Boeing Company.
28 IARC for 43-12113.
29 Bradley, Gen Mark, USAF (Ret.), "Bradley vs the P-75"; in *Test Flying at Old Wright Field, Stories collected by Ken Chilstrom*, Westchester House, Omaha, NB, 1991, pp.23–26.
30 MAT CMD Memo to AAFRR/NAA Inglewood, CA re: PES-T-1320: Fighter Airplanes Extra Tankage, dated July 13, 1942. The Boeing Company.
31 NAA Interoffice Memos – Rice, w/cc to AAF Materiel Command, dated July 13, 1943. The Boeing Company.
32 NAA files. Memo from C/AS Req.Div. to AC/AS MM and D, dated July 15, 1943. Also Boylon, *USAF-136*, p.117.
33 Memo, Acting Chief/AS Kelly to AC/AS Ops., Comt. & Req.; Subject "Allocations of Aircraft to Reconnaissance Aviation," dated July 15, 1943. Also Ludwig, *LREF*, p.110.
34 Bradley, Gen Mark, USAF (Ret.), "Bradley vs the P-75"; in *Test Flying at Old Wright Field, Stories collected by Ken Chilstrom*, Westchester House, Omaha, NB, 1991, p.26.
35 Chilton logbook, entries dated July 14 through 21, 1943.
36 USAAF Materiel Command telex to Rice, ref. Project Change Order C-348 to NA-102 P-51B Spec to provide 85gal fuel tank to NA-102 and NA-106. Experimental Dept. project logs March 1 through December 17, 1943. The Boeing Company.
37 "History of ASC in European Theater," chapter 5, p.43.
38 Freeman, *TM8WM*, p.25.
39 Memo to AAF Requirements from Gen Saville, dated January 12, 1943. Ludwig, *LREF*, p.100.
40 Parton, *8th AF-Eaker*, pp.218–228. Casablanca notes in Gen Eaker's Diary.
41 Ibid, p.222.
42 Arnold, *Global Mission*, p.26.
43 Bodie, *P-47*, p.146.
44 Ibid, p.146.
45 Freeman, *TM8WD*, p.31.
46 Caldwell, *DFIDOF*, p.36.
47 Freeman, *TM8WD*, p.39.
48 Ibid, p.50.
49 USAF Study 85.

50 Caldwell, *DFIDOR*, pp.56–57.
51 Freeman, *TM8WD*, p.54.
52 Parton, *8th AF-Eaker*, p.266.
53 Bodie, *P-47*, p.392.
54 Freeman, *TM8WD*, pp.58–67.
55 Parton, *8th AF-Eaker*, p.271.
56 Parton, *8th AF-Eaker*, p.279.
57 Caldwell, *DFIDOR*, p.70.
58 Boylon, *USAF-136*, p.90.
59 Freeman, *TM8WD*, p.69.
60 Colin Ford, Historian No. 268 Sqn 1940–1946, via e-mail exchange September 2018.
61 Marshall, James (Bill), *Our Might Always: The 355th Fighter Group in World War II*, Schiffer Publishing, Ltd., Atglen, PA, 2013; Hereinafter Marshall, *355th FG*. Powell, Robert, and Ivie, Thomas, *Blue Nosed Bastards of Bodney, History of the 352nd FG – WWII*, Taylor Publishing, Dallas, TX, 1980; Hereinafter Powell and Ivie, *352nd FG*.
62 Bodie, *P-47*, p.392.
63 Collectively, Copp, *Forged in Fire*, p.420.
64 Caldwell and Muller, *TLWOG*, p.101.
65 Freeman, *TM8WD*, pp.78–84.
66 Nowarra, *Bf 190*.
67 Caldwell, *DFIDOR*, p.93.
68 Ibid, Table B, p.453.

CHAPTER 6

1 NAA Report NA-5818, "Long Range Flight Test with Fuselage and Combat Tanks, P-51B-1-NA Airplane AC-43-12304," dated August 5, 1943. The Boeing Company.
2 IARC for 42-102979. The second P-51C-1-NT, 42-102980, was delivered on August 30, 1943.
3 NAA Drawing Effectivities for change from 1650-3 to 1650-7 on 104-42011 "Equipment Installation – Engine Accessories – Engine Section."
4 NAA files. Mat.Cmd. Ftr.Br.Prod.Eng to Mat.Cmd.Prod. Div., cc NAA Rice, dated August 17, 1943. The Boeing Company
5 Boylon, *USAF-136*, pp.98–100.
6 Freeman, *TM8WM*, pp.239, 241.
7 NAA files. Mat.Cmd. Gen Jones for Maj Gen Branshaw, dated September 3, 1943. The Boeing Company
8 NAA Field Services Bulletin 73-95 Modification of P-51 Series Airplane for Long Range Operation, final revision January 12, 1944. The Boeing Company; Hereinafter *FSB 73-95*.
9 Ibid, p.4.
10 Boylon, *USAF-136*, p.157.
11 NAA files, Memo – Branshaw to NAA re: Packard Merlin 1650-7 engines, dated September 17, 1943. The Boeing Company.
12 NAA 102 and 106 Experimental Department project logs, dated September 19, 1942. The Boeing Company.
13 Ibid, dated July 19, 1942 through September 22, 1943. The Boeing Company.
14 NAA files, Memo -AC/Production Mat. Cmd. Morgan to Rice. Subject: Combat Pressurization for P-51B airplane, dated August 21, 1943. The Boeing Company.
15 NAA files. Memo – AC/Production Mat. Cmd. Morgan to Rice. Subject: Fuselage Self Sealing Tanks in P-51B airplane. Dated August 25, 1943. The Boeing Company.
16 Arnold, *Global Mission*, pp.448–450.
17 McFarland and Newton, *TCTS*, Arnold correspondence to Devers/Eaker, p.146.
18 Boylon, *USAF-136*, p.101.
19 Gen John Huston (USAF-Ret'd), *American Airpower Comes of Age – General Henry H. "Hap" Arnold's WWII Diaries – Vol. II*, Air University Press, Maxwell Field AFB, AL, 2002, pp.48–55; Hereinafter Huston, *AACoA–Vol II*.
20 Minutes of Eighth Air Force wing and group CO Meeting, dated October 16, 1943; HD 523.03 and Boylon, "USAF-136," p.102.
21 Letter, Portal to Arnold October 24, 1943. Referenced p.189, Horkey, *P-51*.
22 Boylon, *USAF-136*, p.12. Also USAFHRC, USAF HD 519.511.
23 Parton, *8th AF-Eaker*, pp.319–320.
24 Spaatz correspondence USAF HD 519.511.
25 Rust, *15th AF*, p.5.
26 NAA files, copy of letter K. B. Newell to Branshaw, dated October 5, 1943. The Boeing Company.
27 Chilton logbook and notes, dated November 3 through 30, 1943.
28 NAA Gehrkens cable to NAA-Inglewood following November 19, 1943, 9th AF HQ Conference. The Boeing Company.
29 Blake, Steve, *354th FG – Pioneer Mustang Group*, Schiffer Publishing, Ltd., Atglen, PA, 2008, p.32; Hereinafter Blake, *354th FG*.
30 NAA WSN, Vol. 2, #14, dated November 20, 1943. The Boeing Company.
31 Telex Memo to US Air Depots from Branshaw, dated November 24, 1943.
32 NAA WSN Update November 1943. The Boeing Company.
33 Fry and Ethell, *4th FG*.
34 NAA Weekly Service News, dated January 1, 1944. The Boeing Company.
35 IARC for P-51D-1-NT, accepted 30 December 1943.
36 Caldwell and Muller, *TLWOG*, p.106.
37 Freeman, *TM8WD*, pp.84–86, Caldwell, *DFIDOR*, p.94.
38 Caldwell, *DFIDOR*, p.100.
39 Speer, Albert, *Inside the Third Reich: Memoirs by Albert Speer*, Scribner, a Division of Simon & Schuster, Inc., 1970, p.286; Hereinafter Speer, *Third Reich*.
40 Ibid, pp.114–115.
41 Freeman, *TM8WD*, p.102.
42 Copp, *Forged in Fire*, p.172.
43 Freeman, *TM8WD*, p.106; Caldwell, *DFIDOR*, p.112.

44 Ibid, p.121.
45 Spaatz Correspondence, dated November 29, 1943, USAF HD 519.511.
46 Rust, *15th AF*, pp.5–6.
47 Blake, *354th FG*, pp.32–37.
48 Caldwell. DFIDOR, p.133.
49 Caldwell, *DFIDOR*, p.143.
50 Memo to Technical File – Ninth Air Force, E. C. Walton – US Mission for Economic Affairs. Subj: P-51B Assembly and Operational Programs in ETO. Ref: Conference at Ninth Air Force HQ, dated November 9, 1943. NAA Files via The Boeing Company
51 Caldwell, *DF-IDOR*, p.145.
52 NAA Cable, Gehrkens to Rice, dated November 29, 1943. The Boeing Company.
53 Blake, *354th FG*, p.38.
54 Copp, *Forged in Fire*, p.449.
55 Rust, *15th AF*, p.9.
56 Freeman, *TM8WM*, p.252.
57 Wesley Craven and James Cates, *Army Air Forces in World War II, Vol. III, Europe: From ARGUMENT to D-Day*, University of Chicago Press, Chicago, 1951, p.8; Hereinafter Craven and Cates, *AAF–WWII, Vol III.*
58 Minutes of General Staff meeting, dated November 29, 1943, File 520.161-1 HRC, p.79.
59 Rust, *15th AF*, p.9.
60 Freeman, *TM8WD*, pp.159–161.
61 Caldwell, *DFIDOR*, pp.169–172.
62 Bodie, *P-38*, p.65.
63 Field Services Facts, Lockheed-Vega Customer Service Division, November 19, 1943.
64 Bodie, *P-38*, p.63.
65 Freeman, *TM8WM*, pp.116–117.
66 Bodie, *P-47*, pp.391–392.
67 Ibid, *P-47*, pp.390–392.
68 Ibid, p.259.

CHAPTER 7

1 NAA "O" Report. The Boeing Company.
2 Minutes of Eighth Air Force Commanders Meeting, dated January 11, 1944, HRC File 520.141-1.
3 Fighter Narrative of Operations, Eighth Air Force Mission Summary F.O. 190, dated January 24, 1944.
4 Schmid, Generalmajor Joseph, "The GAF vs. the Allies in the West, 1943–1945: 1 Jan 44–31 Mar 1944," USAFHRC K113.
5 Craven and Cates, *TCTS*, p.157.
6 Caldwell and Muller, *TLWOG*, p.146.
7 NAA files, Cable and letter to NAA Frank Lyons, NAA Field Service Manager – from Maj Charles Krouse, VIII ASC, dated January 4, 1944. The Boeing Company.
8 Collectively, the January statistics cited for the Eighth and Fifteenth Air Forces and the Luftwaffe were drawn from Freeman, *TH8WD*, pp.161–183; Rust, *15th AF*, pp.11–15; Caldwell, *DFIDOR*, pp.173–194; Fighter Group Histories including Fry and Ethell, *4th FG*, pp.34–36; Powell and Ivie, *352nd FG*, pp.49–72; Blake, *354th FG*, pp.51–68, Appendices C and E; Marshall, *355th FG*, pp.45–47, Appendices B and H; Olmstead, "357th FG," pp.29–31 plus Appendices. Eighth Air Force Victory Credits Board, dated June 1945.
9 Collectively, the February statistics cited for the Eighth and Fifteenth Air Forces and the Luftwaffe were drawn from Freeman, *TM8WD*, pp.173–190; Rust, *15th AF*, pp.11–15; Caldwell, *DFIDOR*, pp.195–219; Fighter Group Histories including Fry and Ethell, *4th FG*, pp.36–40; Powell and Ivie, *352nd FG*, pp.41–45; Blake, *354th FG*, pp.69–92, Appendices C and E; Marshall, *355th FG*, pp.47–51, Appendices B and H; Olmstead, "357th FG," pp.42–51, plus Appendices. Dr. Frank Olynyk's Victory Credits database and Eighth Air Force Victory Credits Board, dated June 1945.
10 Caldwell and Muller, *TLWOG*, p.153, re: Schmid, "Fighter Staff Conference, April 18, 1944."
11 Marshall, *355th FG*, p.339.
12 Blake, *354th FG*, p.95.
13 Caldwell, *DFIDOR*, pp.220–225.
14 Marshall, *355th FG*, p.52.
15 Collectively, the March statistics cited for Eighth and Fifteenth AF and the Luftwaffe were drawn from Freeman, *TM8WD*, pp.191–212; Rust, *15th AF*, pp.11-15; Caldwell, *DFIDOR*, pp.220–249; Fighter Group Histories including Fry and Ethell, *4th FG*, pp.41–47; Powell and Ivie, *352nd FG*, pp.45–49 ; Blake, *354th FG*, pp.93–114, Appendices C and E; Marshall, *355th FG*, pp.51–56, Appendices B and H; Olmstead, "357th FG," pp.51–70, plus Appendices. Dr. Frank Olynyk's Victory Credits database and Eighth Air Force Victory Credits Board, dated June 1945.
16 Dr. Frank Olynyk's Victory Credits database.
17 NAA project files, Chilton logbooks for November 1943 through March 31, 1945. The Boeing Company.
18 Chilton logbook and flight test notes for March, 1944.
19 Collectively, the April statistics cited for Eighth and Fifteenth AF and the Luftwaffe were drawn from Freeman, *TM8WD*, pp.212–234; Rust, *15th AF*, pp.16–24; Caldwell, *DFIDOR*, pp.250–282; Fighter Group Histories including Fry and Ethell, *4th FG*, pp.47–51; Powell and Ivie, *352nd FG*, pp.115–172; Blake, *354th FG*, pp.115–142 and Appendix E; Marshall, *355th FG*, pp.52–64 and Appendix B, pp.49–72; Olmstead, "357th FG," pp.72–77 plus Appendices. Dr. Frank Olynyk's Victory Credits database and Eighth Air Force Victory Credits Board, dated June 1945.
20 NAA Weekly Service News, Volume 2, Number 33, dated April 1, 1944. The Boeing Company.
21 AAF MC Report, Gen Price, Chief-Prod. Eng. Section Rpt B, dated April 4, 1942; and Packard letter to NAA dated April 29, 1944. NAA files. The Boeing Company
22 Memo from Commanding General AFSC, to MM&D Prod. Div, and Prod.Eng.Div, dated April 29, 1944. NAA files via The Boeing Company

23 Caldwell, *DFIDOR*, p.292.
24 Speer, *Third Reich*, p.346.
25 Speer, *Third Reich*, p.348.
26 Totals derived from USAF Study 85 and Dr. Frank Olynyk's WWII USAAF Victory Credits database.
27 Dr. Frank Olynyk, published data for American Fighter Aces Association.

APPENDICES

1 See the various theories presented by LaPlace, Theodorsen, and Kutta-Joukowski for transformation of a flow about a rotating circle in a freestream flow.
2 Horkey, *The Real Stuff*, pp.99–100.
3 Richard T. Layman, Historical Program Director-NASA, to author Roger Howe, dated October 1, 1993. NASA Files "P-51 Mustang," Langley Research Center, Hampton, VA.
4 Horkey, *The Real Stuff*, p.99.
5 NACA Advanced Confidential Report ACR No. L5A30, "Summary of Drag Results from Recent Langley Full-Scale Tunnel tests of Army and Navy Airplanes", by Roy H. Lange, February 1945 at Langley Memorial Aeronautics Laboratory, Langley, Virginia. P.11.
6 Ibid.
7 NACA Advanced Confidential Report ACR No. L5A30, "Summary of Drag Results from Recent Langley Full-Scale Tunnel tests of Army and Navy Airplanes", by Roy H. Lange, February 1945, at Langley Memorial Aeronautics Laboratory, Langley, Virginia. P.11.
8 NACA Memorandum Report for the Army Air Forces Materiel Command "Tests of the North American P-51B airplane in the NACA full-scale tunnel", by Charles H. Kelly, December 1943, at Langley Memorial Aeronautics Laboratory, Langley, Virginia. Pp.7-8.
9 Combined Drag values from NAA NA-5534 (P-51B-1), NA-8449 (P-51D-5) and NA-8284A (P-51H-1) Performance Calculations Reports.
10 From NA-5534, pp.15-16.
11 From NA-8449, pp.19-20.
12 From NA-8284A, pp.38-39.
13 Gruenhagen, *Mustang*, pp.72–73.
14 Letter to Bill Marshall from Robert Gruenhagen, dated December 28, 2018.
15 Birch, *R-R & Mustang*, pp.31, 134–135.
16 Meredith, F. W.: "Cooling of Aircraft Engines. With Special Reference to Ethylene Glycol Radiators Enclosed In Ducts," Aeronautical Research Council R and M 1683, 1935.
17 Lednicer and Gilchrist, *P-51*, pp.6–10.
18 Ibid, p.10.
19 Ibid, p.10.
20 Dean, *AOHT*, P-38 data p.135, P-47 data p.285, P-51 data pp.328–329.
21 Maximum Range from USAAF Flight Tests for 10,000ft, zero wind, no fuel reserve for each gross weight and fuel load-out.
22 Combat radius however determined by fuel consumed for warm up, take-off, climb to 25,000ft at maximum continuous power, cruise at most economical range settings for RPM and Military Power, drop tanks to engage in combat for five minutes WEP, 15 minutes. Military Power, cruise home and have 30 minutes' fuel reserved. Pp.599, 600.
23 AAF Memorandum Report FS-M-19-187A.
24 Bob Chilton.
25 NAA Report NA-8231, Flight Test Performance XP-51F, dated July 10, 1944. The Boeing Company.
26 Gruenhagen, *Mustang*, pp.190–191.
27 Collectively, Gruenhagen, Mustang, pp.189–191; NAA Reports NA-5534 P-51B-1 Performance Calculations p.11; NA-8449 P-51D-5 Performance Calculations pp.14–16; Dean, AOHT, pp.328–329
28 Steve Brooking, e-mail dated March 22, 2019 and Colin Ford, e-mails dated September 2019.

INDEX

References to images are in **bold**.